Knowledge Shaping

Renaissance Mind

Studies in the History of Knowledge

Edited by
Valentina Lepri

Board members:
Alexandra Baneu (Romanian Academy of Science), Monica Brinzei (CNRS), Giancarlo Casale (European University Institute), Danilo Facca (Polish Academy of Sciences), Sara Miglietti (Warburg Institute), Justyna Kiliańczyk-Zięba (Jagiellonian University), Fárkas Gabor Kiss (Eötvös Loránd University), Denis Robichaud (University of Notre Dame, Indiana), Michael Stolberg (University of Würzburg)

Editorial staff:
Olga M. Hajduk (Polish Academy of Sciences),
Katarzyna Rusinek-Abarca (Polish Academy of Sciences)

Volume 1

Knowledge Shaping

Student Note-taking Practices in Early Modernity

Edited by
Valentina Lepri

DE GRUYTER

The open access publication of this volume has been funded by the ERC Consolidator Grant Project "From East to West, and Back Again: Student Travel and Transcultural Knowledge Production in Renaissance Europe (c. 1470-c. 1620)" (Project number 864542).

ISBN 978-3-11-221506-7
e-ISBN (PDF) 978-3-11-107272-2
e-ISBN (EPUB) 978-3-11-107326-2
ISSN 2751-1383
DOI https://doi.org/10.1515/9783111072722

This work is licensed under the Creative Commons Attribution 4.0 International License. For details go to https://creativecommons.org/licenses/by/4.0/.

Creative Commons license terms for re-use do not apply to any content (such as graphs, figures, photos, excerpts, etc.) not original to the Open Access publication and further permission may be required from the rights holder. The obligation to research and clear permission lies solely with the party re-using the material.

Library of Congress Control Number: 2023941105

Bibliographic information published by the Deutsche Nationalbibliothek
The Deutsche Nationalbibliothek lists this publication in the Deutsche Nationalbibliografie; detailed bibliographic data are available on the Internet at http://dnb.dnb.de.

© 2025 with the author(s), editing © 2025 Valentina Lepri, published by Walter de Gruyter GmbH, Berlin/Boston. This book is published with open access at www.degruyter.com.
This volume is text- and page-identical with the hardback published in 2023.

Cover image: Portrait of a Gentleman in his Study by Lorenzo Lotto,
ca. 1527, Gallerie dell'Accademia in Venice, Wikimedia Commons
Printing and binding: CPI books GmbH, Leck

www.degruyter.com

Table of Contents

Valentina Lepri
The Student's Mind and His Notes: A Preface —— 1

First Part: **Note-Taking and the Study Discipline**

Valentina Lepri
Note-Taking with Method: Remarks on the Theories of Knowledge in Early Modern *De ratione studii* Manuals —— 9

Gábor Förköli
***Copia* and Historical Note-Taking in an Academic Environment: The Scholarly Manuscripts of the Hungarian Historiographer Péter Révay —— 29**

Danilo Facca
Aristotle Excerpted and Disput[at]ed: Leiden 1602–1603 —— 69

Luisa Brotto
What Student Agency at the Academy of Zamość? Remarks on Some Political Oratory Texts —— 93

Kristi Viiding
"Put it in your mind or in the notes": Instructions for Taking Notes in Early Modern Law Studies —— 119

Second Part: **Students' Curiosity and Choices**

Matthias Roick
Aristotle Up-Front: A Student's Notes on the Title Page of Jacques Lefèvre d'Étaple's *Introduction to Aristotle's Ethics* —— 145

Alicja Bielak
The Notebook that Stood Trial for Heresy: Antitrinitarianism among Polish Students in Tübingen in 1550s —— 173

Farkas Gábor Kiss
Transmission and Transformation of Knowledge: Valentine Nádasdi's Miscellany from the University of Paris or the Chances of Christian Kabbalah and Neoplatonism on the Ottoman Frontier —— 229

Index of Names —— 251

Valentina Lepri

The Student's Mind and His Notes: A Preface

It has been keenly observed that humanism was, along with other things, a world of anthologies (Sottili 2000, 603). On closer inspection, the observation could be extended to the entire Renaissance era, which began by transcribing documents from classical Greek and Latin antiquity into elegant parchment codices and continued into the 16th century, when paper became more available thanks to the impetus of printers and the resulting growth of the paper industry.

Alongside the spread of printing in the early modern age, there also flourished a world of manuscript anthologies, the taxonomy of which is varied and corresponds to different human and professional experiences.[1] Among the first to appear were the Family Books and *Zibaldoni* in Italy in the 15th century, which developed the genre of the account book, a mercantile document that arose in the late Middle Ages to manage the finances of a business. To the roster can be added the travel diaries of explorers and the notebooks of physicians in which illnesses and remedies were recorded. Some documents related to religious life were also kept in the form of notebooks, such as *Rapiaria*, which originated in Modern Devotion, where notes, quotations, and sayings were collected to be used as a guide for spiritual exercises.

Philology and codicology have largely been concerned with documents of these types, and the central issues for them have revolved around describing them correctly and reconstructing the history of their creation. In the field of the history of ideas, on the other hand, the aim was primarily to read the development of a thought or doctrine as through the notebook, seen as the laboratory originating that thought or doctrine (Yeo 2021). So far, studies have focused on documents belonging to leading scientists and men of letters, and there is still a lack of general perception of how widespread and important the experience of composing note-

---

Note: Institute of Philosophy and Sociology, Polish Academy of Sciences, Warsaw, Poland. This research has been made possible thanks to ERC Consolidator Grant n. 864542, "From East to West, and Back Again: Student Travel and Transcultural Knowledge Production in Renaissance Europe (c. 1470–c. 1620)."

[1] An overview of the various typologies of miscellaneous notebooks, including those mentioned in this foreword, can be found in the valuable glossary compiled by Angus Vine (2019, 243–245).

books with different annotations was for understanding the production of knowledge in that period.

This volume focuses on a peculiar kind of notebook than those reviewed up to this point and which was produced by university students in early modern Europe. Compared with their peers attending university in the medieval period, these students had an alternative to the *pecia*, the documents containing their lectures that teachers for centuries had been dictating to professional copyists. With the increasing use of paper, even young people could independently jot down what was said in class, adding to their lecture notes whatever they found useful for their education or interesting, if not simply curious and amusing. Their notebooks contained a variety of works, fragments of them, sentences, or simple words. They have rarely been studied as book units since most of their authors had modest biographies or even remain unknown. To date, studies on these materials have only concentrated on a few individual works within the collections,[2] neglecting the strategy by which texts and textual fragments were selected and the logic through which the notebooks were organized.

The eight chapters that make up this volume explore students' note-taking practices behind the creation of their notebooks from two different angles, namely study disciplines and curiosity.

Chapter 1, which is by the author of this preface, considers instructions on note-taking methods that students could receive from manuals of various kinds. A particular genre of manuals circulated intensively in the 16th century in collective printed volumes that aimed to reinforce study methods by reflecting different pedagogical models. In these volumes, significant space was also devoted to note-taking techniques and practical advice to improve comprehension and the development of memory and knowledge. The chapter presents an initial overview of the corpus of these instructions, focusing mainly on the most influential authors of this genre, Rudolph Agricola, Erasmus of Rotterdam, and Juan Luis Vives.

The second chapter focuses on the note-taking activity of the Hungarian historiographer Péter Révay (1568–1622) when he was studying at the Lutheran Gymnasium in Strasbourg. The chapter's author, Gábor Förköli, examines a corpus of commonplace book manuscript notes composed by extrapolating textual fragments on moral and historical topics. The selection of documents testifies that Révay received a Jesuit education that harmonized a humanistic approach to dialectics with a more typical peripatetic curriculum. Moreover, through that youthful

---

[2] For example, they were used to study the fortunes of Italian humanism in German lands by Ludwig Bertalot, the dissemination of Leonardo Bruni's work by Gualdo Rosa, and that of Petrarch by Agostino Sottili.

note-taking workshop, the weight that Ciceronian ethics had exerted in his moral and political evaluation of historical examples emerges, where the Ciceronian categories of *honestum* and *utile* had become for Révay the essential criteria for judging historical models both in the notebooks and in his later works.

The third chapter considers annotation activities in relation to their study area to answer the question of how university disciplines were able to influence both the content and structure of their notebooks. The notes could relate to the student's main discipline of study or to another area in the orbit of the student's interest, as in the case of the first chapter, authored by Danilo Facca, describing the work of a Pomeranian medical student enrolled at the University of Leiden in the early 1600s. He does not jot down lectures on medicine in his notebook, but rather on Aristotelian natural philosophy and practical philosophy. To do so, he adopts a structure in the form of questions, which open up hypotheses about the genesis of the notebook and its purpose. Facca identifies two peculiar student practices as the models through which the student would draw inspiration to construct his notes. The first is *collegium* or class discussion according to rules of academic *disputatio*, and the second is that of sorting the materials obtained from a systematic perusal of books and aimed at reusing what has been transcribed. From an intellectual history point of view, the two practices roughly correspond to two meanings of the term dialectic: the traditional one in the classical tradition and the one elaborated within the framework of post-Ramist thought.

Chapter 4 by Luisa Brotto instead investigates the activity of note-taking in relation to the discipline of jurisprudence in the context of the Zamość Academy. The Academy's program and further evidence reveal that students were fully involved in the life of the institution, especially through the practice of rhetoric in public sessions. A core of handwritten notes by the student Andreas Sredzinski preserves a number of arguments for and against a set of legal theses he defended in a public session at the Academy in 1614. A *Laus iurisprudentiae* was added to them soon afterwards, the composition of which was carried out by selecting excerpts from orations of established authors. Brotto speculates that the excerpts were chosen and combined to create a new text, better suited to the occasion and perhaps more in keeping with the rules of epideictic oratory. Sredzinski's notes and other manuscript evidence examined in the chapter open the hypothesis that students' creativity was not independent of the supervision of their teachers, who probably encouraged them to explore and use classical and contemporary literature in their interest.

Chapter 5 considers the relationship between note-taking practices and study discipline from the perspective of theoretical instruction as addressed in the first chapter. Kristi Viiding presents a manuscript compendium that its author, the Livonian humanist and jurist David Hilchen (1561–1610), had conceived as a methodical manual for law studies for use by the sons of Polish and Lithuanian nobles. Called *Dikaiographia* (o *Dikaiomatheia*), the manual provided instructions on how to complete an entire course of Roman law in two years and also on how lecture notes were to be taken in the context of legal education. Viiding dwells in particular on how and what Hilchen suggested to jot down regarding Roman law studies.

The volume's second area of research focuses on the students' curiosity and choices by considering them expressions of a self-learning practice not necessarily linked to a discipline of study or instructions from teaching.

This is shown, for example, by the personal notes of Michał Zaleski, a Polish student at Tübingen and the focus of Chapter 6. The author, Alicja Bielak, presents the case of Zaleski's notebook, which was found in the aftermath of his murder in 1559.

While at the time, this was a key element in the investigation and particularly in understanding the crime's motives, Bielak draws attention to the dual nature of the notes. They preserve as many marginal notes concerning the manuscript of a work by Spanish theologian Miguel Servet (1511–1553) as those concerning Zaleski's own *Locus communis* and focus on the positions of Servet and the Italian jurist and propagator of antitrinitarianism Matteo Gribaldi Moffa (1505–1564). The notebook opens a previously unpublished perspective on Polish students' interests in discussions of the Trinity, of which Zaleski's notes constitute one of the earliest known traces.

There are circumstances in which students in Renaissance and early modern Europe exercised their note-taking practices directly on books, ideally transferring their notebooks to between the pages of printed volumes. The margins of a given book became a virtual space for a notebook in which the relationship between university authorities remarks and student commentary is drawn closer. Chapter 7, authored by Matthias Roick, examines such a circumstance by exploring a textbook annotated by its student owner. It is an exemplar of Jacques Levèfre d'Étaples' *Introduction to the Nicomachean Ethics*, printed in Vienna in 1501 and now preserved at the Herzog August Bibliothek in Wolfenbüttel. Unlike other chapters in this volume, there is very little information about the authorship of the manuscript notes, yet they are able to illustrate how students worked with the texts, and in particular with Aristotle and the *Ethics*. Starting with the notes on the title page, Roick's analysis reveals that the student had entered into dialogue with the philosophical text by acting as writer, listener, and reader. In other words, the act of note-taking was not simply an act of adding (para-)text to text. It was a shaping of the text with an attempt to make it available to the individual studying it.

Chapter 8 presents a case study in which pedagogical, rhetorical, religious, and, in particular, Neoplatonic philosophical knowledge was collected in a notebook by the Observant Franciscan Valentinus (Bálint) Nádasdi during his studies in Paris around the mid-16th century. Chapter author Gábor Farkas Kiss highlights that the work of selecting authors and books was supported by a strategy of transformation and reuse of works in peculiar intellectual contexts such as Hungary's northeastern borderlands between Transylvania and the Ottoman Empire. There Nádasdi had established himself by becoming a preacher in the court of Andreas Báthory, the region's military leader.

The chapters in the volume highlight two aspects that emerge from the analysis of students' note-taking practices in the early modern period: the first relating to the subject-matter, the notebook, and the other to its author, the student. Although made up of texts of various genres, subjects, and lengths, the notebook is a book unit in its own right, as its creator conceived it. Extrapolating a text from a notebook collection and focusing attention on it is useful for reconstructing the history of that text's fortunes, but it allows only a partial understanding of the student's goals. Considering student notebook as a unitary book may appear contradictory with their internal characteristics marked by multi-textuality, but it is the only way to reveal the learning and knowledge reworking processes underlying their creation. In sum, to understand the student's activity in creating some personal knowledge, it is necessary to consider the notebook in its entirety.

Students' notes are able to reveal the students' own minds and their original contribution to the broad early modern debate on the *ordo* and *methodus* of knowledge. For if the high-profile thinkers of the time were animated by the attempt to establish a method applicable to all study disciplines, it was the students who first experimented through their notes with theorized methods and other solutions. In other words, university professors were persuaded that medieval scholasticism was now unsatisfactory for handling the growing mass of information and knowledge; they began discussing new ways to handle it—think, for example, of Ramism—and it is precisely in the notebooks of their students that the first fruits of that debate on method can be observed. Therefore, it would be wrong to consider them only insignificant traces, as they may turn out to be better indicators of the features of a historical-intellectual phenomenon than major events.

In this particular case, the complexity surrounding reflection on knowledge production and organization in the early modern era can only be understood by reconstructing the intellectual activities of all the individuals who took part in it. These individuals included students, and the main purpose of this volume is to highlight that they were not mere recipients in the process of understanding and building their own knowledge; on the contrary, they intervened in it by appropriating it and doing something new each time.

The book also aims to direct readers' attention towards a poorly considered theme in the history of knowledge, namely, curiosity as an impulse to know and to collect relevant information. Observing students' note-taking practices, we can see the flow of ideas through them and, more importantly, that the learner was not a simple user of knowledge but an active agent with respect to it. In understanding, the learner was also capable of manipulating the contents of knowledge itself, driven by study needs and his own curiosity.

Bibliography

Sottili, Agostino (2000): "Università e Umanesimo." In: Morena, Antonio, Mond-Dopchie, Monique, Wiegand, Hermann, Schnur, Rhoda, Green, Roger, Iurilli, Antonio, and McCutcheon, Elizabeth (Eds.): *Acta Conventus Neo-Latini Abulensis. Proceedings of the Tenth International Congress of Neo-Latin Studies, Avila 5–9 August 1997.* Tempe: Arizona Center for Medieval and Renaissance Studies, 603–610.

Vine, Angus (2019): *Miscellaneous Order. Manuscript Culture and the Early Modern Organization of Knowledge.* Oxford: Oxford University Press.

Yeo, Richard (2021): "Notebooks." In: Blair, Ann, Duguid, Paul, Goeing, Anja-Silvia, and Grafton, Anthony (Eds.): *Information. A Historical Companion.* Princeton and Oxford: Princeton University Press, 636–640.

First Part: **Note-Taking and the Study Discipline**

Valentina Lepri

Note-Taking with Method: Remarks on the Theories of Knowledge in Early Modern *De ratione studii* Manuals

Abstract: The 16th century saw a peculiar genre of manual flourish throughout Europe conceived to provide students with instructions on how to learn methodically. The manuals circulated intensively in printed collective volumes and reflected different pedagogical models along with a moral flavor. However, significant space was also devoted to practical advice, such as techniques for taking notes, for the enhancement of understanding, preserving, and developing knowledge, as well as memory. My chapter presents a general overview of such instructions, mainly focusing on the most influential authors of this genre, Rudolph Agricola, Erasmus of Rotterdam, and Juan Luis Vives.

1 Introduction: Manuals on Study Method in the 16th Century

In the early modern era, university students took varied notes during their years of study in manuscripts that abound today in archives throughout Europe. Indeed, the transition from the 15th to the 16th century witnessed the demise of the *pecia* system (Destrez 1935; Pollard 1978; and Murano 2005) and the gradual prevailing of the use of taking notes personally in university environments.

During the Middle Ages, in all European universities, lectures were prepared by professors and transcribed by professional copyists into units called *pecies*, named for the booklet that was obtained by folding an entire parchment into parts. The *pecies* were then sold to students according to rates set by universities in a system that went unhindered for centuries.

The printing industry had certainly fostered the phenomenon of students compiling their own notebooks, because of the growth of paper availability. The unprecedented availability of paper allowed students to produce a large number of documents and contents of them were a mirror of their study experience

---

Valentina Lepri: ORCID: 0000-0001-6504-7684. Institute of Philosophy and Sociology, Polish Academy of Sciences, Warsaw, Poland. This research has been made possible thanks to ERC Consolidator Grant n. 864542, "From East to West, and Back Again: Student Travel and Transcultural Knowledge Production in Renaissance Europe (c. 1470–c. 1620)."

 Open Access. © 2023 the author(s), published by De Gruyter. This work is licensed under the Creative Commons Attribution 4.0 International License. https://doi.org/10.1515/9783111072722-002

with notes of various kinds. Single words, phrases, quotations of various lengths, lecture notes, transcripts of works or parts of works on study subjects, or simply things of interest to the author (Bertalot 1975; Gargan 2011; and Forner 2016).

While creating their notebooks, students also strove to memorize and order the knowledge they jotted down in order to find it ready and still accessible even after many years. In doing so, they could rely on various models—primarily those of their teachers, who in turn organized didactics by following different criteria for the selection and presentation of topics in their lessons. From an institutional point of view, Jesuit schools were particularly attentive to guiding students in their way of note-taking, and in their manuals, there were numerous instructions on how to study and how to make notes (Blair 2010, 70 and 77–80; Nelles 2007; Nelles 2010). Among the texts that offered this kind of guidance for students was also a peculiar type of manual in the form of a treatise, which had as its subject the method of study and enjoyed marked editorial attention in the 16th century. It took the form of a letter or speech addressed either to the student or to his tutor, covering only a few dozen pages. Because of its brevity, it circulated in printed editions in the form of collections by various authors.

Manuals appear and have some fortune as early as the 15th century, and prominent authors, mainly Italian humanists, along with their works were the focus of important studies in the mid-20th century and even more recently (Garin 1953; Garin 1957; Garin 1958, and Kallendorf 2001).

The features of this literary genre, however, changed profoundly in the transition from one century to the next, so much so that one could almost speak of two distinct genres. In the early days, the texts were a defense of classical letters that promoted humanistic education and were accompanied by extensive overviews of works recommended for the various disciplines of study.[1] In the 16th century, on the other hand, providing a method for learning is added to the previous scheme, which includes a chapter on the use of notebooks and ways to take notes.

With a few exceptions,[2] these tracts were absent from 15th century manuals, becoming predominant in the 16th century. Among the first to draw attention to this genre was Ann Moss, who in her seminal study devoted to commonplace books (Moss 1996)[3] had pointed out the significance and editorial success of

---

[1] For example, Leonardo Bruni's (1370–1444) *De studiis et litteris liber ad Baptistam de Malatestis* written between 1422 and 1429 (Kallendorf 2001).
[2] For instance, Rudolph Agricola's *De formando studio*.
[3] It has been noted that even in the previous century the purpose of manuals was to provide students with material to create their own commonplace books (Kallendorf 2002, XIV), but how to organize these notebooks found no place in the authors' discussions.

these works during the *Cinquecento*, which also contained valuable information on the characteristics of the commonplace books themselves.[4] Indeed, if the collections did not fail to touch on pedagogical, philosophical, and religious issues, it is the epistemological aspects they explored that make them unique in the treatise production of the period.

Editors and printers who disseminated the printed miscellanies did not direct readers' attention to the authors' described mechanisms of learning, emphasizing rather the moral training of the young and the connection between excelling in a discipline and improving as a human being. Their *focus* was on ethical-religious education, as evidenced by the dedication letters and other texts added to the manuals, often orations, which responded to the educational needs of the Reformation and Counter-Reformation in matters of morality.

Erasmus' *De civitate morum puerorum* was, for example, sometimes added to his *De ratione studii ac legendi interpretandique auctores liber*; similarly, Juan Vives' text *De ratione studii puerilis Epistolae duae* was often found included in the same author's *Introductio ad sapientiam*, a work that offered rules of righteous behavior.[5] The editorial orientation does not rule out that the authors devoted ample space in their works to the ethical education of young people. However, the moral dimension emphasized in the editions probably contributed to overshadowing an intriguing aspect of the manuals—namely, the description of the best method of study. This chapter focuses on that aspect, considering the period from the 1530s to the end of the century, which corresponds to the phase of the greatest dissemination of these collections of manuals in print. Far from being an exhaustive overview, it concentrates instead on just a few salient instructions for learning profitably to show the constant recurrence of the themes of memory, knowledge, and their practical implementation through the princely tool of learning, the notebook.

The selection of authors comprising the volumes was also varied and did not necessarily follow chronological criteria or religious leanings. We count, for exam-

---

4 Chapter 6 of her book deals with "Commonplace-Books at School," and here the author warns that ways to make and use commonplace-books at school were described in the manuals of *De ratione studii*.
5 The USTC surveys 24 editions of Vives' *De ratione studii puerilis*, of these only three are volumes containing only this work; in all other editions, the text is introduced to two other works composed during Vives' stay in England extending from 1523 to 1528: *Introductio ad sapientiam* (first ed. 1524) and *Satellitium animi*, the second of which is dedicated to Mary Tudor, sister of Henry VIII. This 18-chapter work was influenced by the author's recent work on Augustine and, consequently, by a Platonized view of the sapient. According to the author, the road to wisdom is in two stages: one stage in which one knows oneself and another stage in which one knows God (Vives 2001, 287–298).

ple, six editions between 1531 and 1555 that put together Agricola, Melanchthon, and Erasmus, but we also have a version that replaces Erasmus with the pamphlet *Ad indoctum et multos libros ementem* by the Greek writer Lucian.[6] The transition between one type of manual in the 15th century and the other type popular in the following century also included transitional and hybrid editions, which contained elements of both. This is the case, for example, with some Basel editions that added to the authors just mentioned such illustrious figures of the late Middle Ages and early Italian Humanism as Petrarca, Aeneas Silvius Piccolomini, and Giovanni Pico della Mirandola.[7]

There are, however, the constant presences of Rudolph Agricola, Erasmus, and Juan Vives in the prints, and the motivation behind the frequency with which they appear in the volumes on study method opens up various hypotheses.[8] Among the most famous humanists in northern Europe in the 16th century, they gradually replaced the Italian authors who excelled in the genre in the previous century in the printed editions of manuals. They were certainly united by a marked focus on rhetorical and dialectical themes, criticizing formal scholastic logic as a tool for collecting arguments (Vasoli 1965; Rummel 1995; Nauta 2016). The new humanistic-style logic embraced grammar, dialectic, and rhetoric and was discussed extensively in Agricola's *De inventione dialectica*, Erasmus' *De duplici copia, verborum ac rerum*, and Vives' *De disciplinis* (Agricola 1515; Erasmus 1512; and Vives 1531). These works also met with joint fortune from an editorial point of view, as the editors of their publications often commented on one by resorting to the other.[9] As you will see in a moment, these major works of the three humanists are also the key to understanding their manuals on the method of study, as their doctrines were expressed more extensively in them.

Finally, Agricola, Erasmus, and Vives were like a kind of authorities within the volumes that contained the study method manuals because they were the ones

---

6 USTC 683738. Published by Setzer of Haguenau (France) in 1524, then in Venice and in Paris, both in 1527, and again in Venice in 1529. Lucian was translated by and a beloved author to both Melanchthon and Erasmus (Thompson 1939; Geri 2011, 165–208; and Fantappiè and Riccucci 2018).
7 USTC 691263, USTC 625903.
8 In Erasmus' case, however, the texts included in the collections varied. Together with Agricola and Melanchthon, in fact, the second book of *De copia* was circulated, while in the other editions his *De ratione studii*.
9 This happens, for example, in *De inventione dialectica*, effectively referred to as the logic of plausibility (Jardine 1988, 38–57: 38), especially in Chapters 5–7 of the third book, where the editors identified parallels with *De copia*. Nor had it escaped the editors' notice that Agricola echoed in Vives' works and that in *De tradendis disciplinis*, which is the second part of *De disciplinis*, Quintilian for the ancients and Agricola for contemporaries were referred to as models of style and language (Mack 1993, 304–306 and 314–315).

most often cited by the other authors included in the editions. Among the examples is the case of the theologian and famous German botanist Otto Brunfels (1488–1534), who in his *De disciplina et institutione puerorum paraenesis* (Brunfels 1529), after a few paragraphs with instructions for virtuous conduct, presented two sections designed as summaries and entitled respectively "De ratione studii Ex Rudolpho Agricola" and "Quae singa optimae indolis ex Erasmo atque Politiano." For all these reasons, their views will also be the ones considered in these pages.[10]

2 Memory and Knowledge Experiences

In the volumes under consideration in this study, memory and knowledge are described within a unified process that all authors structure in diachronic stages. The notebook represents the working ground where actions related to the exercise of memory and knowledge converge and are carried out.

Memory is always anticipated by an act of understanding by the subject of what he wants to remember. Rudolph Agricola, for example, warns in his *De formando studio* that it is necessary first to grasp clearly what one is learning and then to retain firmly what he has grasped. The advice is addressed in the form of a letter to his friend and esteemed composer Jacobus Barbirianus and written when Agricola briefly taught at the University of Heidelberg.[11] Comprehension, in turn, comes through careful reading and is multilevel, involving the meaning of words, the rhetorical construction of discourse, up to the hidden meanings of the text. When faced with what is not understood, one should not change paths because "to progress you need assiduity, nor indignation." The author recommends reviewing the obscure text after some time, as "one day teaches another"[12] and sometimes enough time and other readings help to understand and then remember something initially unclear.

Although for Agricola, memory depends first and foremost on nature, nature can be assisted by art. More specifically, holding things in our minds requires ex-

---

10 Quotes from their works are taken from the critical editions (Agricola 2002, 210–219, Erasmus 1971, 111–151; Erasmus 1978, 665–691; and Vives 1782; 256–280). English versions of passages from Vives' text are mine because they are not yet available in modern editions.

11 The letter to Jacobus Barbireau of Antwerp on June 7, 1484, which later became the text of *De formando studio* is number 38 in the humanist's complete correspondence (Agricola 2002). Only 3 letters from Agricola to Barbirianus have survived, and they have been studied by Elly Kooiman (Kooiman 1988).

12 "Diligentia enim, ad profectum est opus .... Dies enim (quod dicere soleo) diem docet" (Agricola 2002, 210–211).

ercising maximum concentration, then calling them to mind as much as possible, and finally having a mind free of worries. Referring back to Sallust, he notes that when a mind is pressed to the limit it is certainly powerful, but this is a quality that can hardly be maintained if it is distracted by many worries (Agricola 2002, 212–213).

As with Agricola, understanding and memory play together for Erasmus, in that one cannot remember what one has not first understood. His *De ratione studii ac legendi interpretandique auctores liber* contains several memory-related recommendations for the dedicatee, his friend Pierre Vitre,[13] which can be condensed into the three essential actions of understanding, system, and care, "*intellctus, ordine, cura*":

> For memory largely consists in having thoroughly understood something. Then system sees to it that we can recall by an act of recovery even what we have once forgotten. Furthermore, care is of the highest importance, not only here but in all things. That being so you must repeatedly re-read very carefully what you want to remember. Next, we must regularly tax ourselves with its recall so that if something happens to elude us it can be reinstated (Erasmus 1978, 671).[14]

Once memorized one must have an information retrieval system—that is, one must be able to bring back to mind what one has momentarily forgotten. "Care" involves both understanding the information and organizing it, which must be carried out with rigor and continuity, exercising the ability to remember. It involves meditating carefully over what one has memorized and is reminiscent of Quintilian's *ruminatio* (Quintilian 2001, X.1.19).

To strengthen these three activities, Erasmus suggests an exercise that applies the system of *loci* in a concrete way:

> It will be of considerable help if you take things which it is necessary but rather difficult to remember—place-names in geography, for instance, metrical feet, grammatical figures, genealogies, and so forth—and have them written as briefly and attractively as possible on charts and hung up on the walls of a room where they are generally conspicuous even to those engaged in something else. In the same way you will write some brief but pithy sayings

---

[13] The first part of the work provides information of a theoretical manner that takes up key points from *De copia*, while the second part advices about authors and works to be included in studies prevails.

[14] "Siquidem magna memoriae pars est penitus intellexisse, tum ordo facit ut etiam quae semel exciderint quasi postliminio in animum revocemus. Porro cura omnibus in rebus, non hic tantum plurimum valet. Itaque quae meminisse velis, ea sunt attentius et crebrius relegenda, deinde saepius a nobis ipsis exigenda, ut si quid forte suffugerit, restituatur" (Erasmus 1971, 118). This passage is repeated on page 149.

such as aphorisms, proverbs, and maxims at the beginning and at the end of your books; others you will inscribe on rings or drinking cups; others you will paint on doors and walls or even in the glass of a window so that what may aid learning is constantly before the eye (Erasmus 1978, 671).[15]

Books, objects, and even rooms become tools for memory, and the world is filled with written words, allowing learning opportunities to be expanded to every moment of the day. It is worth noting here the prominence that Erasmus assigns to the combination of visual memory and associative and somewhat empathic memory and to the use of writing hand as a medium that boosts mnemonic abilities.

The physical dimension of the experience of memory is emphasized by other authors of study method manuals and particularly by Juan Vives. His *De ratione studii puerilis Epistolae duae* (Queras 1968) has a practical guide character compared to other texts he devoted to education and the order of disciplines, such as his major work, *De disciplinis*.[16] The manual consists of two letters written during the author's stay in England (1523–c. 1528) and addressed respectively to Charles Mountjoy, son of the influential courtier William Blount, 4th Baron Mountjoy, and to Queen Catherine of Aragon, who wanted some instructions for her daughter Mary's tutor. The work was printed in 1524 and designed to educate the youngest, as Charles and Mary, both born in 1516, were still in their infancy.[17]

In the first letter, addressed to Charles, Vives begins by saying that without memory there is no knowledge, as any effort to acquire it becomes useless. It is like putting water in a pierced jar, a *"pertusum dolium"* (Vives 1782, 271), referring to the myth of the Danaids condemned by Zeus to carry and pour water into a barrel with a pierced bottom for eternity. He also warns that memory requires not only mental requirements, such as a propensity for constant exercise, but physical ones—namely, a healthy body. The person who wishes to remember must have good eating habits and a proper lifestyle, for instance, moderating drinking and

---

15 "Adjuvabit non mediocriter, si quorum necessaria quidem, sed subdifficilis erit memoria, veluti locorum quos tradunt cosmographi, pedum metricorum, figurarum grammaticarum, genealogiarum, aut si qua sunt similia, ea quam fieri potest brevissime simul et luculentissime in tabulas depicta, in cubiculi parietibus suspendantur, quo passim et aliud agentibus sint obuia. Item si quaedam breviter sed insigniter dicta, velut apophthegmata, proverbia, sententias, in frontibus atque in calcibus singulorum codicum inscribes, quaedam anulis aut poculis insculpes, nonnulla pro foribus et in parietibus aut vitreis etiam fenestris depinges, quo nusquam non occurrat oculis, quod eruditionem adiuvet" (Erasmus 1971, 118–119).
16 Compared to other manuals, Vives' is structured in titled paragraphs, and it is precisely the titles that allow for an overview of the topics touched upon in the text as they are enucleated in the title.
17 Vives himself will become Princess Mary's tutor in 1527.

getting enough sleep, as if the health of the body matches that of cognitive abilities. The instructions for exercising and enhancing memory recall those of Erasmus in referring to the use of the hand. Vives explains that "more adhere to memory the things that we have written ourselves with our own hand than those that have been written by others."[18] He then urges the student to take (*excerpat*) the concept or simply the word he wants to memorize out of its context by noting it down, both to remember it and to reuse it.[19]

In the same way that comprehension paves the way for memory, in the manuals, the various definitions of knowledge go hand in hand with reflection on the importance of the method of study, without which no knowledge can be had. The defense of the value of the study method is then followed by a review of the most important actions to obtain it, ranging from the act of selecting information to the pursuit of pleasure. In some cases, a description of the most appropriate mood for the attainment of knowledge is also added.

For Erasmus, having a method in study provides a competitive advantage in any action and particularly in the field of literary studies. To clarify this point, he uses the metaphor of war, remarking that in battle, it is always better to have order and organization than force and a powerful attack:

> Do we not observe that skill makes easily possible the lifting of huge weights, which otherwise no degree of force could move? Similarly, in warfare it does not matter so much how large your forces are, or how massive your attack, as how good your dispositions are and what order you maintain in the battle. And those who are familiar with short cuts reach their destination much sooner than those who take the river-bank or the shoreline as their guide, as Plautus remarks (Erasmus 1978, 665).[20]

The best way to acquire a "winning" method is to have the best possible teacher, but in the absence of the best teacher, the student will have to self-study the best authors.[21] The educational plan begins with the study of Greek and Latin grammar

---

[18] "magis haerent memoriae quae nos ipsi manu nostra scripsimus, quam quae alii" (Vives 1782, 258).

[19] The source here seems to be *De institutio oratoriae:* "Non est inutile iis quae difficilius haereant aliquas adponere notas, quarum recordatio commoneat at quasi excitet memoriam" (Quintilian 2001, 11, 2, 28).

[20] "An non videmus ingentia pondera, si artem ad adhibeas, minimo tolli negocio, quae nullis alioqui viribus moueri poterant? Quemadmodum et in bello non perinde refert quantis copiis quantisque viribus hoftem adoriaris, ut quam probe instructo exercitu, quo confilio quoque ordine pugnam capessas. Ac multo celerius quo tendunt perveniunt ii qui semitas compendiarias norunt, quam qui amnem, ut ait Plautus, ducem sequuntur" (Erasmus 1971, 111).

[21] Among the Greek grammarians, one must choose, for example, Theodorus Gaza or Constantine Lascaris, and among the Latin, Diomedes.

in that order, as already suggested in Quintilian's *De institutio oratoriae*.[22] Among the various study disciplines, grammar plays a key role for Erasmus because it is also linked to a gnoseological view in which human knowledge is defined as being of two kinds, of words and of things.

Knowledge moves first from understanding words and then to understanding things with an order of importance according to which knowledge of the latter is the greatest. Erasmus thus takes part in reflection on the relationship between *voces* and *res* that is not limited to the medieval discussion of universals, because it is already found extensively in Greek philosophy through Plato, Aristotle, and Porphyry. The topic was systematically addressed in his *De copia* from a rhetorical perspective, and the *De ratione studii* makes constant reference to *De copia*, as well as sharing its first printing in Paris in 1512. In both texts, the author's concerns were not logical and metaphysical, and even in the short manual on the method of study, rhetoric aspires to guide the method of study for all disciplines.

The hand, as we have seen, is the tool that activates and amplifies memory, yet Erasmus specifies that writing must also always be selective:

> I have never approved of youths writing down every word they hear, for this practice leads them to neglect the cultivation of memory, allowing for the fact that some may want to make a few brief notes of certain things, but that only until such time as their memory has been strengthened and they no longer desire the prop of the written word" (Erasmus 1978, 691).[23]

What is jotted down in the notebook or on the walls of a room must be the result of choice, and selection becomes the space within which the student reworks information to make it his or her own knowledge. Selection could ideally be added to the actions that structure memory, understanding, system, and care, thus completing the Erasmian method of study.

---

22 Ample space is devoted to how to teach these subjects, and in her study, Moss emphasized the influence that some short manuals had on the rhetorical workings of ornamentation, such as the *Tabulae de schematibus et tropis* by Petrus Mosellanus (Peter Schade, c. 1493–1524; Mosellanus 1516) and the *Epitome troporum ac schematum etgrammaticorum et rhetorum, ad auctores turn prophanos turn sacros intelligendos* by Johannes Susenbrotus (1485–1542; Susenbrotus 1542). In elementary classes, composition exercises were supported by these manuals that explained the mechanisms of rhetorical figures along with examples that students could memorize and use to practice. The former used examples from classical authors, while Susenbrotus from the Bible and was conceived by him as a supplement to Mosellanus' manual that eventually replaced it in curricula in northern European Protestant schools beginning in the second half of the 16th century (Moss 1996, 140–141).

23 "Mihi nunquam placuit ut omnia dictata scribant adolescentes, fit enim hoc pacto ut memoria cultus negligatur, nisi si qui pauca quaedam notulis velint excipere, idque tantisper donec usu confirmata memoria, scripti non desiderent adminiculum" (Erasmus 1971, 146).

Just as Erasmus retrieves salient passages from his *De copia* to define learning, so Agricola discusses the topic by introducing the reader to some essential points from his *De inventione dialectica* (1475–1480). The fact is not surprising since this work of his, considered the most important within his oeuvre, is a textbook focused on writing, reading, and thinking (Mack 1993, 120).

Agricola warns that in order to grasp the greatest result from studies as well as to have scientific knowledge, one must take a further step after grasping and retaining clearly and unambiguously what one is learning. One must develop an ability—Agricola never uses the term "method"—to produce something that is one's own with respect to what one is learning. In other words, Agricola asks how we can ensure that our studies are not simply information sorted and stored in our minds, but on the contrary become seeds to be put in the soil that will produce many fruits: "If you are not capable of handing over anything else to our contemporaries besides what we have learned, what then is the difference between ourselves and a book?"[24] This thought was not posed here for the first time, as both Agnolo Poliziano (1454–1494) and Erasmus similarly argued that what was to be gained by studying a plurality of authors and texts was the power to express oneself (Moss 1996, 105).

To produce knowledge, Agricola believes that two actions are needed. The first is the arrangement of headings (*capita*) retrieved from rhetorical topics, used for the identification of arguments and the arrangement of them in the discourse. The second is a reading in which two systems are adopted. In the first, words used in a given text are analyzed in relation to other terms the author could have chosen; in the second, topical invention is applied to the key words of a given topic: "if anyone expands on these things extensively, through all dialectical topics (in as far as these apply to the nature of each thing), he will find himself with absolutely vast means both of inventing and of speaking" (Agricola 2002, 214–215, and Mack 1993, 127).

Agricola's reflections on the ordering of the *capita* of the information that the subject gradually acquires are only summarized in the manual by the author, who refers the curious reader to a more extensive discussion contained in *De inventione dialectica*. Here, they allow us to introduce the last component of the method of study outlined in the manuals: the notebook. In this case, it would be more accurate to speak in the plural, i.e., of notebooks, since different types of documents are described in the editions according to the nature of the notes they contain.

---

24 "Quod si nihil ipsi ad posteros mandare poterimus, nihil extra ea, que didicimus, ad presentes proferre, quid tandem inter librum et nos intererit?" (Agricola 2002, 212–213).

3 The Notebook as a Space for Action

In *De formando studio*, the notebook is shaped like a commonplace book, and Agricola dwells on the ways in which the student can make it in order to have the content available at all times (Jardine 1988). Each page of the notebook should have "some fixed headings, such as virtue, vice, life, death, learning, ignorance, friendliness, hatred, and other similar things that are universally and publicly in use (so to speak) for all purposes."[25] Whenever reading something, the student is required to jot down on the corresponding page all sentences or stories related to the topic described in the title. According to the author, it is important to question two aspects during the act of note-taking. The first is whether or not a piece of information deserves to be jotted down, thus enhancing the selection process, as also observed in Erasmus' manual. The second aspect, on the other hand, concerns finding and identifying the correct page on which to place the information one has decided to note (Moss 1996, 107–113 and 119–126 as well as Mack 2011, 73 and 116).

The specific features of the commonplace book and the way it is constructed are taken up and developed by Melanchthon and Erasmus. The former is also present in the editions on the method of study with *De locis communibus ratio*—a text already present in *De rethorica libri tres* (1519)—and in the opening pages declares his deference to Agricola's *De formando studio* and Erasmus' *De copia* (Melanchthon 695–698; Erasmus 1988, 258–263; and Mack 1993, 320–333). Erasmus suggests the use of a notebook when dealing with the topic of selection, which must always accompany writing: "in order to enhance the value of that exercise, he should have at the ready some commonplace book of systems and topics, so that wherever something noteworthy occurs he may write it down in the appropriate column. I have indicated how this ought to be done in the second part of my *De copia*. But if someone suffers from a lack of time or books, Pliny alone will furnish an immense amount of information, Macrobius and Athanaeus much, and Gellius a variety of things" (Erasmus 1978, 672–673).[26]

---

[25] "Ut certa quedam capita habemus, cuiusmodi sunt virtus, vicium, vita, mors, doctrina, ineruditio, benivolentia, odium et reliqua id genus, quorum usus fere communis ad omnia et tamquam publicius sit" (Agricola 2002, 212–213).

[26] "Atques id quo cumulatiore fructu faciat, ante locos et ordines quosdam ac formulas in hoc paratas habet, ut quicquid usquam inciderit annotandum, id suo asscribat ordini. Sed hoc qua ratione fieri oportebat, in secundo De copia commentario demostravimus. Verum si cui vel ocium vel librorum copia defuerit, plurima Plinius unus suppeditabit, multa Macrobius et Athenaeus, varia Gellius" (Erasmus 1971, 120). Erasmus states here that he has already illustrated this method in *De copia*; it is the section contained in the second book entitled *Assembling Illustrative Material* (Eras-

It is worth noting that the notebook is not suggested for the student's learning activity but to effectively carry out teaching. This should not be surprising because the dedicatee of his handbook, his friend Vitre, is a teacher. In this context, the notebook makes it possible to selectively and neatly collect the topics the teacher wants to teach to which he or she adds, in corresponding columns, authors and excerpts as appropriate *exempla*. It is worth recalling here that Erasmus, in proposing the metaphor of the study method as a well-organized battle, believed it was essential to have the best possible teacher at hand. In other words, it is the teacher who must first build his own notebook, so that the student is then able to acquire a method of study.

References to Pliny the Elder (c. 24–79), Macrobius (c. 385–c. 430), Athenaeus of Naucratis,[27] and Aulus Gellius (c. 125–c. 180) show Erasmus' thorough knowledge of the use of annotating in the classical world and composing anthological texts, offering the most emblematic examples. Gellius and Pliny, with his *Naturalis historia*, are probably the names most frequently mentioned in these manuals and already present in the works of the humanists of the previous century (Locher 1986). In Agnolo Poliziano's reflections devoted to the way of making miscellanies, for example, the *Noctes Atticae* by Gellius were carefully considered (Vine 2019, 15). Pliny, on the other hand, was modeled by the Italian humanist and author of a successful text on study method, Guarino Guarini (1374–1460), also known as Guarino Veronese:

> Whenever you set out to read, keep ready a notebook as a faithful depository, in which to write down all that you come to notice and choose, so that you make it almost a catalog of the things collected. Thus, as often as you have determined to repeat the selected sentences, so as not to go through the whole book again, you will have your notebook ready, which like a useful and assiduous secretary will supply you with what you require. This expedient was always held to be so fruitful by the most celebrated fathers of studies, as well as by their pupils, that with many others our Pliny says that he never read any book without transcribing its noteworthy things (Garin 1953, 189–191).[28]

---

mus 1978, 635–648)—this part appears in several printings of study method manuals as a substitute of *De ratione studii*.

27 At the Bodleian Library (Sign. Auct. I, R. inf. I.I), there is a copy of the princeps edition of the *Deipnosophistae* (Athenaeus Naucratites 1514) that belonged to Erasmus, which contains numerous manuscript notes that show an intensive use of the text in the preparation of the various editions of the *Adagia* (Margolin 1982).

28 My English translation. Guarino Guarini writes these recommendations to Lionello D'Este in a letter dated 1434: "ogni volta che ci si metta a leggere, tenere pronto un quaderno come un fedele depositario, in cui scrivere tutto quello che si venga notando e scegliendo, in modo da farne quasi un catalogo delle cose raccolte. Così tutte le volte che avrai stabilito di ripetere le sentenze trascelte, per non scorrere di nuovo l'intero libro, avrai pronto il tuo quaderno che come un segretario

It is important to point out that the notebook described in the editions is an anomalous commonplace book with a multifaceted nature. Specifically, as its internal structure changes—that is, depending on the type of notes it contains—its physical characteristics also change. This peculiarity is depicted by Vives, who presents three notebooks to which correspond different formats and contents.

In the first notebook, the student writes in his or her own handwriting short sentences: "Prepare for yourself a little booklet of blank paper in which you will write those little sentences in your own hand which you will send to memory and which will be for you like a manual/dagger."[29] This notebook will be like one's own manual, or one could understand *"enchiridia"* as dagger, echoing Erasmus' use of the term. It is clear that what is proposed is not even a primitive form of a commonplace book because within it the annotations are not organized in places, much less connected to each other. The model recovers the characteristics of medieval *florilegia*, and the goal is merely to support memory. This is accomplished both by making the notebook a constantly updating container and by exercising memory (*memoriae mandatura est*) by writing, which, as we have seen, is an act capable of activating one's mnemonic capacities.

The second type of notebook has a larger format: "Let the learner also keep with her a somewhat larger notebook in which she personally notes down the useful words for everyday life, rare or elegant, found as she goes along in the authors she reads, and also the witty and pleasing sentences or those that are serious or acute, which may constitute an example for her life."[30] In this case, by choosing a larger notebook format, its contents seem to be subject to some arrangement for Vives distinguishes categories in describing the various notes. However, he does not speak of *"capita"* or *"loci"* that identify topics, but rather of types of words and phrases. The categories that structure this type of notebook refer back to vocabulary and grammar and do not aim to provide described elements of reality as is the case with a phrase-book, a private jotter, or a commonplace book (Moss 1996, 134–137).

---

utile e assiduo ti fornirà quanto richiedi. Questo accorgimento fu sempre ritenuto cosí fruttuoso dai piú celebri padri degli studi, come dai loro alunni, che con altri molti il nostro Plinio dice di non avere mai letto alcun libro senza trasceglierne le cose degne di nota" (Garin 1953, 191).
29 "Conficiat sibi libellum ex vacua charta, in quo sua manu conscribat sententiolas, quas memoriae mandatura est, eritque ei vice cujusdam enchiridii" (Vives 1782, 266), the suggestion is addressed to Princess Mary.
30 "Habeat librum vacuum majusculum, in quem manu sua con jiciat tum verba, si qua, inter legendum graves auctores, inciderunt vel utilia usui quotidiano, vel rara, vel elegantia; tum loquendi formulas argutas, venustas, lepidas, eruditas; tum sen tentias graves, facetas, acutas, urbanas, falsas; et historias ex qui bus exemplum vitæ suae possit petere" (Vives 1782, 268). The passage is in the "Annotationes" paragraph still addressed to Princess Mary.

The third type of notebook is defined by Vives as a "pure paper book of the right size" (*librum chartæ puræ justæ magnitudinis*), and addressing the student, he recommends that this should be in a certain order: "which you shall divide into certain places, and as nests, in one of them you shall note the words used for daily use, both of the soul and of the body, our actions, games, clothes, times, dwellings, and food; in another rare information, and in another wittily, and in another skillfully uttered; in another sayings and formulas of speech, or which few understand, or which are often used; in another maxims; in another holidays; in another witty sayings; in another the difficult passages of writers, and all such other things as shall be seen by you or your teacher; thus you shall have carefully recorded and arranged all these things, so that you know not only the book: you should read, re-read, memorize, and commit to memory, so that the actions contained in the writings will be no less in your bosom than in the book, and will come to you as often as you need: for it does not profit much to possess books full of erudition and then to have a crude soul."[31]

The structure of these sections suggests a more elaborate version of a notebook even though the "headings" are still not topics but continue to be types of expressions as in the previous case. Note here also the exhortation to appropriate content with reference to corporeality, in which the notebook is no longer just one's own manual but becomes part of the body of its compiler. The recommendation of the use of the notebook has long endured in Vives' writings, returning even in *De tradendis disciplinis* where a fourth, certainly more articulate notebook model appears on which it is worth dwelling:

> The boy should also have a larger book in which he can put all the notes expounded and developed at length by the teacher, also what he reads for himself in the best writers, or the sayings which he observes used by others; and just as he has certain divisions and heads in his note-books, so let him make indexes of these places for himself and distinguish them by headings in order to know what he shall enter into each division (Vives 1913, 108).[32]

---

31 "Compones tibi librum chartæ puræ justæ magnitudinis, quem in certos locos ac velut nidos partieris: in uno eorum annotabis vocabula usus quotidiani, velut animi, corporis, actionum nostrarum, ludorum, vestium, temporum, habitaculorum, ciborum: in altero vocabula rara, exquisita: in alio idiomata et formulas loquendi, vel quas pauci intelligunt, vel quibus crebro est utendum dum: in alio sententias: in alio festive, in alio argute dicta: in alio proverbia: in alio scriptorum difficiles locos , et quæ alia tibi aut institutori tuo videbuntur: sicque hæc omnia habebis annotata et digesta, ne solus sciat liber: tibi legenda, relegenda, memoriæ mandanda atque infigenda sunt, ut non minus scripta gestes in pectore, quam in libro: et occurrant, quoties erit opus: parum enim prodest libros habere eruditos, si pectus habeas rude" (Vives 1782, 272). These instructions are addressed to Charles in the section "Annotationes."

32 "haberit majorem codicem; eodem referet tum quae a praeceptore acceperit copiosius dicta et fusius, tum quae ipse sua opera apud magnos scriptores legerit, vel ex aliis dicta observarit; et que-

By adding transcriptions of texts considered useful or interesting to lecture notes and short notes, the notebook increasingly becomes a laboratory open to experimentation. It is reminiscent of Gellius' *Noctes Atticae* and, at the same time, of the handwritten notebooks produced by students in that time and commonly found in archives today. Indexes are added, the distinction in *loci* of commonplace books appears, but there are also transcriptions of works or parts of works typical of miscellaneous manuscripts.

From the brief overview of notebooks described in the manuals, their role does not appear to be confined to that of a more or less orderly archive. The notebook is the space of action in which knowledge is selected—as Agricola and Erasmus advise—organized, becomes the object of dialectical analysis, stratified, and finally diversified, if we include in the discourse also the typology described in *De tradendis disciplinis*. The picture that eventually emerges is that of a flexible tool that can be adapted to the various needs and stages of learning.

4 Conclusion: Developing Theories of Human Knowledge

As noted above, memory, learning, and the notebook that houses their contents are constant themes in 16th-century *"ratione studii."* Agricola, Erasmus, and Vives first and foremost address the problem of knowledge, what it is, and how to affect it. Their reflections contribute to a picture that is certainly varied, but with sometimes overlapping points of view. The other authors included in the collections reiterate their positions, favoring one or even more than one—Agricola and Erasmus, for example, often appear associated—depending on the academic background and religious orientation of the author in question.

The study method described in the manuals is looking for its own theory of knowledge through the sermocinal arts, the *artes sermocilales*—that is, that part of the liberal arts consisting of grammar, dialectic, and rhetoric.[33] In this area, the activities by which the student amplifies memory and develops knowledge also include the involvement of the physical and affective spheres. Indeed, they re-

---

madmodum in hoc suo veluti calendario sedes et nidos habet quosdam, ita si velit singulorum nidorum nota pinget sibi, quibus ea distinguet in scriptoribus, quae in quemque est locum relaturus" (Vives 1785, 310) *De tradendis disciplinis*, third chapter of the third book.

33 My aim is not to prove that these humanistic texts refer to or make a contribution to philosophical theories of knowledge, but I believe that the study methods they propose involve a reconsideration of the cognitive functions (transmission, acquisition, organization of knowledge) involved in the process of learning.

quire a healthy body and a mind clear of worries, as indicated by Agricola and Vives, as they are fostered by empathic participation on the part of the learner. One writes in one's own hand, notes everywhere, and must always read in an active and engaged manner. The comprehensiveness of the cognitive experience is one of the most intriguing aspects of the manuals bringing the three authors together. Emotional involvement includes the need to take pleasure in the experience at hand—that is, in the learning process. The exhortation to find delight constantly returns in the manuals and involves every aspect of recalling and knowing, be it annotating, reading, or even relating to one's teacher because "you will learn more easily if you love the teacher."[34]

Including pleasure in learning certainly recalls the "Miscere utile dulci" of the Horatian motto (Horace 1926, 343–346), in which the purpose of poetry and, in general, of art is to teach by providing pleasure. It also resonates with the *De liberis educandis* (Plutarchus c. 1470) by the pseudo Plutarch, which, thanks to its popularizer and already mentioned Guarino Veronese, had a wide influence in 16th-century pedagogical thought. Keeping to the rhetorical ground, it is also not possible to overlook the fact that in both Cicero's *Orator* and Quintilian's *De institutio oratoriae* it is recalled that, along with the essential quality of "*docere*," the skilled orator must also "*delectare*" and "*movere*."[35]

No doubt the examples of Horace, Pseudo Plutarch, and classical rhetoric have elements in common with what is described in the manuals and may have provided some degree of inspiration, even if on closer inspection they do not completely fit with it. Here the student is not urged to elicit physical and emotional involvement in someone—that is, toward an audience as the teacher would do with the class and the speaker with the audience. This is an opposite motion in that sensory experience moves inward toward the subject, as if the orator should procure pleasure in order to improve his or her rhetoric. In other words, affection and emotional transport are presented as intrinsic to learning, not only in the sense that they accompany it, but also because they enhance it and make its effects more stable.

The physical dimension that characterizes the method of study does not spare even the notebook, which is described beginning with its materiality. It is first and

---

34 "Facilius disces, si amaris docentem" (Vives 1782, 271); see also: "danda est opera ut exempla sint interdum gravia, quae sancte illam erudiant; interdum festiva, quae delectent; admiscebuntur castae et purae aliquae fabellae, quae animum ejus reficiant, et redintegrent, tum etiam excitent" (Vives 1782, 263).

35 It has been observed that Agricola wrote more than the widely known rhetoric manuals of the time about "moving and pleasing," particularly in the second and third books of the *De inventione dialectica*. On the other hand, he is also clear in stating that "teaching" is the rhetorician's most important goal (Mack 1993, 123, and Mack 2019, 129–130).

foremost represented as an extension of its creator, both as his manual/dagger and as a part of him. Through the use of the notebook, the student also moves from having a *silva rerum* to having a *hortus* due to different arrangements of information within the notebooks and, hand in hand, possesses notebooks that have a different materiality.[36] To a phrasebook more or less close to the *florilegia* corresponds a certain notebook—to a headbook containing a taxonomy of words and expressions (rare, common, pleasant, serious, etc.) another. Along with these models, there also appears the commonplace book, the headings of which may have a moral focus, or moral and disciplinary according to Melanchthon's usage (Moss 2005, 35–49: 38).

The rules for improving memory, cognitive skills, and constructing one's notebook draw, as noted above, on the sermocinal arts, but their purpose is not to improve communication skills. In other words, dialectic and rhetoric do not enrich the student's oratory, rather they amplify his or her ability to describe reality, of which note-taking is a crucial activity and, for that reason, is also the object of instruction. It has been rightly pointed out that note-taking in the early modern age was a task guided by multiple models compared to today. Standards for organizing one's knowledge on paper were provided by classical examples, educational practices, or practices from the chancery and administrative worlds (Yeo 2014; 13; Vine 2019, 37). In the case of the manuals on study method, we do not simply see an attempt at a synthesis between various models. It is the proposal of a new model in which humanistic rhetoric and dialectic do not merely exert an influence on the instructions concerning the composition of notebooks and note-taking, but become tools for developing theories of human knowledge on which to base the method.

The role of the humanists in the development of modern learning through a new interpretation of the sermocinal arts has already been the subject of studies that have portrayed the ongoing stimulus of humanism in the philosophical field and in the technical-scientific disciplines (Grafton and Jardine 1986). To the picture should also be added the production of *De ratione studii* manuals, which allows us to observe the phenomenon from a novel perspective, that of the weight of humanistic dialectics in the practice of note-taking.

The creation of notebooks by students in the Renaissance and the early modern period corresponded to a production of knowledge for personal use; that is, it is a form of self-learning. For this reason, it is important to assess the logic in the arrangement of their contents to establish the dynamics of their implementation and to identify the epistemic-genetic model(s) underlying them. Indeed, we still

---

36 The popularity of this metaphor in the *Cinquecento* is attributed to early modern dialecticians and recalled by Cesare Vasoli in his studies (Vasoli 1965 and 1968).

do not know what inspired the organization of their notebooks. In recent years, some important research has been concentrating on this issue, focusing precisely on the ways in which students of the time constructed their body of knowledge and arranged it in their notebooks. Scrutinizing in depth the nature, objectives, and philosophical influences of 16th-century manuals on study method is useful for enriching our knowledge around a substantial mass of primary sources that have not yet been fully explored, such as students' notes in the Renaissance period. Relating the norms contained in the manuals to the solutions adopted in the notebooks can indeed offer a key both to properly measure the impact of the former, the manuals, in their time and to decipher the structure and practices for making the latter, the notebooks.

Bibliography

Primary Sources

Agricola, Rudolph (1515): *De inventione dialectica*. Leuven: Dirk Martens.
Agricola, Rudolph (2002): *Letters*. Fokke Akkermen and Adrie van der Laan (Eds. and Trans.). Assen: Van Gorcum.
Athenaeus Naucratites (1514): *Deipnosophistou ten polumathestaten pragmateian nun exesti soi es gnosis elthein*. Venice: Aldo Manuzio and Andrea Torresano. USTC 811383.
Brunfels, Otto (1529): *De disciplina et institutione puerorum paraenesis*. Paris: Robert Estienne. USTC 184843.
Erasmus, Desiderius (1512): *De duplici copia rerum ac verborum commentarii duo; de ratione studii et instituendi pueros commentarii totidem; de puero Jesu concio scholastica et quaedam carmina ad eandem rem pertinentia*. Paris: Josse Bade. USTC 143923.
Erasmus, Desiderius (1542): *De civitate morum puerilium*. Strasbourg: Jakob Frölich. USTC 625537.
Erasmus, Desiderius (1971): "De ratione studii." In: *Opera omnia*. Vol. I/2. Jean-Claude Margolin and Pierre Mesnard (Eds.). Leiden: Brill, 111–151.
Erasmus, Desiderius (1978): *Collected Works*. Vol. XXIV. Betty I. Knott (*De copia*) and Brian McGregor (*De ratione studii*) (Eds. and Trans). Toronto: University of Toronto Press, 307–365.
Erasmus, Desiderius (1988): "De copia." In: *Opera omnia*. Vol. I/6. Betty I. Knott (Ed.). Leiden: Brill, 21–281.
Horace (1926): *Satires. Epistles. The Art of Poetry*. Henry Rushton Faircloug (Trans). Cambridge.: Harvard University Press.
Melanchthon, Philipp (1854): "De locis communibus ratio." In: *Corpus Reformatorum*. Vol. XX. Heinrich Ernst Bindseil (Ed.). Braunschweig, cols. 695–698.
Mosellanus Petrus (1516): *Tabulae de schematibus et tropis*. Augsburg: Ulhart.
Plutarchus (c. 1470): *De liberis educandis*. Guarino Veronese (Trans). Padua: Printer of Platea.
Quintilian (2001): *The institutio oratoria*. Donald A. Russell (Ed. and Trans.). Cambridge: Harvard University Press.

Susenbrotus, Johannes (1542): *Epitome troporum ac schematum et grammaticorum et rhetorum, ad auctores turn prophanos turn sacros intelligendos.* Zurich: Christoph Froschauer. USTC 653063.
Vives, Juan Luis (1524): *Introductio ad sapientiam. Satellitium sive symbola. Epistolae duae de ratione studii puerilis.* Leuven: Petrus Martens. USTC 404738.
Vives, Juan Luis (1531): *De disciplinis libri XX.* Antwerp: Michael Hillenius Hoochstratanus.
Vives, Juan Luis (1782, 1785): *Opera omnia.* Vols. I and VI. Gregorio Mayans (Ed.). Valencia: In Officina Benedicti Monfort, Domini Archiepiscopi Thypographi.
Vives, Juan Luis (1913): *On Education. A translation of the* De tradendis disciplines *of Juan Luis Vives.* Foster Watson (Ed.). Cambridge: Cambridge University Press.
Vives, Juan Luis (2001): *Introductio ad sapientiam. Introducción a la sabiduría.* Isamel Roca Meliá and Angel Gómez-Hortigüela (Eds. and Trans). Valencia: Ayuntamiento de Valencia.

Secondary Sources

Bertalot, Ludwig (1975): "Humanistisches Studienheft eines Nürnberger Scholaren aus Pavia (1460)." In: Kristeller, Paul Oskar (Ed.): *Studien zum italienischen und deutschen Humanismus.* 2 Volumes. Rome: Edizioni di Storia e Letteratura, 83–161.
Blair, Ann (2010): *Too Much to Know: Managing Scholarly Information before the Modern Age.* New Haven: Yale University Press.
Destrez, Jean (1935): *La pecia dans les manuscrits universitaires du XIII$_e$ et du XIV$_e$ siècle.* Paris: Éditions Jacques Vautrain.
Fantappiè, Irene and Riccucci, Marina (Eds.) (2018): "Luciano di Samosata nell'Europa del Quattro e del Cinquecento." In: *Italianistica. Rivista di letteratura italiana* (Special Issue) 47. No. 2.
Forner, Fabio (2016): "Le miscellanee universitarie e la loro diffusione oltralpe." In: *Mélanges de l'École françaises de Rome—Moyen Âge* 128. No. 1, 71–83. DOI: 10.4000/mefrm.2967.
Gargan, Luciano (2011): "'Dum eram studens Padue.' Studenti-copisti a Padova nel Tre e Quattrocento." In: Gargan, Luciano: *Libri e maestri tra Medioevo e Umanesimo.* Messina: Centro Interdipartimentale di Studi Umanistici, 557–577.
Garin, Eugenio (Ed.) (1953): *L'educazione umanistica in Italia: Testi scelti e illustrati.* Bari: Laterza.
Garin, Eugenio (1957): *L'educazione in Europa (1400–1600): Problemi e programmi.* Bari: Laterza.
Garin, Eugenio (1958): *Il pensiero pedagogico dello umanesimo.* Florence: Giuntine.
Geri, Lorenzo (2011): *A colloquio con Luciano di Samosata. Leon Battista Alberti, Giovanni Pontano e Erasmo da Rotterdam.* Milan: Bulzoni.
Grafton, Anthony and Jardine, Lisa (1986): *From Humanism to the Humanities: Education and the Liberal Arts in Fifteenth-and Sixteenth-Century Europe.* Cambridge: Harvard University Press.
Jardine, Lisa (1988): "Distinctive Discipline: Rudolph Agricola's Influence on Methodical Thinking in the Humanities." In: Akkermen, Fokke and Vanderjagt, Arjo J. (Eds.): *Rudolphus Agricola Phrisius, 1444–1485.* Leiden: Brill, 38–57.
Kallendorf, Craig W. (Ed.) (2001): *Humanist Educational Treatises.* Cambridge: Harvard University Press.
Kooiman, Elly (1988): "The letters of Rodolphus Agricola to Jacobus Barbirianus." In: Akkerman, Fokke and Vanderjagt, Arjo J. (Eds.): *Rodolphus Agricola Phrisius 1444–1485.* Leiden: Brill, 136–146
Locher, A. (1986): "The Structure of Pliny the Elder's Natural History." In: French, Roger and Greenaway, Frank (Eds.): *Science in the Early Roman Empire: Pliny the Elder, His Sources and Influence.* London: Croom Helm, 20–29.

Mack, Peter (1993): *Renaissance Argument: Valla and Agricola in the Traditions of Rhetoric and Dialectic.* Leiden and New York: Brill.

Mack, Peter (2011): *A History of Renaissance Rhetoric 1380–1620.* Oxford: Oxford University Press.

Mack, Peter (2019): "How Did Renaissance Rhetoric Transform the Classical Tradition." In: Baker, Patrick, Helmrath, Johannes, and Kallendorf, Craig (Eds.): *Beyond Reception: Renaissance Humanism and the Transformation of Classical Antiquity.* Berlin: De Gruyter, 126–149.

Margolin, Jean-Claude (1982): "Erasme et Atenée. Le chantier d'un humaniste pressé, in From Wolfran and Petrarch to Goethe and Grass." In: Green, Dennis Howard, Johnson, Leslie Peter, and Wuttke, Dieter (Eds.): *Studies in Literature in Honour of Leonard Forster.* Baden-Baden: V. Koerner, 213–247.

Moss, Ann (1996): *Printed Commonplace-Books and the Structuring of Renaissance Thought.* Oxford: Oxford University Press.

Murano, Giovanna (2005): *Opere diffuse per "exemplar" e pecia.* Turnhout: Brepols.

Nauta, Lodi (2016): "The Critique of Scholastic Language in Renaissance Humanism and Early Modern Philosophy." In: Muratori, Cecilia and Paganini, Gianni (Eds.): *Early Modern Philosophers and the Renaissance Legacy.* Springer International Publishing: Switzerland, 59–79.

Nelles, Paul (2007): "*Libros de papel, libri bianchi, libri papyracei,* Note-Taking Techniques and the Role of Student Notebooks in the Early Jesuit Colleges." In: *Archivum Historicum Societatis Jesu* 76, 75–112.

Nelles, Paul (2010): "Seeing and Writing: The Art of Observation in the Early Jesuit Missions." In: *Intellectual History Review* 20. No. 3, 317–333. DOI: 10.1080/17496977.2010.492612.

Pollard, Graham (1978): *The Pecia System in the Medieval Universities.* In: Parkes, Malcolm Beckwith and Watson, Andrew G. (Eds.): *Medieval Scribes, Manuscripts and Libraries, Essays presented to Neil Ripley Ker.* London: Scolar Press, 145–161.

Quera, Miguel Bertrán (1968): "Resumen y comentario al documento pedagógico de Juan Luis Vives: de ratione studii puerili." In: *Revista española de pedagogía* 103, 191–200.

Rummel, Erika (1995): *The Humanist-Scholastic Debate in the Renaissance and Reformation.* Cambridge: Harvard University Press.

Thompson, Craig (1940): "The Translations of Lucian by Erasmus and St. Thomas More, Ithaca (New York)." In: *Revue belge de Philologie et d'Histoire* 18. No. 4, 855–881. DOI: 10.3406/rbph.1940.1569.

Vasoli, Cesare (1965): "Ricerche sulle 'dialettiche' del Cinquecento." In: *Rivista Critica di Storia della Filosofia* 20. No. 2, 115–150.

Vine, Angus (2019): *Miscellaneous Order. Manuscript Culture and the Early Modern Organization of Knowledge.* Oxford: Oxford University Press.

Yeo, Richard (2014): *Notebooks, English Virtuosi, and Early Modern Science.* Chicago: The University of Chicago Press.

Gábor Förköli

Copia and Historical Note-Taking in an Academic Environment: The Scholarly Manuscripts of the Hungarian Historiographer Péter Révay

Abstract: This chapter is a case study on the Hungarian historiographer Péter Révay (1568–1622) by discussing his method of note-taking acquired during his years of education. In addition to three volumes of lecture notes from his time spent at the Jesuit college of Vienna, Révay composed a commonplace book with excerpts from his readings about moral topics at the Lutheran gymnasium of Strasbourg. These documents attest that he received a Jesuit education harmonizing a humanist approach to dialectics with a traditional peripatetic curriculum, while his commonplace book from Strasbourg is interpreted through the optics of Johannes Sturm's pedagogical ideas, focusing on paroemiology and Ciceronian eloquence. The chapter demonstrates that the apparently aleatory structure of the commonplace book derives from the teaching methods of Melchior Junius, Révay's master. Finally, I argue that Cicero's moral categories, i.e. *honestum* (righteous) and *utile* (expedient) were fundamental to Révay in his evaluation of historical examples.

1 Introduction: Ciceronian Copiousness and Note-Taking in History

"Political decision is, first of all, a question of choosing the right exemplum, the right proverb adapted to the circumstances" states Florence Buttay in her masterful book about the political allegory of Fortuna (Buttay-Jutier 2008, 373). To be prepared for the caprices of this blind goddess, political leaders must have a wide range of historical models and prudential maxims at their fingertips. The more varied this virtual treasury is, the better it serves its purpose. If some of its elements offer truths which contradict one another, all the better because they

---

Gábor Förköli: ORCID: 0000-0001-8653-9792. Institute of Philosophy and Sociology, Polish Academy of Sciences, Warsaw, Poland. This research has been made possible thanks to ERC Consolidator Grant n. 864542, "From East to West, and Back Again: Student Travel and Transcultural Knowledge Production in Renaissance Europe (c. 1470–c. 1620)."

∂ Open Access. © 2023 the author(s), published by De Gruyter. [CC BY] This work is licensed under the Creative Commons Attribution 4.0 International License. https://doi.org/10.1515/9783111072722-003

help statesmen discover the many facets of political reality. For Renaissance political rhetoric, examples and proverbs were contradictory because politics was itself contradictory, and deliberations searched not for apodictic but dialectic truth. Concerning the moral implication and the efficiency of a political decision, examples and precepts did not enable certainty, only a certain degree of probability, yet their methodical accumulation with a circumspect analysis of each political situation was considered to validate their application.[1] To achieve this efficiency in knowledge management, numerous precepts and examples are needed. This quantitative capacity was designated *copia*.

The term originates from Cicero's rhetorical treatises (*De inventione*, 1,1; *De oratore*, III, 31, 125), where orators are encouraged to achieve a copiousness in verbal expression and in subject matter (*verba* and *res*), and where rhetorical exploit is described as a matter of parity between these two kinds of richness: to an opulent factual knowledge belongs an equally rich vocabulary. In the Renaissance, the concept of *copia* was popularized by authors like Rudolphus Agricola (*De formando studio*) and Erasmus (*De duplici copia*), who encouraged students to compose notebooks of excerpts and to index the matter with commonplaces or keywords.[2] Commonplacing is employed in various disciplines, including the assimilation of political wisdom. Models and exact instructions for this activity are abundant in the early modern literature. It is not difficult to read Justus Lipsius' *Politics* as a collection of classical quotations arranged into thematical groups by the author (Waszink 2004, 49–78 and 152–155, and Tucker 2011, 163–192). In Jean Bodin's famous theoretical work on historiography, the *Methodus ad facilem historiarum cognitionem*, understanding history or employing its lessons in practice appears as a matter of knowledge management. It is not incidental that the French author discusses structuring historical data through commonplacing in his work (Vasoli 1970, Vasoli 1974; Couzinet 1996a; and Couzinet 1996b, 130).

Based on handwritten notebooks, this chapter reconstructs a particular late humanist method for historical note-taking. I will focus on Péter Révay (1568–

---

[1] About politics as a science of the contingent, see Pocock 1975, 3–30 and Najemy 2014, 1131–1164. About the probability of moral arguments in the early modern era, see Franklin 2001. Some emphasize, rather than stressing the uncertainties of political conclusions, that post-Machiavellian political thought praised a systematic accumulation of historical knowledge based on inductive reasoning from historical data. This view of history, linking the experience of the past to practical use, shared similar epistemological premises with Francis Bacon's scientific method focused on regular observation (Almási 2016).

[2] About Erasmus' idea of *copia* and its Ciceronian origins, see Cummings 2014. About commonplace books, a large secondary literature is available. See, for instance, Moss 1996; Cevolini 2006; and Cevolini 2016.

1622), a Lutheran nobleman and historiographer from Hungary, who carefully preserved handwritten annotations from his learning years. He studied at schools where copiousness was a central concept in rhetorical training which was also one of the main scholarly gateways to access knowledge of state affairs in the early modern period when politics and statecraft were not yet conceived as autonomous academic disciplines independent from ethics and the study of ancient historians.[3] These schools were the Jesuit college of Vienna and the academy of Strasbourg founded by Johannes Sturm, a famous advocate of Ciceronian eloquence.

2 Péter Révay, the Historian of the Hungarian Crown Jewels

Son of the royal master of the doorkeepers, Mihály Révay, Péter was born in the castle of Holíč (today in Slovakia) into a Lutheran family of the Hungarian aristocracy.[4] After his elementary studies, he and his brother Ferenc enrolled at the Jesuit college of Vienna where he dated his first letter to his father on June 9, 1585. He stayed in the Habsburg capital until 1588. At the end of this year, his name appeared on the list of the newly inaugurated magisters of the academy of Strasbourg, which was more convenient for Révay's religious affiliation. Despite his rapid graduation, he spent three more years at the Lutheran institution. Having returned to Hungary, he participated in several military and diplomatic missions related to the Long Turkish War (1591–1606). Nevertheless, he remained faithful to his literary interest. He shared an admiration for Lipsius with a close friend of his, the mannerist poet János Rimay (c. 1570–1631), and he even wrote a letter to the Flemish thinker on July 27, 1592.

His Lutheran faith never seemed to be a burden to his career, yet the greatest political turmoil of his life became the touchstone of his fidelity to the Austrian house: it was the insurrection led by István Bocskai, elected prince of Hungary and Transylvania between 1605 and 1606. Although Bocskai proclaimed to be the protector of causes Révay could have identified with—religious liberties against the violent Catholic Counter-Reformation and respect of Hungarian constitutional traditions—Révay continued to serve the legitimate monarch. However, in 1607, he became a confidant of Archduke Matthias, the brother of Emperor Rudolph II, King

---

[3] For instance, the emergence of the science of statecraft from the rhetorical and poetical analysis of ancient historiography is duly described through the example of the 16th-17th century history of the German Protestant university of Helmstedt by Klein 2017, 251–272.

[4] For his biography, see Bónis 1981.

of Hungary. Matthias assumed the delicate task of appeasing the Hungarian states and orders, considering himself to be more competent than his elder brother. The conflict was resolved when the emperor finally renounced the Hungarian throne and Matthias succeeded him in 1608. As a sign of his benevolence, the new king ordered the return of the Holy Crown of Hungary from Prague. Together with its return, Révay was appointed one of the two crown guards (*conservatores coronae*), who oversaw the security of the artifact. Révay was most proud of this title, which he bore until his death.

As an irreplaceable historical relic, the Holy Crown had a specific importance in royal legitimacy, insofar as no other crown could be used at coronations in the Kingdom of Hungary.[5] Or, at least, that was the tradition advocated by Révay, who made the crown the central theme of his two historical works. Although modern historical research dates the crown to a later period, discussing many problems about its origin, it was evident to Révay that the crown originally belonged to Stephen I, the first Christian ruler of Hungary; hence, its history was linked to the conversion of Hungary.

In his two major works, Révay relates the history of Hungary from the perspective of the Holy Crown. In his earlier *De sacrae coronae regni Hungariae ortu, virtute, victoria, fortuna* […] *commentarius* (1613) or, in short, *Commentarius*, he relates the numerous peripeties of its story including transportations and thefts (Révay 1613). Révay argues for a direct correlation between the fate of the realm and the destiny of the Holy Crown, for this latter mediates the benevolent influences of divine Providence and apparently has its own agency as a living being: as long as the dignity of the crown as a sacred object is respected, the prosperity of the community is assured. In this respect, the crown incarnates the legal traditions which must be observed by the ruler. In the *De monarchia et sacra corona Regni Hungariae centuriae septem*, written around 1619–20 and published posthumously in 1659, Révay's text is more of a political history of Hungary (Révay 1659).[6] Nevertheless, the author still reserves the same mediating role for the diadem, emphasizing also a Protestant point of view of the origins of Hungarian Christianity: to strengthen the idea of Hungarian autonomy within the Habsburg Empire, the book modified the generally accepted legend, according to which the crown was given to Stephen I by Pope Sylvester II, by inventing a Greek origin for the object

---

[5] The history of the Holy Crown and the rites of the coronation are thoroughly described in Bak and Pálffy 2020. The early modern ideology regarding the use of the Holy Crown, including Révay's role, is analyzed by Teszelszky 2009; Teszelszky 2010; Teszelszky 2014; and Fundárková and Teszelszky 2016.

[6] For a recent critical edition, see Révay 2021.

in order to minimize the role of the Latin Church in the Christianization of the Hungarians (Tóth 2014, 127–138, and 2016, 43–56).

Révay's history can also be read as a theoretical work. Some sections of the work remind the reader of the mirrors for princes genre. To emphasize the moral and political lessons of history, the book orients the attention of the reader by means of cursive letters in the main text and of frequent marginalia, highlighting precepts, formed as an adage (*sententia*), or historical events which might serve as examples (*exempla*) to illustrate these precepts in practice in the framework of Révay's specific ideological goal. Researchers have identified many of his inspirations in this field. One of them was Bodin's *Methodus*, which, according to Kees Teszelszky, taught Révay how to coordinate precepts of political wisdom with historical examples both antique and modern (Teszelszky 2009, 217–232; cf. Bartoniek 1975, 398–399). Although Révay never quotes Bodin on the matter of *exempla*, it is a well-established fact that he read both the *Methodus* and the *Six livres de la République*; for instance, his *De Monarchia* assimilated Bodin's numerological considerations, including the idea that every period of five-hundred years induces a cataclysm in an empire. As naïve as Bodin's quasi-mathematical speculations seem to us, it was not at all contradictory to his efforts to use historical empirical data to refute erroneous visions of human history—such as the protestant theory of the four monarchies—and to identify general tendencies (Bartoniek 1975, 396 and 402; Bónis 1981, 68–69; and Tóth 2021b, 162).[7]

As an admirer of Lipsius, Révay could follow the model of the author's *Politics*, which was itself a commonplace collection of political wisdom, as well as his *Monita et exempla politica*.[8] In the intellectual circle Révay was active in, Antonio Guevara's *Relox de Príncipes* was very popular as well, and since 1610, a part of the grandiose book had been available in Hungarian (Guevara 1610).[9] Several sentences of Révay's *De Monarchia* come from Guevara, and a few quotations can be identified from Erasmus' *Adagia* and the political commonplace book of the Huguenot theologian Lambert Daneau (*Politicorum aphorismorum silva*, 1583) as

---

[7] For instance, the multiplications of seven and nine are dangerous—many famous people died at the age of 63 and the same interval might separate historical catastrophes—whereas other numbers are benign. See Desan 1987, 100–112.

[8] This influence concerns both the transfer of neo-stoic ideas and the stylistic impact of the use of examples and proverbs, see Coron 1976; Bónis 1981, 81–92; Teszelszky 2007; Tóth 2014, 128–131; Tóth 2019; and Tóth 2021a.

[9] This translation containing Book II of the original was later extended to the full text of the work: Guevara 1628; Christoph Lackner, a German-speaking magistrate of the West-Hungarian town Sopron, who frequented the same late humanist circles as Révay, published a book with selected adages from the *Relox* in Latin: Lackner 1625. About the presence of the *Relox* in Révay's works, see Tóth 2014, 131–133, and 2021b, 135, 146, and 159–160.

well (Tóth 2021b, 135, 146, 135, 146, and 157–163.). Yet, as appealing as it is to link Révay's process to bookish inspirations, the discussion of his method cannot be limited to the influence of a few authors: using commonplace collections and quoting historical examples were frequent strategies in early modern text production.[10]

In this respect, Révay's studies in his formative years have been neglected. An important opportunity has been missed, given the fact that four volumes of annotations have been preserved from Révay's school years in the Archdiocesan Library of Esztergom. Three of them were made during his philosophical studies in Vienna—*Annotationes in universam logicam et mathesim* (486 folios), *Commentaria in octo libros Aristotelis de Physice auscultatione* (453 folios), *Commentaria in libros Aristotelis de Coelo et Mundo* (366 folios)—and the fourth one, a commonplace book, *Annotationes morales historicae* (279 folios), was based on his readings in Strasbourg.[11] Their presentation demonstrates how deeply Révay cherished these early documents: he had them bound in white leather and placed his monogram and the year of their making in gilt on the binding. That excerpting was not a scholarly constraint to him is proven by an interesting remark made by Raphael Hrabecius, the minister who delivered his eulogy at his funeral: he mentions a certain notebook entitled *Viridarium* (Pleasure-garden) that Révay worked on his whole life. Unfortunately, this manuscript cannot be found today (Hrabecius 1623, F2r; Bónis 1981, 11–12). Of course, the literature is aware of the subsisting volumes.[12] Furthermore, Tóth's critical edition identifies two instances where the *De Monarchia* quotes this commonplace book of his youth (Révay 2021: II, 144–145 [6.74.6], and II, 284–85 [6.152.2]).[13] Nevertheless, their systematic analysis is still waiting.

3 *Copia* at the Jesuit College of Vienna

In Vienna, the town of Johannes Cuspinianus and Joachim Vadian, humanism had firm positions in university education. Accordingly, the erudition of Erasmus was welcomed from the outset in Vienna. The poet Johannes Alexander Brassicanus

---

[10] Cf. with Tóth's conclusion about Révay's use of sentences: Tóth 2021b, 163.
[11] Archdiocesan Library, Esztergom (ALE) MS II. 272; II. 224; II. 273; II. 253. (The size of the four manuscripts is 200 x 150 mm. I followed the chronological order of the studies instead of the order of the shelf marks.)
[12] Bónis used his Vienna manuscripts to reconstruct the chronology of Révay's studies: Bónis 1981, 10.
[13] The second quotation can be found both in the *Annotationes* and in Lambert Daneau's collection.

was appointed professor of rhetoric and jurisprudence at the university, and he openly professed Erasmian views.[14] When Erasmus publicly turned against Luther in his *De libero arbitrio* in 1525, his prestige was strengthened in Catholic Vienna. He was appreciated by humanist priests of the town, including Johann Faber, before religious debates took a turn towards hostility.[15]

When Catholicism found itself in a more defensive position, the hope of avoiding a fatal division of the Church with an inner reform faded. It became less and less appropriate for Catholics to refer to Erasmus, yet his imposing philological oeuvre remained essential to many of them. In 1559, his works were put on the *Index*, and his memory was banned. However, even Catholic authorities felt that his contribution to the humanities could not be neglected, and some of them shared a nuanced opinion which condemned the theologian but appreciated the philologist in Erasmus (Salliot 2017). As for the Jesuits, in the beginning, they used *De copia* and *De conscribendis epistolis* to teach proper style at their schools. Even before the Index of 1559, Ignatius of Loyola expressed his doubts concerning Erasmus, but in 1557, his successor, superior general Diego Laínez, still allowed the teachers of the Society in Padua and in Ingolstadt to use his works (Kainulainen 2018, 541–542).[16]

Erasmian books were indispensable for teaching *copia*. What Catholics could try was to at least get rid of his name, if not his ideas. It is known that Paolo Manuzio, the son of the great typographer Aldo, completed a purged edition of the *Adagia* for Catholic readership ([Erasmus] 1575). As for Erasmus' theoretical work about the topic, in 1556, the French Jesuit André des Freux, who worked in Rome beside Ignatius of Loyola, published his versified adaptation of *De duplici copia* in distiches (Des Freux 1556). Like Erasmus' original, the first part of the didactic poem discussed figures and tropes necessary to achieve linguistic richness, whereas the second part presented a dialectical method of describing various topics.

This latter book was also printed in Vienna (Des Freux 1561), where it was used in teaching as late as in the 1580s by an instructor named Joannes Molensis, who was also Révay's teacher of philosophy according to his notes. Born in Antwerp in

---

14 Gábor Pesti, the Erasmian translator of Aesop's fables in Hungary, contacted him during his stay in Vienna (Gerézdi 1964, 139–140, and Ritoókné Szalay 2002, 169–170).
15 This Erasmian milieu inspired Benedek Komjáti, a Hungarian scholar and a student of Vienna, who translated the epistles of Saint Paul to Hungarian, one of the favorite authors of Erasmus in theology (Gerézdi 1964, 138–139, and Ács 2019, 45–57).
16 Marc Fumaroli (1999, 93) also draws attention to the complicated Jesuit evaluation of Erasmus' works, pointing out that as members of the Republic of Letters, Jesuits could not honestly depreciate all his merits.

1560, he spent his whole Jesuit career at the university of Vienna, where he died in 1613. He graduated as *magister artium* only in the beginning of the 17th century, and he later obtained a doctorate in theology.[17] His name is indicated in a handwritten entry made by a Hungarian student inside a copy of Des Freux's *De copia*, the analysis of which was finished by him in 1583. The successive possessors of the book were István Szuhay (1551–1608), later known as the bishop of Kalocsa, and Demeter Naprágyi (1564–1619), a famous humanist bishop with whom Révay undertook diplomatic missions (Bónis 1981, 19, and Tóth 2021b, 154).[18] Both Szuhay and Naprágyi studied in Vienna and could have been students of Joannes. As for Révay, nothing certain is known about his first years in Vienna, but his education was probably about solidifying oratorial skills, connecting patriotic and rhetorical instruction performed mainly with the help of Cicero's works by Jesuit teachers (Grendler 2019, 15–17). It is not unlikely that he had to study Des Freux's book with Joannes as well.

There is no sign that he had any issues due to his Lutheran affiliation. He even wrote a letter to his father to assure him that he would never abandon the faith of his family (Bónis 1981, 8–9). Whereas Catholic students of Vienna usually concluded sections in their manuscripts by praising the Virgin Mary, Révay consequently used the Protestant formula "*Soli Deo gloria.*"[19] It is true, however, that as a Lutheran, he could not graduate as a master at the university because registration was tied to a public profession of Catholic faith since 1581 (Gall 1965, 17 and 57, and Bónis 1981, 10). That is the reason why he later decided to move on to Strasbourg.

His annotations from his Vienna period are derived from the dictation of the teacher (*dictata*) in the classroom. They cover a typical Jesuit curriculum in philosophy. Providing a traditional exegesis of Aristotle's texts, the curriculum was divided into three main disciplines: logic, physics, and metaphysics. Originally, the curriculum was planned to take three years, though it was not uncommon for it to be reduced to one year due to lack of teaching staff (Grendler 2014, 13, 2016, 23–24, and 2019, 8–9). In this respect, the case of Révay was special: although he

---

17 About his life, see Bónis 1981, 10.
18 The entry which can be read on the verso of leaf 36 is published by Edina Zvara: "Magister Joannes Molensis ultima Feb(ruarii) 1583 finem fecit" (Zvara 2011, 47–71, in particular 65 and 70). The location of the item: Eisenstadt (Austria), Esterházy Library, Zimmer V. mittlere, Kasten 5. Regal 1.
19 For instance, ALE MS II 272, 447r; MS II 224, 453r, MS II 273, 42v. For the sake of comparison, György Dubovszky, who studied in 1590 in Vienna and later became a canon of Esztergom, said grace to both God and the Virgin after his annotations on *Metaphysics* and *De anima:* ALE MS II 308, 259v: "Laus Deo Ter Op[timo] Mariae Beatissi[m]ae / M[atri] Virg[ini]" and 368r: "Laus itaque Deo Virginique matri."

spent only one year with his philosophical studies, the course he accomplished seems to be almost exhaustive. He commenced the study of dialectics with Porphyry's *Isagoge* on January 5, 1587, and he finished it with the *Topica* on July 11, after which he started *Elements* and the *De sphaera mundi*.[20] Natural philosophy, commenced on July 27 and finished in June of 1588, included Aristotle's *Physics, On Heavens, On Generation and Corruption*, and *Meteorology*.[21] On June 25, 1588, Joannes began commenting on *De anima*, and on September 1 *Metaphysics*, but Révay could study this latter work only for a very short period of time, because he left for Strasbourg in the same year.[22] According to his annotations, he was deeply involved in geometrical studies as well, and he copied superb illustrations of logic and of astronomy into his notebook, including not only Porphyrian trees and other charts inherited from medieval scholastics, but also some more uncommon diagrams. Regarding the structure and the content of this course, there are some striking similarities with manuscripts composed by other Hungarian students at Jesuit colleges of Habsburg territories during the same decade: Ferenc Szelepcsényi Pohronc (?–1611), later a canon of Esztergom, and the brothers Martin and Simon Bánovszky studied the same curriculum, but at different institutions. Szelepécsnyi Pohronc was enrolled in Vienna where he was taught by Ludovicus Hantsamus,[23] whereas the brothers Bánovszky attended the lessons of Joannes Grasser in Olomouc.[24]

In all these manuscripts from Vienna and Olomouc, the division into chapters and the figures match with a rather early textbook for dialectics: the *Commentaria in Isagogen Porphyrii, et in omnes libros Aristotelis de dialectica*, also known as the *Louvain commentaries*. First issued in 1535 and regularly reedited in 1547, 1553, and 1568, the textbook was written by a number of authors supervised by Joannes Stan-

---

20 ALE MS II. 272, 1r: "Annotationes in Universam Logicam tradita à Joanne Molense Sacerdote Societatis Jesu Viennae Austriae 5 Janurij Ao 1587"; 447r: "Finis 11 Mensis Julij / A[nn]o D[omi]ni 1587" (end of the *Topica*); after the *Organon*, the numbering of the pages recommences from the beginning: 1r: "In Mathematicas disciplinas"; and it also recommences at the beginning of the *De sphaera:* 1r: "In sphaeram Ioannis de Sacrobosco commentaria."
21 ALE MS II. 224, 1r: "Commentaria in octos libros Ari[stote]lis de phisica auscultatione tradit a P. Ioanne Molense Societatis Iesu. Vien[n]ae Austriae incipit faeliciter 27 Mensis Julij Anno D[omin]i 1587"; ALE MS II 273, unnumbered folios: "Meteorologia / Incipit 8 Junij matu[tina] hora octava Anno d[omi]ni 1588."
22 ALE MS II 273, unnumbered folios: "de Anima 25 die Junij hora 8o matutina A. d[omi]ni 1588" and "Commentaria in Metaphysicam Ar[istote]lis Patris Molensis auspicata 1a die Septemb[ris] hora matutina 8a An[n]o 1588 d[omi]ni."
23 ALE MS II 226a, MS II 274; MS II 226b (1585–87).
24 ALE MS II 227a, 227b, 227c, 227d (1588–89).

nifex at the University of Louvain.[25] The book resulted from a rivalry between the university and the Collegium Trilingue, established in 1517 in the same town. Criticizing Aristotelian contents and methods, this new humanist institution challenged traditional curriculum, and the university had to act. Yet instead of entirely rejecting the humanist approach to dialectics, the professors chose a well-balanced eclecticism embracing Peripatetic philosophy and making some concessions to humanist dialectics. Thus, in accordance with Catholic tendencies of the time, the book adopted a moderated realism, excluding radical nominalists, like Ockham. This also fit Jesuit requirements which can be described as predominantly realist as well. On the other hand, the work also referred to humanist sources. The authors criticized Lorenzo Valla, the notorious enemy of Aristotle, for separating ontological and dialectical issues and condemning metaphysics, whereas they attributed more positive values to other humanists, like Jacques Lefèvre d'Étaples and Rudolphus Agricola, whose *De inventione dialectica* was printed for the first time in Louvain in 1515. Beyond some reproaches, the Louvain commentaries are rather positive with respect to Agricola's work while discussing the first two books of the *Topica*. This implied a more practical and flexible approach of the *loci* of invention that Agricola put in the service of rhetoric persuasion using plausible arguments and copious examples to inductively prove a conclusion in practical domains, such as morality, history, and even politics, rather than in abstract science.[26]

Always considering this practical goal of dialectic and rhetoric, Agricola did not display much interest in ontological problems, such as the debate about universals between realists and nominalists. Yet, despite the lack of any explicit statement on the question, recent scholarship has demonstrated that Agricola's practical aims tacitly imply an epistemological optimism which postulates that topics in logic must correspond to the diverse aspects of ontological reality. Being himself a realist, Agricola was more compatible with the predominantly realist Catholic scholarship of the early modern period than openly anti-metaphysician authors (Braakhuis 1988 and Nauta 2012).

This pragmatic realism manifests itself in the fact that the Louvain commentaries set an encyclopaedical goal. Still following the guidelines of Aristotle's work, the textbook opened the discussion to various materials. For instance, it paid special attention to the habits (*habitus*) and the faculties of the soul. Aristotle discusses *habitus* as intellectual and moral dispositions or qualities of the soul in *Categories* (7–8), in *De anima* (2.5), in *Metaphysics* (5.20, 1022b12–14), and in the

---

25 The consulted edition: Stannifex 1553.
26 About Agricola's evaluation in the Louvain commentaries and the conflict with the Collegium Trilingue, see Papy 1999. About Agricola's dialectical and rhetorical thoughts, see Van der Poel 2007, 2015, and 2018.

Nicomachean Ethics (1.13) (Faucher and Roques 2019.) Since the *Organon* already anticipates this matter explained in detail by his later works, the subject of intellectual habits provides an opportunity to establish a taxonomy of human activities, including sciences and arts as well. This classification is illustrated by one of the many diagrams that Révay's teacher borrowed from the Louvain textbook. According to this diagram, intellectual habits can be related to what is always true (*semper verus*), what is always false (*semper falsus*), or what is sometimes true and sometimes false (*aliquando verus*). The first category covers theological and philosophical wisdom, inferior sciences, and the arts, the second one basically corresponds to ignorance, whereas the third one contains uncertain yet no less important phenomena of human intellectual and verbal activity: opinion and suspicion (Stannifex 1553, 84).[27] Hence, the dialectic in the Louvain commentaries becomes a propaedeutic not only for all scientific disciplines, but also to all possible sources of rhetorical arguments.

This exigence to integrate a large spectrum of discipline into the dialectic framework can also be illustrated by the presence of a peculiar science in the Louvain commentaries. This discipline is physiognomy, and the Louvain authors refer to Jacques Lefèvre d'Étaples to resume its principles for the students (Stannifex 1553, 276–278).[28] Observation of facial features thus was considered to be a valid source of arguments about a person's character, hence an operational part of dialectic. Establishing this kind of connection between abstract science and versatile knowledge could make dialectical problems more understandable to students. Sometimes, playful methods are employed in this curriculum as well. For instance, to dwell on mathematics, his professor used not only the usual *De Sphaera Mundi* by Johannes de Sacrobosco but also a commentary written by the Jesuit Christophorus Clavius on the same work (Clavius 1570). This textbook employed classics as mnemotechnical poems to help the students memorize astronomical facts, such as the name of the constellations in the Zodiac, and Révay's teacher dictated these verses to his students, as the manuscript attests.[29]

To conclude, Révay's Jesuit education in Vienna merged the traditional curriculum with humanism. In the teaching of philosophy, copiousness was key as linguistic and rhetorical training was completed with an encyclopaedical effort which opened the scholastic dialectic towards other disciplines. This education

---

[27] In Révay's manuscript: ALE MS II 272, 139v.
[28] "Descriptio signorum, a Iacobo Stapulensi ex Aristotele et Adamantio Physiognomio collecta."
[29] Clavius quotes Manilius, *Astronomica*, 1, 263–274 as a mnemonic aid for the constellations of the Zodiac (Clavius 1570, 295); in Révay's manuscript: ALE MS II 272, "In sphaeram Ioannis de Sacrobosco commentaria" 24v (in this section about astrology, the numbering of the folios recommences from f. 1r).

was not incompatible with the requirements which were awaiting Révay in Strasbourg. But the documents from his years spent at the protestant gymnasium already reflect his personal preferences, where the student, still following the guidance of his professors, had a certain degree of freedom to choose the materials in his notes.

4 Ciceronian Commonplaces at the Sturmian Gymnasium of Strasbourg

After leaving Vienna, Révay arrived at Strasbourg, one of the most important European strongholds of humanist studies on phraseology (paroemiology). The Lutheran gymnasium was founded by Johann Sturm, a disciple of Ramus in 1538, and although it achieved the rank of university only in 1631, its prestige was recognized even earlier.

The elderly Sturm was still alive when Révay enrolled at the school. In his rhetorical works, including the *De imitatione oratoria*, he professed a Christian humanism that presumed an immediate connection between linguistic purity and the purity of Christian doctrine: skill in languages makes possible a deeper understanding of religious teachings. Sturm's views imply that dialectic can achieve an adequate description of the reality of things, while rhetoric, inseparable from this discipline, can appropriately express it. Imitation and excerpting classics into commonplaces were methods that Sturm highly estimated in regard to these goals (Sturm 1574; Spitz and Tinsley 1995; Moss 1996, 147–154; Arnold 2007; and Arnold 2009). His disciples and colleagues at Strasbourg continued this heritage, especially by cultivating lexicography and paroemiology in classical languages. Melchior Iunius, a teacher of rhetoric, discussed *copia*, excerpting, and commonplacing in his textbook (Iunius 1585, 75–97), while Johann Bentz, author of several commentaries on Cicero, composed Greek and Latin treasuries (Bentz 1581; Bentz 1596a; Bentz 1596b) and published a manual in 1588, which listed commonplace headings that his students had to use while preparing excerpts (Bentz 1588). Strasbourg scholars also published several printed commonplace books, including the *Adagia* of Johann Ludwig Hawenreuter (1573). Joseph Lang was a particularly successful disciple of Sturm. His Greek–Latin–German *Adagia* was prefaced by his old master (Langius 1596), and he also published two further collections: *Loci communes sive florilegium* (Langius 1598) and an updated version of Nanus Mirabellius' famous *Polyanthea* (Nanus Mirabellius et al. 1607). To do justice to the prestige of Strasbourg's paroemiology, it is worth evoking the fact that when in 1618 the protestant gymnasium received a rival in the form of a new Jesuit university founded in the small Alsatian town of Molsheim (Negruzzo 2005; Grendler 2014, 18–20), the Lutherans complained that these Jesuit fathers plagiarized the *Apophthegms* of their late compatriot, Conrad Lycosthenes.[30]

In the 1580s–1590s, Strasbourg paroemiology inspired Hungarian scholars, namely, János Baranyai Decsi (1560–1601), who studied in Strasbourg between 1588 and 1592 and published a selection of Erasmus' *Adages* with the Hungarian equivalents of the proverbs (Baranyai Decsi 1598), and Albert Szenci Molnár (1574–1634), an important Calvinist poet and the author of the first modern Hungarian-Latin dictionary, who composed a hand-written commonplace book based on the system of headings in Bentz' aforementioned textbook.[31] Given their scientific production, these two lexicographers must have deliberately chosen the Strasbourg gymnasium as a place which matched their ambitions in literature.

Révay's intention was to study rhetoric and law in Strasbourg. First, his teacher was Sturm, who had to resign in 1589 because of his Calvinism. Then Révay studied under the supervision of Melchior Iunius, who staged orations on antique models with his students. In 1589, Révay played the role of the praetor in a reenactment of Murena's trial based on Cicero (Iunius 1592b, 250–252, 271, and 281–282), and in 1591, Révay delivered a speech about a case of parricide told by Livy (Iunius 1592a: 38–42), and another one to glorify Cicero (Iunius 1592b, 210–230). In an additional oration, he also praised hunting (Iunius 1592b, 10–14); he also wrote a preface to fellow students' orations, in which they had to decide which one of the four cardinal virtues fits a nobleman best (Iunius 1592b, 115–119). In the same year, he defended a legal disputation about loans (*De mutuo*); this one was exceptionally presided over by the professor of law, Paul Graseck (Révay 1591). The impressive list implies that this training was integrated into a practical education devoted to the young nobility, which could recognize its activities (legal administration and sport) in the curriculum (Eckhardt 1944, 9–18; Bónis 1981, 10–11; and Tóth 2021b, 104–105 and 138n–139n).

Regarding his rhetorical education, his praise of Cicero delivered on January 8, 1591, is the most interesting text. The speech discusses Cicero as the paragon of orators: after presenting his biography by Plutarch, it proposes various perspectives to evaluate Cicero's oeuvre. A major part of the oration consists in a topical classification of Cicero's texts. After this thematic analysis, Révay groups the speeches

---

[30] This accusation of plagiarism appears in a satiric work of an author of Strasbourg: Dachtler 1619, 58.

[31] About Baranyai Decsi's and Szenci Molnár's intellectual surroundings in Strasbourg, see Imre 2009, 28–46. Szenci Molnár's commonplace book with his diary and other documents may be found in Târgu Mureș (Romania), Teleki-Bolyai Library MS To 3619b; see Förköli 2022.

according to their oratorical and stylistic procedures, including digression and amplification.

In Révay's speech, Cicero's subjects are arranged into four larger groups: philosophy, politics, law, and a mixed section which he calls oratorial commonplaces. Inside these topics, he indicates one or two Ciceronian texts as an example for each commonplace.[32] This results in an entire system of headings which might help students read and excerpt the works of the Roman orator. Révay praises this richness of the Ciceronian oeuvre in the following terms:

> What shall I say now about the commonplaces, my respected audience? Cicero complains that, in his age, nobody had catalogued [*repertos*] the orators, who could amplify [*dilatare*] and transform a given reasoning adapted to the needs of the person and the time into a common oration of any kind: he claims that there are most brilliant and almost vivacious sections [in the orations], which contain theses and commonplaces [*Theses et locos communes*]. It can hurt nobody, I think, if they search Cicero's orations for the best rules to invent them [the commonplaces] correctly and wisely, to use them properly and to discuss them copiously [*copiose*], ornately, and eloquently, except those who turn out to be a complete stranger to these orations. There is an excellent commonplace about religion in *Pro Domo sua* and in *De Haruspicum responsis*; about divine providence in the fourth oration against Catilina and in *Pro Milone*; about the power of conscience in *Pro Sexto Roscio* and in *Pro Milone*; about the immortality of soul in *Pro Archia*.[33]

This system was not entirely a personal invention of Révay. He was certainly helped by his teachers and their textbooks. Sturm, for instance, included an overview of the whole Ciceronian oeuvre in his *De imitatione oratoria:* in the supplement of this treatise, he published several scholia which discussed Cicero's and Demosthenes' texts according to their subjects, the types of the arguments they used, and their figures of speech (Sturm 1574). Cicero's works were also published in

---

32 Eckhardt and Bónis noticed the presence of this list of commonplaces in the speech (Eckhardt 1944, 12–13, and Bónis 1981, 11). For the whole system of Ciceronian commonplaces in Révay's oration, see Supplement 1.
33 "Quid de locis nunc communibus ut proferam, expectatis Auditores? Non suo tempore repertos fuisse Oratores Cicero conqueritur, qui dilatare, & à propria ac definita disputatione hominis & temporis, ad communem uniuersi generis traducere Orationem potuerint: luminosas maximè, & quasi actuosas eas esse partes affirmat, quae Theses & locos communes habe[n]t. Horum & rectè prudenterq[ue] inueniendorum, & decorè adhibendorum & tractandorum copiosè, ornatè, oratoriè ratione[m] omnium optimam Ciceronis in Orationibus reperiri, nemo, opinor, inficiabitur, nisi qui in ijsdem hospes planè ac peregrinus extiterit. Est locus communis insignis de Religione, pro Domo, & de Haruspicum responsis: de diuina prouidentia in 4. Catil. & pro Milone: de vi conscientae, pro S. Roscio & Milone: de animae immortalitate pro Archia" (Iunius 1592b, 222).

thoroughly indexed editions in Strasbourg by Sturm and his colleagues.³⁴ In 1581, Cicero's orations were printed in three volumes, containing the emendations and the annotations of the French scholar Denis Lambin. The title page announced that the edition was augmented with "theses or commonplaces" (*thesibus item seu locis communibus*), an expression echoed by Révay in the passage quoted above. Indeed, each volume of the edition ends with an index of contents entitled "Ἀποση- μειώσεις" (annotations) which regroups keywords into four or five categories according to the volume: "Philosophicae," "Γνωμολογίαι" (adages), "Historicae," "Grammaticae," and "Rhetoricae" (Cicero 1581). Révay's thematical groups that he suggests for studying Cicero vaguely resemble this division, but the real *theses seu loci communes* promised by the title page of the edition can be found exclusively at the end of the first volume under the title "Index locorum communium."³⁵ This index was adopted and augmented by Melchior Iunius as well, when he published a commentary on Cicero's orations in 1594. In the book, Révay's teacher extracted 21 commonplace themes from Cicero's orations (*Ex. M. Tul. Ciceronis orationibus loci aliquot communes*).³⁶ By the time of its publication, Révay had returned to Hungary. Yet, it is not unlikely that Iunius used similar methods to teach rhetorical invention when Révay was still in Strasbourg. As Révay's surviving handwritten notes suggest, he indeed had access to Iunius' text before its printed edition, as we shall see below.

Révay formed these annotations into a commonplace book in Strasbourg. They fill about 279 folios, each of them corresponding to a specific heading. Révay was aware of the historical tradition of excerpting: at the beginning of the manuscript, he listed classical and modern authors worth emulating while collecting common-

---

34 That is the case of this volume of Cicero's epistles edited by Sturm: Cicero 1541. In the book, the annotations of the commonplaces are named by the Greek term Ἀποσημειώσεις, like in the edition of Cicero's letters from 1581 (see below).
35 "[D]e fama & existimatione laesa" (*Pro Quinctio*); "de accusatoribus falsis & iniquis calumniatoribus coercendis" (*Pro S. Roscio*); "de patricidii ... crimine" (*Pro S. Roscio*), "de officio magistratus" (*In Verrem* 2); "de difficultate & periculo accusandi" (*In Verrem* 3); "de testimoniis" (*Pro M. Fonteio*); "de scripti & sententiae controuersia" (*Pro A. Caecina*); "de iure iurisq[ue] consultis" (*Pro A. Caecinna*) (Cicero 1581, I, i1r–i5v).
36 The first eight *loci* are the same as Cicero 1581. The rest are the following: "De Animaduersionibus, notationibus & subsciptionibus censorijs" (*Pro. A. Cluentio*), "De Iurisprudentia" (*Pro L. Muraena*), "De Accusatoru[m] autoritate" (*Pro L. Muraena*), "De Literarum studijs" (*Pro Archia Poeta*), "De Laudis atque gloriae studio" (*Pro Archia Poeta*), "De Religionis studio" (*De Harispicum responsis*), "De Gratitudine" (*Pro Cn. Plancio*), "De optimatum conditione & officio" (*Pro P. Sextio*), "De Adolescentum voluptatibus & erratis" (*Pro M. Caelio*), "De Vindicta priuata & vi repellenda" (*Pro Milone*), "De Ratione vera parandae potentiae" (*Philippica* 1), "De Aetate Magistratus" (*Philippica* 5), "De Animaduersionibus ac poenis" (*Philippica* 8) (Iunius 1594).

places: Joannes Stobaeus, Valerius Maximus, Conrad Lycosthenes, and the author of the *Polyanthea*.[37] Despite Révay's involvement in this tradition and his familiarity with well-organized, printed commonplace books, the notebook does not have their well-rounded structure, and there are even some key-words which occur twice. It is true that Révay intended to remediate this redundancy by adding cross-references to the headings. Vague topical groups of headings can be discerned as well, and he also used the simple method proposed by Agricola and Erasmus—that is, organizing keywords into dichotomies, such as vice and virtue.[38]

Nevertheless, there are a few indications that Révay did systematic work. These above-mentioned moral dichotomies originate from an Aristotelian approach which identified virtue as a middle way between vicious extremities: true generosity (*liberalitas*), for instance, is placed between prodigality (*prodigalitas*) and avarice (*avaritia*). On the very first page, Révay designates the source of ethical erudition: the *Epitome doctrinae moralis*, the textbook of the Strasbourg professor Theophilus (Gottlieb) Golius: "Generosity is a virtue that maintains the middle way in asking for, giving, and receiving money; to know more about the topic, see Theophilus Golius' commentary on Aristotle's *Nicomachean Ethics* that I received in Strasbourg in 1588, page 1."[39] The work discussed Aristotelian ethics in a catechetic form (questions and responses), including virtues and vices. Comparing their order in the textbook with the beginning of Révay's annotations, the similarity is striking.

Révay's thoroughness also manifests in the way he treated Cicero's works in the annotations. The Roman orator is clearly the most quoted antique author in the manuscript, and Révay's indications reveal that he used Sturm's edition of

---

[37] ALE MS II 253, [1v]: "Auctores q[ui] locos comunes scripserunt. / Stobaeus / Conradus Lycosthenes / Valerius Max[imus] / Polyanthea / Vitae Ciceronis et Demosth[enis]" (Authors who wrote commonplace books, etc.). This latter entry might be a reference to Plutarch's biography of the two orators. Révay perhaps had a section in mind where the author makes a short remark about note-taking (*Demosthenes*, 2).

[38] For a table of contents, see Supplement 2.

[39] ALE MS II 253, 1r: "Liberalitas est virtus quae mediocritatem servat in expetendis, dandis et accipiendis pecunijs, qua de re plura vide in Comentarijs M. Theophili Golij in Ethica Ar[istote]lis ad Nicomachum, a me excepta anno 1588 Argentorati, pagina—I." All the editions listed in VD16 are posterior to 1588. Révay certainly made a mistake noting the page number; for the quotation, see Golius 1597, 147. The author enumerates on the same page the virtues discussed in Book IV of the *Nicomachean Ethics*: "Liberalitas, Magnificentia, Magnanimitas, Modestia circa honores, Mansuetudo, Veritas, Comitas, et Urbanitas." Golius discusses the extremities of each virtue, identified as vices (*vitia*): accordingly, the two extremities of generosity are *profusio/prodigalitas* and *avaritia* (Golius 1597: 153), those of *magnificentia* are *luxus* and *sordes* (Golius 1597, 160), those of *mansuetudo* are *lentitudo* and *iracundia* (Golius 1597, 172), etc.

the orations in three volumes. While searching for quotations, he proceeded according to the prescriptions he gave in his oratorial praise of Cicero, or as it is chronologically more likely, he used his commonplace collection based on Iunius' method to compose the list of Ciceronian topics in his oration. At first glance, the commonplace system of the speech is very different from the table of contents of the annotations. Yet, if we compare the few headings which are similar in the two sources, we cannot unsee the correspondences. In the speech, Révay proposes to discuss the power of conscience (*de vi conscientiae*) with the help of Cicero's *Pro Sexto Roscio Amerino* et *Pro Milone* (Iunius 1592, 222). Accordingly, he put quotations from these two speeches under the heading "Conscientia" of his commonplace book with the *Pro Aulo Cluentio* speech and a letter to Quintus, Cicero's brother:

> *On behalf of Cluentius:* if conscious is the witness of our best counsels throughout our whole lives, we shall live with no fear and in the greatest honor. *Letter to his brother Quintus:* apart from crime and wrongdoing, nothing can trouble a good man. *On behalf of Roscius Amerinus:* do not believe what you often see in fables, that those who have acted impiously and wickedly are persecuted and frightened by furies with burning torches. They are disturbed by their own fraud and their fear, their own wickedness drives them and afflicts them with madness; the remorse of their own soul frightens them, etc. *On behalf of Milo:* the power of conscience is great, and it is in both parts: it does not frighten those who have done nothing wrong, but it does make those who have committed a crime believe that their punishment is right before their eyes.[40]

About earthquakes (*de terrae motu*), Révay refers to the *De Haruspicum responsis*, Cicero's speech about omens (Iunius 1592b, 217), which also figures in the commonplace book.[41] Sometimes, instead of directly referring to Cicero's text, Révay quotes

---

40 ALE MS II 253, 23r: "Cicero pro Cluentio. Si optimor[um] consilior[um] in omni uita testis conscientia, sine ullo metu summa cum volupta[te] [recte: honestate] vivemus. [Cicero, *Pro Aulo Cluentio*, LVIII, 159.] Et idem ad Q[uintum] Fratrem Ep[istu]la 1. P[rae]ter culpam et peccatum nihil est quod sit viro bono permiscendum. [It is rather a summary than a direct quotation. Révay thought probably on *Epist. ad Quintum fratrum*, 1.1.15–16.] / Idem pro Sexto Roscio Amerino Colum. 33. litt. c. Nolite putare q[uem] ad modum in fabulis saepenumero videtis, eos, q[ui] aliq[uid] impie scelerateq[ue] commiserunt, agitari et perterreri furiar[um] taedis ardentibus. Sua quemq[ue] fraus et suus terror maxime vexat, suum quemq[ue] scelus agitat, amentiaq[ue] afficit, suae malae cogitationes conscientiaeq[ue] animi terrent etc. [*Pro Sexto Roscio*, 67] / Cicero Pro Milone Col. 179 litt. a. Arg[entorati] fol. 113. Magna vis est conscientiae, et magna in utraque partem: ut n[e]q[ue] timeant qui nihil commisserint, et poena[m] semp[er] ante oculos versari putent qui peccarint" (*Pro Milone*, XXIII, 61). The number of the folio matches the annotated edition of 1581 (Cicero 1581, III, 113r).
41 "Do not believe what happens in fables, that a god from heaven goes to the assembly of men, lives on earth, and talks to men; on the contrary: he warns people, when he sends fearful events,

a *dictata*, a text dictated by Melchior Iunius, and the *Theses et loci communes Ciceronis*, which was the title of an annotation in the 1581 edition of Cicero's orations, as we have seen. This applies to the heading "Homicidium, Parricidium" in the manuscript,[42] where he mentions Cicero's *Pro Roscio* in accordance with his speech where he proposed to study the punishment of parricide (*De parricidij poena*) via the same oration (Iunius 1592b, 223). Révay proceeds similarly when he refers to the *Pro Roscio* to discuss false accusations and calumniators both in his speech (*De accusatorum multitudine & improbitate*, Iunius 1592b, 223) and in his commonplace book (*Accusatores, Calumniatores, Obtrectator*).[43] Révay must have known the *Pro Roscio* very well: Roscius was accused of murdering his father, and, as we have seen, Révay delivered a speech about a similar topic under Iunius' supervision. Both the *locus* of false accusations and the *locus* of parricide that Révay cites from Iunius' *dictata* and Cicero's commonplaces can be matched with corresponding sections of the index in the edition of 1581 and of Iunius' book from 1594.[44] It is thus more than likely that the text dictated by the teacher

---

when thunder strikes, and horrible things are announced by an earthquake," ALE MS II 253, f. 59r: "Cicero in oratio[ne] de Haruspicu[m] Responsis fol. Arg. 258: Non, inq[ui]t, ut in fabulis fieri solet deus aliq[ui]s e caelo coetus ho[mi]num adit, uersatur in terris, loq[ui]tur cum hom[ini]b[us], tum monet h[omi]nes, cum res metuendas mittit, intonatur sonitus, terraemotus nunciantur horribiles" (*De Haruspicum responsis*, XXVIII, 62; cf. Cicero 1581, II, 258v).

42 "See also the text dictated by Iunius from *Theses et loci communes Ciceronis*, where you can find several nice things about this topic from Plato, Aristotle, Plutarch, Seneca, Cicero, and Demosthenes, and also those provided by himself [Iunius] about the matter on page 11 and 12; see the oration about parricide imitating Cicero's On behalf *Roscius Amerinus*," ALE MS II 253, f. 84r: "Vide etiam dictata d. Iunij de Thesiu[m] et locor[um] communiu[m] Cic[er]onis in orationib[us] tractatione et usu, ubi reperies varias venustas hac de re, ex Platone, Ar[istote]lle, Plutarcho, Seneca, C[icer]one, Demosthene et ex ipso etia[m] inre allatas fol. 11o. Et ibidem fol. 12o oratione[m] de parricidio ad imitation[em] C[ice]ronis p[ro] Roscio Amerino."

43 "See in the dictated text, what we have made [?] from the *Theses et loci communes Ciceronis*, the commonplace about false accusers and about the coercion of testimonies—made after the oration *On behalf Roscius Amerinus*," ALE MS II 253, 229r: "Vide in dictatis, q[uae] [unreadable] de Thesiu[m] et locor[um] communium Cice[ro]nis etc., locum co[m]munem de accusatorib[u] falsis et testimonionib[us] coërcendis (depromtum ex oratione p[ro] Roscio Amerino fol. 27 v. 23) folio 6°."

44 "[D]e parricidii ... crimine ... Locus est in orat. eadem pro. S. Roscio ..." (Cicero 1581, I, i1v–i2r: About the crime of parricide, there is a locus in his oration *On behalf of Roscius*); "de accusatoribus falsis, & iniquis calumniatoribus coercendis ... Locus est in orat. pro S. Roscio ..." (Cicero 1581, I, i1v: about the false accusers and the unjust coercion of calumniators, there is a locus in *On behalf of Roscius*); "Locus communis de parricidii crimine. Ex Oratione pro Sex. Roscio Amerino" (Iunius 1594, 30: commonplace about the crime of parricide from *Roscius*); "Locus communis de accusatorum falsorum et calumniatorum licentia coercenda. Ex Oratione Ciceronis pro Sext. Roscio Amer-

to his students during Révay's studies at the Strasbourg gymnasium was similar to the work he published in print a few years later.

The Ciceronian erudition remained crucial in Révay's works. His *De Monarchia* contains quotations from the same corpus of Cicero's orations as his notebook. Like his commonplaces and his eulogy for the Roman rhetor, his book manifested an interest in Cicero's opinions about prodigious signs, and he did not miss to echo the *Pro Murena* speech as a nice memory of the part he had played in the trial staged in Iunius' class.[45]

During his years in Strasbourg, Cicero was one of Révay's guides to political prudence. Under the title "Historia, Historicus" of his commonplace annotations, he noted several phrases from the Roman orator, including a simple piece of wisdom: "In the *Perfect Orator* [sic!], Cicero claims that ignoring what happened before you were born is equivalent to remaining a child forever."[46] Knowing history is essential for political activity, as Aristotle says in one of the quotations—"Aristotle writes that past things thoroughly written are most useful for public deliberation"[47]—but the political value of history does not reside solely in its rhetorical potential. Referring also to a Hungarian humanist and senior contemporary, Joannes Sambucus (1531–1584), who must have been a personal and patriotic

---

ino" (Iunius 1594, 15: commonplace about false accusers and the coercion of calumniators from the oration for *Roscius*).

45 An exclamation about human inconstancy: "Alas, what a slippery road the world offers to [human?] nature" (Cicero, *Pro Coelio*, 41; Révay 2021, I, 374 [3.17.7]: "Proh quam multas mundus naturae vias lubricas ostendit"). The text evokes a comet as "being always a bad omen" preceding the defeat of Sigismund of Luxembourg by the Ottomans: "cometas semper calamitatum praenuntios fuisse" (Cicero, *De natura deorum*, 2.5.14, and Révay 2021, I, 456 [5.9.4]). The same topic is present both in the *Annotationes* (ALE MS II 224, 352r: "Divinatio") and in his praise of Cicero (in the locus "de coeli ardoribus, Cometis, fulminibus" where he recommends the third speech against Catilina: Iunius 1592b, 217). And discussing the risks of an armed crowd during a political rally, Révay quotes the *Pro Murena*: "There is no maritime storm, no Western wind which would cause as much commotion, as many diverse waves, as the perturbations and troubles caused by assemblies—especially armed assemblies" (Révay 2021, II, 264 [6.142.3]: "Nullum fretum, nullus zephyrus, tot motus, tantas tam varias habet agitationes fluctuum, quantas perturbationes et aestus habet ratio comitiorum, potissimum armatorum"; cf. Cicero, *Pro Murena*, 35).

46 ALE MS II 253, 44r: "Cicero in Perfecto Oratore [inserted from above: Col: 368. litt. e] nescire, inquit quid anteq[uam] natus sis acciderit est semper puerum esse" (Cicero, *Orator ad M. Brutum*, 34.120; despite Révay's indication of the page number, I could not identify the edition used by him amongst the Strasbourg editions of Cicero).

47 ALE MS II 253, 44r: "Aristoteles lib. 1. Rh. Cap. 4. Ad publica consilia, diligenter perscriptam rerum gestarum esse scribit perutilem" (Aristotle, *Rhetoric*, I, 4, 1–13).

choice for him,⁴⁸ Révay gathered here several quotations which affirm the political uses of history: "The main utility of history resides in the fact that it can make one cautious and wise by the means of the peril of others and without their own peril, and you can use the examples you receive from it for anything you want."⁴⁹ If this discipline is powerful, it is because it can provide a multitude of examples from the past, more than what a lifetime of experience can do, and it has an advantage over real political action in that it is not dangerous. To prepare an individual against the turmoil of politics, the number and the variety of these examples is key, as Nikolaus Reusner affirms in a treaty about political eloquence, quoted here as well:

> History is an eternal treasury of examples and it is like a picture or a theatre of all human life corresponding with every age and time, the main power of which is its capacity to make us farsighted and circumspect in every aspect of life with examples and various decisions and results.⁵⁰

Cicero's influence is also manifest under a heading called "Honestum" of the notebook. At this *locus*, Révay quotes from the *De officiis* to discuss the relation between honesty and utility (*utile et honestum*):

> If the eyes could discern honesty, says Plato, it would stimulate a miraculous love of wisdom in us. See also book 3 of *De Officiis* where the author discusses excellent maxims about how to preserve utility and honesty. He proves for philosophers and orators that honesty must be preferred to usefulness ... Column 524 proposes some examples of the Romans and stories that prefer honesty to utility.⁵¹

---

48 "The utility, the task, and the subject of history are elegantly described by Joannes Sambucus in his preface to Bonfini," ALE MS II 253, 44r: "Historiae utilitatem officium atque p[ro]positum describit eleganter Joannes Sambucus in p[rae]fation[em] Bonfinij." Joannes Sambucus was a physician in the imperial court of Vienna, a humanist, and a collector of manuscripts; for more about him, see Almási and Kiss 2014 as well as Gastgeber and Klecker 2018. He published, amongst other works, the Hungarian history of King Mathias' Italian historiographer, Antonio Bonfini. Révay could have used one of these two editions: Bonfini 1568 or Bonfini 1581.
49 ALE MS II 253, 44r: "Historiae utilitas p[rae]cipua periculis alior[um] sine periculo suo cautum sapientemq[ue] fieri, exempla inde capere omnigena q[uae] ad usum tuum qualibet in re traducas." The *Polyanthea*, from which Révay probably took this quotation, attributes it to the *Bibliotheca historica* by Diodorus Siculus (Nanus Mirabellius and Amantius 1574, 368).
50 ALE MS II 253, 44r: "Historia est perpetuus thesaurus exemplorum et pictura ac veluti theatrum totius vitae humanae omnibus mundi aetatibus ac temporibus congruens, cuius ea vis est ut exemplis et varietate consioliorum et eventuum ad omnem vitae usum nos providos et circumspectos efficere possit," Cf. Reusner 1595, 22v.
51 ALE MS II 253, 358r: "Honestum si oculis cerneretur mirabiles amores, ut ait Plato, excitaret sapientiae. V[ide] Ciceronis lib. 1. Off[iciorum] Col. 465. lit. s. [Cicero, *De officiis*, I, 5, 15] / V[ide]

Révay's reference to Book III of Cicero's work is particularly interesting. According to Stoic teaching, no dishonest deed can be useful, at least in the long term. Affirming the absolute inseparability of righteousness and efficiency in moral and political actions, Cicero discusses contracts, simulation and dissimilation, and truth and lies in politics and in business. A very large section of this part is devoted to keeping promises and vows: can a political decision maker break his word if it is useful for the state? Cicero acknowledges very few cases in which promises are allowed to be broken. A coerced promise, for instance, is no valid excuse for him, and even a pledge given to our enemies must be kept. The only exception is a vow given to an illegitimate enemy, such as pirates; yet one should keep their promises made to a legitimate military opponent.[52] An honest man keeps his oath, even if given to unfaithful people (*infideli*):

> Therefore, those who discuss these problems with more rigor make bold to say that moral wrong is the only evil, while those who treat them with more laxity do not hesitate to call it the supreme evil. Once more, they quote the sentiment: "None have I given, none give I ever to the faithless." It was proper for the poet to say that, because, when he was working out his Atreus, he had to make the words fit the character. But if they mean to adopt it as a principle, that a pledge given to the faithless is no pledge, let them look to it that it be not a mere loophole for perjury that they seek (Cicero 1913, 385).[53]

By the 16th century, these *infideli* had been identified with non-Christian enemies, in particular with the Ottoman invaders. In the *Six livres de la république* (V, 6), Bodin raises the question of contracts and oaths in the context of Muslim-Christian relations, concluding in accordance with Cicero that natural law applies to treaties between parties of different religions. The subject of righteousness and usefulness

---

etia[m] lib. 3 Off. [inserted from above: 519 lit. b. etc.] Col. 521 lit. d & sequ[entes] qu[in]que Col. Ubi de utilitate et honestate deservanda p[rae]cepta aliqua egregia tractat etc. Honestatem utilitati p[rae]ferendam ... philosophis & raetorib[us] p[ro]bat ... / Et Col. 524 lit. c affert aliquot ex[em]pla Romanor[um] & Historias q[uae] honestum utilitati pr[ae]tulerunt."

52 Cicero, *De officiis*, III, 29.106–108 (the distinction between pirates and legitimate military opponents), III, 30.110 (about coerced promises).

53 "Itaque nervosius qui ista disserunt, solum audent malum dicere id, quod turpe sit, qui autem remissius, ii tamen non dubitant summum malum dicere. Nam illud quidem: / Neque dedi neque do infideli cuiquam / idcirco recte a poeta, quia, cum tractaretur Atreus, personae serviendum fuit. Sed si hoc sibi sument, nullam esse fidem, quae infideli data sit, videant, ne quaeratur latebra periurio" (Cicero, *De officiis*, III, 29.106). The embedded quotation ("Neque dedi neque do infideli cuiquam") is a fragment from *Atreus*, Lucius Accius' lost tragedy. This passage is quoted and condemned by religious authorities who consider oath-breaking as a sort of blasphemy against God's name, amongst them Calvin (in his commentary on Deut. 10:20: "In nomine eius iurabis": Calvin 1882, 562).

also appears in the *Methodus* as commonplaces which can be employed to excerpt history. He suggests that one should keep a notebook filled with historical *exempla* which are to be marked with the adjectives *honestum* and/or *utile*. If an example of the past corresponds to both categories, then it is both morally acceptable and politically fruitful, and it may be followed by a scrupulous statesman (Melani 2006, 95–96, and 2012, 146–148).

In Strasbourg, Révay probably did not know Bodin yet, but later, one of the *République*'s examples could have drawn Révay's attention, though he must have known it from many other sources—namely, the peace treaty that was concluded between the Kingdom of Hungary and the Ottoman Empire in the town of Szeged, Southern Hungary in 1444. By signing this treaty, confirmed with his oath taken on the Gospel, King Władysław I (Władysław III as King of Poland) quit the anti-Ottoman league forged between the pope and the Emperor of Byzantium. The papal nuncio, Cardinal Giulio Cesarini, convinced him to attack the Turks anyway. This campaign led to the fatal battle of Varna, where the king died. In protestant historiography, this tragedy was often interpreted as an instance of divine punishment for oath-breaking provoked by Catholic machinations, but even standing on the ground of natural law, failing to comply with a treaty was repulsive to authors like Bodin.[54] Révay commemorates this event in both of his works. In the *Commentarius*, his description is rather neutral, but in the *De Monarchia*, he manifests his denominational partiality by adding a scandalous detail which emphasizes the sacrilegious nature of the conduct of the Catholics in this matter: according to Révay, Sultan Murad II received a piece of sacred host as a warrant of the treaty from the Christians, and he had it with him when he implored for divine vengeance during the battle (Révay 2021, I, 509–510 [5.31.9]). No other historian of Hungary reports this odd circumstance. Beyond anti-papal allegations, Révay also takes recourse to the Ciceronian vocabulary of *honestum* and *utile* while interpreting the event: "May advisors take care not to give princes advice which is against equity and *honesty*, for such attempts are *fruitless* for those who are counselled and for those who

---

[54] The popularity of the battle in anti-Catholic pamphlets and in jurisprudential arguments on treatises is largely due to a wide-spread epigram, i.e., a fictious epitaph of King Władysław. The poem is also reproduced by Révay: "Cannae was made famous by the Romans and Varna by me with my fall. Mortals, learn that oaths must not be violated. Had the prelates not commanded me to break the alliance, now the Pannonian region would not bear the yoke of the Scythians [i.e., Turks]" (Romulidae Cannas, ego Varnam clade notavi, / Discite mortales non temerare fidem. / Me nisi pontifices iussissent, rumpere foedus, / Non ferret Scythicum Pannonis ora iugum) (Révay 2021, I, 510 [5.31.13]). It was recently shown that its author was Christophorus Manlius (1546–1575), a poet active in Lausitz (Szentmártoni Szabó 2012, 183–186).

counsel."[55] Discussing the king's death as a divine punishment like many other authors, Révay also echoes the Ciceronian terms: what seems to be useful is not always honest, and what is dishonest is never useful.

In Révay's work, *utile* and *honestum*, as the basic categories in this Ciceronian branch of "virtue politics" (Hankins 2019, 31–62), reflect a moral engagement which cannot permit any noble goal to justify violent means. Their role is clear in the description of the historical agency of the Holy Crown: the artifact mediates God's punishment for the abuse of power. For instance, the reign of King Béla I is described as a mixture of useful and dishonest: his rule was rather good, but he seized power in a murderous way, which was unpleasant for the crown. As a divine punishment, his throne collapsed and killed him while he was sitting on it in 1063 (Révay 2021, I, 283 [1.171.2]). Another passage reveals that although the duality of *honestum* and *utile* is a condition *sine qua non* of moral and political success, they are not sufficient: other deliberations (political in the strict sense of the term) are necessary as well. In this section, Révay explains why the alliance offered by King Béla IV to the Cumans did not work despite the ruler's good will: "Although Béla's decision seemed to be both honest and useful, it was not fortunate for either of the parties."[56] On the other hand, the harmony of righteousness and usefulness is key to the prosperity of the realm: according to Révay, Louis I contributed to the *honest* reputation of the Hungarian and his reign was *useful* for the state. He also knew how to *be of use* in a *righteous* way:

> Because his government was not only salutary for the heroism and the good reputation of the Hungarian but also useful for the other countries of the Christian commonwealth, for the king who excelled with his courageous acts, and on whom as by a rope the condition of the realm was depending, was of use not only for his own in a righteous way, but he also ruled over those who resisted the power of the Holy Crown.[57]

The semantic field of *honestum* enables martial "beauty" and glory to be linked to *utile* as well. That happens in a passage where Révay discusses the victorious battle

---

55 "*Videant itaque consultores, ne principibus contra aequi, et **honesti** rationes suadeant: nam talia molimina **improspere** cedunt, et illi, qui paret, et qui consulit*" (Révay 2021, I, 510 [5.32.3]; italics in the original, the bold letters are mine).
56 "Sed hoc Belae licet honestum et utile videbatur esse consilium, neutri parti felix fuit" (Révay 2021, I, 354 [3.6.7]).
57 "Eius quippe gubernatio non solum Hungaricae virtuti, et *nomini honesto* apprime salutaris, sed et reliquis provinciis christianae reipublicae summe *utilis* extiterat, quando rex rebus fortissime gestis insignis, et a cuius salute, velut filo pendebat multorum status regnorum, non solum suis *recte profuit*, sed etiam hostibus imperii Monarchiae Sacrae Coronae praefuit" (Révay 2021, I, 408 [4.16, 5]. The italics are mine).

of Székesfehérvár and the recapture of the castle of Fülek from the Ottomans in 1593, during the Long Turkish War: "at that time, there was another victory, as beautiful and splendid as useful for the Hungarian."[58]

5 Conclusion: Methodological Remarks

In Strasbourg, Révay was already receptive to Bodin's methodological recommendations about structuring and evaluating historical data. The Ciceronian approach to oratorial and civic matters, which both characterized Jesuit education and Sturmian protestant humanism, had prepared him well. In fact, it is more plausible that, contrary to what some researchers have formerly suggested, he did not have to rely on Bodin when he elaborated his approach of coordinating *exempla* of the past and using them to phrase political advice. To conclude, a study of pedagogical procedures implemented in his education and of unprinted sources, such as handwritten commonplace books, might be as fruitful as studying the influence of important classics of the history of ideas, because it reveals how they shaped knowledge, not only in the framework of studies, but also with a long-term effect on one's mindset.

Studying Révay's annotations in the mirror of his other academic texts and later literary production facilitates a few methodological observations. Recent contributions about commonplace books and excerpts emphasized the optical layout of early modern annotations. Echoing Ong's thesis that note-taking in the post-Ramist period had an exceptional capacity to display the relationship between notions and data in a geometrically organized way on the plane of the paper, this approach suggests that the very structure of early modern knowledge management has been externalized in annotations, consequently this inner structure is identical with that of the visible elements of the documents. For example, Élisabeth Décultot, a specialist in Winckelmann's annotations, qualifies excerpts as "the organisational charts" (*organigramme*) of their owners' thinking (Décultot 2003, 28), whereas Alberto Cevolini argues that early modern commonplace books are "forgetting machines" because they outsource memory from the human mind to the medium of paper (Cevolini 2016). It is true that some of these evaluations take printed commonplace collections into consideration as well, in which case a clear arrangement of information was key to the usefulness of the book. The structure of privately used manuscripts, however, does not always justify this kind of optimism. Despite

---

[58] "Nam et altera illa non minus pulchra et solennis quam utilis eodem tempore Hungaris contigerat victoria" (Révay 2021, II, 290 [6.154.2]).

the presence of keywords, the principle of their organization does not surrender easily to researchers, but as the example of Révay demonstrates, the reconstruction of the student's pedagogical surroundings and his own interests can help in finding order where there does not seem to be any.

Supplement 1:
Cicero's commonplaces in Révay's *Oratio ... de laudibus M. Tul. Ciceronis*

Page	Main subject	Locus	Text recommended
215	Philosophy	"de virtutibus imperatoriis"	"In Maniliana"
		"de corporis & fortunae bonis"	"pro domo"
		"de officiorum finibus"	"pro Muraena"
		"de amicitia"	"pro Plancio"
		"de religione"	"libr. 4 in Verrem pro Cluentio & Domo"
		"de patriae charitate"	"in Haruspicum responsis & 13. Philip."
		"de fortitudine"	"4. Catil. & Miloniana"
		"de Gratitudine"	"post reditum in Senatum & ad Quirites, de Prouinciis consularibus"
		"de veritate"	"pro Caelio"
		"de Seueritate"	"libro 3. & 5. in Verrem"
		"de Clementia"	"pro Marcello & Ligario"
		"de inuidia"	"pro Cluentio, Plancio, Balbo. 10. & 14. Philip."
216	Politics	"de diuina prouidentia in imperiis constituendis"	"locus de Haruspicum responsis"
		"miseriae illorum [imperiorum]"	"Respub"; "pro domo"
		"de Magistratuum conditione laboriosa"	"pro Flacco"
		"de salute communi rebus anteponenda priuatis"	"pro Sylla"
		"de Iudicum officio ac potestate"	"pro Quintio, Roscio 1 & 4. in Verrem, pro Fonteio, Cluentio, Muraena, Rabirio Posthumo"
		"de largitionibus vitandis"	"2 in Verrem"
		"de vigilantia & circumspectione"	"pro Plancio"
		"de Tyrannide fugienda"	"1. & 2. Philip."
		"de multitudinis inconstantia"	"pro Q. Roscio Comaedo, Domo, Plancio"
		"de ratione verae parandae gloriae"	"1. Philipp."
		"de Nobilium conditione atque officio"	"pro S. Roscio, Sextio, Cluentio"

Continued

Page	Main subject	Locus	Text recommended
		"de legatorum priuilegiis"	"primo, in Verrem & de Haruspicum responsis"
		"de Consilij ac sententiae mutatione"	"pro Plancio, Balbo 12. Philipp."
		"de dissensionum"	"in Repub. causis. 2. Agraria & Haruspicum responsis"
		"de libertate defendenda"	"2 Agraria 4. Catilinaria 3. 4. 8. 10. 13. Philip.
		"de mora & procrastinatione vitanda"	"Philipp. 3. 5. 6."
		"de conuiciis & maledictis aliorum ferendis"	"pro Roscio Comaedo, Muraena, Plancio, de Haruspicum responsis"
		"de domus cuiusque immunitate"	"pro Domo"
217	Physics	"de corporis lineamentis"	"pro Cluentio"
		"de coci natura & victus consuetudine"	"2 Agraria"
		"de rerum naturalium fragilitate"	"11. Philip."
		"de immoderatis tempestatibus"	"pro Sexto Roscio"
		"de terrae motu"	"in Haruspicum responsis"
		"de coeli ardoribus, Cometis, fulminibus"	"3. Catilinaria"
	Law	"de curatione ac potestate"	"Agraria"
		"de prouinciis Consularibus"	"In Vatiniu[m] & Pisone[m]"
		"de Coloniis"	"pro Balbo"
		"de ambitu"	"p[ro] Muraena"
		"de vi"	"pro Domo, Sestio, Milone"
		"de pecunijs repetu[n]dis"	"pro Rabirio Posthumo & Balbo"
		"de proscriptis"	"lib. 1. in Verre[m] & pro Cluentio"
		"de seruis alienis retentis"	"pro Rabirio"
218		"de ciuium Romanorum pulsation"	"libr. 5 in Verrem"
		"de re fumentaria"	"in Verrem"
		"de ciuitate"	"pro Balbo & Archia poëta"
		"de Accusatoribus"	"pro S. Roscio, pro Muraena & 2. in Philip."

...

Page	Main subject	Locus	Text recommended
222	Oratorial subjects (commonplaces)	"de Religione"	"pro Domo, & de Haruspicum responsis"
		"de diuina prouidentia"	"in 4. Catil. & pro Milone"
		"de vi conscientiae"	"pro S. Roscio & Milone"
		"de animae immortalitate"	"pro Archia & Milone"
		"de improborum poenis ac supplicij"	"pro Roscio, Catilinaria 1. 4. & 8. Philip."
		"de rerum humanarum inconstantia & mutatione"	"5. & 11. Philip."

Continued

Page	Main subject	Locus	Text recommended
		"de gratitudine"	"pro Plancio"
		"de domus cuiusque religione ac sanctitate"	"pro Domo"
		"de Senatus grauitate & constantia"	"in 7. Philip."
		"de Iudicis sapientis officio"	"pro Cluentio"
		"de seueritate in puniendis delictis"	"Catil. 5. 1. 4. pro Sextio"
		"de Nobilium ingenio & co[n]ditione"	"pro Quintio, S. Roscio, Sextio"
		"de gratitudine"	"pro Plancio"
223		"de lentitudine ac remissione bonorum, sedulitate contra improborum"	"pro Sextio"
		"de poenitentia & erroris agnitione"	"Philip. 2"
		"de ratione emergendi in Repub."	"pro Sextio & 1. Philip."
		"de viris popularibus"	"2. Agraria"
		"de periculi & mortis fuga honesta"	"pro Sextio"
		"de πολυπραγμοσυνη"	"10 Philip."
		"de exilio"	"pro Cecinna 2. Agraria, Sylla, Milone"
		"de Comitiorum inconstantia"	"pro Muraena"
		"de Epicureorum & Stoicorum doctrina"	"ibidem" [Pro Muraena]
		"de Statuis & monumentis benemeritorum"	"9. Philip."
		"de Iuris ciuilis dignitate & praestantia"	"pro Cecinna & Cluentio"
		"de accusatorum multitudine & improbitate"	"pro S. Roscio"
		"de parricidij poena"	"ibidem" [Pro S. Roscio]
		"de officij & honoribus iuuenum"	"5 & 11. Philip."
		"de difficultate gerendi Magistratus"	"pro Flacco"
		"de Agriculturae praestantia"	"pro Roscio"
		"de vi armis repellenda"	"pro Milone"
		"de peregrinitate"	"pro Sylla"
		"de Censoria animaduersione"	"pro Cluentio"
		"de testimonijs"	"pro Roscio Comoedo, Fonteio, Sylla"
		"de Tyrannorum conditione misera"	"1. Philip."
		"de leuitate certarum nationum"	"pro Flaccio"
		"de conditione hominum nouorum"	"lib. 5. in Verrem"
		"de sententiae mutatione"	"pro Plancio"
		"de bonorum proscriptione"	"pro Quintio"
		"de obtrectatoribus & calumniatoribus"	"pro Plancio"
		"de eloquentia"	"pro Muraena"
		"de arte Poëtica"	"pro Archia"

Supplement 2:
The table of contents of Révay's commonplace book from Strasbourg

Munificientia, Liberalitas, Benignitas	1r
Prodigalitas, Prodigus	2r
Avaritia	3r
Magnificentia	4r
Magnanimitas, Fortitudo	5r
Pusillanimitas	6r
Superbia, Arrogantia	7r
Modestia	8r
Ambitio	9r
Mansuetudo, Clementia	10r
Ira, Iracundia	11r
Eloquentia, Orator	12r
Studia, Doctrina	13r
Philosophia	14r
Joci, Facetia, Ludi	15r
Respublica, Regnum	16r
Disputatio	17r
Orator, Eloquens, Eloquentia	18r
Ingenium	19r
Epistola	20r
Magistratus, Princeps	21r
Fama, Existimatio	22r
Conscientia	23r
Victoria	24r
Exordium	25r
Adhortatio, Monitio	26r
Senectus	27r
Laus	28r
Continentia	29r
Jactantia, jactator	30r
Mors	31r
Ingratitudo	32r
Crudelitas	33r
Urbs, Civitas	34r
Facilitas, Comitas, Humanitas, Lenitas	35r
Excidium	36r
Veritas	37r
Mendacium	38r
Proditio, Proditor, Defectio	39r
Scurrilitas	40r
Facies, Persona	41r

Metus	42r
Prodigia, Miracula	43r
Historia, Historicus	44r
Pudor, Verecundia	45r
Labor, Diligentia, Studium, Sedulitas	46r
Conversatio	47r
Humorositas, Facilitas, Comitas, Lenitas	48r
Consuetudo, Usus	49r
Fluvius, Amnis, Inundatio	50r
Curiositas	51r
Credulitas, Facilitas	52r
Largitiones, Munera, Magist[ratorum] venditio	53r
Suspicio, Diffidencia	54r
Amicitia, Amicus	55r
Justicia	56r
Mores	57r
Homo	58r
Terrae motus	59r
Grando, Pluvia, Tempestas	60r
Medicus, Medicina	61r
Ebrietas, Ebrius	62r
Natio	63r
Adulator, Adulatio	64r
Levitas, Insconstantia	65r
Bellum	66r
Pax	67r
Fortuna	68r
Virtus	69r
Divitia, Dives	70r
Audacia	71r
Nobilitas, Nobilis	72r
Legati	73r
Peregrinatio, Peregrini	74r
Solitudo, Mona[c]hus	75r
Gratitudo, Pietas	76r
Sacrilegium	77r
Silentium, Taciturnitas	78r
Consolatio	79r
Avaritia	80r
Magistratus, Princeps	81r
Libertas	82r
Servitus	83r
Homicidium, Parricidium	84r
Turca	85r
Ars	86r
Subditus	87r
Servus	88r

Decorum	89r
Jurisprudentia, Jurisperitus	90r
Castitas, Pudicitia	91r
Leges	92r
Miles sive ars militaris	93r
Judicium, Judex et Judicis iniusti poena	94r
Maeror, Masticina, Dolor	95r
Gaudeum	96r
Sobrietas	96r [sic!]
Voracitas, Edacitas	97r
Libido, Venus, Adulteria	98r
Severitas	99r
Otium, Recreatio, Ludus	100r
Testis, Testimoniu[m]	101r
Aetas	102r
Doctrina, Eruditio, Studia, Litterae	103r
Imperator, Dux	104r
Fortitudo, Magnanimitas	105r
Natura	106r
Patrimonia, Haereditas	107r
Juventus, Adolescentia	108r
Senectus	109r
Gloria, Laus	109r [sic!]
Foenerator, Foenus, Usura	200r [sic]
Prudentia	201r
Utilitas	202r
Voluptas	203r
Agricultura	204r
Anima	205r
Memoria, Oblivio	206r
Exilium	207r
Coniugium, Coniunx, Uxor, Nuptiae	208r
Convivium	209r
Luxus, Luxuria	210r
Aristocratia, Optimates	211r
Populus, Democratici, Democratia	212r
Honor	213r
Egestas, Paupertas	214r
Concordia	215r
Invidia	216r
Coniugiu[m], Matrimoniu[m]	217r
Impietas, Blasphemia	218r
Patria	219r
Tumultus, Seditio	220r
Oratio, Precatio	221r
Indoctis, Inscitia	222r
Praeceptor	223r

Discipulus	224r
Tributum, Vectigal	225r
Exercitatio	226r
Ludus, Rectreationes	227r
Parentes	228r
Accusatores, Calumniatores, Obtrectator	229r
Precatio, Deus et nominis divini invocatio	230r
Furtum, Fur	231r
Morbus, A[e]grotatio	232r
Impietas	233r
Odium, Discordia	234r
Domum, Donatio	235r
Politicus	236r
Somnis	237r
Foemina, Mulieres, Matrona	238r
Speculatio	239r
Religios[us], Religio	240r
Fug[a]citas vel Inconstantia rer[um] humanar[um]	241r
Musica	242r
Stratagema	243r
Venatio	244r
Poena	245r
Physica	245r [sic!]
Geometria	246r
Mathematica, Astronomia	247r
Annus	248r
Imagines, Statuae	249r
Episcopus, Episcopatus	250r
Papa, Pontifex, Pontificatus	251r
Educatio	252r
Summum bonum	253r
Vindicta, Poena	254r
Temperancia	255r
Pictor, Pictura	256r
Patientia, Moderatio	257r
Ultio, Vindicta privata	258r
Ebrietas	259r
Equestris ars	260r
Funus	261r
Foelicitas	262r
Iusiurand[um]	263r
Leges	264r
Lingua	265r
Scelus, Peccatum, Error, Flagitiu[m]	266r
Fuga	267r
Cupiditas nov[orum], Concupiscentia	268r
Detractio, Obtrectatio, Calumniator	269r

Tyrannus, Tyrannis	270r
Amor subditor[um], Amor paternis	271r
Scientia	272r
Senator, Consiliarius	273r
Sapiens, Sapientia	275r [sic!]
Incontinentia	276r
Medicus	277r
Mercatura	278r
Bellum	279r
Appellatu[m]	280r
Magistratus, Princeps	281r
Iudex	282r
Monarchia, Regnum, Rex	283r
Constantia, Perseverantia	284r
Crudelitas	285r
Occasio	286r
Tutor, Tutela	287r
Ignavia	288r
Arma	289r
Magia, Magicus	290r
Peculatus	291r
Inimicitia	292r
Chorea	293r
Gloria	294r
Vestitus	295r
Stultitia, Stultus	296r
Magistratus	297r
Academia, Schola	298r
Testamentu[m]	299r
Filij, Liberi	300r
Infamia, Infamis	301r
Gladiatoria, Palestra	302r
Templum	303r
Peregrinatio, Peregrini	304r
Bonor[um] Communicatio	305r
Obscuritas	306r
Pastor	307r
Ignobilitas	308r
Poësis, Poëta	309r
Auctoritas	310r
Fortuna	311r
Fatum	312r
Festinatio, Celeritas	313r
Temeritas	314r
Procrastin[atio], Cunctatio	315r
Bona externa seu fortunae	316r
Robor seu vires corporis	317r

Forma, Formositas	318r
Dies natalis, Festu[m], Dies festi	319r
Corporis exercitationes	220r [recte: 320r]
Natatio	221r [recte: 321r]
Sagitandi ars seu usus	322r
Aucupium	323r
Nox	324r
Dissimulatio, Occultatio, Simulatio	325r
Amicitia, Amicus	326r
Obedientia	327r
Consultatio, Deliberatio	328r
Foedus, Societas	330r [sic!]
Ira, Iracundia	331r
Mors	332r
Infernus	333r
Mulier, Faemina, Matrona	334r
Frugalitas	335r
Primogenitura	336r
Magistratus, Princeps	337r
Alea	338r
Somnium	339r
Adulator, Adulatio	340r
Sepultura, Epithafiu[m]	341r
Electio	342r
Bellum	343r
Senectus	344r
Asylum	345r
Eventus	346r
Fortuna	347r
Leges	348r
Irrespondentia	349r
Bibliotheca	350r
Ignorantia	351r
Divinatio	352r
Divina Providentia, Deus	353r
Ars militaris, Miles	354r
Vis, Violentia	355r
Mors	356r
Divortium	357r
Honestum	358r
Pecunia	359r
Monomachia	360r
Dives, Divitia	361r
Avaritia	362r
Iniusticia	363r
Iniuria	364r
Philosophia	365r

Ebrietates 365r [sic!]
Aranu[m], Fiscus 366r

Bibliography

Primary Sources

Manuscripts

Archdiocesan Library, Esztergom
MS II 226b
MS II 227a
MS II 274
MS II 308
MS II. 224
MS II. 226a
MS II. 227b
MS II. 227c
MS II. 227d
MS II. 253
MS II. 272
MS II. 273

Printed Sources

Baranyai Decsi, János (1598): *Adagiorum Graecolatinoungaricorum chiliades quinque*. Bardejov: Jakob Klöss.
Bentz, Johann (1581): *Thesaurus elocutionis oratoriae grecolatinus novus ex optimorum autorum resolutione, ad orationis utriusque elegantis uberem copiam delectumque facilem, secundum ordinem naturae in locos LXXVI distinctus*. Basel: Eusebius Episcopius. USTC 697050.
Bentz, Johann (1588): *Locorum communium, comparandae rerum et exemplorum copiae, accomodatorum, genera IIII. Ad usum studiosorum, in Argentinensi Academia, collecta*. Strasbourg: Antonius Bertramus. USTC 673526.
Bentz, Johann (1596a): *Thesauri latinitatis purae compendium primum*. Strasbourg: haered. Berhard Jobin. USTC 697028.
Bentz, Johann (1596b): *Thesauri latinitatis purae compendium alterum*. Strasbourg: haered. Berhard Jobin. USTC 697027.
Bonfini, Antonio (1568): *Antonii Bonfinii Rerum Ungaricarum decades quatuor cum dimidia*. Basel: Johannes Oporinus. USTC 611992.
Bonfini, Antonio (1581): *Rerum Ungaricarum decades quatuor cum dimidia*. Frankfurt am Main: Andreas Wechel. USTC 611994.

Calvin, Jean (1882): *Ioannis Calvini Opera quae supersunt omnia*. Vol. XXIV. Guilielmus Baum, Eudardus Cunitz, and Eduardus Reus (Eds.). Braunschweig: Schwetschke.
Cicero, Marcus Tullius (1541): *M. Tullii Ciceronis alterum epistolarum volumen [...] cum praefatione Ioan. Sturmij ad Vuolfgangum Abbatem Campidunensem: Cum indice & Pauli Manutij annotationibus*. Strasbourg: Wendelin Richel.
Cicero, Marcus Tullius (1581): *Orationum M. T. Ciceronis volumen primum [secundum, tertium] ex emendatione Dionysii Lambini: Nunc primum brevibus, sed utilibus argumentis singularum orationum: thesibus item seu locis communibus, si qui occurrunt, eorumque tractatione*. 3 Volumes. Strasbourg: Josias Richel and Jacques Dupuy. USTC 681246.
Cicero, Marcus Tullius (1913): *De Officiis*. Walter Miller (Ed. and Trans.). Cambridge: Harvard University Press.
Clavius, Christophorus (1570): *In Sphaeram Ioannis de Sacro Bosco commentarius*. Rome: Victor Helianus. USTC 822861.
Dachtler, Gottlieb (1619): *Relatio ex Parnasso*. Strasbourg: Christoph von der Heyden. USTC 2005110.
Des Freux, André (1556): *De utraque copia, verborum et rerum praecepta, una cum exemplis dilucido breuique carmine comprehensa*. Rome: Antonius Bladus. USTC 826597.
Des Freux, André (1561): *De utraque copia, verborum et rerum praecepta, una cum exemplis dilucido breuique carmine comprehensa*. Vienna: Raphael Hoffhalter. USTC 630106.
[Erasmus, Desiderius] (1575): *Adagia quaecumque ad hanc diem exierunt, Paulli Manutii studio, [...] ab omnibus mendis vindicata, quae pium, et veritatis Catholicae studiosum lectorem poterat offendere*. Florence: Iuntas. USTC 828315.
Golius, Theophilus (1597): *Epitome doctrinae moralis ex decem libris Ethicorum Aristotelis ad Nicomachum*. Strasbourg: haered. Josias Richel. USTC 652990.
Guevara, Antonio (1610): *Horologii principum, az az az feiedelmek oraianak masodik koenyve (The second book: The alarm clock of princes)*. János Draskovich (Trans.). Graz: Georg Widmanstadt. USTC 871383.
Guevara, Antonio (1628): *Feiedelmeknec serkentö oraia (Alarm clock of princes)*. András Prágai (Trans.). Bardejov: Jakob Klöss Jr. USTC 871199.
Hawenreuter, Johann Ludwig (1573): *Adagia classica scholis Argentinensibus digesta*. Strasbourg: Josias Richel. USTC 609154.
Hrabecius, Raphael (1623): *Oratio funebris in solennibus exequiis [...] Petri de Rewa*. Košice: Daniel Schultz. USTC 871764.
Iunius, Melchior (1585): *Methodus eloquentiae, comparandae, scholis aliquot Rhetoricis tradita*. Strasbourg: Christian Müller. USTC 675871.
Iunius, Melchior (1592a): *Orationum, quae Argentiensi in Academia exercitii gratia scriptae et recitatae ab illustribus, generosis, nobilibus et aliis [...] pars prima*. Strasbourg: Lazarus Zetzner. USTC 681250.
Iunius, Melchior (1592b): *Orationum [...] pars secunda*. Strasbourg: Lazarus Zetzner. USTC 681253.
Iunius, Melchior (1594): *Ex. M. Tul. Ciceronis orationibus loci aliquot communes, eum in finem selecti atque explicati, ut eorundem tractandi ratio appareat*. Strasbourg: Lazarus Zetzner. USTC 654988.
Lackner, Christoph (1625): *Aphorismi politici pro principe, republica, pace, bello, oeconomia, et bonis moribus ex Horologio principum, in decadas*. Tübingen: Eberhard Wild. USTC 2111016.
Langius, Joseph (1596): *Adagia sive sententiae proverbiales graecae latinae, germanicae*. Strasbourg: Josias Richel. USTC 609156.

Langius, Joseph (1598): *Loci communes sive florilegium rerum et materiarum selectarum: praecipue sententiarum, apophthegmatum, similitudinum, exemplorum, hieroglyphicorum*. Strasbourg: haered. Josias Richel. USTC 673448.

Nanus Mirabellius, Dominicus and Amantius, Bartholomaeus (1574): *Polyanthea, hoc est opus suavissimis floribus clebriorum sententiarum tam Graecarum quam Latinarum*. Cologne: Maternus Cholinus. USTC 684670.

Nanus Mirabellius, Dominicus, Amantius, Bartholomaeus, Tortius, Franciscus, and Langius, Joseph (1607): *Polyanthea nova, hoc est, opus suavissimis floribus celebriorum sententiarum tam graecarum quam latinarum refertum*. Frankfurt: Lazarus Zetzner. USTC 2027428.

Reusner, Nikolaus (1595): "De sapiente perfecto, sive homine vere politico." In: Reusner, Nikolaus: *Orationum panegyricarum volumen secundum*. Jena: Tobias Steinmann, 1r–43v. USTC 678078.

Révay, Péter (1591): *Disputatio de mutuo, materia non minus difficili quam utili, in Inclyti Argentoratensium Academia exercitii causa a ... Petro de Rewa ... Ungaro conscripta, et praeside ... Paulo Graseccio I. U. D. Mense Martio defensa*. Strasbourg: Anton Bertram.

Révay, Péter (1613): *De sacrae coronae regni Hungariae ortu, virtute, victoria, fortuna [...] commentaries*. Augsburg: Christoph Mangus. USTC 2042349.

Révay, Péter (1659): *De monarchia et Sacra Corona regni Hungariae*. Frankfurt: Matthias Götz.

Révay, Péter (2021): *De monarchia et Sacra Corona regni Hungariae centuriae septem: A Magyar Királyság birodalmáról és Szent Koronájáról szóló hét század*. Gergely Tóth (Ed.). 2 Volumes. Budapest: Bölcsészettudományi Kutatóközpont Történettudományi Intézet.

Stannifex, Johannes (Ed.) (1553): *Commentaria in Isagogen Porphyrii, et in omnes libros Aristotelis de dialectica [...] in inclita Academia Lovaniensi [...] composita*. Leuven: Servatius Sassenus. USTC 404939.

Sturm, Johann (1574): *De imitatione oratoria libri tres*. Strasbourg: Bernhard Jobi. USTC 667900.

Secondary Sources

Ács, Pál (2019): *Reformations in Hungary in the Age of the Ottoman Conquest*. Göttingen: Vandenhoeck & Ruprecht.

Almási, Gábor (2016): "*Experientia* and the Machiavellian Turn in Religio-Political and Scientific Thinking: Basel in 1580." In: *History of European Ideas* 41. No. 7, 1–25. DOI: 10.1080/01916599.2016.1161531.

Almási, Gábor and Kiss, Farkas Gábor (2014): *Humanistes du Bassin des Carpates II: Johannes Sambucus*. Turnout: Brepols.

Arnold, Matthieu (2007): "Le projet pédagogique de Jean Sturm (1507–1589): originalité et actualité." In: *Revue d'histoire et de philosophie religieuses* 87. No. 4, 385–413.

Arnold, Matthieu (2009): *Johannes Sturm (1507–1589): Rhetor, Pädagoge und Diplomat*. Tübingen: Mohr Siebeck.

Bak, János M. and Pálffy, Géza (2020): *Crown and Coronation in Hungary 1000–1916 A.D.* Budapest: Research Centre for the Humanities–Hungarian National Museum.

Bartoniek, Emma (1975): *Fejezetek a XVI–XVII. Századi magyarországi történetírás történetéből (Chapters from the history of 16th–17th century Hungarian historiography)*. Budapest: Magyar Tudományos Akadémia Irodalomtudományi Intézete.

Bónis, György (1981): *Révay Péter*. Budapest: Akadémiai Kiadó.

Braakhuis, Henricus A. G. (1988): "Agricola's View on Universals." In: Akkerman, Fokke and Vanderjagt, Arjo J. (Eds.): *Rodolphus Agricola Phrisius 1444–1485*. Leiden: Brill, 237–247.

Buttay-Jutier, Florence (2008): *Fortuna: Usages politiques d'une allégorie morale à la Renaissance*. Paris: PUPS.

Cevolini, Alberto (2006): De arte excerpendi: *Imparare a dimenticare nella modernità*. Florence: Olschki.

Cevolini, Alberto (Ed.) (2016): *Forgetting Machines: Knowledge Management Evolution in Early Modern Europe*. Leiden: Brill.

Coron, Antoine (1976): "Justus Lipsius levelezése a magyarokkal és Révay Péter kiadatlan levele Lipsiushoz [J. L.'s correspondence with Hungarians and P. R.'s unpublished letter to L.]." In: *Irodalomtörténeti Közlemények* 80. No. 4, 495–496.

Couzinet, Marie-Dominique (1996a): "La *Methodus ad facilem historiarum cognitionem:* histoire cosmographique et méthode." In: Zarka, Yves Charles (Ed.): *Jean Bodin: Nature, histoire, droit et politique*. Paris: Presses Universitaires de France, 23–42.

Couzinet, Marie-Dominique (1996b): *Histoire et méthode à la Renaissance: Une lecture de la* Methodus ad facilem cognitionem *de Jean Bodin*. Paris: Vrin.

Cummings, Brian (2014): "Encyclopaedic Erasmus." In: *Renaissance Studies* 28. No. 2, 183–204. DOI: 10.1111/rest.12049.

Décultot, Élisabeth (2003): "Introduction: L'art de l'extrait: définition, évolution, enjeux." In: Décultot, Élisabeth (Ed.): *Lire, copier, écrire: Les bibliothèques manuscrites au XVIIIe siècle*. Paris: CNRS Éditions, 7–28.

Desan, Philippe (1987): *Naissance de la méthode (Machiavel, La Ramée, Bodin, Montaigne, Descartes)*. Paris: A.-G. Nizet.

Eckhardt, Sándor (1944): *Magyar szónokképzés a XVI. századi Strasszburgban* [Teaching rhetoric to Hungarians in the 17th century Strasbourg]. Budapest: Magyar Tudományos Akadémia.

Faucher, Nicolas and Roques, Magali (2019): "The Many Virtues of Second Nature: Habitus in Latin Medieval Philosophy." In: Faucher, Nicolas and Roques, Magali (Eds.): *The Ontology, Psychology and Axiology of Habits (Habitus) in Medieval Philosophy*. Cham: Springer, 1–23. DOI: 10.1007/978-3-030-00235-0_1.

Förköli, Gábor (2022): "From Commonplacing to Expressing Confessional Identity: The Sturmian Paroemiology in Strasbourg and the Hungarian Albert Szenci Molnár" In: *Journal of Latin Cosmopolitanism and European Literatures* 9, 32–68. DOI: 10.21825/jolcel.v6i0.11801.

Franklin, James (2001): *The Science of Conjecture: Evidence and Probability before Pascal*. Baltimore: Johns Hopkins University Press.

Fumaroli, Marc (1999): "The Fertility and the Shortcomings of Renaissance Rhetoric: The Jesuit Case." In: O'Malley, John W., S.J., Bailey, Gauvin Alexander, Harris, Steven J., and Kennedy, T. Frank, S.J. (Eds.): *The Jesuits: Cultures, Sciences, and the Arts 1540–1773*. Toronto: University of Toronto Press, 90–106.

Fundárková, Anna and Teszelszky, Kees (2014): "Wirklichkeitsgetreue Darstellungen Der Ungarischen Krone Um 1608." In: Cziráki, Zsuzsanna, Fundárková, Anna, Manhercz, Orsolya, Peres, Zsuzsanna, and Vajnági, Márta (Eds.): *Wiener Archivforschungen: Festschrift Für Den Ungarischen Archivdelegierten in Wien, István Fazekas*. Vienna: Institut für Ungarische Geschichtsforschung in Wien, 133–141.

Gall, Franz (1965): *Alma Mater Rudolphina 1365–1965: Die Wiener Universität und ihre Studenten*. Vienna: Austria Press.

Gastgeber, Christian and Klecker, Elisabeth (Eds.) (2018): *Johannes Sambucus: János Zsámboki: Ján Sambucus (1531-1584): Philologe, Sammler und Historiograph am Habsburgerhof*. Vienna: Praesens.

Gerézdi, Rabán (1964): "Érasme et la Hongrie." In: Sőtér, István and Süpek, Ottó (Eds.): *Littérature hongroise—Littérature européenne: Études de literature comparée publiées par l'Académie des Sciences de Hongrie à l'occasion du IVe congrès de l'Association Internationale de Littérature Comparée*. Budapest: Akadémiai Kiadó, 129–154.

Grendler, Paul F. (2014): "Jesuit Schools in Europe: A Historiographical Essay." In: *Journal of Jesuit Studies* 1. No. 1, 7–25. DOI: 10.1163/22141332-00101002.

Grendler, Paul F. (2016): "The Culture of the Jesuit Teacher 1548–1773." In: *Journal of Jesuit Studies* 3. No. 1, 17–41. DOI: 10.1163/22141332-00301002.

Grendler, Paul F. (2019): *Jesuit Schools and Universities in Europe 1548-1773*. Leiden: Brill.

Hankins, James (2019): *Virtue Politics: Soulcraft and Statecraft in Renaissance Italy*. Cambridge: Harvard University Press.

Imre, Mihály (2009): *"Úton járásnak megírása": Kulturális emlékezet, retorikai-poétikai elvek érvényesülése Szenci Molnár Albert műveiben* ["Writing travel": Cultural memory and the presence of rhetorical and poetical principles in Sz. M. A.'s works]. Budapest: Balassi Kiadó.

Kainulainen, Jaska (2018): "Virtue and Civic Values in Early Modern Jesuit Education." In: *Journal of Jesuit Studies* 5. No. 4, 530–548. DOI: 10.1163/22141332-00504003.

Klein, Boris (2017): *Les Chaires et l'esprit: Organisation et transmission des savoirs au sein d'une université germanique au XVIIe siècle*. Lyon: Presses universitaires de Lyon.

Melani, Igor (2006): *Il tribunale della storia: Leggere la "Methodus" de Jean Bodin*. Florence: Olschki.

Melani, Igor (2012): "'De rebus singulis rectius judicare': Usi della storia, antropologia politica, formazione del funzionario nella *Methodus* di Jean Bodin." In: Zecchini, Giuseppe and Galimberti, Alessandro (Eds.): *Storici antichi e storici moderni nella* Methodus *di Jean Bodin*. Milan: Vita e Pensiero, 133–172.

Moss, Ann (1996): *Printed Commonplace-Books and the Structuring of Renaissance Thought*. Oxford: Clarendon Press.

Najemy, John M. (2014): "The 2013 Josephine Waters Bennett Lecture: Machiavelli and History." In: *Renaissance Quarterly* 67. No. 4, 1131–1164. DOI: 10.1086/679779.

Nauta, Lodi (2012): "From Universals to Topics: The Realism of Rudolph Agricola, with an Edition of His Reply to a Critic." In: *Vivarium* 50. No. 2, 190–224. DOI: 10.1163/156853412X644614.

Negruzzo, Simona (2005): *L'armonia contesa: Identità ed educazione nell'Alsazia moderna*. Bologna: Il Mulino.

Papy, Jan (1999): "The Reception of Agricola's *De inventione dialectica* in the Teaching of Logic at the Louvain Faculty of Arts in the Early Sixteenth Century." In: Akkerman, Fokke, Vanderjagt, Arjo J., and van der Laan, Adrie H. (Eds.): *Northern Humanism in European Context, 1469-1625: From the "Adwert Academy" to Ubbo Emmius*. Leiden: Brill, 167–185.

Pocock, John Greville Agard (1975): *The Machiavellian Moment: Florentine Political Thought and the Atlantic Republican Tradition*. Princeton: Princeton University Press.

Ritoókné Szalay, Ágnes (2002): "Erasmus és a XVI. századi magyarországi értelmiség [Erasmus and Hungarian intellectuals of the 16th century]." In: Ritoókné Szalay, Ágnes: *"Nympha super ripam Danubii": Tanulmányok a XV–XVI. századi magyarországi művelődés köréből*. Budapest: Balassi Kiadó, 161–174.

Salliot, Natacha (2017): "Érasme dans les controverses religieuses entre protestants et catholiques sous le régime de l'Édit de Nantes." In: Perona, Blandine and Vigliano, Tristan (Eds.): *Érasme et la France*. Paris: Classiques Garnier, 383–393.

Spitz, Lewis William and Tinsley, Barbara Sher (1995): *Johann Sturm on Education: The Reformation and Humanist Learning*. Saint Louis: Concordia Publishing House.

Szentmártoni Szabó, Géza (2012): "'Romulidae Cannas,' avagy egy ál-Janus Pannonius-vers utóélete, eredeti szövege és valódi szerzője ['Romolidae Cannas,' or the posterity of a Pseudo-Janus Pannonius poem, its text, and its actual author]." In: Békés, Enikő and Tegyey, Imre (Eds.): *Convivium Pajorin Klára 70. születésnapjára*. Debrecen and Budapest: Debreceni Egyetem, 183–194.

Teszelszky, Kees (2007): "Révay Péter és Justus Lipsius eszméi a történelemről és a nemzeti identitásról (P. R. and J. P.'s ideas on history and national identity)." In: Bitskey, István and Fazakas, Gergely Tamás (Eds.): *Humanizmus, religio, identitástudat: Tanulmányok a kora újkori Magyarország művelődéstörténetéről*. Debrecen: Kossuth Egyetemi Kiadó, 106–113.

Teszelszky, Kees (2009): *Az ismeretlen korona: Jelentések, szimbólumok és nemzeti identitás (The unknown crown: Meanings, symbols, and national identity)*. Pannonhalma: Bencés Kiadó.

Teszelszky, Kees (2010): "The Hungarian Roots of a Bohemian Humanist: Johann Jessenius a Jessen and Early Modern National Identity." In: Trencsényi, Balázs and Zászkaliczky, Márton (Eds.): *Whose Love of Which Country: Composite States, National Histories and Patriotic Discourses in Early Modern Central Europe*. Leiden: Brill, 315–332.

Teszelszky, Kees (2016): "The Crown of Hungary before and after the Hungarian Crowning: The Use of the Holy Crown of Hungary in Hungarian Revolts and Habsburg Representation between 1604 and 1611." In: *Hungarian Studies* 30. No. 2, 167–173. DOI: 10.1556/044.2016.30.2.3.

Tóth, Gergely (2014): "Lutheránus országtörténet újsztoikus keretben [A Lutheran history of the country in a neo-stoic framework]." In: Tóth, Gergely (Ed.): *Clio inter arma: Tanulmányok a 16-18. századi magyarországi történetírásról*. Budapest: MTA BTK Történettudományi Intézet, 117–147.

Tóth, Gergely (2016): *Szent István, Szent Korona, államalapítás a protestáns történetírásban (16-18. század) [Saint Stephen, the Holy Crown, and the foundation of the Hungarian state in protestant historiography (16th-18th century)]*. Budapest: MTA BTK Történettudományi Intézet.

Tóth, Gergely (2019): "Állhatatosság és politika: Justus Lipsius munkásságának hatása (és hatástalansága) Révay Péter műveire [Constance and politics: The influence [and the lack of influence] of J. L.'s oeuvre on P. R.'s works]." In: *Irodalomtörténeti Közlemények* 123. No. 5, 567–584.

Tóth, Gergely (2021a): "Quisquis est in aulis magnorum principum... Udvari tanácsosok, Habsburg uralom és a régi magyar királyi királyi udvar emléke Révay Péter *De monarchia* című munkájában [Courtly councilors, Habsburg reign, and the memory of the old Hungarian royal court in P. R.'s *De monarchia*]." In: Békés, Enikő, Kasza, Péter, and Gábor Kiss, Farkas (Eds.): *Latin nyelvű udvari kultúra Magyarországon a 15-18. században*. Szeged: Lazi Könyvkiadó, 117–128.

Tóth, Gergely (2021b): "A Lutheran Magnate's Political Testament in the Language of History: Péter Révay's *De Monarchia*." In: Révay, Péter: *De monarchia et Sacra Corona regni Hungariae centuriae septem: A Magyar Királyság birodalmáról és Szent Koronájáról szóló hét század*. Gergely Tóth (Ed.). Vol. I. Budapest: Bölcsészettudományi Kutatóközpont Történettudományi Intézet, 101–194.

Tucker, George Hugo (2011): "Justus Lipsius and the *Cento* Form." In: de Bom, Erik, Janssens, Marijke, van Houdt, Toon and Papy, Jan (Eds.): *(Un)masking the Realities of Power: Justus Lipsius and the*

Dynamics of Political Writing in Early Modern Europe. Leiden: Brill, 163–192. DOI: 10.1163/ej.9789004191280.i-348.40.

Van der Poel, Marc (2007): "Humanist Rhetoric in the Renaissance: Classical Mastery?" In: Verbaal, Wim, Maes, Yanick, and Papy, Jan (Eds.): *Latinitas Perennis I: The Continuity of Latin Literature.* Leiden: Brill, 119–138. DOI: 10.1163/ej.9789004153271.i-224.12.

Van der Poel, Marc (2015): "Aristotle in Rudolph Agricola's *De Inventione Dialectica.*" In: Celentano, Maria Silvana, Chiron, Pierre, and Mack, Peter (Eds.): *Rhetorical Arguments: Essays in Honour of Lucia Calboli Montefusco.* Hildesheim: Georg Olms, 341–352.

Van der Poel, Marc (2018): "Introduction." In: Agricola, Rodolphe: *Écrits sur la dialectique et l'humanisme.* Marc van der Poel (Ed. and Trans.). Paris: Classiques Garnier, 13–47.

Vasoli, Cesare (1970): *Jean Bodin, il problema cinquecentesco della Methodus e la sua applicazione alla conoscenza storica.* Turin: Edizioni di filosofia.

Vasoli, Cesare (1974): "Il problema cinquecentesco della *'Methodus'* e la sua applicazione alla conoscenza storica." In: Vasoli, Cesare: *Profezia e ragione: Studi sulla cultura del Cinquecento e del Seicento.* Naples: Morano, 595–647.

Waszink, Jan (2004): "Introduction." In: Lipsius, Justus: *Politica: Six Books of Politics or Political Instruction.* Jan Waszink (Ed. and Trans.). Assen: Van Gorcum, 3–213.

Zvara, Edina (2011): "Ismert könyvgyűjtők tulajdonosi bejegyzései az Esterházy-könyvtárban [Possessor entries of known bibliophiles in the Esterházy library]." In: *Magyar Könyvszemle* 127. No. 1, 47–71.

Danilo Facca
Aristotle Excerpted and Disput[at]ed: Leiden 1602–1603

Abstract: An anonymous manuscript of the Toruń University Library contains an exposition of Aristotle's *libri naturales* and *Nichomachean Ethics*. It was compiled by a Pomeranian student of medicine at Leiden University in the early 1600s, who selected these questions out of some of the most influential interpreters of Aristotelian philosophy at the turn of the 17th century in Reformed Central Europe: Zabarella, the Jesuit *Conimbricenses*, Casmann, and Keckermann. Other relevant authors are Jean Fernel and Francisco Valles. The article examines the intellectual framework provided by Leiden University (and the Gdańsk and Stettin Gymnasia). It is the genesis and the process of composition of the text which is analyzed in more detail, in an attempt to illustrate the material constitution and intended function of the book. It emerges that the text derives from two different student practices, that of class discussion (*collegium*) and that of systematic ordering of materials obtained from book-mining.

1 Introduction: From Manuscripts to Curricula

Scholars of early modern academic teaching are certainly aware of the importance of "dialectical" practices within the curricula. Not only did the awarding of a degree follow a public examination during which the candidate was called upon to defend *theses*, but it can be said that an important, if not predominant, part of

---

Danilo Facca: ORCID: 0000-0002-2752-6964. Institute of Philosophy and Sociology, Polish Academy of Sciences, Warsaw, Poland. This research has been made possible thanks to ERC Consolidator Grant n. 864542, "From East to West, and Back Again: Student Travel and Transcultural Knowledge Production in Renaissance Europe (c. 1470–c. 1620)."

Acknowledgements: I would like to thank Dr. Andrzej Mycio and his colleagues of the Manuscripts and Old Print Section of the Library of Nicolaus Copernicus University in Toruń for their competent help in consulting the manuscripts.

Notes: The census and classification of these materials has been carried out mainly in Germany, starting with the older works of Ewald Horn and Hermann Mundt to the more recent ones by Hanspeter Marti. For further bibliographical indications the reader can refer to some more recent works: Gindhart and Kundert 2010; Weijers 2013; Gindhart, Marti, and Seidel 2016; and Friedenthal, Marti, and Seidel 2021. As can be seen, these collected works are sometimes inspired by the idea of the *longue durée* of academic dialectical practices in the West, in others the specificity of modern disputatio is emphasized.

∂ Open Access. © 2023 the author(s), published by De Gruyter. This work is licensed under the Creative Commons Attribution 4.0 International License. https://doi.org/10.1515/9783111072722-004

his course of study consisted precisely in the exercise of the ability to question certain assertions or to account for others either by argument or by reference to texts of "authorities." Among the direct effects of the pervasive presence of these practices is the huge number of published *disputationes*, which in merely quantitative terms constitutes perhaps the largest part of the legacy of printed texts derived from academic environments (gymnasiums and universities). Research has long been conducted with the aim of surveying, classifying, and analyzing the formal aspects and intellectual content of this vast production, work that seems to me to still be ongoing and not destined to end soon.

In addition to the printed *disputatio*, which is the final result of precise rules and conventions and thus a highly standardized "product," a testimony to the dialectical aspects of teaching procedures also comes from manuscripts, the importance of which has been recognized with increasing awareness over the last decades. These sources are mostly a product that comes straight out of the hands of the students themselves and testifies less to the prevailing conventions of a given academic environment and more to the intellectual and practical needs of their editor or owner and the writing strategies to carry them out. As we shall soon see, we cannot simply refer to the practice of note-taking or compiling reference books (about which enough has already been written anyway[1]) but should rather think of a variety of activities. This circumstance requires a case-by-case approach to individual documents in attempting to shed light on the process by which the text took its final shape. A further necessary step is to relate the analysis of the process of composition to the practical and intellectual motivations that determined it, also taking into account the academic context with its institutional and cultural idiosyncrasies.

2 The Manuscript 120/II at the Nicolaus Copernicus University in Toruń: Provenance, Structure, and Philosophical Background

One such attempt is undertaken here by examining a manuscript dating from the early 17th century and connected on the one hand to the University of Leiden and

---

1 As to the literature, I simply mention Ann Blair's (2010) classic monograph. For a perspective closer to the one adopted here, I refer to the research carried out during the last few years in the framework of a project at Leuven University entitled *"Ad fontes!" in the Classroom: Teaching Latin, Greek and Hebrew Texts in the Early Modern Southern Low Countries* (https://sites.google.com/view/leuvenstudentnotes2020/project-team, last accessed May 14, 2023).

on the other to the Pomeranian area—namely, ms 120/II, which is preserved at the Toruń University Library (Biblioteka Uniwersytetu Mikołaja Kopernika). The text is anonymous and is mainly devoted to the natural philosophy, although reading it soon makes it clear that the author was someone about to study medicine. This seems evident to me if we consider that among the most frequently cited authors, if we exclude those we can classify generically as philosophers, such as Otho Casmann, Bartholomäus Keckermann, Jacopo Zabarella, and the *Conimbricenses*, there is a marked presence of famous authors of medical matters such as Francisco Valles, Jean Fernel, Andreas Vesalius, François Valleriola, and Johannes Jessenius (not to mention Galen and Avicenna): *sternit philosophia medicinae viam*, stated the first of this company, who like many of his colleagues did not disdain to deal with exquisitely philosophical problems (Valles 1556, 3r). The author also seems to have approached his work in this spirit.

On the provenance of the manuscript there are currently no certain indications, other than that it belongs to the holdings that Polish bibliographers refer to by the term "secured" (*zabezpieczone*)—that is, deriving from German archives and libraries that found themselves within the redefined borders of the Republic of Poland after 1945 (Mycio 2012 and 2020). There are no visible signs of provenance other than the stamp of the university and library of Toruń. In the same collection of the Toruń library, however, there are three other manuscripts (sign. 105/I, 106/I, 215/I) on medical matters, which share a family resemblance with 120/II. A study by Ulrich Schlegelmilch (2016), which I consider exemplary for the new direction of study on early modern manuscripts I have just mentioned, identified Andreas Hiltebrand (1581–1637), a humanist and doctor from Stettin, as the compiler of the first two notebooks (105/I and 106/I) while he was a medical student in Leiden in the years 1603–1605, just after having studied in Lipsia (Aurnhammer 2015, 202–203). As Schlegelmilch has shown, one of the volumes (105) contains the protocols of meetings of small groups of students that were held at the home of Pieter Pauw, a famous professor of medicine at Leiden and also rector of the university in those years. Since the hands that drafted 105 and 120/II appear different and since, as we shall see, some parts of ms 120/II date from 1602, when Hiltebrand was not yet in Leiden, it does not seem possible to attribute the compilation of the latter to him.[2] It cannot be ruled out, however, that he knew of it or even that it was part of his personal library and thus later, and together with the other three volumes, passed from there into the manuscript funds of the Stettin Gymnasium and later into those of the University of Toruń (Mycio 2020, 195). Later, we will provide a hypothesis about the author of ms 120/II. Further research

---

2 [Du Rieu] 1875, col. 70, reports Hiltebrand enrolling in the medical faculty in June 1603.

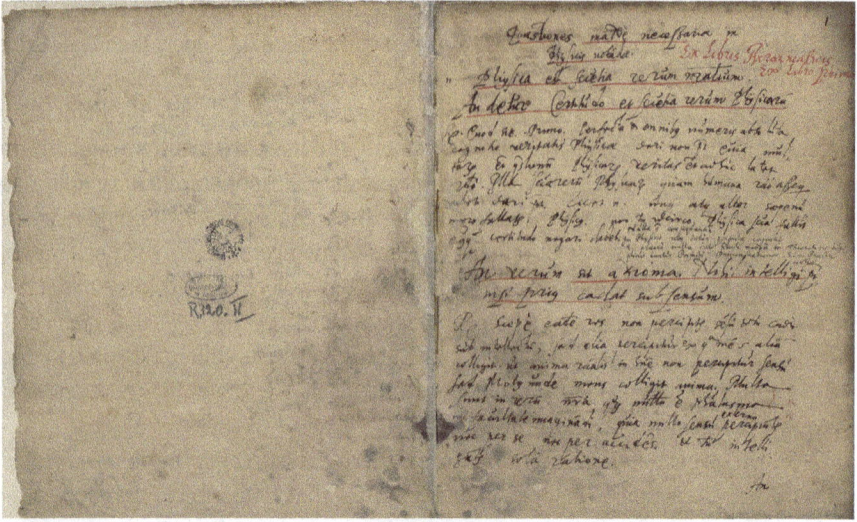

Fig. 1: The beginning of the *Physics* (The Toruń University Library, MS 120/II, f. 1v)

will be able to tell us more about these points; here it is sufficient for us to attest to its hitherto undetected kinship with the aforementioned group of three manuscripts.

Apart from the blank guard sheets inserted later, the manuscript consists of *folia* numbered 1 to 202 and measuring about 16.8 x 20.5 cm, some of which are left blank (28r–29r and 34v–35v). In one case a smaller piece of paper was added in order to supplement the existing text (between 133v and 134r). The whole is divided into 7 sections, each of which has also a separate numeration, and contains a course in philosophy articulated according to Aristotle's *libri naturales* with the addition of a summary of the main points of the *Nicomachean Ethics*. The only part that appears to be a foreign body, but which might be useful in identifying the author or owner of the compilation, consists of a few pages redacted by another hand and bearing what appears to be a prediction about the life of a son (*natus*) born after 1615 and extending into the 70s (46v–49v). The explicit declares that "this is a general and most careful explication of our Son. God paternally confirms all good things and with clemency keeps away the bad ones. Amen."[3]

---

3 "Et haec est generalis exolutio diligentissima Nati nostri. Deus confirmet paterne bona cuncta et clementer avertat mala. Amen." "Clarification" or "explication" may have been meant by "*exolutio*." The text is organized topically: *thema, causae efficientes, adiuncta, opposita*.

A simple synopsis reproducing the structure of this course with the chronological and geographical indications provided in the text will help us follow the considerations explored below:

1) *Physica* 1–4	1/08/1602	
Quaestiones	1/09/160	s.l.
2) *De coelo*	20/10/1602	
Observationes et quaest.	31/10/1602	s.l.
3) *De ortu et interitu*	16/01/1603	
Observ. et quaest.	6/02/1603	s.l.
4) *De anima*	1/07/1603	
Quaest. et observ.	6/08/1603	Lugduni, *Studio privato*
5) *Metereologica*	1/01/1603	
Observ.	21 or 22/01/1603	Stetini
6.1) *Parva Naturalia*	1/08/1603	
Observ. et quaest.	9/08/1603	Lugduni
6.2) (*Miscellanea naturalia*)		
I) *Quaestiones quaedam physyco medicae* [...] *ex Collegio Conimb. et Casmanni Physiologia excerptae*		
	20/03/1603	Stetini
From the 7th *quaestio* on	1/07/1603	Lugduni
II) *Quaestiones ex cursu phil. Keckermanni*		s.l
	(after 1604?)	
III) *Axiomata quaedam physica ex acroamaticis*		s.l.
	(after 1604)	
7) *Ethica Nicomachea*		
Observ. quaedam et quest.	1/07/1603 *coepi*	Lugduni

Let us begin by saying that—with the exception of the seventh part—this organization of the subject mirrors that of numerous textbooks on natural philosophy of the time. In particular, it essentially coincides with that of two reference works circulating at Leiden University in those years. The first is the *Physicae seu naturalis pilosophiae institutiones* by Cornelius Valerius (Cornelis Woutersz, 1512–1578; Valerius 1593 and 1598), formerly Justus Lipsius' professor in Louvain. This text first saw the light of day in Antwerp in 1567 but is best known for its 1593 Marburg edition, which was accompanied by various explanatory elements and, in particular, the notes of the celebrated Rudolf Goclenius in order to offer a brief and perspicuous "synopsis" of the subject. The second, which is the most likely reference for the author of ms 120/II, is the *Physiologiae peripateticae libri sex* by Marburg professor Johannes Magirus (1560–1596), a former student in Padua where he came into contact with the Italian Aristotelian tradition. This work, much longer than the previous one, was published in 1597 and had enjoyed great popularity in universities at least until the mid-17th century (Magirus 1597 and 1603).[4] The agreement between ms 120/II and these two treatises, even within each of the sections, is quite precise, but with one difference: in Valerius and Magirus, meteorology is collocated after the section on generation and corruption and before the section on the soul, and the subjects are arranged in this same way in the handbook by Gilbert Jack (ca 1578–1628), professor of philosophy at Leiden in the years when ms 120/II was written.[5] The inverted position of these parts, as it appears in ms 120/II, is common to other successful physics texts of the period, though Bartholomäus Keckermann's *Systema Physicum* and Franco Burgersdijk's *Idea philosophiae naturalis* seem to be particularly relevant to us here. The former became famous for his activity as a teacher in the Gdańsk Gymnasium and as an author of handbooks; the latter studied at Leiden and became a professor there from 1619.[6] It is worth noting that the section on ethics placed at the end of the manuscript is not something found in the handbooks and treatises I have mentioned, setting it apart in that regard. In any case, I am inclined to think that it was Magirus' text that was constantly before the eyes of our author: first, because it is mentioned several times in ms 120/II (e.g., 8v, 156v, and 160r) and, second, because it proceeds in a manner more akin to the latter—namely, by presenting the debate between schools and authorities on the main points of natural philosophy, whereas Valerius merely provides notions and principles in the form of dogmatic assertions.

As for the philosophical orientation inspiring the compilation, we meet the eclectic Aristotelianism notoriously characteristic of the University of Leiden in the decades following its foundation (1575). The more or less explicitly negative opinion that historians express about this trend, branding it "conservative," should not obscure the fact that it performed the positive function of integrating even quite heterogeneous intellectual orientations into a common platform of natural philosophy. Ms 120/II represents a good example of this function, as we find discussed therein, in general with approval for their views, representatives of Aristo-

---

[4] The 1597 edition has a different title, *Physica peripatetica, etc.* (Magirus 1597), and does not present commentaries. They are already present in the subsequent editions (the latest one I could find is Magirus 1603). Beginning with a Wittenberg edition in 1609 (Magirus 1609), the *Institutiones* is printed together with the *Enchiridion metaphysicum* by Danish Lutheran theologian Caspar Bartholin, a significant integration that marks the distance from the Melanchthon-style natural philosophy that had been dominant in university courses up to that time.

[5] This handbook has been edited several times in progressively augmented form. The first edition is Jacchaeus 1614.

[6] Keckermann 1610 and Burgersdijk 1642. See also Burgersdijk 1652, a collection of disputations in which the sequence is *Physics, On Heaven, On Generation and Corruption, On Soul, Meteorology,* and *On Cosmos*. On Jack, Burgersdijk, and the teaching of Aristotelian physics, see Ruestow 1973, Chapter 2.

telianism in its secular (Zabarella, Arcangelo Mercenario) and Counter-Reformation (Bento Pereira, the *Conimbricenses*) versions, of "sacred" or "Mosaic" philosophy of nature (Valles, Casmann), of reformed humanistic philosophy (Melanchthon), of Neoplatonic medical philosophy (Jean Fernel[7]), outsiders like Girolamo Cardano and Giulio Cesare Scaligero, and also physicians without a definite philosophical profile (Andreas Vesalius, François Valleriola, Laurent Joubert, etc.). Unsurprisingly, with all the manuals cited above, ms 120/II shares a distrust of metaphysics and philosophical theology, as is evident not only from the absence of a specific section, but also from the fact that the first section based on Aristotle's *Physics* is limited to the doctrine of principles (form, matter, privation, time, place, etc.) while ignoring the quasi-theological speculations that correspond to the second part of the treatise. Deserving our attention is the favor with which the compiler proposes and defends (with arguments also drawn from Genesis) a doctrine of the soul that conceives the latter not only as a form of the body, but as a substance in itself and, as such, a potentially autonomous entity with respect to the body (98r for the idea, derived from Casmann 1594, 1, of the "hypostatic union" between the rational soul and the body).[8] Finally, of note are two passages in which views attributed to Ramus are refuted. In one (8v) his assertion that privation, as a *non ens*, could not be considered among the principles of natural phenomena is rebutted. The reference to the Frenchman's *Scholae physicae* is only indirect, for the passage is actually transcribed almost exactly from Magirus' *Institutiones*. Here are the passages (Magirus 1603, 55):

---

7 Fernel's conceptions of *forma totius* as well as of *abditae rerum causae* are particularly important (f. 60r).

8 I mention the only digression beyond the territory of natural philosophy *iuxta propria principia*, that is, the question of whether the human soul thus understood is of celestial provenance or passes to the conceived through the seed of the parents and at the act of conceiving. It is answered by affirming the latter horn of the alternative by means of the following argument: if the soul created by God had remained immune from contamination with the body for an extended period of time and was infused into it only at a later moment, it would succeed in healing the body's weaknesses and freeing it from sin. Instead, we note (an Augustinian motif) that the original corruption of human nature drives us to sin as soon as we are born (f. 70r–72r).

Ms 120/II	Magirus
Dic unum argumentum Rami. Non ens principium rei naturalis esse nequit. At privatio est non ens quia est pura negatio. Ergo non est principium. Respondeo: privatio non est omnino NON ENS, neque pura negatio quia hic plus quam in logicis significat. Et licet non si principium rei tamen est principium generationis. Plura vide in Magirus l. 1 c. 2 p. 46 et 47	... audiamus nunc argumenta, quibus nonnulli privationem de coetu principiorum proscribere tentant. 1.Non ENS principum rei naturalis esse nequit. At privatio est non ens, quoniam, ipso Aristotele teste, est negatio. Non igitur est principium. Respondeo: Privatio non est omnino non ens, neque est pura negatio. Plus enim hic quam in Logicis significat, sed quid reale ponit et quamvis non sit principium rei, est tamen prinicipium generationis.

The refutation of Ramus' well-known argument ("Aristotle in the *Physics* and *Metaphysics* 'says the same things' he has already said in his logical treatises") is accompanied by a second passage contained in a note that was added to the main text (17r). This note is interesting not only as an indication of an unfriendly attitude towards Ramus' views but also for pointing to a different milieu than Leiden. It is actually a quotation from a compendium of natural philosophy first published in Basel in 1561 and authored by George Liebler (1524–1600), a professor of natural philosophy and ancient languages in Tübingen. This textbook, not canonical in Leiden, was among the readings in use at the *Paedagogium* in Stettin, at that time a secondary school of preparation for the university.[9] Let us now place side by side the passus from ms 120/II and Liebler's text, in the 1596 edition (Liebler 1596, 89–90), from which the quotation is probably taken:

---

[9] I refer to Wehrmann 1894, 68. In general on this school, see Gaziński 2016. Unfortunately, I could not take into account the recent publication of Borysowka and Gierke 2022. Liebler's *Epitome* was published several times, and in expanded form starting with the 1573 Leipzig edition in order to counter Ramus' *Scholae Physicae* (1565). It is likely that the editor of the ms 120/II had in his hand precisely this edition, since in the others on 89 the here quoted passage is not found.

ms 120/II	Liebler 1596
NB: Ramus ob[iecit]: actio et passio ad Logicam pertinet. At idem motus est actio et passio. E[rgo] motus ad Logicam et non physicam pertinebit. Re[spondet] Liblerius: licet in Logica quid sub communi ratione tractatur, tamen non id vere ad eandem pertinebit. Sic enim omnes disciplinae ad illam referri posset, ac praeter logicam nulla esset disciplina. Liblerus p. 89.	Atque ex ho capite Ramus effici putat, motum ad logicam pertinere, atque ob id e physicis eiciendum, hoc videlicet syllogysmo: Actio et passio ad logicam pertinet, ut Aristoteles in Categoriis et Topicis perspicue testatur. At motus idem, est actio passioque, in movente actio, in mobile passio, ut hoc capite testatur Aristoteles. Motus igitur Aristotele autore et assertore logica res est, ideoque a physicis ad logicam removeatur. Atqui non, si quid sub communi quadam et populari ratione in logicis tractatur, ob id eius accuratiorem cognitionem nulla peculiaris scientia sibi vendicabit. Hoc enim si asseratur, praeter logicam nulla erit scientia, cum in logicis et de essentiis et de quantitatibus, et de qualitatibus, et de relatis, quae omnium propemodum artium et scientiarum subiecta sunt, tractetur.

Ramus' specific "panlogism," his claim to reduce *scientiae reales* to collections of concepts and thus to the discipline of logic, is targeted here. However, as any Aristotelian knows, properly speaking, logic is not a discipline but an "instrument," since it deals only with "second" notions and not first or real ones. These are motifs that the contemporary *Schulphilosophie* will elaborate fully in the very first decades of the 1600s, stimulated by the theoretical challenge brought by Ramus.

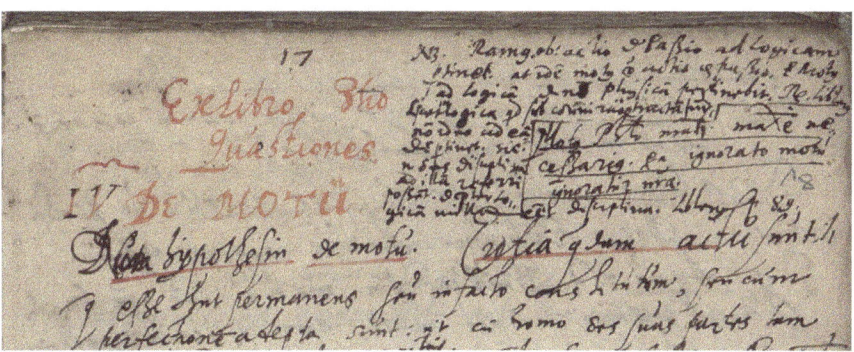

Fig. 2: A note on Ramus (The Toruń University Library, MS 120/II, f. 17v)

3 The Genesis of the Text

However, more than the reconstruction of ideological orientations in a document such as this, which holds no surprises from what we already knew about the teaching of philosophy in Leiden in the decades leading up to the 1619 turning point (Dibon 1954, 1–79, and Hotson 2020, 21–59), it is the material aspects of the constitution of the volume that draws our attention. The reconstruction proposed here is, of course, partly a matter of conjecture based both on the scant direct indications in the text and on other paleographic and codicological clues.

As can be seen from the table above, the beginning and end of the sections are marked with dates (day/month/year) and in six cases with the name of the locality. The period covered by the composition of the text is about one (academic) year, from the beginning of July 1602 to the end of July 1603, but except for the first two, the sequence in which the sections are disposed in the volume does not correspond to the chronological sequence of their composition (if the dates refer to composition, see below). I have accordingly derived a further table from the first—one that reconstructs the chronology of the writing of the manuscript:

When		Where
1602	**August**	
	Physica	(?)
	October	
	De coelo	(?)
1603	**January**	
	Meteor.	Stetini
	January-February	
	De gen. et corr.	(?)
	March	
	Quaestiones quaedam	
	physico-medicae n. 1–6	Stettin
	from July n. 7–23	Lugduni
	July	
	Ethica Nicomachea	Lugduni
	July-August	
	De anima	Lugduni (*Studio privato*)
	August	
	Parva nat.	Lugduni
	after January 1606	
	Quaestiones ex Keckermanno	
	Axiomata	(?)

On the basis of the discrepancy between the chronological sequence of the composition of the parts and the sequence in which they are physically arranged in the book, I hypothesize that the author *preliminarily* established a systematic arrangement of the subject matter, which in essence is the one derived from the reference texts recalled above, and then, at different times, proceeded to "fill in" this general scheme with the corresponding materials. In fact, chronological order and material succession coincide only in regard to the first two parts (*Physics* and *On Heaven*). That this was the genesis of the book seems to me to be confirmed by the circumstance whereby the individual thematic sections were composed using different reams of paper.[10] This in fact seems to me to be compatible with the hypothesis that they were first composed independently of each other and assembled at a later time. Moreover, the indications of the cities, though incomplete, tell us that the writing of the text took place in at least two different places. To be precise, the location for the first two parts composed between August and October 1602 is missing, while the indications for 1603 suggest a continuous winter stay in Stettin and an analogous stay in Leiden in the summer.

But what do the dates and places refer to? On the basis of the other Toruń manuscripts of medical subjects quoted above, Schlegelmilch has reconstructed the work of the *collegia disputationis* (disputation colleges/seminars), which, as was the widespread custom in the schools and universities of the time, were organized privately by a professor, usually in the form of extracurricular meetings, and gathered small groups of students who practiced their skills in disputing. During these meetings, they were taking up the same roles of *respondens/defendens* and *opponens* that were taken up, for instance, in public disputations *pro gradu*. One of the Toruń manuscripts described by Schlegelmilch records the protocols of these sessions, which as a whole were intended as an organic system encompassing all the essential issues of the discipline (in that case, medicine and pathology). The manuscript testifies to the widespread practice of preparing collections of disputations from these reports or other systematically organized materials that could come in handy not only in the course of studies, but also in the post-academic period in the pursuit of the profession, usually medical or legal. It is worth noting that the term *observationes*, which appears in another manuscript considered by Schlegelmilch (106), designates nothing more than *excerpta*—that is, points taken from canonical literature and structured as *loci communes* (Schlegelmilch 2016, 81–7).

---

10 The difference in paper is visible, for instance, in the transition from the file containing *De gen. et corr.* to the one containing *De an.*, f. 65v–66r or from *De an.* to *Meteor.*, f. 101v–102r.

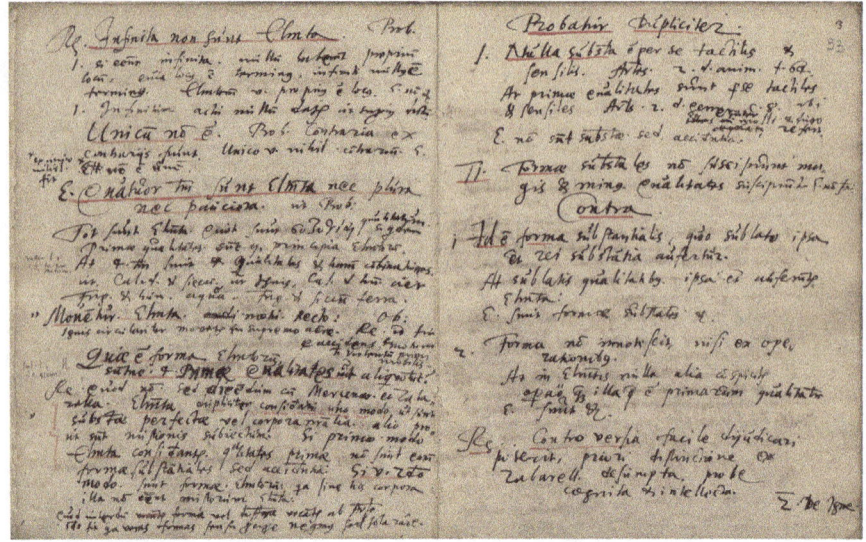

Fig. 3: Probatur, contra, respondeo… (The Toruń University Library, MS 120/II, ff. 52v–53r)

Now, returning to ms 120/II, with all the relevant differences (if only for the fact that the subject matter here is merely philosophical and one can expect reduced extracurricular or professional usefulness if compared with analogous medical notebooks), the process of its formation must have been similar. Certainly, the texts are not protocol accounts of seminars of small student communities, as in the case of the texts studied by Schegelmilch. However, given the common and widespread practice of holding *collegia* in Leiden (and probably also in Stettin), given also the numerous textual indicators that refer to verbal exchanges of interlocutors confronting each other (see examples in the next paragraph), a more or less distant relationship to discussions *actually* held or to be held in extracurricular philosophical seminars is a plausible hypothesis. In other terms, the compiler has given these parts a "dialectical" form on the basis of or in view of *viva voce* discussions. This certainly does not exclude that he supplemented the text with points (objections and responses) customarily found in the literature: the two activities—book mining and live discussions—are not mutually exclusive and indeed could have coexisted and reinforced each other. Whatever the case, my hypothesis is that the dates and places I reported in the tables refer not so much to when and where the sessions of the seminars actually took place but are instead indicators related to the act of drafting the manuscript. If true, the expression *Studio privato* at the beginning of the section *De anima* (f. 66r) would refer not so much to meetings that took place, for example, at a professor's house, but to individual work done by the student in compiling the book. In any case, whether the author worked on raw materials provided by meeting protocols (such as those in Toruń ms 105) or was carrying out research and selection work on published texts, or whether he combined both, manuscript 120/II corresponds to a stage of desk work—namely, of transcribing, correcting, and sorting. If one were to examine a random page of the manuscript, one would see that the spatial composition is regular and orderly, with titles and salient parts underlined in red and few corrections, which in my opinion is indicative of further refinement work subsequent to the first draft [see f. 114v–115r as an example]. In short, I tend to believe that the author, by pointing out dates and places, wanted to leave indication of precisely this latter stage of work of his, resulting in "a kind of handbook" (Ashmann 1995, 89; see also Schlegelmilch 2016, 83).

If we then look more closely at the structure of these pages, we find that a certain pattern recurs in them, which moreover corresponds to the title that generally appears in the single sections: *observationes et quaestiones*. The former denote a theme, an argument expounded in assertive form: "Physica est scientia rerum naturalium" (1r); "Subiectum physicum est corpus naturale quatenus naturale" (2r); or as a response to a request: "Dic divisionem physicae!" (2v); or a question: "Quis est numerus principiorum?" (3v), followed and illustrated by a set of arguments and authorities drawn from the literature on the subject. "*Quaestions*," on the other hand, are characteristically introduced by alternative interrogative particles: *An ...? Estne ...?*, followed by the formula *Re[spondeo] quod sic/non* and here too with arguments and authorities supporting or refuting the thesis discussed.

To sum up, I would say that any random page of the manuscript is the result of two different kinds of activity: one being that of *excerpere*, or deriving from other books a set of dogmatic *loci communes* expressed in an assertive form or as a response to a question, and the other being that of rephrasing of discussions that actually took place in school classes or were even only imagined, to the solution of which contribute *pro et contra* arguments drawn from past or present authorities, explicitly cited or not. Let us consider that the deepest structure of many printed works of the period intended for academic use was no different. Casmann's work cited above is exemplary, the title of which recalls the dualism between *praelectiones* and *disputationes*, not to mention the structure of the individual chapters, in which a series of dogmatic ("methodical") statements are followed by *questiones controversae*.[11]

---

11 In works of this kind the terminology is quite varied, a certain stabilization of it is the effect of Keckermann's reforms (Hotson 2007, Chapter 4).

Summing up all these considerations, I would therefore say that the manuscript presents three layers of composition, which roughly correspond to three poles of activity on the part of the author and give the measure of his contribution to the organization of philosophical-medical knowledge:
- A macro-structure, corresponding to the topical scheme provided by Aristotle's books and arranged according to a pattern common in the treatises of the time.
- A medium structure, provided by the network of *observationes*, eclectically drawn from the manuals and treatises in vogue (Zabarella, *Conimbricenses*, Casmann, Fernel, Valles, Keckermann, etc.) and expressed in the form of *principia, praecepta, axiomata*, etc.
- A micro-structure, consisting of the addressing of single dogmatic points through *quaestiones* that are also topical and sometimes referred to an authority.

One would also have to add an analysis of the annotations added to the manuscript after its final arrangement, which would raise the question of its post-academic life. Since we would be entering a period when the author was no longer a student, I limit myself to one observation: for a volume on a medical topic such as the one Schlegelmilch considered, its usefulness at a later stage was quite plausible as a place to report *observationes*, this time no longer understood as excerpts from readings but as pieces of experiences derived from direct encounters with the sick people. And indeed, this was the function of the text compiled by Hiltebrand, who actually practiced as a physician in the early decades of the 1600s in Pomerania. In the case of a volume on natural philosophy, this further function is presumably of less importance and is basically limited to the reporting of further readings by the volume's owner, with a few exceptions (see the "Ramist" notes above).

4 The Different Pattern of Section 6a

There is a section in manuscript 120/II that deserves some focused attention, as it presupposes a different composition strategy. It is the one indicated in the table as 6a, consisting of three parts. The first is further divided into 23 points (132r–168v), of which the first 18 deal with topics that could roughly be said to be of "physiology" (the term had recently been introduced by Fernel with the meaning of the study of organ functions), then going on to metals, mineral stones, and insects. Its composition does not differ from the rest of the volume as we have described it, with "dogmatic" and "dialectical" parts. From the second part (168v–175v), de-

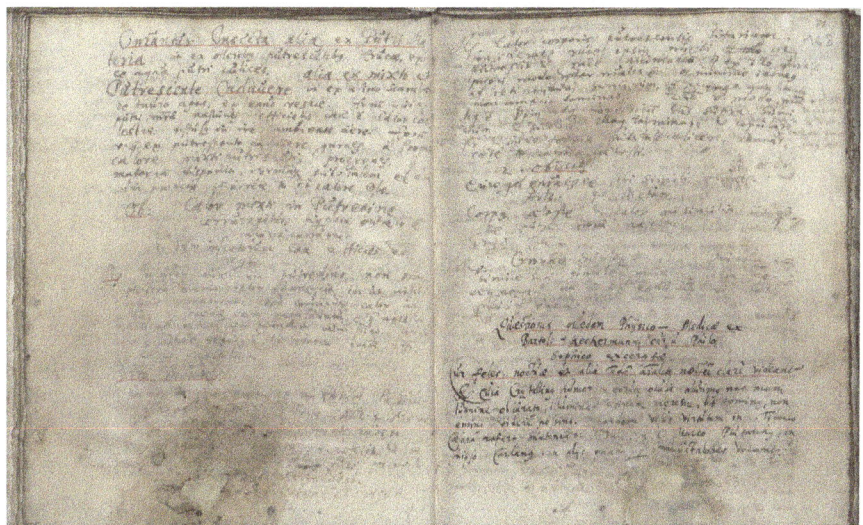

Fig. 4: The beginning of the Miscellaneous section (The Toruń University Library, MS 120/II)

rived from Keckermann's *Cursus philosophicus*, things change. The "miscellaneous" content is articulated in points (to quote the first three on the topic of "sight": Why do felines see at night? Why do some bring the book closer to their eyes to read and others push it away? Do moles lack sight?) in the form of simple direct questions (*Cur... An ... Unde ... Quaenam sit causa ...*) followed by more or less complex answers, but lacking the disputative articulation signaled with typical markers (*respondeo, obicio, concludo, distinguitur*, etc.). So, I would say that in these cases, the question form of the headings has no dialectical value, since they are in effect simple titles introducing a given theme (the paradigm could be the Aristotelian *Problemata*). Moreover, the hand that wrote these sections does not look like the one that composed the previous parts.

The lack of a disputative substratum is even more evident in the third subsection (176r–182v), affixed to a separate fascicle of sheets, which has been annotated by a different hand. Here we find a collection of "physical axioms taken from those of Beda the philosopher, very necessary and very useful *to be read*," where the author presents a selection of philosophical sentences arranged in alphabetical order, drawing them from one of the most successful florilegia of the second half of the

16th century, though without adding to these sentences the brief commentaries that usually accompanied them.¹²

My impression is that these three parts were added to the already complete body of the manuscript, and more precisely to the section on the *Parva Naturalia*, which in itself is of miscellaneous nature, or likely to be supplemented with materials of different subject matter and provenance. That these are supervening materials seems clear, and likewise that the two subsections derived from Keckermann and pseudo-Beda are the fruit of simple book-mining. In the case of the former, we find an important clue in the heading—namely, that this part is taken from the Gdańsk professor's *Cursus philosophicus*. To be more precise, the reference is to a printed book presenting a systematic series of *Quaestiones Disputatae* that took shape in the margins of *Praelectiones*—that is, curricular and public lectures given at the Gdańsk Gymnasium in early 1603 and published in January 1606.¹³ Theoretically, the author of these subsections could have participated in these activities (lectures and disputations), but a marginal note on f. 170r (*Vide Kecker. in cursu philosoph.*, 162) demonstrates that he simply worked from the published book. My conclusion is that this section was composed and included with the other files of the manuscript only after January 1606. As for pseudo-Beda's *axiomata*, there is no such evidence. Nonetheless, it seems clear that they are the product of bookwork, independent of the lively discussions held in *collegia* or sessions of disputations. On the whole, however, whatever their origin, these materials still play into the basic idea that governed the composition of the volume—namely, that of offering as systematic and comprehensive a picture as possible of the issues usually raised in natural philosophy. A work in which a physician might be interested, and also a semi-blanc platform open to additions and sedimentations of further materials, a functionality that a printed handbook could not offer or could only offer within given limits.

In the margin of these considerations, I return for a moment to the question of the author and owner of the book. If, as it seems to me, the hand that compiled the last two part of the miscellany section is different from the one which wrote the rest, and if the composition of these two parts took place later, it can be assumed that they were added by someone to whom the manuscript came into possession after August 1603 and who added to it his own materials (the two subsections). Or alternatively, it could be assumed that the book did not change hands and that the author took these materials from someone else, judging them appropriate as *ad-*

---

12 176r: "Axiomata quaedam physica ex Bedae Philosophi axiomatibus desumpta valde necessaria et *lectu* utilissima" (italics mine). On pseudo-Beda, see Schmitt 1987, 532–533.

13 Keckermann 1606. In the preface "to the reader," we find interesting indications on the interaction between the teaching *ex cathedra* and the disputing activity of the *auditores*.

denda to the sixth section on the *Parva Naturalia* in the book he had composed. It is hard for me to speculate about the identity of the author and possible later owner. The chronological and geographical indications in the text point to someone from Pomerania, as indeed many students at Leiden University came from this area until at least the early 17th century (Pękacka-Falkowska 2020). If I were allowed to make a tentative guess about the author of the core of the book (the six sections), I would suggest a name that often pops up in the sources. I mean to speak of Matthaeus Radecius (Radetius, Radecke), who appears among the enrolled at Leiden on June 16, 1604, in the faculty of medicine with an entry specifying him to be 20 years of age and qualifying him as *"Dantiscanus."* This is thought to be the son of the more famous Socinian activist Matthaeus Radecke (1560–1612) (Tazbir 1986) and also the same person who appears as the author of a *Lobgedicht* in Latin in honor of Andreas Hiltebrand in the *Disputatio medica de crisibus et diebus decretoribus* published in 1605 and discussed by Hiltebrand himself on March 16 of that year under the praesidium of Aelius Everhardus Vorstius, extraordinary professor of natural philosophy at Leiden Medical School. And the same person is probably the one who figures as *respondens* in the disputation held at the Gdańsk Gymnasium on January 24, 1604, with Keckermann as *praesaes*, presenting a number of very interesting theses on Francesco Patrizi's philosophy of nature.[14] More problematic is that this is the same Matthaeus Radecius *"Dantiscanus Borussus, Ecclesiae Christii neophytus"* and *"Theologiae et Philosophiae studiosus"* who on May 4, 1603, had publicly discussed forty five theses drawn from the Nicene symbol (Eglin 1603) as *respondens* in Zurich, although his being the author cannot be ruled out on that account, as the dates of the manuscript do not cover the period between April and June. Further investigation, especially paleographic, could support or refute this conjecture.

5 Conclusion: Leiden 1603

It is now time to highlight those historical circumstances that can explain the author's effort to undertake such a long and complex work.

"Viewed from the standpoint of philosophical pedagogy rather than philology, Leiden is not the unmoved centre around which the system turns: it is a satellite of Heidelberg, Marburg, Herborn, and indeed the academic *gymnasium* in Danzig"

---

[14] Keckermann. 1606, 330–343; "Disputatio extraordinaria de thesibus quibusdam Acroamaticis, contra Franciscum Patricium directis, quam favente Deo opt. max. sub praesidio clarissii viri domini Bartholomaei Keckermanni philosophiae professoris in Gymnasio Dantiscan publice proponit ad diem 24 Ianuarii, Anni 1604 Matthaeus Radecius Dantiscanus."

(Hotson 2020, 40). This is how Hotson recently clarified Leiden's position within the "post-Ramist" school system that had been forming in the years between the French professor's death and those of Keckermann's activity in Gdańsk. In spite of the historiographical myth that had exaggerated the role and importance of this university and saw it as the spearhead of the academic world of the *zweiter Reformation*, the lack of international appeal of its educational institutions suggests otherwise (Hotson 2020, 21–30). For having chosen a policy that favored the humanistic elitism advocated by Lipsius and which regarded the schoolbook syntheses that had made the fortunes of the centers where Ramism had spread as pedagogical and intellectual degeneration (*compendia dispendia* was the derogatory motto that came into vogue), Leiden had effectively closed itself off from the reform of higher education and, at the same time, from the demand for a modern university or quasi-university education of an ever-growing student population coming mainly from the bourgeois elites of Central Europe (Hotson 2020, 41–46). One of the consequences of this "pedagogical Counter-Reformation," which thwarted the work of Rudolf Snell, one of the most talented pedagogues of the time at the disposal of the University of Leiden, was the very low volume of locally produced textbooks, which was made up for by purchasing those produced in those years at an industrial rate and quantity by Keckermann in not-so-far-away Gdańsk (Hotson 2020, 40).

To remain in the field of natural philosophy, consider that the first compendium by one of the Leiden professors who taught this subject in the years in which our manuscript was written would not be printed until 1614 (Jacchaeus 1614). In short, if even the study of "physics" was considered preliminary and essential to that of medicine, students did not have an adequate supply of inexpensive volumes with which to prepare. The presence of recently published Keckermannian materials in the manuscript is noteworthy in this regard, providing what is certainly some of the earliest evidence of the leadership exercised at the time in the educational-publishing field by the Gdańsk Gymnasium. The author of ms 120/II, in order to make up for this shortage, *fecit de necessitate virtutem.*

This text seems to derive from extra-curricular activities, such as "colleges" and private readings, freely undertaken by its author, rather than from mandatory or curricular courses.[15] In the situation described above, the author understood that thanks to the knowledge and experience accumulated through these activities it was possible to arrive in a span of a year or so at one's own volume that would

---

15 At Leiden, the student was free to follow his own curriculum and there was no requirement, as there was in Paris, to receive the title of *magister artium* to enter higher studies: "as a consequence, students frequently left the philosophy curriculum unfinished as they rapidly moved on to the more advanced disciplines" (Ruestow 1973, 11).

have the dual function of systematically framing the entire discipline and also of providing a convenient material basis for further expansion and thus serving beyond the end of his studies, the same function offered by those octavo volumes printed far from Leiden.

There is another aspect that makes a text like this different from and not easily replaced by a printed textbook. In general, in a course *ad usum studiosorum*, contained in a printed book and signed by a holder of a university chair, dogmatic and expository forms prevail, resulting in an assemblage of well-ordered principles, assertions, precepts, canons, and so on. Instead, the prevailing and most characteristic feature of the physics course as we read it in the manuscript is the dialectical forms: questions and objections, answers and solutions; we find here essentially the same subject matter but in the form in which it appeared during the learning process and from the perspective of the student—that is, the one who, according to the teaching conventions of the time, was constantly urged to "give reason" to the contents he was learning. In fact, his specific task was not so much handling this content as acquired data, but rendering it "scientific," in the sense this adjective had at the time—that is, supported by reasons, evidence, and arguments in order to resist critique and to be *magis remotus a contradictione*. In a notebook such as this one, we thus see less the function of a "forgetting machine" meant to cope with an excess of knowledge (considered in essence as bits of information) (Cevolini 2016; Blair 2010) and more that of training for the acquisition of a fundamental intellectual habit, which is that of defending or attacking a thesis in the course of a disagreement.

Therefore, it seems to me that the traditional concept of dialectic prevails in the manuscript, the one that was alive in *collegia* and *disputationes* and is expressed in the form of arguments in which the one who avoids contradiction or proves the contradictions of the opponent wins. As we have seen, however, the other meaning is not lacking either, the more modern, Ramist and post-Ramist meaning, referring to an *ars disserendi* that teaches how to derive concepts and order them "methodically" in the mental space of memory, the blank space of a sheet of paper, or that of many sheets stitched together in a fascicle or several fascicles. An anonymous student of the early 1600s thus left us an interesting record of this polarity so characteristic for the time and also a testimony to the way he played with it in order to gain that knowledge to which he aspired.

Bibliography

Primary Sources

Manuscripts

BUMK (Biblioteka Uniwersytetu Mikołaja Kopernika) Toruń, rkps 120/II

Printed Sources

Burgersdijk, Franco (1642): *Franconis Burgersdici Idea philosophiae naturalis sive methodus definitionum et controversiarum physicarum, editio novissima*. Leiden: Elsevier.

Burgersdijk, Franco (1652): *Collegium physicum, disputationibus XXXII absolutum; totam naturalem philosophiam compendiose proponens. Autore M. Francone Burgersdicio philosophiae professore, cum Syllabo disputationum respondentium nomina exprimente. Editio secunda, Autoris manu aucta.* Leiden: Elsevier.

Casmann, Otho (1594): *Psychologia anthropologica sive animae humanae doctrina, methodice informata, capitibus dissecta, singulorum capitum disquisitionibus ac controversarum quaestionum ventilationibus illustrata, partim Scholasticis Praelectionibus, partim vero Disputationibus, cum publicis, tum privatis in illustri Comitis Benthemici , etc., Schola Steinfurtensis tractata ab Othone Casmanno*. Hanau: Guilelmus Antonius.

Eglin, Raphael (1603): *Tetradis Catecheticae pars altera, quae est de Symbolo Apostolico, in quo promissiones Evangelii per fidem in Christum apprehendendae nobis proponuntur, quaestionibus et responsionibus comprehensa, et publicae disputationi in schola Tigurina propositae, auctore et praeside Raphaelo Eglino Iconio, Ecclesiaste Tigurino, respondente Matthaeo Radecio Dantiscano Borusso, Ecclesiae Christy Neophyto. Disputabitur ad diem 4 Maij horis solitis in majoris collegij auditorio aestivo publice*. Zürich [s.n.]

Jacchaeus, Gilbertus (1614): *Institutiones Physicae Iuventutis Lugdunensis studiis potissimum dicatae Authore Gilberto Iacchaeo*. Leiden: Iacobus Patius.
USTC: 1507216.

Keckermann, Bartholomäus (1606): *Disputationes philosophicae physicae praesertim, quae in Gymnasio Dantiscano ad Lectionum Philosophicarum cursum paulo plus biennio publice institutae et habitae sunt, sub praesidio Bartholomaei Keckermanni philosophiae in eodem Gymnasio professoris, ita scriptae ut scientiae naturalis methodicum compendium, simul et de praecipuis materiis utiliora iucundiora Problemata continerent*. Hanau: Guilelmus Antonius. USTC: 2027200.

Keckermann, Bartholomäus (1610): *Systema Physicum septem libris adornaturm et anno Christi 1607 publice propositum in Gymnasio Dantiscano, a Bartholomaeo Keckermanno, SS. Theologiae Licentiato, et Philosophiae ibidem Professore*. Hanau: Guilelmus Antonius. USTC: 2028565.

Liebler, Georg (1596): *Epitome Philosophiae Naturalis, ex Aristotelis summi philosophi libris ita excerpta, ut eorum capita breviter et dilucide eplicet, et ad eosdem cum fructu legendos praeparare studiosos possit. Multis locis auctior et emendatior, quae etiam Scholarum Petri Rami in octo libros Acroamaticos Aristotelis errores passim detegit, per Georgium Lieblerum, professorem Phys. in Schola Tubing*. Leipzig: [Michael Lantzenberger].

USTC: 653026.
Magirus, Johannes (1597): *Physica peripatetica ex Aristotele, eiusque interpretibus collecta, et in sex libros distincta, in usum Academiae Marpurgensis, studio et opera Iohannis Magiri doctoris Medici, et Physiologiae Professoris Ordinarii.* Frankfurt: Zacharias Palthenius.
Magirus, Johannes (1603): *Johannis Magiri, medicinae doctoris, et in Academia Marpurgensi Professoris olim ordinarii, Physiologiae Peripateticae Libri VI, cum commentariis, in quibus praecepta illius perspicue eruditeque explicantur, et ex optimis quibusque peripateticae philosophiae interpretibus, Platone, Aristotele, Zabarella, Archangelo Mercenario, Thomae Erasto, Iacobo Schegkio, Scaligero, Vico Mercurio, Contareno Cardinale, Hermolao Barbaro, Francisco Patritio et aliis disceptantur. Editio Nova, ab innumeris mendis repurgata, pluribusque in locis ex manuscripto Auctoris aucta.* Frankfurt: Wolffgang Richter.
Magirus, Johannes (1609): *Johannis Magiri Physiologiae peripateticae libri sex, cum commentariis [etc., ut 1603] disceptantur. Accessit Caspari Bartholini Malmogii Dani Enchiridion Metaphysicum ex Philosophorum Coriphei Aristotelis, optimarumque eius interpretum monumentis adornatum. Editio quinta.* Wittenberg: Iohannes Gorman.
Valerius, Cornelius (1593): *Physicae seu naturalis philosophiae Institutiones Cornelii Valerii ultrajectini. In usum Scholae Philosophicae Marpurgensis, cum generali Physices Synopsi, capitumque in paragraphos distinctione, eorundemque argumentis, jam denuo editae opera et studio Hermanni Wolfii, Medicinae Doctoris, et Physices in modo dicta Acad. Professoris. Quibus accesserunt excellentissimi viri Rodolphi Goclenii notae in singular capita doctissimae.* Marburg: Paulus Egenolphus.
USTC: 684024 and 684026.
Valles, Francisco (1556): *Controversiarum medicarum et philosophicarum Libri decem. Autore Francisco Vallesio Covarruviano, doctore et professore Complutensi.* Alcalá de Henares: Ioannes Brocarius.

Secondary Sources

Ashmann, Margreet (1995): "Teaching in *collegia:* the organization of disputationes at universities in the Netherlands and in Germany during the 16th and 17th centuries." In: Romano, Andrea (Ed.): *Universitá in Europa. Le istituzioni universitarie dal Medio Evo ai nostri giorni. Strutture, organizzazione, funzionamento.* Messina: Soveria Mannelli, 99–114.
Ashmann, Margreet (2000): *Collegium und Kolleg. Der juristische Unterricht an det Universität Leiden 1575-1630 unter besindere Berüsichtigung solcher Regelungen.* Frankfurt am Mein: Klostermann.
Aurnhammer, Achim (2015): "Andreas Hiltebrand—ein pommerscher Dichterartz zwischen Späthumanismu und Frühbarock." In: Kühlmann, Wilhelm and Langert, Horst (Eds.): *Pommern in der Frühen Neuzeit: Literatur und Kultur in Stadt und Region.* Tübingen: Max Niemeyer, 199–225.
Blair, Ann (2010): *Too Much to Know. Managing Scholarly Information before the Modern Age.* New Haven and London: Yale University Press.
Borysowka, Agnieszka and Gierke, Michał (2022): *Album studiosorum Pedagogium Książęcego w Szczecinie (1576–1666).* Szczecin: Książnica Pomorska.
Cevolini, Alberto (Ed.) (2016): *Forgetting Machines: Knowledge Management Evolution in Early Modern Europe.* Leiden: Brill.

Dibon, Paul (1954): *La philosophie néerlandais au siècle d'or*, t. I. *L'enseignement philosophique dans les universités à l'époque précartésienne (1575–1650)*. Paris, and Amsterdam, London, and New York: Elsevier.

Facca, Danilo (2020): *Early Modern Aristotelianism and the Making of Philosophical Disciplines*. London: Bloomsbury Academic.

Du Rieu, Willem Nicolaas (1875): *Album studiosorum Academiae Lugduno Batavae MDLXXV–MDCCCLXXV. Accedunt nomina curatorum et professorum per eadem secula ... Nomina lectorum qui in Academia Lugduno Batava docuerunt ... Nomina studiosorum Academiae Lugduno Batavae ....* The Hague: Martinus Nijoff.

Friedenthal, Meelis, Marti, Hanspeter, and Seidel, Robert (Eds.) (2021): *Early Modern Disputations in an Interdisciplinary and European Context*. Leiden: Brill.

Gaziński, Radosław (2016): "Paedagogium Książęce (lata 1544–1667)." In: Niedzielski, Piotr and Tarczyński, Waldemar (Eds.): *Akademicki Szczecin XVI–XXI wiek*. Szczecin: Wydawnictwo Naukowe Uniwersytetu Szczecińskiego, 15–46.

Gindhart, Marion and Kundert, Ursula (Eds.) (2010): *Disputatio 1200–1800. Form, Funktion und Wirkung einrs Leitmediums universitärer Weissenkultur*. Berlin and New York: De Gruyter.

Gindhart, Marion, Marti, Hanspeter, and Seidel, Robert (Eds.) (2016): *Frühneuzeitliche Disputationen Polyvalente Produktionsapparate gelehrten Wissens*. Cologne: Böhlau.

Hotson, Howard (2007): *Commonplace Learning. Ramism and its German Ramifications, 1543–1630*. Oxford: Oxford University Press.

Hotson, Howard (2021): *The Reformation of Common Learning. Post-Ramist Method and the Reception of the New Philosophy, 1618–c. 1670*. Oxford: Oxford University Press.

Mycio, Andrzej (2012): "Nowożytne rękopisy w zbiorach Biblioteki Uniwersyteckiej w Toruniu." In: *Czasy Nowożytne* 25, 193–205.

Mycio, Andrzej (2020): "Rękopisy szczecińskiego Gimnazjum Mariackiego w zbiorach Biblioteki Uniwersyteckiej w Toruniu." In: *Przegląd Zachodniopomorski* 35/64. No. 2, 189–201. DOI: 10.18276/pz.

Pękacka-Falkowska, Katarzyna (2020): "The Medical Faculty at the University of Leiden and its Graduates from the Polish-Lithuanian Commonwealth. Some Introductory Remarks." In: *Biuletyn Polskiej Misji Historycznej/Bulletin der polnischen historischen Mission* 15, 97–138. DOI:10.12775/BPMH.2020.004.

Ruestow, Edward G. (1973): *Physics at Seventeenth and Eighteenth Century-Leiden: Philosophy and the New Science in the University*. The Hague: Martinus Nijhoff.

Schlegelmilch, Ulrich (2016): "Andreas Hiltebrands Protokoll eines Disputationscolegiums zur Physiologie und Pathologie (Leiden 1604)." In: Gindhart, Marion, Marti, Hanspeter, Seidel, Robert (Eds.): *Frühneuzeitliche Disputationen Polyvalente Produktionsapparate gelehrten Wissens*. Cologne: Böhlau, 49–88.

Schmitt, Charles (1987): "Auctoritates, Repertorium, Dicta, Sententiae, Flores, Thesaurus, and Axiomata: Latin Aristotelian Florilegia in the Renaissance, In: Wiesner, Jürgen (Ed.): *Aristoteles Werk und Wirkung. Paul Moraux gewidmet, Zweiter Band: Kommnetierung, Überlieferung, Nachleben*. Berlin and New York: De Gruyter, 516–537.

Tazbir, Janusz (1986): "Mateusz Radecke." *Polski Słownik Biograficzny*. Vol. XXIX. Wrocław, Warsaw, Krakow, Gdańsk, and Łódź: Zakład Narodowy imienia Ossolińskich and Wydawnictwo Polskiej Akademii Nauk, 671–672.

Wehrmann, Martin (1894): *Geschichte des Marienstifts-Gymnasiums 1544–1894. Festschrift zum dreihundertfünfzigjährigen Jubiläum des Königlichen Marienstifts-Gymnasiums zu Stettin am 24. und 25. September 1894.* Szczecin: Druck von Herrcke und Lebeling.

Weijers, Olga (2013): *A History of Disputations Techniques from Antiquity to Early Modern Times.* Turnhout: Brepols.

Luisa Brotto

What Student Agency at the Academy of Zamość? Remarks on Some Political Oratory Texts

Abstract: This chapter inquires into possible forms of student agency in some surviving documents of the Academy of Zamość. The academy program and other testimonies reveal that the students were highly involved in the life of the academy, especially through the practice of rhetoric in public sessions. My goal is to investigate whether the students actively contributed to producing notes and speeches. The surviving documents can also provide insights into possible cooperation between students and teachers, hence into educative relations in university environments. Throughout the essay, I examine two brief handwritten texts from a codex probably belonging to a student, and I briefly recall another oration from the Biblioteka Ordynacji Zamoyskiej library fund. Overall, these documents point to the existence of a 'guided' student agency: the students' creativity was not independent of the supervision of teachers and tutors, who possibly encouraged them to explore and appropriate classical as well as contemporary literature.

1 Introduction: Student Agency in Lecture Notes and Orations

Investigating early modern students' notes in order to trace manifestations of student agency leads to addressing complex documents, which result from a variety of factors. Lecture notes and university-related writings collected in notebooks–such as reported disputations, sermons, and orations–pose specific challenges to contemporary scholars. Unlike personal private notes, these texts rarely disclose the lives and personalities of the students that produced them. Their structure and content are the product of institutionally imposed duties, contents and learning techniques derived from pre-existing traditions, and personal initiative.

A careful study of this kind of writings can shed light on the learning mechanisms of the students, thus showing that the teachings were received and reshaped through a process of appropriation. These documents can also provide insights into the educational relations between teachers and students, and between fellow

---

Luisa Brotto: ORCID: 0000-0002-3382-6699. NAWA (Polish National Agency for Academic Exchange) Ulam-Seal of Excellence Fellow (Application PPN/SEL/2020/1/00005).

∂ Open Access. © 2023 the author(s), published by De Gruyter. [CC BY] This work is licensed under the Creative Commons Attribution 4.0 International License. https://doi.org/10.1515/9783111072722-005

students, possibly revealing different forms of collaboration. For instance, tutors and teachers could have supported students when they wrote their speeches, e.g., by offering advice in choosing certain sources, by encouraging imitation or more critical thinking.

Another aspect that should be explored is the role of the texts after they were produced. Although students' notes and notebooks were sometimes intended as "disposable" texts, which lost their relevance once the students finished their studies (Burlinson 2010, 242–243), many of them had a life beyond the university careers of their authors and owners. Studies have shown that lecture notes could circulate within universities and sometimes even become the basis for the production of printed works (Blair 2008). Students could sometimes keep their notes as a valuable record of their studies and as materials they could consult at later stages of their life.

To inquire into modes of student agency in student university writings and to address the social dimension behind these texts, this chapter focuses on the teaching and learning practices of an innovative educational institution situated in the Polish-Lithuanian Commonwealth: it examines documents belonging to, and possibly produced by, students of the Academy of Zamość.

After briefly describing the educational project of the academy and illustrating some features of the surviving manuscripts regarding its teaching activities, I focus on a handwritten codex created in 1615 and belonging to the *studiosus* Andreas Sredzinski. By thoroughly analyzing an oratory piece that is part of the codex, I retrace the student's exploration and selection of both ancient and recent sources that led him to compose the oration. Additional references to notes and other oratory pieces point to the fact that students were encouraged to apply their acquired knowledge of classical texts in producing speeches that were probably delivered during public sessions, thus constituting both a test and a shared occasion for learning.

2 The Academy of Zamość: A Brief Overview of Some Recent Studies

Founded in 1594 by Chancellor Jan Zamoyski (1542–1605), a prominent political and military authority within the Polish-Lithuanian Commonwealth, the Academy of Zamość was an innovative institution designed to impart an effective political education to young noblemen through the study of classical texts. This educational project was rooted in the public life of the Commonwealth, since it aimed to prepare the Polish-Lithuanian youth for public political confrontation, thus leading students to develop various oratory and debating skills, while also mastering legal and political notions.

Even though medicine and theology were also taught at the academy, politics and law constituted the main core of the educational program, especially during the first decades of its activity. Professors such as Adam Burski (1560–1611) and Tomasz Drezner (1560–1616), established authorities in moral philosophy and law, respectively, held courses on Aristotle's *Nicomachean Ethics*, Justinian's *Institutiones*, ancient rhetoric, and history.

In the past decades, an increasing number of studies have been devoted to the educational activities carried out at the Academy of Zamość, thus shedding new light on both the intellectual and practical aspects of its life. Intellectual historians have inquired into the educational choices of the founder, reported in the academy program, and into the extant manuscripts regarding the lessons held by the academy professors.[1] Furthermore, studies have been devoted to reconstructing the educational practices and habits of both teachers and students. Such a purpose has led to examining the life of the small institutions that were part of the academy: the printing house, the library, and the dormitory have become the subject of specific inquiries.[2]

The surviving manuscripts relating to the teaching activities can be further examined to uncover possible forms of student agency and cooperation between students and teachers. Based on my analysis, I intend to argue that the notes resulting from lessons, access to library books, and the composition of orations were all part of an educational mechanism that promoted a "guided" form of student agency:

---

[1] In addition to providing the first English translation of the academy program, the monograph by Valentina Lepri (Lepri 2019) has examined its structure and retraced a possible influence of Johann Sturm's theories on the overall organization of the academy, thus adding further material to the studies of Jan Karol Kochanowski (Kochanowski 1900). Specific studies have been devoted to eminent professors. To name only a few, the preparation and the role of the teachers have been addressed by Chachaj 1996. On philosophical teachings and especially on Adam Burski, see Dąmbska 1974 and 1978, Szymanski 1988, Facca 1999b and 2000, Ryczek 2017, Półćwiartek-Dremierre 2020, and Lepri 2021. On Szymon Birkowski (1574–1626), professor of moral philosophy and metaphysics, see Facca 1999a. As to the study of law at the academy, see Kuryłowicz and Witkowski 1980, Kuryłowicz 1996 and 1999; and Dyjakowska 2000a, 2000b, and 2003. Cieslak 1957 and Bukowska 1960 are devoted to the work of Tomasz Drezner as a jurist. On the teaching of theology and the religious life of the academy, see Kumor 1996 and Dyjakowska 2001.

[2] The structure and history of the academy library have been examined in Horodyski 1951 and Makowski 2005a, 2005b, 2012a, and 2012b. The activity of the printing house of the academy has been addressed in Myk 1994a, 1994b, and 1996. In addition to publishing the *Album stutentów* of the academy, Henryk Gmiterek has devoted studies to life within the academy, with special focus on ceremonies and rituals, the life of underprivileged students, and the organization of the dormitory. See Gmiterek 1976, 1999/2000, and 2005.

the goal of the educational practices at the academy was to gradually lead students to scholarly independence within well-established frameworks provided through teaching.

3 Features of the Extant Notes Regarding Teaching Activities

As far as we know today, most of the surviving manuscripts related to the academy's educational activities are part of the Biblioteka Ordynacji Zamojskiej library fund at the Polish National Library.[3] The majority of them convey commentaries to classical texts carried out by the academy professors during the first decades of the 17th century–probably resulting from their courses. Therefore, they are especially useful for reconstructing the work of the first generation of professors, chosen directly by the founder Zamoyski, and determined to carry out his conception of education by promoting the study of rhetoric, ethics, and law as part of a more general political expertise.

Aside from a few exceptions, the manuscripts have a rather polished outline. They report classical texts mostly in their entirety, divided into passages and accompanied by corresponding commentary, which sometimes contains examples, or recalls classical sources relating to the main text. The contents of the manuscripts mirror the peculiar humanist approach of the academy professors—namely, the idea that earnest assimilation of classical texts could lead the students to succeed better in matters of public and practical life.

The handwriting is rather neat, with very few corrections. The titles are displayed carefully and are sometimes decorated, although usually very simply. Accurate diagrams are often displayed at the end of the commentaries or after individual parts and chapters.[4] Very accurate drawings, and graphics that require geometrical drawings, also appear in some of the manuscripts. The *marginalia* do not report personal comments and annotations. Rather, they are mostly educational: they summarize the main points of the text, recall some sources, or provide Latin transcriptions of Greek words.[5]

---

[3] Among the exceptions is Vasyl Stefanyk National Scientific Library of Ukraine, MS 384, whose existence was kindly indicated by Dr. Hanna Mazheika, and the codex from Biblioteka Jagiellońska that constitutes the object of my analysis.

[4] See, for instance, Polska Biblioteka Narodowa BOZ MS 141, 49v; Polska Biblioteka Narodowa BOZ MS 1515–1516, 144v; and Polska Biblioteka Narodowa BOZ MS 1526, 14v.

[5] See, for instance, Polska Biblioteka Narodowa BOZ MS 141, 15r–v, 20v.

Given the precision of the notes, it could be argued that they are second-order versions created after the lessons, or extremely polished first-order writings. As to their possible creators, some of notes can be traced back to teachers, while others have been attributed to students, who may have reported the lectures they attended or commissioned the creation of manuscripts. A group of manuscripts in the Biblioteka Ordynacji Zamojskiej fund has been linked to Tomasz Zamoyski (1594–1638), the son of the founder.

Overall, the manuscripts relating to the Academy of Zamość present scholars with issues common to other lecture notes of the time: although they could have been created by the students themselves, the involvement of "invisible helpers," namely, entrusted note-takers, cannot be ruled out (Blair 2016, 265). The possible contribution of the teachers is also to be taken into consideration: the manuscripts may have been copied from official notes published by the teachers themselves; alternatively, some of the teachers may have encouraged the creation of manuscripts by the students (Blair 2010a, 315). In any case, the notes definitely played a role in the students' education and in the life of the institution. For instance, the manuscripts belonging to Tomasz Zamoyski were probably available to other academy professors, tutors, and perhaps some students. They were passed down to the following generations until they became part of the library.[6]

Whereas lecture notes constitute the majority of the surviving manuscripts, a few oratory pieces are also present. A volume in the Biblioteka Ordynacji Zamojskiej fund contains a number of fragments of lecture notes and some speeches. The notes could be preparatory stages for more accurate transcriptions or, alternatively, partial copies of previously existing lecture notes. The speeches could be writing and oratory exercises.[7] Moreover, a handwritten volume preserved in Kraków conveys different kinds of materials, namely, notes relating to a disputation, an oration, and some lecture or study notes.

4 The Volume of Andreas Sredzinski, a Possible Student at the Academy

The handwritten volume that belonged to Andreas Sredzinski, part of the manuscript collection of Biblioteka Jagiellońska, deserves a special place among the documents of the Academy of Zamość, as it provides significant insights on the educational activities and learning practices of its owner. The volume consists of 351

---

6 On the features of these manuscripts, see Makowski 2005a, 84–85.
7 It is the volume Polska Biblioteka Narodowa BOZ MS 1525.

chartae and contains a heterogeneous series of texts connected to the activity of Sredzinski as a student.

The first is *Dikaiomatheia* (Biblioteka Jagiellońska, MS 2279 AA VII 61, 1–121), a work by the Livonian humanist David Hilchen (1561–1610), who spent many years in Zamość and, despite not being a professor, clearly had the opportunity to exert an influence over some of the students.[8]

The other texts appear to be written by a different hand, which, although it cannot be proved with certainty, might be that of Sredzinski himself. The name "Andreas Sredzinsky" appears at the bottom of two blank pages (220r and 320r). Thus, it is reasonable to infer that the volume belonged to him. Although all the texts are handwritten, one printed sheet is included (137). Released by the printing shop of the academy, it certifies that Sredzinski, presented as a *studiosus philosophiae*, publicly defended a series of legal theses in a session presided over by professor Tomasz Drezner.[9]

The theses are mostly taken from Justinian's *Institutiones* and *Digesta*; the only exception is a thesis on marriage taken from the *Canones* on the reformation of marriage from the Council of Trent.[10] The choice of these legal theses proves the relevance of Roman law to the students' education at the academy. Such a choice clearly mirrors the will of the founder as stated in the academy program, which prescribed that civil law be taught in addition to Polish law (see *Fundatio Academiae Zamoscensis*, in Lepri 2019, 143).

---

[8] The work by Hilchen is analyzed for the first time in the chapter of this volume authored by Kristi Viiding.

[9] Biblioteka Jagiellońska MS 2279 AA VII 61, 137r: "Has Theses Deo iuvante propugnabit Andreas Sredzinski Philosophiae in Academia Zamoscensi Studiosus Praeside Thoma Dresnero I. V. D. Anno Domini M. DC. XIV. Mensis Iunii die VIII Hora I."

[10] Biblioteka Jagiellońska MS 2279 AA VII 61, 137r: "1. Iurisprudentia est divinarum atque humanarum rerum scientia, iusti atque iniusti cognitio. §. Iurisprudentia Instit. De iustitia et iure. 2. Consuetudo est, ius non scriptum, moribus utentium comprobatum. §. Constat autem. Instit. De iure naturali, gentium, et civili. l. de quibus ff. de legibus. 3. Ius civile saepe mutari solet, vel tacito consensu populi, vel alia postea lege lata. §. sed naturalia. Instit. De iure naturali, gentium, et civili. 4. Omnes ius civile, vel ad personas pertinet, vel ad res, vel ad actiones. § omne ius. Institut. De iure naturali, gentium et civili. 5. Omnes homines aut liberi sunt, aut servi. In principio Institut. De iure personarum. 6. Libertas inaestimabilis res est. §. cum ergo. Instit. quibus ex caussis manumittere non licet. 7. In nuptiis contrahendis requiritur consensus tantum eorum, qui easdem contrahunt. Concilium Tridentinum. De refermatione matrimonii. 8. Pupilus potest suam conditionem meliorem facere sine tutore, deteriorem vero, non aliter quam cum tutoris autoritate. In principio Instit. De autoritate tutorum. 9. Rerum, quaedam in nostro patrimonio sunt, ut res profanae; quaedam extra patrimonium, ut res sacrae. In principio Instit. De rerum divisione. Et § nullius autem eodem ut supra. 10. Quod ante nullius, id naturali ratione occupanti conceditur. §. fere igitur. Instit. De rerum divisione."

The handwritten texts that immediately follow the printed sheet are connected to the defense of the legal theses. Arguments against each of the ten theses are reported, along with possible solutions. The document gives the reader a glimpse of what was probably said by Sredzinski on that public occasion. The arguments are followed by an oratory piece, a *Laus iurisprudentiae*, which I analyze below.

The other handwritten texts collected in the volume are about rhetoric. An *Artis dicendi compendium* (155–204) illustrates the art of rhetoric through questions, starting with general ones on the nature of rhetoric, then moving on to analyzing its parts and more specific issues. The *Compendium* is followed by three commentaries—respectively, to Hermogenes' *De formis dicendi* (221–259), the first two books of Cicero's *De oratore* (263–305), and Cicero's *Oratio pro Sexto Roscio Amerino* (321–350). Unlike other extant handwritten commentaries from the Academy of Zamość, the texts collected by Sredzinski do not report the name of any professors. Dates referring to when the courses were held, or to the composition of the manuscript, are missing as well. Therefore, it is not possible to precisely ascertain whether these texts resulted from lessons held at the academy or from independent study. Nonetheless, when analyzing the commentaries on Hermogenes, Thomas Conley pointed out that *De formis dicendis* was the subject of academy courses, as confirmed by the existence of a partial commentary attributed to Adam Burski (see Conley 1994, 281). What is more, the texts paired with commentaries that Sredzinski collected are mentioned in the academy program as part of the mandatory teachings on rhetoric (see *Fundatio Academiae Zamoscensis*, in Lepri 2019, 145). Therefore, it can perhaps be assumed that the commentaries resulted from the lessons attended by the student. Like other surviving notes from the academy, the ones by Sredzinski are extremely polished and well-ordered, most likely the result of careful copying and editing of previous notes.

This choice of texts could somehow summarize Sredzinski's experience as a student at the academy and displays what we are entitled to believe to be some of its most valuable moments. What is more, it suggests what disciplines and what sets of skills the student deemed important to his later professional life. Considering that, based on the information on the printed sheet, Sredzinski was a *studiosus philosophiae*, the fact that he defended theses concerning civil law and seemed to particularly value rhetorical texts shows that law, rhetoric, and moral philosophy were considered strictly intertwined at the academy.

A further observation can be made: the binding of the volume is from the early 17th century. An inscription located on the pastedown indicates that the texts were probably bound together in 1615, one year after Sredzinski defended the legal theses. The date of the binding thus reinforces the idea that the volume was conceived as a reminder of relevant parts of the student's education, and a long-term tool—a set of scholarly materials he could always consult if needed (Blair 2010b, 63).

As to the identity of Andreas Sredzinski, the *Album studentów* of the Academy reports that an "Andreas Stanislai Sredzinski" from the district of Przemyśl enrolled in the academic year 1609–1610; his name is followed by that of a possible relative, "Christophorus Stanislai Sredzinski" (Gmiterek 1994, 72). This information complies with indications found in the printed sheet conveying the legal theses: the document is opened by a dedication to the student's father, whose name was Stanisław Sredzinski.[11] Based on the genealogy of the Sredzinski family provided by Szymon Okolski in his *Orbis Polonus*, it seems that an Andreas Sredzinski pursued literary studies, held political positions such as that of royal secretary, and later became a member of the clergy.[12] This brief inquiry into Andreas Sredzinski's origins and life suggests that in his younger years he was exactly the kind of stu-

---

11 Biblioteka Jagiellońska MS 2279 AA VII 61, 137r: "Generoso et magnifico domino D. Stanislao Sredzinski Andreas Sredzinski patri suo charissimo F. S. P."

12 Okolski 1641, 87: "Andreas quintus filius Stanislai, qui post studia literaria, ad Spiritualis vitae cultum animum diligenter adiecit. ... A Serenissimo Rege Sigismundo III, in Secretarium R. Maiestatis electus, multoties Iudex Parlamenti, et Nuntius a R. Maiestate ad Comitia particularia missus, et ad Compositionem inter status ab Illustriss. et Reverendiss. D. Ioanne Pruchnicki, Archiepiscopo Leopol. atque ipsius Ven. Capitulo deputatus fuit. Demum Praepositus Praemyslien. et Officialis Leopolien. creatus, in Episcopum Nicopolien. et Suffraganeum Leopolien. inauguratus est." In addition to mentioning the aforesaid legal theses, Estreicher's *Bibliographia Polska* notes that an Andreas Sredzinski composed a preliminary poem to Piotr Ciekliński's Polish translation of Plautus's *Trinummus*, (Ciekliński 1597) and a preliminary epistle to Szymon Szymonowić's *Imagines diaetae Zamoscianae* (Szymonowić 1604; see Estreicher 1933, 146). According to Okolski's genealogy, the younger brother of Andreas was Christophorus, an information that seems to comply with the record in the *Album studentów*: both brothers could have enrolled during the academic year 1609–1610. Andreas Sredzinski, son of Stanisław, is not to be confused with and older and most renowned Andreas Sredzinski, deeply involved in the life of the Academy of Zamość. Based on Okolski's text, the latter was the son of Faelix Sredzinski. See Okolski 1641, 88: "Andreas alter filius [Faelicis], Secretarius R. Maiestatis, et Ioannis Zamoyscii strenuus miles, singulis expeditionibus praesens. Huic Zamoyscius consanguineam suam de armis Ielita, Annam de Łaznino, in matrimonium collocavit." On this Andreas Sredzinski and his close connections to Jan Zamoyski, see Tygielski 1990, 15, 102, and 107. It is possible that he was the author of the earlier texts mentioned in *Bibliographia Polska*. As a matter of fact, Okolski reports the existence of another Andreas Sredzinski, son of Albertus Sredzinski (Okolski 1641, 87). It is perhaps worth mentioning that an "Andreas Sredzinsky" enrolled at the Academy of Zamość in 1615–1616, but the record on the *Album studentów* does not convey any information about his origins and family (Gmiterek 1994, 90). On the Sredzinski family, see again Okolski 1641, 83: "Sredzinscii, de Srednie in Palatinatu Russiae, in districtu Chelmensi. Antiqua familia, militari et patriae obsequiis continuo dedicata. Quapropter a Serenissimis Regibus, qui omnem Rempublicam duraturam religione et militari advertunt, publicis praemiis remunerati sunt."

dent the Academy of Zamość was intended for. Coming from a family of military men, with an inclination for literary studies and a political career before him, he could benefit from the acquisition of rhetorical as well as philosophical and political skills.

The works collected in the volume have already raised the interest of scholars (see Conley 1994). My goal is to focus briefly on the report of the legal theses defended in June of 1614 and more extensively on the *Laus iurisprudentiae*, probably conceived for that same occasion. These documents display a process of appropriation of scholarly notions and sources that were revisited and reenacted by the student during the public event.

5 The *Theses* and the *Laus iurisprudentiae* as Possible Examples of "Guided" Student Agency

A preliminary examination of the list of arguments raised against the legal theses and their solutions reveals that they were not the result of original work. A possible source is a collection of disputations by Jean de la Reberterie, a law professor at the University of Paris during the second half of the 16th century. Leaving a more detailed analysis of the theses to a future study, here I limit myself to presenting a brief example. To argue against the sixth thesis—namely, that human freedom does not have a price and cannot become an object of trade—Sredzinski points out that in the case of slavery human freedom was in fact sold, by quoting Justinian's *Institutiones* (*De iure personarum*) and *Digesta* (*De statu hominum*). This objection is then rejected by declaring that servitude, and not freedom, is what is actually sold in this kind of transactions. Another argument against the main thesis is made by referring to *Digesta* (*De his, qui effuderint vel deiecerint*), where the accidental killing of a free man is sanctioned with a fine. In this case as well, Sredzinski pointed out that human freedom was not actually bought and sold. Rather, it is a financial punishment. Such considerations demonstrate, once and for all, that freedom is never the object of economic transactions. The exact same arguments had already been provided by Jean de la Reberterie in his *Disputationum libri*.[13]

---

13 Reberterie 1581, 39v: "Libertas inaestimabilis est §. cum ergo Instit. Quibus ex caus. manumit. non licet. Obiectiones. Doctissime respondens, argumentor in hoc propositum, quo contendis libertatem inaestimabilem esse. Et si huic tuae opinioni ni subscrivere videatur Poëta Satyrographus cum ait, 'Non bene pro toto libertas, venditur auro': nihilominus hanc sententiam falsam esse sic doceo. Quicquid emi et vendi potest id in aestimationem cadere nemo est cui dubitet. Atqui libertas emi et vendi potest, ut docet Imperator in §. cum autem 2. Inst. de iur. personar. vers. venundari passus est, tunc enim certo pretio aestimatur l. servorum, in princip. in vers. venire, D. de stat.

It can accordingly be argued that Sredzinski's defense of the legal theses largely followed a path provided by previous sources. It is also safe to assume that his teachers allowed the student to draw inspiration from manuals of disputations, approved of these practices, and possibly encouraged them. If the theses were both chosen and examined based on pre-existing materials, the public defense performed by the student was a moment of reenactment of consolidated knowledge. Although it is possible that the student was also invited to improvise and build on the arguments that they could find in the existing literature, his agency was clearly "guided," directed towards the assimilation of specific contents and methods.

The *Laus iurisprudentiae* can perhaps provide further evidence as to the kind of student agency occurring within the academy. In a passage of the *Laus*, the student addresses his knowledgeable audience and asks that his work be judged as the product of humble and yet profound commitment to his studies. The author is not explicitly mentioned in the printed sheet. However, given that the oration is referred to as an introduction to a further presentation on legal matters, it can be argued that it was delivered (or written to be delivered) on that occasion, most likely by Sredzinski himself.[14]

A brief overview of the oration clearly shows that the text is a "mosaic" of passages drawn from different works, taken out of their original contexts and combined to create a new speech. *Iurisprudentia* is portrayed as an all-encompassing kind of knowledge, capable of providing answers to both theoretical and practical matters pertaining to social life. The authority of Aristotle is recalled in order to remind the audience that human beings are meant for action as much as they are meant for knowledge.[15] By adapting Cicero's praise of civil law as developed

---

hominum. Igitur libertas aestimabilis res est. Deinde si quis liberum hominem occiderit, 50. aureorum poena damnatur, l. 1 § sed cum liber, D de his qui deiecer. vel effud. vers. 50. aureorum condemnatio fit. Igitur liber homo aestimatur, et ita nulla est tua thesis. Solutiones. Doctissime iuris Antecessor, respondeo, qui patiebatur se venundari, non vendebatur ut liber, sed ut servus, cum liberi hominis nulla sit aestimatio. Quod attinet ad l. 1 § sed cum liber, Iurisconsultus ibi docet, liberum hominem non aestimari, se poenam quidem 50 aureorum statui in eum, qui liberum hominem interfecit."

14 Biblioteka Jagiellońska MS 2279 AA VII 61, 148r: "Atque eius quidem brevis navigationis meae fructum opeculasque hodie ostendere, et coram vobis expromere visum mihi est … Sed antequam thesauros hos iuris vobis promam, iuvat … Deae eius formam pauliper contemplari. Itaque bona vestra venia pauca quaedam … de Iurisprudentiae laudibus praefabor." The metaphor of sailing appears also in the *Conclusio* that follows the arguments *pro* and *contra* the legal theses, suggesting possible continuity between these texts; see Biblioteka Jagiellońska MS 2279 AA VII 61, 145v.

15 Biblioteka Jagiellońska MS 2279 AA VII 61, 147r: "Si enim recte princeps Peripatheticorum Aristoteles hominem non ad intelligendum solum, sed ad agendum etiam natum esse protulit, quae tandem e numero optimarum artium ita sine fronte sit ut ex hoc Mustaceo palmarium sibi quaerere, adeoque laudem iurisprudentiae praeripere debitam audeat?"

by the character of Lucius Licinius Crassus in the first book of *De oratore*, the author points to the superiority of law over philosophy, due to the former's ability to provide more linear, equally profound answers, and to concretely improve human moral and social life.[16] Despite its practical attitude, the discipline of law is portrayed as capable of elevating the human soul: the holy teachings of the law can lift human beings over their own mortality and lead to a gradual approximation to divine nature.[17] Law is said to plant the seeds of virtue and to provide personal comfort as well as social order.

6 The Sources and Their Combination

Already in the first pages of the oration, in addition to several explicit quotations from Cicero, the reader can find entire paragraphs borrowed from more recent oratory pieces. It is worth noting that the author drew material from late 16th century oratory literature, that is, from late humanism, rather than from primary sources. For instance, to highlight the relevance of law over philosophy, he adapted a passage that appears to come from the *Oratio de fructu et utilitate philosophiae moralis* by the German professor Gregor Bersman (1538–1611), dean of the Gymnasium Franciscum in Zerbst. By attributing the idea that *disciplina morum* is the most relevant knowledge that can be grasped by the human faculties to the Stoic philosopher Aristo of Chio, Bersman intended to present his reader with a praise of ethics. Instead, the author of the *Laus iurisprudentiae* employs those same words to put moral philosophy in the background and formulate a praise of law, thus intentionally changing their original meaning.[18]

---

16 Biblioteka Jagiellońska MS 2279 AA VII 61, 147r–v contains several quotations from *De oratore*, I, 188–197.
17 Biblioteka Jagiellońska MS 2279 AA VII 61, 147r: "Sed etiam pleraeque artes, illud maximi loco beneficii nobis conferunt, quod optimis earum institutis excultum ingenium, ad vitae eius obeunda laudabiliter munia quodam modo aptius evadat: haec vero iuris scientia cum hoc ipsum abunde, tum illud etiam auctarii vice plena adiicit manu, ut mortalitas nostra sanctissimis legum praeceptis instructa, divinae quodam modo adaequetur naturae."
18 Biblioteka Jagiellońska MS 2279 AA VII 61, 148r: "Aristonem Chium nobilem olim philosophum qui ob eximium sermonis leporem syrenis cognomen invenit, dicere saepe solitum accepimus, eorum quae philosophi in scholis scrutando inquirant, quaedam ad nos pertinere, alia supra nos eminere, alia nil prope nos attangere. ... Ipsam demum morum disciplinam, tanquam normam vitae, morum praeceptricem eo loco ponebat, ut haec sola ad nos pertinere, haec sola et par, et digna studio nostro videretur esse." These sentences are nearly exact quotations of the beginning of the aforementioned oration in Bersman 1576. The preeminence of law over philosophy due to the practical nature of the former was particularly emphasized in one of the opening chapters

The tendency to borrow and adapt passages from pre-existing materials becomes more evident throughout the oration. More than half of the praise of law is taken from the *Oratio de laudibus iustitiae* by the French humanist Marc-Antoine Muret (1526–1585), a prominent figure of French Renaissance culture who combined the study of rhetoric and that of moral philosophy, while also dedicating some well-received oratory pieces to civil law. Through Muret's words, the praise of law is placed within an utterly naturalistic framework. The author of the *Laus* observes that laws are first found in nature, since they provide a healthy balance among the components of the universe. While they fulfill their goal perfectly in the superlunar realm, laws are imperfectly applied to the sublunar realm due to the essential imperfection of matter.[19] By taking up a classical comparison between medicine and justice—and still quoting Muret's oration—the author argues that physical health and moral virtue are forms of justice, whereas sickness and vice are both manifestations of injustice.[20]

The observations on the existence of harmony among different elements in nature provide a naturalistic foundation for the notion of *aequitas*—that is, the moral, legal, and political principle which consists in granting to different individuals or parties what is most appropriate to them.[21] Such a principle—different

---

of Tomasz Drezner's *Institutionum iuris Regni Poloniae libri IV*, published in 1613 (Drezner 1613, 5–6). It could be argued that this work influenced the views expressed in the *Laus jurisprudentia*. According to the printing sheet in the handwritten volume, Drezner himself presided the seance during which Sredzinski disputed the legal theses (Biblioteka Jagiellońska MS 2279 AA VII 61, 137r).

19 Biblioteka Jagiellońska MS 2279 AA VII 61, 149r: "Iustitiae originem a coelo esse perhibent veteres; illic eam et vigere, et ex omni aeternitate viguisse .... In iis autem, quae orbi lunae subiecta sunt, absolutam illam quidem et ex omni parte perfectam iustitiam materiae vitio cerni non posse." See Muret 1789, 76.

20 Biblioteka Jagiellońska MS 2279 AA VII 61, 149v: "Omnia namque mala, omnia damna, omnis pernicies tam animis quam corporibus ex iniustitia evenit: salus contra et incolumitas, omne denique bonum a iustitia proficiscitur: nam cum in corporibus nostris quatuor sint, quae quatuor elementis respondent, igni flava bilis, animae sanguis, aquae pituita, bilis atra terrae: quamdiu haec cum aequalitate quadam inter se permista sunt, quamdiu certis quibusdam aequalitatis continentur legibus, tamdiu valemus vigemusque; cum eorum aliquid limites excedit, dum aut maius aut minus iusto est, aut se a communione ceterorum segregavit, nonne subito conflictamur morbis, tandemque interimus." See Muret 1789, 77.

21 Biblioteka Jagiellońska MS 2279 AA VII 61, 150v: "Nam et convenerunt homines et una vitam colere decreverunt, cum aequi se iure usuros, et quod suo sibi labore peperissent, eo sine metu fruituros esse, neque moenibus magis quam legibus a vi atque ab iniuria tutos se fore confiderent: hinc etiam quamdiu id observatur, tam diu amice inter se ac concorditer vivunt; simul atque ab aequitate disceditur, partes, factiones, secessiones, seditiones et bella civilia exsistunt." See Muret 1789, 80. On the history of the notion of *aequitas*—notably presented by Aristotle in the fifth book of his *Nicomachean Ethics*, 1137a32–1138a3—in early modern legal thought, see Maniscalco 2020.

from equality—is considered capable of preserving the natural differences existing within social contexts. Allowing every component to be as its best, it is conceived as a key element for the creation of social concord. Thus conceived, laws are crucial in maintaining united and peaceful political bodies, and civil law becomes an antidote to all kinds of social divisions. The notion of *iustitia* is linked to those of *veritas, fides, pax,* and *amicitia,* to point out that a good education, a strong religion, and the search for social concord complete the constructive action of law.[22]

Muret's text displayed a personal formulation of concepts well-spread in Renaissance conceptions of natural law and drew inspiration from the Platonic as well as the Aristotelian and Ciceronian traditions. By quoting his words, the author of the *Laus* assimilates what was already a complex work as to both theoretical contents and rhetorical structure. A contemporary reader might be inclined to view such a choice as an attempt to rely on ready-mixed interpretations and analyses, instead of facing classical culture directly. However, it should also be noted that quoting recent texts also constitutes an opportunity to get in touch with later traditions and their outcomes, thus providing different ways of addressing the past.

Despite quoting *Oratio de laudibus iustitiae* so extensively, the *Laus iurisprudentiae* introduces a significant change: what Muret wrote about the virtue of justice is now attributed to law. By declaring that law is "written justice," the focus shifts from a moral principle to the actual, concrete possibility and ability to produce just legislations.[23] This move is particularly emphasized towards the end of the oration: the end of Muret's oration is omitted from the *Laus iurisprudentiae*; instead, the author adds different considerations and examples. Once again, the additions do not constitute original work, but they result from his own choices in the matter of style and content.

For instance, some examples are taken from one *Praefatio* to Cicero's *De legibus* written by Jean Passerat (1534–1602), professor of eloquence at the prestigious Collège Royal in Paris during the second half of the 16th century. In addition to a Greek quotation from the *Orphic Hymns* and Homer's *Odyssey,* the Laus *iurisprudentiae* displays some examples taken from ancient history to illustrate how laws

---

22 This constellation of terms was further illustrated—once again following Muret's oration—through some verses from Horace's *Odes* (IV, 5), which allow the reader to bear in mind the pillars of human security. See 151r as well as Muret 1789, 80–81.
23 Biblioteka Jagiellońska MS 2279 AA VII 61, 152v–153r: "Si vos eius ulla tenet rei admiratio scire vos velim, me ea in sententia semper fuisse, cum iurisprudentia ex fontibus iustitiae derivetur, et ad eandem tanquam ad caput suum praecepta sua referat, ob eam ita auctam communionem quicquid de iustitia diceretur, idem dici de iurisprudentia, communesque laudes continere. Quid enim Iurisprudentia aliud quam scripta iustitia est?"

should be honored. Among others, the *Laus* mentions two Spartan kings: Demaratus, who respectfully accepted his own deposition by declaring that even a king should submit to law, and Archidamus, who stated that obedience to law was crucial to maintaining the power of Sparta.[24]

The political examples taken from Passerat clearly emphasize the preeminence of law over other forms of political authority: praise is bestowed on kings and officials who choose not to use their power arbitrarily and who acknowledge the authority of legislators and magistrates. The author of the *Laus* may have chosen to include those very examples in his oration precisely to highlight this conception of power.

Consequently, towards the end of the *Laus*, the reader finds praise of Justinian as the founder of civil law. Part of that praise is a reference to the *Praefatio* of his *Institutiones*—namely, that "Imperial Majesty must not only be distinguished by arms, but also be protected by laws."[25] Through this quotation, another *topos* of Medieval and Renaissance political literature is invoked: the dichotomy and necessary coexistence of arms and laws. Such a reference indicates that in the final pages of the oration, its author focuses more closely on the human and practical nature of law. The references to a cosmic justice gradually fade and lead to an acknowledgment that law sometimes needs to be affirmed by means of force. Nonetheless, the argumentation developed throughout the text undoubtedly stresses the preeminence of law over despotic use of power and invites the readers to conceive of social life in terms of a search for balance and mediation rather than violent conflict. By importing elements from other authors and works that were missing in Muret's original text, the author of the *Laus* partially shapes its oration according to his own goals and needs. The combination of the sources, together with the theoretical and rhetorical outline it generates, is therefore the product of his choices. The contents of this oratory piece appear to mirror some of the leading

---

24 See Biblioteka Jagiellońska MS 2279 AA VII 61, 152r. Such examples, together with others regarding ancient history and poetry, seem to be taken directly from Passerat 1606, 162–163.

25 Biblioteka Jagiellońska MS 2279 AA VII 61, 153r: "Merito Iustinianus omnium Maximus imperator, pace et bello Imperatoriam maiestatem, et armis decoratam, et legibus armatam initio Institutionum suarum esse debere protulit. Noluit Imperator rerum a se in bello gestarum praeclare et feliciter preconem agere; non id sibi laudi dicere, quod Alemanos vicerit, Gothos profligavit, Francos superavit, duros Martis sectatores Alanos domuerit, Vandalos ferocitate tumentes compescuerit, in Africa et alibi plurima clarissima victoriarum trophaea erexerit; verum principis esse boni laudatique Imperatoris exemplo suo ostendere voluit, adeoque autoritate sua velut praecipere nil Regibus, Principibus, Imperatoribus convenientius esse, quam legum notitiam, quibus et se ipsos et subditos intra officium honesti, iustique contineant facile." The praise of Justinian could be partially taken from the *Oratio pro armis habita a Detlevo Ranzovio nobili Holsato* in Junius 1597, 403–404.

values of the Polish-Lithuanian Commonwealth, thus implicitly portraying its idealization. The idea that sovereigns should obey the laws of their countries mirrors the Commonwealth's own political order, where the elected king and shared governance with a parliament of noblemen.[26] In that context, searching for mediation and agreement became a key factor in the development of political life. Even the reference to a controlled use of arms might be an echo of the influence that military families such as the Zamoyskis and Sredzinskis had over the political life of the country.

As mentioned above, the author, most likely the *studiosus* Andreas Sredzinski, chose to combine recent rather than classical sources. Throughout the oration, it becomes clearer that this choice led him to explore contemporary oratory literature, which he had to examine carefully in order to select the passages that would be most useful for his own speech.

7 A Virtuous Weave of Books, Notes, and Speeches

It can perhaps be argued that the academy professors themselves encouraged writing practices such as Sredzinski's as a means for the students to broaden their knowledge, refine their literary and oratory taste, and increase their critical awareness. The academy program clearly states that the students were required to take part in public events on Sundays, at least once a month. Their performances on such occasions were considered tests to ascertain their progress. Therefore, Sredzinski's defense and oration were part of consolidated institutional rites.

According to the original programs, disputations were not the only public events taking place at the academy: the students were also expected to perform reenactments of ancient political forms of association, such as the Roman senate or *comitia*. In such situations, classical orations could be recited, and the composition of new orations by the students was encouraged as well (*Fundatio Academiae Zamoscensis*, in Lepri 2019, 146). The relevance of theatrical performances within the academy was also highlighted by the Italian diplomat Bonifacio Vannozzi (1549–1621), secretary to the Papal legate, who visited Zamość in 1596. Vannozzi reported that during his stay, the students held theatrical reenactments of ancient Roman history. According to his testimony, although the topics were decided in ad-

---

26 See Grześkowiak–Krwawicz 2021. This political form had consequences on the legal system of the Commonwealth. On the reduction of royal jurisdiction under the reign of Stefan Batory, see Roşu 2009.

vance, it was up to the students to set up the events (Gmiterek 1999, 154, and Niemcewicz 1839, 187).

Based on such reports, the reenactments of ancient assemblies held at Zamość could be connected with the tradition of university drama, familiar from prestigious French and English universities (see, for instance, Cartwright 1999 and Lavéant 2012). Johann Sturm (1507–1589), whose educational theories strongly influenced the structure and activities of the academy (see Lepri 2019, 21–23), fostered educational theatre by observing that what "privately seems obscure" could be "seen and understood" through public representations (Spitz and Tinsley 1995, 248). Since at the Academy of Zamość, the students were given the possibility to revisit past notions and traditions by organizing reenactments of ancient political forms, it seems safe to say that such occasions were an opportunity for the expression of student agency and even creativity.

Furthermore, a few observations resulting from the analysis of the *Laus iurisprudentiae* suggest that the teachings and the literary resources offered by the academy were employed by the students when composing oratory pieces. First of all, it seems that the main works that compose this oratory "mosaic" were part of the library of the academy. Unfortunately, the scarcity of surviving books from the academy library makes it difficult to look for traces left by their readers in physical volumes. Some information is provided by the first known catalogue of the library, the *Regestrum omnium librorum, qui extant in Bibliotheca Academiae Zamoscensis*, which dates back to the second half of the 17th century: it was first created in 1675 and later augmented through several additions. Although the *Regestrum* does not offer a perfect record of the state of the collection in the 1610s, it can be argued that texts by relevant authors of the previous century had probably already been acquired by then. The section of the library catalogue devoted to politics and oratory includes references to Muret's and Passerat's *Orationes* (Polska Biblioteka Narodowa BOZ MS 1544, 79v). Since the quoted books probably belonged to the library, it could be imagined that students had access to the library books—directly or through the mediation of their teachers—and could draw materials from them in order to complete the tasks required for their education.

While the library provides some information on the cultural stimuli the students were exposed to at the academy, other clues on how the students at Zamość worked on their oratory pieces may come from surviving notes and commentaries. Once again, Sredzinski's volume may provide some information on this matter. As mentioned above, the rest of the volume contains various texts, all providing precepts on rhetoric: a *Compendium artis dicendi* and commentaries to Hermogenes' *De formis dicendi*, Cicero's *De oratore*, and *Oratio pro Sexto Roscio Amerino*. The instructions given in the notes, as part of the original classical text or of the teachers' commentaries, might have been taken into consideration during the composition of the *Laus*.

The *Laus iurisprudentiae* belongs to the epideictic genre, largely devoted to solemn praises or reprimands. Some of its general features appear to comply with Hermogenes' precepts for achieving grandeur and solemnity. In his *De formis dicendi*, as he listed the topics that required a solemn style, Hermogenes noted, among others, "justice or moderation ... or what is law."[27] Thus, Hermogenes had explicitly placed all praises of law in the oratory category of solemnity. The author's choice to quote mainly other epideictic speeches, such as Muret's praise of justice, could indicate that he intended to make sure the main features of the genre were displayed in his oration.

In providing some indications as to how an epideictic speech should be written, Hermogenes highlighted that the topic was to be approached "generally and universally," without references to specific situations. Consequently, one's arguments should not be presented in a form that looked too personal. The same applied to the choice of examples, which should be authoritative and prestigious, with possible references to poetry (Hermogenes 1987, 20–23). Again, Sredzinski appears to follow these instructions, not just by choosing Muret as his main source, but also by selecting apt examples, such as Passerat's references to ancient poets and kings and the praise of Justinian, an undisputed authority as an emperor as well as a legislator. These very general observations aim to suggest that the notes on rhetorical classical texts provided both a theoretical framework and practical writing tips that the students were expected to consider in creating speeches of their own.

Consequently, a hypothetical scenario can be outlined based on the presence of Sredzinski's main sources in the academy library and on the possible influence of the notes on the *Laus iurisprudentiae*. The theoretical framework provided by the teachers during the lessons—communicated in writing through the notes—and the exploration of the sources in the library could be viewed as complementary elements of the educational process. They both influenced a mildly creative production of texts that were publicly presented during the disputations and theatrical reenactments, which were conceived by the institution itself as an integral part of the students' learning practices. The idea of education resulting from such practices aims to both foster student agency and channel it into forms that were considered particularly instructive. The documents I have examined so far do not allow one to establish with certainty to what point the students were guided by their professors or tutors in the process of writing the speeches and selecting

---

27 Hermogenes 1987, 20. See Biblioteka Jagiellońska MS 2279 AA VII 61, 230r–v.

the sources. However, it seems safe to conclude that they were encouraged to sometimes work on their own, to achieve the knowledge and ability to master humanist culture, and thus relative intellectual independence within that specific tradition.[28]

8 A Surviving Oration against Civil Conflicts

The existence of other documents similar in structure to Sredzinski's *Laus iurisprudentiae* could support the hypothesis that composing orations by selecting and combining pre-existing sources was a widespread practice among the students of the Academy of Zamość. In the aforementioned volume BOZ 1525, which contains fragments of notes of various kinds, one can find a few documents that appear to be parts of oratory pieces.[29] As an example, I will briefly describe a short text condemning civil struggle.

Although BOZ 1525 is attributed to Tomasz Zamoyski by the *Inwentarz* of the manuscript from the Biblioteka Ordynacji Zamojskiej (Kocówna and Muszynska 1967, 82), the fragments are written by many different hands. It could be argued that the texts were all somehow related to the education of Zamoyski, possibly written by tutors or secretaries. If that was the case, since Tomasz Zamoyski completed his studies in 1614, the text I am considering (BOZ 1525, 137r–142v) could have been created shortly before the *Laus iurisprudentiae*. However, given the lack of information on the matter, the text is to be considered anonymous. The handwriting is rather neat, and a different hand appears to have made a few corrections.

The short text is a commentary on a passage from the *Iliad* (IX, 63–64), reported in Greek, declaring those who cause internal struggles in their communities to be outlaws who disown their family and homeland. The commentary, however, is not an erudite inquiry, but rather an occasion for a rhetorical invective. Not unlike the *Laus iurisprudentiae*, the text appears to be an epideictic speech the goal of which is to deprecate sedition and civil wars in general, while conversely praising human sociability and reasonability.

What makes this text peculiar is the fact that almost every sentence is taken from a work by Cicero. Its author, whoever it was, selected passages from different works and recombined them, thus rephrasing some leitmotifs of Ciceronian moral

---

28 Educational assistance by the teaching staff and cooperation among students were and would be increasingly promoted in many European universities. See, for instance, Miert 2009, 123–124, and Prögler 2013, 102–105.
29 See n. 7.

and political thought. The Homeric verses in Greek are followed by a quotation from the *Thirteenth Philippic*, where the main political figures in the civil war that occurred in Rome are all equally condemned.[30] Through a series of expressions from the Pseudo-Ciceronian *Rhetoric to Herennius*, the author represents the damage that civil wars cause to the very symbols of social life, such as the temples, the fortifications, and the tombs of the ancestors.[31] A comparison is drawn between the feral condition of those who create such circumstances, and the fully human condition of those who engage in social life under the banner of reason. The author takes up a passage from *De officiis* to state that reason and discursive ability distinguish human beings from beasts and act as social bonds capable of holding communities together.[32] The praise of these two eminently human features is further developed by adapting the famous praise of philosophy as a guide for human life presented in Cicero's *Tusculanae disputationes*. Such praise is now referred to reason, whereas eloquence and its ability to establish its power over human minds is celebrated through a reference to *De oratore*.[33]

Through this brief description, I aim to point out the existence of other texts which display composition strategies similar to those of the *Laus iurisprudentiae*. Whereas Sredzinski's text combined recent sources, in this case classical sources were employed. Texts like this one, the aim of which was probably an exercise in Ciceronian expressions and thought, might have been produced in preparation for a public reenactment.

---

30 Polska Biblioteka Narodowa BOZ MS 1525, 137v–138r: "Nam neque privatos focos, nec publicas leges, nec libertatis iura cara habere ... quem discordiae, quem caedes civium, quem bellum civile delectat, eumque ex numero hominum eiciendum puto, ex finibus hominum exterminandum. Itaque sive Sulla sive Marius sive uterque sive Octavius sive Cinna sive iterum Sulla sive alter Marius et Carbo, sive quis alius civile bellum optavit, eum detestabilem civem rei publicae natum iudico". See Cic. *Phil. XIII*, 1.
31 Polska Biblioteka Narodowa BOZ MS 1525, 138r–v: "Qui revulsis maiorum sepulchris, deiectis moenibus, inriut in Rempublicam? Qui spoliatis templis, optimatibus trucidatis, matribusfamilias, et ingenuis sub suam libidinem subiectis, urbibus acerbissimo incendio conflagratis, miserandum cinerem patriae suae quae illum genuit, aluit, fovit, omnibus bonis cumulavit, potest videre?" See *Rhet. Her.* 4.12.
32 Polska Biblioteka Narodowa BOZ MS 1525, 138v–139r: "Haud enim iniuria Aud. natura duobus magnis vinculis ratione scilicet et oratione humano generi datis, hominem conciliat homini, ad orationis, et ad vitae societatem, ingeneratque in primis praecipuum quendam amorem in eos qui procreati sunt: impellitque ut hominum coetus et celebrari inter se, et a se obiri velit." See Cic. *Off.* 1. 1.12.
33 Polska Biblioteka Narodowa BOZ MS 1525, 140r–v: "O vitae ratio dux, o virtutis indagatrix, expultrixque vitiorum. Quid non modo nos, sed omnino vita hominum sine te esse potuisset? Tu urbes peperisti .... Te vero o eloquentia quid praestabilius potest esse? Quae tenes hominum coetus, mentes allicis, voluntates impellis." See Cic. *Tusc.* 5.5 and *De or.* 1.30.

In composing the text on civil struggles, the author probably relied on collections of Ciceronian maxims. It is worth mentioning that, as pointed out by Danilo Facca and Valentina Lepri, around the time of the possible composition of this oration two different printed volumes had been released by the academy printing shop. A work called *Elementa seu loci ex Ciceronis libris desumpti*, explicitly dedicated to the students of eloquence and philosophy at the academy, was printed in 1609; in 1611, professor Szymon Piechowicz published his *Narrationes, Sententiae, Similia ex libris Ciceronis* (see Facca, Lepri 2016, 86; Lepri 2019, 107). The short timespan between the two publications suggests that during those years works of that kind had an audience within the academy. Therefore, they might have been conceived as tools for specific educational practices, and their use could have been recommended by the teachers as a means to master classical culture more easily.

Through the described practices, the students rehearsed Ciceronian maxims, experimented with them, and experienced their use directly, thereby internalizing rhetorical formulas as well as moral and political views. Thus, the anonymous condemnation of civil struggles could very well be an outcome of guided student agency, the expression of which was encouraged during public events at the academy.

9 Conclusion: Note-Taking, Imitation, and Interpretation

The analysis of the oratory pieces from the first decades of the activity of the Academy of Zamość—and especially the volume that belonged to Andreas Sredzinski—offers insights into the educational practices and the role of student agency at this institution. As we have seen, the practice of creating speeches based on classical models was part of academy life already according to the original program outlined by the founder, possibly inspired by other European examples of pedagogical theatre.

Simulated disputations and orations were also a well-established scholarly exercise, rooted in a pedagogical tradition that, stemming from the experience of early humanists such as Guarino Veronese (1374–1460), viewed imitation as a particularly effective way of learning (Grafton and Jardine 1986, 7 and 22). The creation of oratory pieces by students was also connected with the growing use of commonplaces and collections of maxims documented throughout the 16th and 17th centuries (Blair 2010b). Resulting from well-established traditions, the examined orations indicate that at the Academy of Zamość, the tools of traditional oratory education led to the practice of writing and speaking through the words of other authors. Furthermore, they clearly show that along with topics and expressions from the past, present forms of speaking and thinking were also reenacted, and thus inquired into by the students.

The contents of the orations constitute concrete examples of the political education imparted by the academy. In a simple form accessible to the students and mediated by classical culture, topical political issues were addressed, such as the nature of power, the relationship between law and force, and the search for strategies to achieve concord. As to the teaching and learning methods, I have suggested that the orations point to the existence of a "guided" student agency—since the students created writings of their own according to pre-established models and instructions, as part of their classes and duties and, possibly, under the guidance of their teachers. The originality of those texts results from what sources are selected and from the way in which they are combined: these aspects of their works are a product of the choices and views of the students.

This kind of student agency conforms to a conception of education aimed at achieving intellectual independence—thus echoing Johann Sturm's idea that education should ideally allow the student to become his own teacher, through a gradual process of empowerment (Spitz and Tinsley 1995, 241; see Tinsley 1989). However, it should also be noted that the outcomes of such student agency were somehow pre-oriented by the need of meeting specific standards and goals, and partially determined by the existing hierarchy between professors and students. Accordingly, the goal of the Zamość educational system appears to have been precisely the search for a fruitful balance between promoting intellectual independence and shaping the students' views, thus encouraging a kind of creativity that could operate within the political and cultural systems of the Commonwealth and disclose its innovative potential within existing frameworks.

Bibliography

Primary Sources

Manuscripts

Biblioteka Jagiellońska
MS 2279 AA VII 61

Polska Biblioteka Narodowa,
Biblioteka Ordynacji Zamoyskiej MS 141

Polska Biblioteka Narodowa,
Biblioteka Ordynacji Zamoyskiej MS 1515–516

Polska Biblioteka Narodowa,
Biblioteka Ordynacji Zamoyskiej MS 1525

Polska Biblioteka Narodowa
Biblioteka Ordynacji Zamoyskiej MS 1526

Polska Biblioteka Narodowa
Biblioteka Ordynacji Zamoyskiej MS 1544

Vasyl Stefanyk National Scientific Library of Ukraine
Baworowski Fund MS 384

Printed Sources

Bersman, Gregor (1576): *Orationes duae, una, de cura loquendi, altera, de fructu et utilitate philosohiae moralis*. Leipzig: Iohannes Rhamba excudebat.
Ciekliński, Piotr (1597): *Potroyny z Plauta*. Zamość: Marcin Lęski.
Drezner, Tomasz (1613): *Institutionum iuris Regni Poloniae libri IV*. Zamość: Marcin Lęski.
Junius, Melchior (1597): *Orationum quae argentinensi in Academia exercitii gratia scriptae et recitatae [...] pars sexta*. Strasbourg: Lazarus Zetzner.
Muret, Marc-Antoine (1789): *Opera omnia*. Vol. I. David Ruhnken (Ed.). Leiden: Luchtmans.
Okolski, Szymon (1641): *Orbis Poloni tomus II*. Kraków: Franciscus Caesarius.
Passerat, Jean (1606): *Orationes et praefationes*. Paris: David Douceur, USTC 6015116.
Piechowicz, Szymon (1611): *Narrationes. Sententiae. Similia. Ex libris M. Tullij Ciceronis*. Zamość: Typographia Academiae.
Reberterie, Jean de la (1581): *Disputationum Iuris libri quatuor*. Wittenberg.
Szymonowić, Szymon (1604): *Imagines diaetae Zamoscianae*. Zamość: Martinus Lenscius.

Secondary Sources

Blair, Ann M. (2008): "Student Manuscripts and the Textbook." In: Campi, Emidio, Angelis, Simone de, Goeing, Anja-Silvia, and Grafton, Anthony (Eds.): *Scholarly Knowledge: Textbooks in Early Modern Europe*. Geneva: Droz, 39–73.
Blair, Ann M. (2010a): "The Rise of Note-taking in Early Modern Europe." In: *Intellectual History Review* 20. No. 3, 303–316. DOI: 10.1080/17496977.2010.492611.
Blair, Ann M. (2010b): *Too Much to Know. Managing Scholarly Information before the Modern Age*. New Haven and London: Yale University Press.
Blair, Ann M. (2016): "Early Modern Attitudes toward the Delegation of Copying and Note-Taking." In: Cevolini, Alberto (Ed.): *Forgetting Machines. Knowledge Management Evolution in Early Modern Europe*. Leiden and Boston: Brill, 265–285. DOI: 10.1163/9789004325258_013.
Bukowska, Krystyna (1960): *Tomasz Drezner, polski romanista XVII wieku, i jego znaczenie dla nauki prawa w Polsce* [*Tomasz Drezner, a 17th century Polish romanist, and his relevance to Polish legal studies*]. Warsaw: Wydawnictwo Prawnicze.

Burlinson, Christopher (2010): "The Use and Re-Use of Early Seventeenth-Century Student Notebooks: Inside and Outside the University." In: Daybell, James and Hinds, Peter (Eds.): *Material Readings of Early Modern Culture. 1580-1700.* London: Macmillan, 229-245.

Cartwright, Kent (1999): *Theatre and Humanism. English Drama in the Sixteenth Century.* Cambridge: Cambridge University Press.

Chachaj, Marian (1996): "Wykształcenie Profesorów Akademii Zamojskiej [The training of the professors of the Academy of Zamość]." In: Gmiterek, Henryk (Ed.): *W kręgu akademickiego Zamościa [In the milieu of the Academy of Zamość].* Lublin: Wydawnictwo Uniwersytet Marii Curie —Skłodowskiej, 113-142.

Cieślak, Tadeusz (1957): "Polski procesualista z przełomu XVI-XVII wieku. Tomasz Drezner [A Polish expert in procedural law between the late 16th and the 17th century. Tomasz Drezner]." In: *Czasopismo Prawno—Historyczne* 9. No. 1, 75-82.

Conley, Thomas M. (1994): "Some Renaissance Polish Commentaries on Aristotle's *Rhetoric* and Hermogenes' *On Ideas.*" In: *Rhetorica. A Journal of the History of Rhetoric* 12. No. 3, 265-292. DOI: 10.1525/rh.1994.12.3.265.

Dąmbska, Izydora (1974): "Adam Burski i jego *Dialectica Ciceronis* [Adam Burski and his *Dialectica Ciceronis*]." In: Dąmbska, Izydora (Ed.): *Znaki i myśli: wybór pism z semiotyki, teorii nauki i historii filozofii [Signs and thoughts: a selection of articles on semiotics, scientific theory and history of philosophy].* Warsaw: Państwowe Wydawnictwa Naukowe, 211-221.

Dąmbska, Izydora (1978): "Filozofia w Akademii Zamojskiej [Philosophy at the Academy of Zamość]." In: Szczucki, Lech (Ed.): *Filozofia i myśl społeczna XVI wieku [Philosophy and social thought of the 16th century].* Warsaw: Państwowe Wydawnictwa Naukowe, 87-114.

Dyjakowska, Marzena (2000a): "Badania porównawcze nad *Corpus Iuris Civilis* i ustawodawstwami obcymi w pracach profesorów Akademii Zamojskiej [Comparative studies on the *Corpus Iuris Civilis* and foreign legal systems in the works of the professors of the Academy of Zamość]." In: Dębiński, Antoni (Ed.): *Starożytne kodyfikacje prawa [Ancient legal codes].* Lublin: Katolicki Uniwersytet Lubelski, 153-186.

Dyjakowska, Marzena (2000b): *Prawo rzymskie w Akademii Zamojskiej w XVIII wieku [Roman law at the Academy of Zamość in the 18th century].* Lublin: Wydawnictwo KUL.

Dyjakowska, Marzena (2001): "Wyznaniowy charakter Akademii Zamojskiej (1594-1784) [The religious character of the Akademia Zamojska (1594-1784)]." In: *Studia z Prawa Wyznaniowego* 3, 51-76.

Dyjakowska, Marzena (2003): "Comparative Research on *Corpus Iuris Civilis* in Dissertations of Professors of Academy of Zamość." In: *Review of Comparative Law* 8, 191-215.

Estreicher, Karol (1933): *Bibliografia Polska. Tom 29 (Sok.-St.).* Kraków: Polska Akademia Umiejętności.

Facca, Danilo (1999a): "Filosofia e retorica nel commento al Timeo di Szymon Birkowski." In: *Verbum: Analecta neolatina,* 1, 48-58.

Facca, Danilo (1999b): "Philosophical Pedagogy in Early Seventeenth-Century Poland: *Method* and *Accumulation* in the Philosophical Teaching of Adam Burski." In: *Acta Comeniana* 13, 83-97.

Facca Danilo (2000): *Humanizm i filozofia w nauczaniu Adama Burskiego [Humanism and philosophy in the teachings of Adam Burski].* Warsaw: Polska Akademia Nauk, Instytut Filozofii i Socjologii.

Facca, Danilo (2002): "Kultura późnego renesansu w nauczaniu filozofii w Akademii Zamojskiej [Late Renaissance culture in the teachings of philosophy at the Academy of Zamość]." In: Hanusiewicz, Mirosława, Dąbkowska, Justyna, and Karpiński, Adam (Eds.): *Świt i zmierzch baroku [Sunrise and Sunset of the Baroque].* Lublin: Towarzystwo Naukowe KUL, 11-24.

Facca, Danilo and Lepri, Valentina (2016): "In the Shadow of Cicero. An Early Modern Think-tank at the Academy of Zamość." In: Marciniak, Katarzyna and Olechowska, Elżbieta (Eds.): De amicitia.

Transdisciplinary Studies in Friendship. Warsaw: Zakład Graficzny Uniwersytetu Warszawskiego, 55–63.

Gmiterek, Henryk (1976): "Bursa Starnigela przy Akademii Zamojskiej [Starnigel's student residence at the Academy of Zamość]." In: *Rocznik Lubelski* 19, 21–38.

Gmiterek, Henryk (1994): *Album studentów Akademii Zamojskiej. 1595–1781*. Henryk Gmiterek (Ed.). Warsaw: Polska Akademia Nauk, Instytut Historii Nauki.

Gmiterek, Henryk (1999, 2000): "Uroczystości akademickie w Zamościu w XVI–XVIII wieku [Academic celebrations in Zamość between the 16th and 18th centuries]." In: *Annales Universitatis Marie Curie-Skłodowska* 54/55, 149–158.

Gmiterek, Henryk (2005): "Początki Akademii Zamojskiej [The beginnings of the Academy of Zamość]." In: Kondraciuk, Piotr, Kuśnierz, Jerzy, and Urbański, Andrzej (Eds.): *Jan Zamoyski wódz-mecenas-polityk 1542–1605* [*Jan Zamoyski Chief-patron-politician 1542–1605*]. Zamość: Muzeum Zamojskie, 73–82.

Grafton, Anthony and Jardine, Lisa (1986): *From Humanism to the Humanities. Education and the Liberal Arts in Fifteenth and Sixteenth-Century Europe*. Cambridge: Harvard University Press.

Grześkowiak-Krwawicz, Anna (2021): *The Political Discourse of the Polish-Lithuanian Commonwealth. Concepts and Ideas*. Daniel J. Sax (Trans.). New York and London: Routledge.

Hermogenes (1987): *On Types of Style*. Cecil W. Wooten (Trans.). Chapel Hill and London: University of North Carolina Press.

Horodyski, Bogdan (1951): "Zarys dziejów Biblioteki Ordynacji Zamojskiej [Notes on the history of the library of the Zamoyski feud]." In: Budzyk, Kazimierz and Kawecka-Gryczowa, Alodia (Eds.): *Studia nad książką. Poświęcone pamięci Kazimierza Piekarskiego* [*Studies on the book. In memory of Kazimir Piekarski*]. Wrocław: Wydawnictwo Zakładu Narodowego im. Ossolińskich, 243–251.

Kochanowski, Jan Karol (1900): *Dzieje Akademii Zamojskiej (1594–1784)* [*History of the Academy of Zamość (1594–1784)*]. Kraków: Druk W.I. Anczyca i Spółki.

Kocówna, Barbara and Muszyńska, Krystyna (1967): *Inwentarz rękopisów Biblioteki Ordynacji Zamojskiej. Sygn. 1–2051* [*Inventory of the manuscripts of the Library of the feud of Zamoyski, 1–2051*]. Warsaw: Biblioteka Narodowa.

Kumor, Bolesław (1996): "Wydział Teologiczny Akademii Zamojskiej 1648–1784 [The faculty of theology of the Academy of Zamość. 1648–1784]." In: Szczygieł, Ryszard and Urbański, Andrzej (Eds.): *Akademia Zamojska w dziejach i życiu miasta* [*The Academy of Zamość in the history and life of the city*]. Zamość: Muzeum Okręgowe w Zamościu, 65–173.

Kuryłowicz, Marek (1996): "Prawo rzymskie w studiach i koncepcjach akademickich Jana Zamoyskiego [Roman law in the studies and academic concepts of Jan Zamoyski]." In: Gmiterek, Henryk (Ed.): *W kręgu akademickiego Zamościa* [*In the milieu of the Academy of Zamość*]. Lublin: Wydawnictwo Uniwersytetu Marii Curie-Skłodowskiej, 95–112.

Kuryłowicz, Marek (1999): "Nauczanie prawa w Akademii Zamojskiej w świetle wybranych *tekstów źródłowych* [The teaching of law at the Academy of Zamość in light of selected textual sources]." In: Bardach, Juliusz and Kuryłowicz, Marek (Eds.): *Pomniki prawa doby Renesansu w Europie Środkowo Wschodniej* [*Monuments of Law in Renaissance Central-eastern Europe*]. Warsaw: OBTA, 191–248.

Kuryłowicz, Marek and Witkowski, Wojciech (1980): "Nauczanie prawa w Akademii Zamojskiej. 1594–1784 [The teaching of law at the Akademia Zamojska. 1594–1784]." In: *Palestra* 7, 38–56.

Lavéant, Katell (2012): "Le Théâtre dans la Formation Oratoire des Écoliers au XVIe Siècle." In: *Revue de Synthèse* 133, 235–250. DOI: 10.1007/s11873-012-0185-4.

Lepri, Valentina (2019): *Knowledge Transfer and the Early Modern University. Statecraft and Philosophy at the Akademia Zamojska (1595–1627)*. Leiden and Boston: Brill.

Lepri, Valentina (2021): "Minor Virtues? The *Nicomachean Ethics* and the Teaching of Rhetoric at the Akademia Zamojska." In: *History of Universities* 34. No. 2, 125–136. DOI: 10.1093/oso/9780192857545.003.0008.

Makowski, Tomasz (2005a): *Biblioteka Ordynacji Zamojskiej. Od Jana do Jana* [*The library of the Zamoyski feud. From Jan to Jan*]. Tomasz Makowski (Ed.). Warsaw: Biblioteka Narodowa.

Makowski, Tomasz (2005b): "Zarys dziejów biblioteki Jana Zamoyskiego [History of Jan Zamoyski's library. An outline]." In: *Zamojsko-Wołyńskie Zeszyty Muzealne* 3, 91–100.

Makowski, Tomasz (2012a): "A Brief History of Jan Zamoyski's Library." In: Östlund, Kristen (Ed.): *I lag med böcker. Festskrift till Ulf Göranson*. Uppsala: Uppsala Universitet, 243–251.

Makowski, Tomasz (2012b): "Siedziba i organizacja biblioteki Jana Zamoyskiego, kanclerza i hetmana wielkiego koronnego [The premises and organisation of the library of Jan Zamoyski, royal chancellor and grand hetman]." In: *Rocznik Biblioteki Narodowej* 43, 352–361.

Maniscalco, Lorenzo (2020): *Equity and Early Modern Legal Scholarship*. Leiden and Boston: Brill.

Miert, Diek van (2009): *Humanism in an Age of Science. The Amsterdam Athenaeum in the Golden Age. 1632–1704*. Leiden and Boston: Brill.

Myk, Sławomir (1994a): *Drukarnia Akademii Zamojskiej jej dzieje i wydawnictwa* [*The print shop of the Academy of Zamość. Its history and publications*]. Lublin: Wydawnictwo Lubelskie Nowe.

Myk, Sławomir (1994b): "Zamojska oficyna akademicka w świetle nowych źródeł [The print shop of the Academy of Zamość in light of new sources]." In: Szyszka, Bogdan (Ed.): *Akademia Zamojska i jej tradycje* [*The Academy of Zamość and its tradition*]. Zamość: Muzeum Okręgowe, 84–102.

Myk, Sławomir (1996): "Edytorzy i nakładcy druków zamoyskich. XVI–XVIII wiek [The editors and founders of the Zamość publications. The 16th and 17th centuries]." In: Gmiterek, Henryk (Ed.): *W kręgu akademickiego Zamościa* [*In the milieu of the Academy of Zamość*]. Lublin: Wydawnictwo Uniwersytetu Marii Curie-Skłodowskiej, 303–314.

Niemcewicz, Julian Ursyn (1839): *Zbiór pamiętników historycznych o dawnej Polszcze. Tom II* [*A collection of historical memoirs about old Poland. Volume 2*]. Leipzig: Breitkopf & Haertel.

Prögler, Daniela (2013): *English Students at Leiden University. 1575–1650. Advancing your abilities in learning and bettering your understanding of the world and state affairs*. Burlington: Ashgate. DOI: 10.4324/9781315579801.

Roşu, Felicia (2009): "Monarch, Citizens, and the Law Under Stefan Batory. The Legal Reform of 1578." In: Friedrich, Karin and Pendzich, Barbara M. (Eds.): *Citizenship and Identity in a Multinational Commonwealth. Poland-Lithuania in Context, 1550–1772*. Leiden and Boston: Brill, 17–47. DOI: 10.1163/ej.9789004169838.i-311.9.

Ryczek, Wojciech (2017): "Renesansowe teorie figuratywności (III): Adam Burski [Renaissance theories of figurativeness (III): Adam Burski]." In: *Pamiętnik Literacki* 108, 121–136.

Spitz, Lewis William and Tinsley, Barbara Sher (1995): *Johann Sturm on Education. The Reformation and Humanist Learning*. Saint Louis: Concordia Publishing House.

Szymański, Mikołaj (1988): Dialectica Ciceronis *Adama Burskiego: Problemy warsztatu filologicznego renesansowego* [*The* Dialectica Ciceronis *by Adam Burski: On the study of Stoic logical matters through the philological tools of a Renaissance scholar*]. Warsaw: Polska Akademia Nauk, Instytut Filozofii i Socjologii.

Tinsley, Barbara Sher (1989): "Johann Sturm's Method for Humanistic Pedagogy." In: *Sixteenth Century Journal* 20. No. 1, 23–41. DOI: 10.2307/2540521.

Tygielski, Wojciech (1990): *Politics of Patronage in Renaissance Poland. Chancellor Jan Zamoyski, his supporters and the political map of Poland. 1572–1605.* Warsaw: Wydawnictwa Uniwersytetu Warszawskiego.

Kristi Viiding

"Put it in your mind or in the notes": Instructions for Taking Notes in Early Modern Law Studies

Abstract: This chapter presents two Latin guidelines for taking notes for future professional legal activity, from 1592 in Riga and c. 1606 in Zamość, written by the Livonian-Polish humanist and lawyer from Riga, David Hilchen (1561–1610), who had studied law and rhetoric in German universities (Ingolstadt, Tübingen, Heidelberg) but did not promote. Yet he was very successful in practice: he composed the draft of the Livonian Land Law in 1599 and many other regulations for the city of Riga between 1586 to 1599. In 1595, he was one of the representatives of the King of Poland in an international dispute with Brunswick over the inheritance of Princess Sophia. His special interest was the law of succession. From 1603, he lived in exile in Zamość. My main aim is to demonstrate the importance of the prescriptive genre of ratio studiorum for the research of notebook practice.

1 Introduction: Special Reasons for Taking Notes in Legal Education

The turn of the 16th and 17th centuries marked various transitions in the legal systems of Northeastern Europe. There was a permanent need for new legislation, especially in the border area, called Old Livonia in the Middle Ages and separated into Estonia, Livonia, and Courland since 1561, to define the limits and privileges of the (1) constantly changing supreme powers, like the Polish-Lithuanian Commonwealth, Denmark, Sweden, and the local Baltic German, Estonian, and Latvian population, (2) between the cities and noble landowners as well as (3) between the Lutheran and Catholic churches. In the same decades, statutory law tried to gain supremacy over medieval customary law. In both of these parts of the legal culture, but also at every stage of the legal proceedings and court practice, written form has become increasingly common: from the summons, prosecution, defense, taking and giving of evidence to the judgment and appeal, and sometimes even to the execution of a sentence, for example, in the form of a public apology (Schmidt 1895; Pihlajamäki 2017; and Oestmann 2022 et al.).

Kristi Viiding: ORCID: 0000-0003-2488-7163. Under and Tuglas Literature Centre of the Estonian Academy of Sciences.

Implementing the new legal requirements of society, professional learned lawyers, well versed in written legal procedures and ready to draft laws themselves, were of crucial importance. Yet there did not exist a local university with a law faculty in Northeastern Europe until 1632,[1] nor was law taught at the local cathedral schools, gymnasia, not to mention the city schools in Tallinn (Reval) and Riga.[2] However, the biggest cities gave stipends to the sons of their citizens for studies abroad, and lawyers were trained elsewhere in European universities (Tering 1996 as well as 2008, 572–586). The choice of foreign university often depended on the religious affiliation of the hometown or community. In the period from 1561 to 1632, the destinations of law students were Rostock, Frankfurt/Oder, Wittenberg, Helmstedt, Heidelberg, Tübingen, Leipzig, and Ingolstadt in Germany, Padua and Bologna in Italy, Königsberg in Prussia, and in exceptional cases also Vienna, Würzburg, and Rome. At least ten Estonian, Livonian, and Curonian students attained the title of *dr.iuris* or *dr.utr.iuris*[3] in these early modern decades before establishment of the first local law faculty in Tartu (Tering 2018).

To encourage fellow Livonians as well as young Lithuanians and Poles to study law in these changing circumstances, not only financial support but also methodological advice from more experienced countrymen, who had finished their law studies abroad and who were active as lawyers after that, was crucial.[4] This kind of guidance could not take place at universities, as only *doctores (utriusque) iuris* had the privilege to teach future lawyers publicly—that is, *venia legendi*

---

[1] For the predecessors of legal education and failed attempts to provide legal education in the region in the Middle Ages, see the introduction in Blaese 1962, 14–18. There was, however, no lack of professionals with a legal education in Northeastern Europe in the Middle Ages among the landlords, clerics, or notaries, but their education from Western European universities was limited to canon law (Blaese 1962, 28–32). Despite many efforts to open a faculty of law at the Jesuit Academy of Vilnius (established 1579), it did not happen until 1641 (see, e. g., Jovaiša 2018, 370). About the first law faculty at the University of Tartu, then called Academia Dorpatensis (1632–1656, Academia Gustaviana; 1690–1710, Academia Gustavo-Carolina), there exists no updated overview after Kiris and Leesment 1982, 196–199.

[2] For the study programs in Tallinn City School, see Vestring 1603 in Schiemann 1887, 10–25; on Tallinn Gymnasium, see Vulpius 1635; and on Riga Cathedral School, see Eck, Hilchen, and Rivius 1597.

[3] Gotthard Welling (1546–1586) 1574, Johann Tecno(n) (*fl.* 1565–1613) 1582, Christoph Sturtz (fl. 1575–1602) 1584, Heinrich Berg (fl. 1574–1626) 1584, Caspar Dreiling (1572–1632) 1603, Paul Rennenkampf (*fl.* 1598–1604) 1604, Ludwig Hintelmann (1578–1643) 1607, Heinrich zum Dahlen (*fl.* 1601–1608) 1608, Johann Friedrichs (1583–?) 1609, Georg von Lohn (d. 1634) 1606.

[4] According to Blaese 1962, 65, the majority of Estonian, Livonian, and Curonian law students who returned from their studies abroad became practitioners, not law professors. Of the learned jurists of Livonian origin, only Christoph Sturtz and Johann Flügel became professors: Sturtz in history in Rostock in 1586 (Tering 2018, 681) and Flügel in law in Riga in 1640 (Tering 2018, 304).

(Köbler 1978, 484; Schott 1978, 489). Yet private advice in written and even in printed form was obviously allowed for other jurists. Obviously, such guidance better reflected the practical needs and challenges of law, as they were given by trusted and often even familiar persons.

The purpose of the following chapter is to observe, on the basis of two Latin study guides from Livonia and Poland from 1592 and c. 1606 respectively, whether and how the overall transition to written form in legal culture is reflected in legal education at the same time. The focus is primarily on the relationship between oral and written learning methods and the forms of written learning: lecture notes, different types of notebooks, and their suitability for different learning content. The more general question is thus if and how the change from the old customary law to the learned reception-related process (Luts-Sootak 2022, 224) also renewed the learning methods of law in the region. Both case studies concern the teaching of Roman law:[5] the first reflects recommendations for law studies at a German university, the second at home under the guidance of a private teacher. The link connecting the two case studies is their author, the Livonian-Polish humanist and lawyer from Riga, David Hilchen (Heliconius; 1561–1610).

After a brief overview of the life and activities of the author of these works, I will analyze the main positions of both instructions, contextualizing them primarily on the basis of historical and personal background, as the intentions of the

---

5 Since the late Middle Ages, in the Western Europe the academic study of law entailed alongside canon law the mastery of Roman legal texts, terms, and ideas. The methodological focus was on the analytical exegesis of the individual books and titles of the Corpus Juris Civilis and the glosses and commentaries on them (so-called *mos italicus*). Gradually the teaching of the Roman law gained purchase beyond the academic centers in North-Central Italy and South-Western France and applied humanist practices with their pedagogical reform program: return to the pure Roman sources without glosses and commentaries as well as the most comprehensive general education (Latin and Greek) of the jurists (*mos gallicus*). In the German-speaking regions, Roman law was adopted from the mid-15th century, with the way in which the *Corpus Juris Civilis* was applied being referred to as *usus modernus pandectarum*. The common teaching format of the Roman law in the 16th century were the formal lectures, dictated by professors from their written notes and amplified with illustrative examples, and followed by the students annotating them in their notebooks word for word (see, e.g., Hagemann 1992, *passim*). In addition to the lectures on the legal principles built on dialectic and logic, which provided future lawyers with tools for administration and dispute resolution, oral disputations also played an important role in the academic law studies and were obligatory for obtaining an academic degree in Roman law as part of *doctor utriusque juris*. Although Philipp Melanchthon wrote a plea for Roman law in his speech *Oratio de legibus* (1525) and ensured its reception in Protestant countries as well, the Catholic dissertations focused more often on questions of Roman law than their Protestant counterparts (Scholz 2022, 308). For the tradition of study guides structuring the studies of the Roman law of beginners in the early modern period see, e.g., Troje 1977, 718–730.

author can be determined thanks to his voluminous written heritage (correspondence, legal texts, speeches, poems) and intensive research on it in recent decades. Since the *Ratio studiorum* printed in Riga in 1592 has survived in only one copy, which has not yet been digitized,[6] and the study guide *Dikaiomatheia* from 1606 has survived in one manuscript copy in Bibliotheca Universitatis Jagellonicae (MS 2279 AA VII 61),[7] the article contains transcriptions of the most important parts of these study guides.

2 David Hilchen and His Activities as an Advisor

David Hilchen, born in Riga in 1561 and first educated in the local cathedral school, studied law and rhetoric from 1580 to 1585 at three German universities (Ingolstadt, Tübingen, Heidelberg) but did not promote to *doctor iuris*.[8] During his studies, his special interest was the law of succession: he held four private and two public disputations about it (Hilchen 1584 and Hilchen 1585). After his return to Livonia, he was the city secretary (1585–1589) and legal councilor (*syndicus*) (1589–1600) in Riga, from 1595 the secretary of the Polish king, and from 1596 the notary of Wenden district. In 1591, he was ennobled by Jan Zamoyski. In 1600–1603, he took part in the Polish-Swedish war in Livonia on the Polish side; in 1603–1610, he lived in exile in Zamość.[9] In 1600, he was accused by the City of Riga of treason. He was tried in Riga and appealed to the King of Poland; by 1609, he was acquitted by the Polish King Sigismund III.[10]

---

[6] The information in the Universal Short Title Catalogue presenting it as a lost book is not correct —a copy exists in Riga, in the Academic Library of the University of Latvia with the signature H 4, R2053 (22). The study guide is not mentioned in the central bibliography of academic publications in the German language area (Erman and Horn 1904) either.

[7] The photocopy is in the Marburg Herder Institute for Historical Research on East Central Europe, MS DSHI 100 Ramm-Helmsing 184.

[8] For an example of him being referred to as a *dr.iur.* in Polish historiography, see, e.g., Starowolski 1625, 75; in Baltic German historiography, see Blaese 1936, 41.

[9] The earlier tradition of his biography is written from either a Baltic German (Bergmann 1803 and 1825) or a Polish perspective (Leliwa 1880) and relies on the respective sources, while ignoring the sources of the other side. In the 1930s, Herta von Ramm-Helmsing tried to write a synthesis relying on both sources, but before World War II, she managed to publish only the first part of Hilchen's biography, dealing with the Livonian years (Ramm-Helmsing 1936). For the updated biography, see Viiding 2021, 11–36, and Viiding, Siimets-Gross, Hoffmann, and Klöker 2022, 297–302.

[10] For his proceedings, see Siimets-Gross and Viiding 2020; Luts-Sootak 2022; and Siimets-Gross and Hoffmann 2022.

As a typical early modern Livonian lawyer, he was successful in practice in legislation and judicial practice. He composed a Livonian land law draft in 1599 (Hoffmann 2007) and many other regulations for the city of Riga between 1586 and 1599 (Ramm-Helmsing 1936, 28–43, and Mahling 2011). In 1595, he was one of the representatives of the King of Poland in an international dispute with Brunswick over the inheritance of Princess Sophia Jagiellonica (Zofia Jagiellonka) (Viiding 2022, 41–43). He can undoubtedly be considered a leading learned legal authority among his contemporary lawyers of Livonian origin.

As recent analysis of Hilchen's correspondence has shown, counseling was one of the central activities of both his professional and personal communication. However, Hilchen did not belong to the spectacular inventors or innovative scientists in any area of his advisory work—such as jurisprudence, administration, and education—but to those who adapted new knowledge for everyday use in the city of Riga and later at Zamoyski's circle (Viiding 2022, especially 27–28).

Hilchen's experience as an advisor in the methodology of law studies had two general motivations. The first is based on his historical experience in Livonia. In the decades before Hilchen's life, almost all previous handwritten and printed legal literature, mainly on canon law, less on Roman law, which was kept in the medieval libraries of educated landowners and monasteries, was dispersed or destroyed. For example, during the Reformation in the 1520s, the monastery libraries in Riga, Tallinn, and Padis ceased to exist, as did the library of the archbishop in Kokenhusen during the Quarrels of the Coadjutors from 1556–1557, and the libraries of the archbishop of Livonia in Ronneburg, the Riga Cathedral, and the Master of the Livonian Order in Wenden as well as the monastery libraries in Tartu during the Livonian-Russian war war from 1558–1583 (Blaese 1962, 35). Even as the local printing houses in Riga and Vilnius were established in the second half of the 16th century, little legal literature was printed in them (Buchholtz 1890 and Narbutienė and Narbutas 2002). So, Hilchen grew up knowing that a proper private library and personal systematic notebook, like an encyclopedic reference work, could be a *conditio sine qua non* to the success of one's professional career in Livonia.

The second is based on his educational experience. Namely, Hilchen continued his studies after the Riga Cathedral School in the traditional form of *peregrinatio academica*, but did not travel alone or with a group of protestant Livonians but in the entourage of the Ruthenian Prince Alexander Olelkowicz Słucki (c. 1560–1591). The entourage consisted of students mainly from eastern parts of the Polish-Lithuanian Commonwealth, whose previous education had been determined not only by their different denominations (representatives of Russian Orthodoxy, Calvinists, and Catholics) but also by different educational backgrounds (Pietrzyk 1997, 135–

136 and Skepjan 2013, 93 and 135–143).[11] Hilchen belonged to this entourage during the first years of the *peregrinatio academica* from 1580 to 1582—that is, from Wrocław, Prague, Ingolstadt, Strasbourg, and Stuttgart to Basel. From Basel, the group went to Rome, while Hilchen went to Tübingen and matriculated there in September of 1582.

At the latest during his study trip, Hilchen should have realized the legal diversity of the early modern Polish-Lithuanian Commonwealth and the fact that Roman law was classified there as a subsidiary law after all local laws (e.g., in Gdańsk after the law of Kulm, Magdeburg, and Saxon law, the law of Gdańsk, the royal constitutions, etc.).[12] Thus, the situation in 16th-century Poland was rather similar to that of medieval Livonia, where Roman law was kept away from everyday legal life and limited to individual chancelleries and notary offices, but different from 16th-century Livonia, where, especially after coming under the rule of Polish-Lithuanian Commonwealth, Sweden or Denmark, Roman law was happily adopted and opposed to the new rulers in order to avoid foreign law being introduced as a subsidiary law (Blaese 1962, 64–66). Due to the constant threat of Russian conquest of Livonia, Hilchen obviously realized the need for the Livonians to cooperate closely with the Polish-Lithuanian Commonwealth, which from the 1580s at the latest also meant closer integration of the two legal traditions—for example, at the level of the judicial system and court officials. It must have been clear to Hilchen that a more in-depth knowledge of Roman law in the Polish-Lithuanian Commonwealth would be useful for the Livonians and would help both legal systems work together more easily.

3 David Hilchen's Guidelines for the Livonian Student

Hilchen wrote and published his first study instructions in the form of a 17-page letter in Riga in 1592 for Theodor (Dietrich) Rigemann the Younger (1571–1605)[13] —that is, to the son of his colleague, the councilor Dietrich Rigemann the Elder

---

11 The other *Aulici Alexandri ducis Slucensis et Copeliensis* were Petrus Zborowski, Georgius Sigowski, Wsiemborius Timienski, Stanislaus Kochanoreski, Foelix Raczinski, Abraham Skorsieski, Ioannes Poklaterzki, Ioannes Wituski, Ioannes Kieltika, Alexander Trisna, Ioannes Koletai, Stanislaus Pierzchalski, and Petrus Timienski (von Pölnitz 1937, 1079).
12 For a discussion of the role of Roman law in Poland, see Godek 2013.
13 The dedication is dated January 1, 1592. For the study guides presented as a letter or as a series of letters, see Troje 1977, 718, for European countries and Martins and Widener 2018, 22, for the United States.

(1529–1597). His addressee was already an adult of 20 or 21 years, who obviously had no previous academic education. A year later, in 1593, Rigemann nevertheless began his studies at the University of Leipzig, and upon his return he became a councilor of Riga in 1597 (Tering 2018, 583; Böthführ 1877, 61). According to Hilchen, however, the recipient's age is just right for learning about certain legal issues, such as *ius tutelare* (Hilchen 1592, Bv).

Although Hilchen admits that much has been written about learning methods in the past, his writing is based solely on his personal learning experience, at least according to his claim (Hilchen 1592, A2v–A3r). As authorities, he only mentions the logic textbook *Institutiones dialecticae libri octo* by the Portuguese cardinal and scholar Pedro da Fonseca SJ (1528–1599). Fonseca and his *Institutiones* clearly point to Hilchen's source, to his short study experience at the Jesuit Academy in Vilnius in 1579—Fonseca was the core author of the philosophy course there (Piechnik 1984, 120). At the same time, the reference to that source shows that Hilchen himself used such a learning model as an adult learner—that is, certainly after the age of 18, as Hilchen studied in Vilnius shortly before his *peregrinatio academica* in Germany.

As mentioned in the title of the program *Ad Theodorum Rigemannum, elegantis ingenii iuvenem Epistola. Qua ratio studendi Philosophiae et cuicumque alteri facultati demonstratur*, his program is universally applicable and effectively prepares the future specialist, no matter what area of life. Thus, for Hilchen, the method of studying law does not differ from the study methodology of other fields (Hilchen 1592, Av).

Hilchen's methodological recommendations are divided into four groups, the balance and interaction of which is of central importance in learning: recommendations prior to the lecture, during the lecture, after the lecture, during the disputation.[14]

During the first three stages, thinking and writing activities in the form of taking notes are interwoven, while in the last stage only memorizing and speaking activities occur. While reading the literature or the previous lecture notes before the next lecture, the purpose of taking notes is to write down the parts that the student thinks he understands. Accordingly, during the lecture he has to listen attentively as to whether his prior notes correspond to the explanations of the professor.[15]

---

14 "Ratio autem haec studiorum est distributa in tempus ante lectionem, in tempus lectionis: post lectionem et tempora disputationum: Ex his bene transactis et collocatis, pendet totus profectus hominis studiosi" (Hilchen 1592, A3r).
15 "Media hora itaque ante lectionem aut circiter, praelegas ea, quae Praeceptorem lecturum putas: in iis, si quae sunt, quae tibi intelligere videris, des operam, vt in lectione attendas: num

During the lecture, the student must fully focus on the teacher with his eyes and attention and must never look at the text of the author being commented on. After all, a teacher's single gesture sometimes helps much more to understand some difficult passages.[16] Further, taking written notes must be so automatic that it does not distract from what is being learned.[17]

Immediately after the lecture, one's first duty is to summarize the content of the lecture with one keyword and capture it firmly in the mind.[18] A thorough repetition follows. First, the student must go through the entire structure of the previous lecture and the most important teachings in his mind.[19] Then, he must find additional explanations and proofs of what was presented in the lecture in the works of the author in question or other books.[20] Only then do some elements of writing follow: you have to come up with your own examples for the rules, laws, definitions, and distinctions presented in the lecture and write them down.[21] In so doing, both supporting and contradictory examples should be found, and it is the contradictory ones in particular that should be written down to be presented to the professor in the next lecture.[22] Repetition can be con-

---

eodem modo explicet et intelligat Praeceptor, nec ne: si quae vero non intelligis: ea vel animo vel scripto annotes: ac postea animaduertas quomodo Praeceptor explicet, atque ita comparatus ad lectionem accedes" (Hilchen 1592, A3r).

16 "In ipsa vero lectione (quae quoad fieri potest, nunquam negligenda est) diligentissime semper attendas Praeceptorem explicantem, nec interim vnquam occuperis circa textum Authoris, aut circa scripta dum explicat Praeceptor. Iuuat etiam ad euagationes mentis cohibendas, fixis oculis intueri Praeceptorem explicantem: excitatur enim magis animus, et saepe ex vno gestu Praeceptoris facile intelligitur, quod difficulter aliquando aut tarde fuisset intellectum" (Hilchen 1592, A3v).

17 "Inter scribendum prodest ita se assuefacere, vt non totus animus semper sit in solis characteribus formandis, sed vt simul dum scribis, possis etiam nonnihil attendere rebus ipsis" (Hilchen 1592, A3v).

18 "Tandem vno quasi indice vel verbo saltem coneris, breuem quandam summam eorum, quae sunt dicta in lectione, animo consignatam tecum domum reportare, quantum quidem fieri potest" (Hilchen 1592, A3v).

19 "In qua quidem repetitione primum breuiter ac (A3v) ruditer reuoluas animo summam totius lectionis quam debes repetere" (Hilchen 1592, A3v–A4r).

20 "Deinde vel ex Authore vel ex scriptis quaeras exactiorem eius intelligentiam, probationem, explicationem, etc" (Hilchen 1592, A4r).

21 Hilchen took examples only from two areas: from theology (one paragraph about faith) and law.

22 "Si lectio indigeat exemplis, praeter ea quae sunt in libro, ipse alia excogites aut etiam scribas, quibus regulas, leges, definitiones item et diuisiones, applices. Cogites etiam: an illa quae ab Authore vel a Praeceptore in Philosophicis praesertim spaciis dicuntur, ita se habeant, vt ipsi dicunt: et ea quasi examines ac coneris inuenire aliqua in contrarium. Quae si inueneris, coneris rursus soluere, vel ex proprio ingenio, vel ex Authoris et Praeceptoris dictis. Et si quidem soluere poteris, bene habet: sin minus, notes in charta, et prima occasione Praeceptori vel alteri soluenda propo-

sidered a success if the student is ready to present the learned material as an oral lecture in front of the professor and fellow students, to explain it more simply to younger students, or hold a disputation about that topic in accordance with commonplaces.[23]

According to Hilchen's instructions, the student first gathers an everyday, portable, chronological notebook of miscellaneous nature with very different types of notes: with excerpts from books, lecture notes, self-invented examples, and with the student's conclusions about what he has learned. In addition, another systematic notebook based on commonplaces had to be set up, which also had to be filled in every day, but even more diligently, so that it could be used for a long time.[24] Hilchen believed, however, that sufficient guidance was available for commonplace books, and he did not consider it necessary to make any further recommendations in this regard.[25]

Considering the scarce academic background of the addressee, Hilchen only touched on the legal education methodology at the level of examples. He has chosen examples from inheritance law, statutory and testamentary succession, and *ius tutelare* (Hilchen 1592, Br–B3r). Apparently, this selection of examples reflected both the author's own education and interests as a newly ennobled person as well as an indication of which areas of law a future lawyer in Livonia had to deal with the most.[26] Hilchen warns of two things when it comes to legal educa-

---

nas: quod idem faciendum est de aliis quibuscunque dubitationibus occurrentibus" (Hilchen 1592, A4r).
23 "Vnum, vt ita semper apud te repetas, quasi eandem lectionem vel in Auditorio repetiturus esses coram Praeceptore et condiscipulis: vel quasi eandem deberes alteri rudiori te, explicare. Actum demum te perfecte repetiuisse et rem integre inuestigasse, existimes, cum ordinem locorum praecipuorum artis disserendi sequutus fueris" (Hilchen 1592, A4v).
24 "Sed in hac adnotatione, de qua toties, oportet te habere duo genera voluminum. Vnum quod contineat res quotidianas aduersarias, ita vt in eadem pagina sint accepta et expensa, data et soluta, confuso quidem ordine, sed aliqua tamen distinctione. Debet enim volumen hoc memoriae quotidianae causa comparari et institui, ita vt ad quaeuis loca deferri possit. Alterum volumen quod erit Bibliothecae et custodiae, debet esse perfectius et in normam Communium locorum redactum, vt accepta semper parata atque in promptu sint. Instituendi itaque sunt hi loci et quotidie implendi" (Hilchen 1592, B3v).
25 "Et iam fortasse expectas vt, quo pacto isti sint comparandi subiiciam: Ad eam etenim rem conficiendam primum delectu diligenti, tum cautione non vna opus est. Verum hic labor a me in praesentia non est flagitandus, non solum quia tam multa de his scripta sunt, vt vix ea in summam omnium ingeniis congruentem, redigi possint, sed eo vel maxime quia sua cuiusque collectio rerum, omnium optima est" (Hilchen 1592, B3v–B4r).
26 The inheritance law, property law, family law, and law of obligations played a key role among the nobility in the German lands and formed the largest cluster of academic disputations until the middle of the 17th century (Scholz 2022, 311–312).

tion: firstly, many people make the mistake of thinking that legal education is only reached after political education (*prudentia civilis*); secondly, there is no need to overload one's study with learning about glosses and commentaries—this makes the process difficult and long.[27] Thus, Hilchen's recommendation for the legal education was based on the then-fashionable *mos gallicus*.

Hilchen organizes the acquisition of legal knowledge on the basis of a system of reasons taken from Aristotle. For each right, the student must find the *causa efficiens, causa materialis, causa formalis, effectus,* and *finalis*. With the help of this formal system, according to Hilchen, it is good for the student to gather information scattered in different books of Roman law—that is, *Institutiones, Pandecta,* and *Codex* (Hilchen 1592, Bv–B2v).

So far, it is clear that in the learning model described by Hilchen to his young fellow citizen in 1592, the highest goal of the student was to achieve the overall academic skills of oral presentation by reading, memorizing, listening, and repeating, and not to prepare a new coherent and well-argued written text, e. g., draft pleadings and many other legal documents, which would be necessary for the next generation of Livonian lawyers for increasingly important written legal procedures, not to mention for legislative activities. Written notes in any form were merely an aid to the main objective.

Since there are no surviving sources from the time of the addressee's studies or later activity in the service of the Riga City council, it is impossible to assess whether and what the young Rigemann took away from Hilchen's guidance.

4 *Dikaiomatheia* for the Lithuanian and Polish Students

The other case is the 14-page Latin manuscript compiled by Hilchen entitled Δικαιομαθεία *Dauide Hilchen Secretario Regiae Maiestatis Illustri domino Joanni Stanislao Sapiehae Supremi Ducatus Lithuaniae Cancellarij filio praescripta* and sometimes also referred to in his letters as *Dikaiographia* or *Elementa iuris*. The Greek title *Dikaiomatheia* (guidance to jurisprudence) is just a humanist promo-

---

27 "Iurisprudentiae quoque studiosi cum magno labore, saepe etiam (vt Imperatoris Iustiniani verbis vtar) cum dissidentia (quae plerunque iuuenes quasi per medium profundum euntes, ab innumeris Ciuilis prudentiae voluminibus auertit) ad id perueniunt, ad quod leuiore via et hac ipsa Methodo ducti, sine magno labore et sine vlla dissidentia peruenire possent. Valeant glossae; valeant opiniones: valeant commenta: nullo loco erunt, si hanc rationem Methodicam, de qua dico, perfeceris" (Hilchen 1592, Br–v).

tional trick: Hilchen has never written a Greek text, not even the shortest poem, and in the few Greek quotations in his letters he used Greek orthography and diacritics rather unsystematically. Hilchen presented himself with this title as a learned expert of law and justice.[28]

Only one handwritten early modern copy of the text survives today—in a collective volume of different teaching materials about law in the Krakow University Library. Hilchen's study guide is at the forefront of this volume, before the manuscript of Tomasz Drezner's scholia *In Institutiones seu Elementa Juris D. Justiniani Sacratissimi Principis*, the printed theses *Positiones ivris ex variis titvlis Institvtionvm desvmptae* by Andrzej Srzedziński, defended and printed in Zamość 1614, and many others.[29] Neither early modern prints of it nor even attempts to print it are known.

This study guide was addressed and sent to young noblemen from Poland and Lithuania. According to the title, the copy in Krakow was sent to Jan Stanisław Sapieha (1588–1635),[30] but in Hilchen's correspondence, there are references to the further copies sent by Hilchen to the brothers Paweł (c. 1593–1632) and Stanisław Orzechowski[31] and their private tutors, the brothers Paweł (d. 1642) and Jan Krok-

---

28 The word was never used in Classical Greek or Latin. Cicero used, however, the compound word with *dicaea-: dicaearchus* (De Leg. 3.14) with the meaning of "a learned listener of Aristotle." In early modern Latin, the compound words *dicaeologia* and *dicaeodotes* were used.
29 For Srzedziński's identification, theses, and other manuscripts in this volume, especially his method to use different sources and notes for the legal issues, see Chapter 4 by Luisa Brotto.
30 Between 1599 and 1600, Sapieha studied at the Jesuit Academy in Vilnius and between 1603 and 1606 at the Jesuit College in Braunsberg. In the years 1606–1607, Sapieha was at the University of Würzburg and then went to France via Frankfurt, where he met Isaac Casaubon. From there, he traveled to Leuven and Nuremberg and returned to Poland in 1609 (Gryko-Andrejuk 2019, 372–373) under the direction of the Livonian nobleman Theodor Fa(h)rensbach. Beata Gryko-Andrejuk suspects that Hilchen's study instruction was written before Sapieha began his studies in Braunsberg but without a reference to her source. According to Hilchen's correspondence, however, the study instructions did not reach the young Jan Stanisław until the second half of 1606 in Würzburg, since Hilchen asked Sapieha for feedback in his letter from January 1607, because he had not yet received any praise or criticism from his father or the son for his instructions. Sapieha was later Marshal of the Lithuanian Tribunal from 1612 to 1621 and Grand Marshal of the Grand Duchy of Lithuania from 1621; after losing the Battle of Walmoza (Wallhof) to Sweden and Gustavus Adolphus in 1626, his mental health began to deteriorate, and he gave up further political and military pursuits (Gryko-Andrejuk 2019, 381).
31 The Orzechowski brothers enrolled at the University of Marburg on December 19, 1603, accompanied by the brothers Jan and Paweł Krokier (Caesar 1980, I, 160), and at Orléans in 1606 (Wotschke 1929, 141). In 1608, they returned to Poland and became supporters of the Arians. Paweł left for Marburg again in 1616 to study chemistry. Since 1617, Paweł was the senior of Lublin and Chełm and since 1618 a Sejm deputy. They belonged to the most influential activists and defenders of Calvinism in Lesser Poland.

ier³² in March 1606, and to Jan Żółkiewski (1595–1623)³³ in March 1607. Their fathers had been good friends and supporters of Jan Zamoyski—the Grand Duke of Lithuania Lew Sapieha (1557–1633), the Polish nobleman and Unitarian Paweł Orzechowski Senior (c. 1550–1612),³⁴ and Zamoyski's supporter and comrade in the Polish-Swedish war in Livonia in 1600–1602, Hetman Stanisław Żółkiewski (1547–1620).³⁵ The recipients of this study guide were about 12–17 years old—that is, remarkably younger then the addressee of Hilchen's Livonian guidance (see the textual evidence in Viiding 2022, 32–34) and almost all of them were on a *peregrinatio academica* in Western Europe at the time. Obviously, only Jan Żółkiewski had not started his studies yet, as in the letters from March 1607, Hilchen recommended himself as a private tutor for Jan under his very program (Hilchen *Epistolarum libri VI*, 70r).

Hilchen's reason for compiling this guide is well documented in his writings: on the one hand, Hilchen believed that without legal knowledge all other knowledge is unimportant (Hilchen, *Epistolarum libri VI*, 78r–v); on the other, he was not pleased that he did not have such a guide during his studies in Germany that would have enabled him to complete his studies faster and more efficiently.³⁶ Hilchen considered it possible that in two years, with the right learning methods, it would be possible to pass the whole of Roman law (Hilchen *Δικαιομαθεία*, 8r).³⁷

In contrast to the instructions of 1592, Hilchen focuses only on jurisprudence when teaching Polish and Lithuanian nobles and provides a systematic approach

---

32 Between the Krokier brothers, Paweł made a career: after staying with his brother Jan as a companion of the Orzechowski brothers in Marburg and Orléans, he was rector of the Unitarian School in Raków of Polish Brethren in 1610–1616 and belonged to the first scholars of the Raków school (Sand 1967, 175). During the rectorate, he wrote a handwritten commentary on ethics by Aristotle, *Commentarii ethici ad libros, qui Bibliothecae latentis numero comprehenduntur*. In 1616 he received his doctorate in Basel as dr.med.

33 Jan Żółkiewski devoted himself to a military career and fell already in 1623 after being wounded in the Țuțora expedition and subsequently imprisoned by the Turks; it has not been possible to find any information about his academic studies.

34 Paweł Orzechowski Sen. (c. 1550–1612) was a Polish nobleman; in 1581–1588, he was a cupbearer in Chełm, in 1588–1612, a subchamberlain in Chełm (Gmiterek 1992, 251), Sejm deputy, Arian, and patron of the Polish Brethren (Lubieniecki 1982, 230). Zamoyski's stepmother came from the Orzechowski family (Tygielski 1990, 32).

35 For their relationship, see Tygielski 2007, passim.

36 "Mihi si olim talis monitor contigisset, uel citius absoluissem" (Hilchen *Δικαιομαθεία*, 10v).

37 Cf. the curriculum written by Bonifacius Amerbach in 1536 for the University of Basel, in which the first two-year phase of study was also dedicated to the *Institutiones* and was intended to prepare the young lawyers sufficiently and successfully for the second phase of study with any professor in Germany so that the students were capable of learning the parts of the law most common in the German nation and most useful in practice (Hagemann 1999, 169).

instead of exemplary guidance. His study program is organized on a monthly basis, with no holidays.[38] Through the first year, the student has to work only with his own tutor, without lectures or disputations at the academy. This was fundamentally different from legal education in German universities in the second half of the 16th century, when lectures were still the main form of teaching (Köbler 1978, 486).

First of all, three months must be dedicated to dialectics and ethics;[39] only then can one transition to Roman law. First, it is important to read the four volumes of Justinian's *Institutiones*, the basic work on Roman law. But it must be done in a simple way, reading only Justinian's own text, without commentary from the later centuries. The novelty of things and the volume of material should not overwhelm the student's mind.[40]

Then comes six weeks of memory training. The student should memorize 200 legal principles, five daily, without missing a single day. These are short Latin sentences based on the *Institutiones* that the student finds in the appendix of Hilchen's guide.[41] For example, "Magistratus debet defendere, non opprimere Ciuitatem" (the magistrate must protect the city, not suppress it) or "Falsae excusationes non sunt audiendae" (false accusations do not have to be heard).[42] They are organized into three groups according to the three objects of law: things, persons, and activities. While learning the rules, the student must have the dictionary *De Verborum significatione* next to him. He has to mark all the words he does not know

---

[38] Cf. the fixed six-month semester cycle as the usual teaching principle of the private law colleges at early modern German universities (Köbler 1978, 486).
[39] "Duo praemittenda sunt: Dialectica et Ethica. Illa, ut methodum tibi compares, quae te per Juris labyrinthum ducat: haec ut fontes Juris concilies. ... Satis est locos argumentorum scire. In Ethicis quintum librum, quo nullus uberior, nouisse" (Hilchen Δικαιομαθεία, 8r). Book V of the *Nicomachean Ethics* is about justice.
[40] "Quid igitur inquies, primum audiam et legam? *Institutiones*, quae sunt elementa Juris. Sed duplici methodo. Prima est, ut quatuor isti libri, leui ac simplici uia, nude ut sunt, omissis glossis, et obsoletarum materiarum titulis, tradantur: alioquin si praeceptor statim ab initio rudem adhuc et infirmum animum incipientis multitudine commentariorum, ac uarietate rerum, praesertim antiquarum, onerauerit, duorum alterum (ut Justinianus Imperator inquit) aut desertorem studiorum efficiet, aut cum magno labore, saepe etiam cum dissidentia, quae plerumque iuuenes auertit, serius ad id perducet, ad quod leiuore uia ductus, sine magno labore, et sine ulla dissidentia perduci potuisset: mora igitur hic inter legendum nulla sit, nec animum tuum attonitum reddat nouitas rerum et magnitudo librorum" (Hilchen Δικαιομαθεία, 8v).
[41] "Ne absterreare: *Institutiones* absoules, si ordo, si constantia sit. Et Regulas Juris finies, si quisque dies officium suum faciat. Sunt regularum Juris duae Centuriae: si singulis diebus quinque regulas memoriae mandaueris, spacio 6. septimanarum utramque centuriam absoules" (Hilchen Δικαιομαθεία, 10v).
[42] Hilchen Δικαιομαθεία, 19v.

with an exact reference there but not yet systematize them to the *loci communes* in his notebooks.[43]

At this point, Hilchen's guidance responds to the potential objection of his student(s) that there will be too much material for such a short period of time. Hilchen recommends to set aside all the principles that are confusing and insignificant to the Polish circumstances. For example, out of the 26 parts of the first book of the *Institutiones*, the student has to go through six;[44] out of the 25 parts of the second book, nine;[45] out of the 30 parts of the third book, eight;[46] and out of the 17 tituli of the fourth book, eleven.[47] According to Hilchen's explanation, this is the most urgent knowledge of the *Institutiones* for a practicing lawyer, as

---

[43] "Obscuriorum porro nominum et Verborum explicatio prolixa facienda non est, sed satis est numerum in titulo de Verborum significatione indicasse, quo eorum interpretatio continetur: eum tu tradas libro iam ante parato, titulumque totum de Verborum significatione habeas pro Nomenclatore" (Hilchen Δικαιομαθεία, 9r).

[44] "Nimis angustum tempus esse dices. Latum erit satis, si obsoleti, minusque in Polonia necessarij tituli omittantur. Qui illi sint quaeris? Ecce dicam. /.../ Sex tibi assigno: reliquos omitte. Primus est de Iustitia. Secundus de Jure naturali gentium et Ciuili. Tertius de Patria potestate. Quartus de Nuptijs. Quintus de Tutelis. Sextus de Curatoribus" (Hilchen Δικαιομαθεία, 9r).

[45] "Secvndvs liber *Institutionvm* continet Titulos 25. Hic nouem tantum titulos a te exigo. Primus est de rerum diuisione. Secundus de seruitutibus. Tertius de usufructu, usu et habitatione. Quartus de Usucapionibus. Quintus de Donationibus. Sextus quibus alienare licet, uel non. Septimus de Testamentis, et Codicillis faciendis, et rumpendis: haeredibus instituendis, et exhaerendis. Octauus de Substitutionibus. Nouus de Legatis. Si pauciores uis, omitte sextum et Octauum, quorum etsi nullus in Polonia usus esse uideat, ego tamen magnum esse puto, et singulariter, octaui tituli de Substitutionibus" (Hilchen Δικαιομαθεία, 9r–v).

[46] "Liber tertivs 30 titvlos complectitur. Hic me liberalem esse agnosces. In tui enim usum octo duntaxat assigno. 1. De haereditatibus, quae ab intestato deferuntur. Velim a praeceptore totam hanc materiam, quam Imperator 13. titulis tractat, uno titulo per regulas certas expediri: habet hoc Grempius in sua Analysi, eum sequere. 2. De Obligationum diuisione: rerum et uerborum obligatione: diuisione stipulationum: inutilibus stipulationibus, et literarum obligationibus. 3. De fideiussoribus. 4. De emptione et uenditione. 5. De locatione et conductione. 6. De societate. 7. De mandato. 8. De obligationibus, quae quasi ex contractu nascuntur, et medis quibus eae tolluntur" (Hilchen Δικαιομαθεία, 9v–10r).

[47] "Liber iv *Institvtionvm* continet 17 Titulos. Hic fateor difficilior est, quia practicus Jurisque processum tradit. Hunc ergo uel totum differri ad alteram methodum, uel ex eo praecipuas saltem materias excerpi tradique uelim: nempe: 1. De obligationibus, quae ex delicto, uel ex quasi delicto nascuntur. 2. De ui bonorum raptorum. 3. De Lege Aquilia. 4. De iniurijs. 5. De Actionibus. Hic titulus prolixus et perplexus est. Ad Grempij Analysin, uel Wolffij erothemata te relego. Sed cum hoc titulos coniungendus est titulus: Si quadrupes pauperiem fecisse dicatur. Tum etiam titulus de perpetuis et temporalibus actionibus, de interdictis, et officio Judicis. 6. De Procuratoribus. 7. De satisdictionibus, siue Cautionibus. 8. De exceptionibus. 9. De Replicationibus. 10. De poena temere litigantium. 11. De publicis Judicijs" (Hilchen Δικαιομαθεία, 10r–v).

every Polish nobleman had to be ready to perform the duties of an assessor in court.

Only after nine months of mainly oral teaching does written work under the supervision of the private tutor begin. Within three months, the student should analyze the structure of the relevant chapters of the *Institutiones*, according to various *causae*, i.e., *causa efficiens, materialis, formalis, finalis, effectus,* and *pugnans,* and visualize it in tables. Hilchen admits that this method of (Ramistic) analysis has been most useful for himself.[48] Thus, he systematically gave a personal touch to his precepts.

Only from the second year will the student work in a team, listening to lectures and disputations, constantly asking questions, reading theses and systematically writing down what is being studied.[49] In addition to the *Institutiones*, he should now examine other sources of Roman law, the *Pandecta* and *Codex*. He must use the structural analysis method for them too.[50]

In the second year, the previous memorization and reading is required, but in addition, listening, discussing, and taking notes also emerge as learning methods.[51]

---

48 "Altera difficilior est: ideo /.../ unum insuper quadrantem anni tibi largior. Necesse igitur, ut si quatuor libri diligentissime atque exactissime euoluantur, et exponantur, omnia ad methodum accommodentur. Sed nulla methodus melior est Analytica. Enarraturus itaque Praeceptor tuus Institutionum libros, omissis interpretum ambagibus, et commentariorum maeandris, singulorum imprimis librorum dispositionem in breuem tabulam contrahat, eamque ductis lineis ob oculos proponat. Singulas uero materias titulis distinctas, methodo Analytica per causas explicet. Et primo quidem semper definitionem nominis et rei, ex titulo de Verborum significatione uel ex Hotomani, aliorumue lexico Iuris inquirat. Tum diuisiones: Causam efficientem tam propinquam, quam remotam: materialem etiam, formalem, finalem, effectus, et pugnantes causas designet: praecipuas sententias ex singulis titulis eruat, et Regulas Juris singulis titulis, et paragraphis applicet. De huius methodi, si recte intelligatur, et accommodetur, commodis, satis nunquam dici poterit, nec quantum mihi contulisse eandem putem, facile equidem dixerim" (Hilchen Δικαιομαθεία, 10v).

49 "Post expeditam auditionem et lectionem in exercitio solertem te esse oportet. Multa tibi ex praeceptore quaerenda sunt, plura a te ipso repetenda: omnia cum aequalibus conferenda. Nec utilius quicquam, quam unam quamque materiam simul ac tradita, euoluta, atque cognita fuerit, in certas praepositiones concludere, et singulis hebdomadis inter aequales praeponere disceptandam. Quae enim singuli didicerint, ea in medium uelut in unum collata aceruum ad unumquemque disserendo redeunt, ac ipso disputationum instrumento perpoliuntur omnia" (Hilchen Δικαιομαθεία, 10v–11r).

50 "Duas principales partes uniuersi Juris specta: Pandectas, et Codicem. /.../ Deinde uero omissis ijs titulis, qui in Institutionibus analytice explicati sunt, concordantes Pandectarum et Codicis, tituli utiles tamen et necessarij coniungendi, et in conclusiones methodo Analytica redigendi, accuratiusque in memoriae thesaurum recondendi sunt" (Hilchen Δικαιομαθεία, 11r–v).

51 "Hic necesse est, ut quamprimum audias, quaeras, intelligas, memoriae commendes, in amicorum quotidianis colloquijs, et congressibus de studijs Juris loquaris, publicis disputationibus inter-

According to Hilchen, notes must be taken not only when reading but when listening and during disputations as well.⁵² Similar to the recommendations given to the Livonian student in 1592, it means that among the students' written heritage lecture transcripts in pure form should be rather seldom, as they are normally mixed with notes obtained from reading and disputing.

For notebooks, Hilchen has three general recommendations: first, they should be filled with careful love, like your own soul; second, although others have made notebooks in the past, everyone has to make their own; thirdly, taking notes is easy to recommend, but it is hard work.⁵³

The student of Roman law needs four different notebooks, depending on the content. The first should contain material on the history of law, the second the results of a structural analysis of the basic texts of Roman law, the third specific arguments and counter-arguments, and the fourth legal terms and their explanations.⁵⁴ He gives longer comments on the first, second, and fourth species.

About the legal history notebook, Hilchen makes recommendations on the level of content: first, it must contain everything that concerns the rulers and officials of ancient Rome;⁵⁵ second, changes to the source texts of Roman law throughout history; third, the small differences between Polish and Roman law; and fourth, the principles of feudal law in Prussia and Livonia as parts of the Pol-

---

sis, prius tamen theses earum recte intelligas, /.../, quod nulla alia re assequeris, quam quaerendo, audiendo, legendo, disputando, scribendo" (Hilchen *Δικαιομαθεία*, 11v).

52 "In lectione attende /.../ Dubia ne te morentur: sed trade omnia libro dubijs peculiariter destinato, tempusque liberum nactus, eorum dissolutionem a praeceptore exige. Ipse etiam ex libris quaere: cum reperisti, stylum cape, excerpe, et uelut annonam in horreum repone" (Hilchen *Δικαιομαθεία*, 11r).

53 "Libros ut animum praecipuarum materiarum cognitione impleas," "Qui labor etsi ab alijs praestitus sit, hic tamen tuum proprium exposco." "In his labor aliquis, sed mihi crede utilis." (Hilchen *Δικαιομαθεία*, 11v).

54 "Sint autem quotuor libri tibi parati et distincti. Unus in quem historiolam Juris Ciuilis consignes. Secundus qui Analysin singularum Materiarum contineat. Tertius in quem praecipuas obiectiones, et responsiones singularum materiarum congeras. Quartus in quo phrases, et uoces Juridicas conserues. In his labor aliquis, sed mihi crede utilis. Trimestris res est" (Hilchen *Δικαιομαθεία*, 11r). Cf. different types of legal notebooks in early modern Britain (Blessin 2020, 29–38 and 40–42): 1. Notebook with legal commonplaces. 2. Classroom commonplace book. 3. Records of oral instruction. 4. Records of moot cases. 5. A commonplace book along with lecture and moot records. 5. Notebooks with legal and non-legal (historical, political, literary, philosophical) texts, provided with legal comments.

55 This instruction on the close connection of legal and political studies refers to the influence of the Academy of Zamość in Hilchen's study guide, cf. Chapter 4 by Luisa Brotto.

ish state.[56] It is in the third and, in particular, in the fourth point that Hilchen therefore requires the teaching of local legislation, which he himself had not been able to study at German universities. This last point is Hilchen's attempt to harmonize legal education in the different parts of the Polish-Lithuanian Commonwealth.

About the second notebook, Hilchen gave some examples of *methodus analytica*. Here, it is impressive how Hilchen advises the student to adapt the subject to himself, using singular first-person verbs: "*sic resolvo*" (I analyze them), "*si numerem*" (if I count), "*reperio*" (I find), "*singulos connoto*" (I notice the details) (Hilchen *Δικαιομαθεία, passim*). With the help of these introductory phrases, the old and universal content of the law became the object of the student's own personal research and discovery.

Finally, there is the fourth type of notebooks with explanations of legal terms and phrases. First of all, it is clear from the examples given by Hilchen that both nouns and verbs need to be clarified. Secondly, for the most part, the exact classical or later source must be added to the definition. Third, the definitions may also include examples from history (e. g. Cicero as *pater patriae*). Fourth, it is also advisable to note changes in the meaning of the word over time (e. g., the use of the word "*perduelles*" in Old Latin instead of the classical word "*hostis*") (Hilchen *Δικαιομαθεία*, 17v–18r).

In conclusion, the learning model described by Hilchen to the Polish and Lithuanian noblemen around 1606–1607 was focused on ascertaining knowledge of Roman law in a formalized and concentrated form, specifically of what was most relevant for the Polish and Lithuanian context through the eyes of a learned foreigner from a newly integrated province of the Commonwealth. The overall academic skills and learning methods are almost the same as in Hilchen's study guide from 1592 to his Livonian fellow (reading, memorizing, listening, and repeating), and the preparation of a new coherent and well-argued written text was still not a necessary aim. The main differences are that Hilchen now mentioned a series of Central and Western European legal experts and that all these authorities

---

56 "Totus de dignitatibus et officialibus Romanorum: sit ergo tibi arbitrarius: praeceptoris autem haec semper cura erit, ut ubi in Pandectis, Codice et Nouellis per posteriorem Imperatorum Constitutiones emendatum quicquam, uel mutatum, aut sublatum est, indicet. Ut sit etiam qui, in quibus Ius Regni Poloniae a Ciuili Romano differat, paucis tibi ostendat, uotum meum est. Sed tu ipse Deo dante aliquando intelliges Jus Romanum a iure, quo in Polonia utimur, accidentijs, non autem substantia differre. Iis sic pertractatis, si quid residui temporis erit, tribues materiae Feudali, cuius etsi in Polonia usus nullus esse uideatur, maximus tamen est, et Duces Prussiae et Liuoniae Vasallos Regni" (Hilchen *Δικαιομαθεία*, 14v).

are representatives of *mos gallicus*.[57] In the written notes, he recommended to use the (Ramist) method of visualization.

Similar to the case of Hilchen's first guide from 1592, there is no further information regarding whether and how his strict and voluminous instruction for the young Polish and Lithuanian nobility was used in learning.

5 Conclusions: Legal Education Methodology Lagging behind Legal Practice

The turn of the 16th and 17th centuries marked the transitional period from the medieval oral customary law to written, learned law in Northeastern Europe, first in legal proceedings and court practice but, with some delay, also in legal education. For Livonia and also Lithuania, where no academic institution for legal education existed until 1632 (1641), private study guides are one possibility for analyzing the stages of this transition.

On the basis of the two Latin instructions written by the Riga humanist and lawyer David Hilchen in 1592 and 1606, it is clear that the learning of law under private tutors and outside of universities was, in the last decade of the 16th century and first decade of the 17th century, mainly in oral form (reading, memorizing, listening, repeating, and disputing as main forms) even despite the elaborated system of different types of notebooks. The notebook was still the main form of the written learning methods. The preparation of a new coherent and well-argued written text, e.g., draft pleadings or other legal documents is not mentioned. In the case of law studies, it can be justified by the fact that spontaneity and the creation of new knowledge was not expected from the students; rather, the practicing of the exact, concise, and clear use of words was recommended. This is in line with the overall traditions of academic legal education at the time, the aim of which was to systematically learn and acquire legal principles, not so much to create new knowledge (Köbler 1978, 486).

Hilchen's case also demonstrates that the genre of study guides and the notes of students were in constant dialogue. One's own critical experience as a student

---

57 Johannes von Borcholdt (1535–1593), Ludwig Gremp von Freudenstein (1509–1583), Franz Hotemann (1524–1590), Joachim Mynsiger von Frundeck (1514–1588), Johannes Schneidewein (1519–1568), Matthias Wesenbeck (1531–1586), Conrad Wolf von Thumbschirn (1604–1667). Only Giulio Pacio de Beriga (1550–1635) represents an intermediate tradition between *mos italicus* and *mos gallicus*.

transformed into changed guidelines for subsequent students, be it by omitting previous prescripts or by recommending particularly effective learning methods.

Bibliography

Primary Sources

Manuscripts

Bibliotheca Universitatis Jagellonicae Cracoviensis, Krakow
MS 2279 AA VII 61

Herder-Institut, Marburg
MS DSHI 100 Ramm-Helmsing 184

Latvijas Valsts vēstures arhīvs, Riga
MS 4038-2-297

Stifts- och landsbibliotek, Linköping
MS Br 43

Printed Sources (books printed before 1800)

Eck, Nicolaus, Hilchen, David, and Rivius, Johannes (1597): *Orationes tres, e quibus duae honoratissima dignitate, tum sapientia et virtute ornatissimorum D.D. Scholarcharum, Nicolai Ekii, Proconsulis et Davidis Hilchen Syndici. Tertia Ioannis Rivii, cum solenni et publico ritu produceretur, ad demandatam sibi ab Amplissimo Senatu Inspectionem Scholasticam Ineundam. Habitae in restitutione seu instauratione Scholae Rigensis XV. C[a]L[enda]S [Sexti]L[e]S [=18 June]. Adiuncta sunt iisdem: primum, publicae doctrinae series, tabellis expressa inque curias V. distributa. Deinde, docendi in singulis curiis, praescripta ratio et demonstratum iter, quod utiliter Praeceptores huius Ludi sequerentur: cum in tradendis artibus, tum in tractando et interpretando omni genere utriusque linguae, Autorum.* Riga: Mollinus. USTC 6910891.

Hilchen, David (1584): *Disputatio de successione ex testamento. Qvam Divini numinis auspicio, praeside clarissimo viro D. Andrea Laubmario, V.I.D. et in celeberrima Tubingensi Academia ordinario professore, praeceptore suo singulariter observando, die 29. Maji hora 6. In auditorio Jureconsultorum, ingenij exercendi gratia, defendere conabitur David Heliconius, Livonus.* Tübingen: Georgius Gruppenbachius. USTC 637088.

Hilchen, David (1585): *De legatis et fideicommissis disputatio in antiqua Heidelbergensi academia sub excellentissimi viri Domini Matthiae Entzellini V.J.D. et professoris ordinarii: Praeceptoris sui omni officio observandi praesidio: ingenii retexendi gratia publice proposita a Davide Heliconio Livono die 20. Februarii horis ante et pomeridiani discutienda.* Heidelberg: Ioannes Spiess.

Hilchen, David (1592): *Ad Theodorum Rigemannum, elegantis ingenii iuvenem Epistola. Qua ratio studendi Philosophiae et cuicumque alteri facultati demonstratur.* Riga: Mollinus. USTC 6910244.

Starowolski, Simon (1625): *Scriptorum Polonicorum Hekatontas; Seu Centum Illustrium Poloniae Scriptorum Elogia Et Vitae.* Frankfurt: Zetter. USTC 2032940.

Vulpius, Heinrich (1635): *Methodica paedias isagoge, pro felici successu gymnasii Revaliensis, a generosis nobilissimis, amplissimis, magnificentissimis, ordinis Esthonici, equestris & urbici, senatoribus, anno 1631. Revaliae laudabiliter fundati, et ab incomparabili heroe, Gustavo Adolpho magno, glorissimo Svecorum etc. rege, et acerrimo Religionis Orthodoxae propugnatore clementer confirmati. Delineata a M. Henrico Vulpio, Lemgovia-Westphalo rectore et inspectore, et authoritate praedictorum Dominorum patronorum, 4. Maij, anni decurrentis, publicata.* Tallinn: Christoph Reusner. USTC 6911474.

Secondary Sources

Bergmann, Benjamin (1825, 1826): "David von Hilchen, ein Beitrag zur Geschichte Livlands, nach Urkunden und literarischen Seltenheiten." In: *Magazin für Russland's Geschichte, Länder- und Völkerkunde* 1 (1825; No. 3, 128–157) and 2 (1826; No. 1, 117–158, and No. 2, 133–148).

Bergmann, Gustav (1803): *Vita Davidis ab Hilchen, Secretarii Regis Poloniae et Notarii Terrestris Vendensis.* Rūjiena: s.n.

Blaese, Hermann (1936): *Bedeutung und Geltung des römischen Privatrechts in den baltischen Gebieten.* Leipzig: Weicher.

Blaese, Hermann (1962): *Einflüsse des römischen Rechts in den Baltischen Gebieten.* Milano: Giuffré.

Blessin, Adams (2020): *Universal Men of Law: Humanism, Literature and Play in the Legal Notebooks of Law Students at the Early Modern Inns of Court (1575–1620).* Thesis submitted for the Degree of Doctor of Philosophy University of East Anglia School of Literature, Drama and Creative Writing. Manuscript.

Böthführ, Heinrich Julius (1877): *Die Rigische Ratslinie von 1226 bis 1876. Zweite vollständig umgearbeitete Auflage.* Riga, Moscow, and Odessa: Deubner.

Buchholtz, Arend (1890): *Geschichte der Buchdruckerkunst in Riga 1588–1888: Festschrift der Buchdrucker Rigas zur Erinnerung an die vor 399 Jahren erfolgte Einführung der Buchdruckerkunst in Riga.* Riga: Müller.

Caesar, Julius (1980): *Catalogus studiosorum scholae Marpurgensis. Pars I–II. Nachdruck von Marburg: Elwert 1875.* Nendeln: Kraus.

Erman, Wilhelm and Horn, Ewald (1904): *Bibliographie der deutschen Universitäten: systematisch geordnetes Verzeichnis der bis Ende 1899 gedruckten Bücher und Aufsätze über das deutsche Universitätswesen. Teil I.* Leipzig and Berlin: Teubner.

Gmiterek, Henryk (1992): *Urzędnicy województwa bełskiego i ziemi chełmskiej XIV–XVIII wieku: spisy* [Officials of the Bełz Voivodeship and the Chełm Region of the 14th–18th Centuries: Censuses]. Kórnik: Polska Akademia Nauk.

Godek, Sławomir (2013): "Prawo rzymskie w Polsce przedrozbiorowej w świetle aktualnych badań [Roman Law in Pre-partition Poland in the Light of Current Research]." In: *Zeszyty Prawnicze* 13. No. 3, 39–64. DOI: 10.21697/zp.2013.13.3.02

Gryko-Andrejuk, Beata (2019): "Choroba psychiczna? Relacje Jana Stanisława Sapiehy z rodziną i otoczeniem [Mental illness? Jan Stanisław Sapieha's relations with his family and surroundings]." In: Dubas-Urwanowicz, Ewa, Kupczewska, Marta, Łopatecki, Karol, and

Urwanowicz, Jerzy (Eds.): *Honestas et turpitudo: magnateria Rzeczypospolitej w XVI–XVIII wieku* [*Honestas et turpitudo: Polish magnates in the 16th–18th Centuries*]. Białystok: Polskie Towarzystwo Historyczne, 371–382.

Hagemann, Hans-Rudolf (1992): "Rechtsunterricht im 16. Jahrhundert: die juristischen Vorlesungen im Basler Amerbachnachlass. " In: *Zeitschrift für Neuere Rechtsgeschichte* 14: 162–190.

Hoffmann, Thomas (2007): *Der Landrechtsentwurf David Hilchens—ein livländisches Rechtszeugnis polnischer Herrschaft.* Frankfurt am Main: Peter Lang.

Jovaiša, Liudas (2018): "Eustachijus Valavičius: nejvertinto herojaus curriculum vitae. Eustachius Wołłowicz: curriculum vitae of an undervalued hero." In: *Bažnyčius istorijos studijos* [*Studies in Church History*] 9, 82–167 and 369–370.

Kiris, Advig and Leesment, Leo (1982): "Õigusteadus [Jurisprudence]". In: Piirimäe, Helmut (Ed.): *Tartu Ülikooli ajalugu: 1632–1982. I. 1632–1798.* [*History of Tartu University: 1632–1982. I. 1632–1798*]. Tallinn: Valgus, 196–199.

Köbler, Gerhard (1978): "Juristenausbildung." In: Erler, Adalbert, Kaufmann, Ekkehard, and Schmidt-Wiegand, Ruth (Eds.): *Handwörterbuch zur deutschen Rechtsgeschichte*. Vol. II. Berlin: Erich Schmidt, 484–488.

Leliwa, Stanisław (1880): "Dawid Hilchen. Szkic biograficzny na tle dziejów inflancko-polskich osnuty [David Hilchen. Biographical sketch against the background of Livonian-Polish history]." In: *Biblioteka Warszawska* 1. No. 157, 1–29 and 383–400.

Lubieniecki, Andrzey (1982): *Poloneutychia*. Linda, Alina, Maciejewska, Maria, Tazbir, Janusz, and Zawadzki, Zdzisław (Eds.). Warsaw and Lodz: Państwowe Wydawnictwo Naukowe.

Luts-Sootak, Marju (2022): "Der Injurienprozess vom Jahr 1600 gegen David Hilchen in Riga als Spiegel der frühneuzeitlichen Rechtsentwicklungen in Livland." In: Viiding, Kristi, Siimets-Gross, Hesi, Hoffmann, Thomas, and Klöker, Martin (Eds.): *Briefe, Recht und Gericht im polnischen Livland am Beispiel von David Hilchen. Letters, Law and Court in Polish Livonia. The Case of David Hilchen.* Münster: LIT, 149–224.

Mahling, Madlena (2011): "Die Kanzleiordnung des Rigaer Rats von 1598. Historischer Kommentar und Edition." In: *Archiv für Diplomatik, Schriftgeschichte, Siegel- und Wappenkunde* 57, 181–204.

Martins, Ryan and Widener, Michael (2018): *Learning the Law: The Book in Early Legal Education: An Exhibition October 1–December 14, 2018.* New Haven: Lillian Goldman Law Library, Yale Law School.

Narbutienė, Daiva and Narbutas, Sigitas (2002): *XV–XVI a. Lietuvos lotyniškų knygų sąrašas = Index librorum latinorum Lituaniae saeculi quinti decimi et sexti decimi*. Vilnius: Lietuvių literatūros ir tautosakos institutas.

Oestmann, Peter (2022): "*Contumacia*. David Hilchen, Ladungsungehorsam und das frühneuzeitliche Prozessrecht." In: Viiding, Kristi, Siimets-Gross, Hesi, Hoffmann, Thomas, and Klöker, Martin (Eds.): *Briefe, Recht und Gericht im polnischen Livland am Beispiel von David Hilchen. Letters, Law and Court in Polish Livonia. The Case of David Hilchen.* Münster: LIT, 225–259.

Piechnik, Ludwik (1984): *Początki Akademii Wileńskiej 1570–1599* [*The beginnings of the Vilnius Academy 1570–1599*]. Rome: Apud Institutum Historicum Societatis Jesu.

Pietrzyk, Zdzisław (1997): *W kręgu Strasburga: z peregrynacji młodzieży z Rzeczypospolitej polsko-litewskiej w latach 1538–1621* [*In the Circle of Strasbourg: About Travels of Youths from the Polish-Lithuanian Commonwealth in the Years 1538–1621*]. Krakow: Biblioteka Jagiellońska.

Pihlajamäki, Heikki (2017): *Conquest and the Law in Swedish Livonia (ca. 1630–1710). A Case of Legal Pluralism in Early Modern Europe.* Leiden: Brill.

Pölnitz, Götz von (1937): *Die Matrikel der Ludwig-Maximilians-Universität Ingolstadt-Landshut-München.* Part I: Ingolstadt. Vol. I: 1472–1600. Munich: Schöpping.

Ramm-Helmsing, Herta von (1936): *David Hilchen (1561–1610). Syndikus in Riga.* Poznań: Historische Gesellschaft für Posen.

Sand, Christophorus (1967): *Bibliotheca Antitrinitariorum. Praefatione et indice nominum instruxit Lech Szczucki.* Warsaw: Państwowe Wydawnictwo Naukowe (facsimile from the first edition in Freistadii: Johannes Aconius, 1684).

Schiemann, Theodor (1887): "*Materialien zur Geschichte des Schulwesens in Reval.* " In: *Beiträge zur Kunde Ehst-, Liv- und Kurlands* 4. No. 1, 1–64.

Schmidt, Oswald (1895): "Rechtsgeschichte Liv-, Est- und Curlands, aus dem Nachlasse des Verfassers hrsg. von Eugen von Nottbeck." In: *Dorpater juristische Studien* 3, 75b–403.

Scholz, Luca (2022): "A Distant Reading of Legal Dissertations from German Universities in the Seventeenth Century." In: *The Historical Journal* 65. No. 2, 297–327, DOI: 10.1017/S0018246X2100011X.

Schott, Clausdieter (1978): "Juristenfakultäten." In: Erler, Adalbert, Kaufmann, Ekkehard, and Schmidt-Wiegand, Ruth (Eds.): *Handwörterbuch zur deutschen Rechtsgeschichte.* Vol. II. Berlin: Erich Schmidt: 488–490.

Siimets-Gross, Hesi and Hoffmann, Thomas (2022): "Ad rem et famam meam. David Hilchens juristische Korrespondenz." In: Viiding, Kristi, Siimets-Gross, Hesi, Hoffmann, Thomas, and Klöker, Martin (Eds.): *Briefe, Recht und Gericht im polnischen Livland am Beispiel von David Hilchen. Letters, Law and Court in Polish Livonia. The Case of David Hilchen.* Münster: LIT, 71–148.

Siimets-Gross, Hesi and Viiding, Kristi (2020): "The Humanist Lawyer David Hilchen in the Polish Livonian and Polish Courts 1600–1609: The Reflection of His Proceedings in Letters." In: *Journal of Legal Studies/Studia Prawnicze KUL* 82. No. 2, 269–299, DOI: 10.31743/sp.5803.

Skepjan, Anastasija (2013): *Kniazi Slutskiya [The Princes of Sluck].* Minsk: Belarus.

Tering, Arvo (1989): "Über die Juristenausbildung der Mitglieder des Hofgerichts in Dorpat (Tartu) 1630–1710." In: *Studia Juridica 4: Historia et Theoria*, 28–57.

Tering, Arvo (1996): "Die Ratsstipendien von Reval und Riga im Zeitraum vom 16. bis 18. Jahrhundert." In: Kotarski, Edmund and Chojnacka, Małgorzata (Eds.): *Literatur und Institutionen der literarischen Kommunikation in Nordeuropäischen Städten im Zeitraum von 16. bis zum 18. Jahrhundert.* Gdańsk: Wydawnictwo Uniwersytetu Gdańskiego, 154–168.

Tering, Arvo (2008): *Eesti-, liivi- ja kuramaalased Euroopa ülikoolides 1561–1798* [*The Students from Estonia, Livonia and Courland in the European Universities 1561–1798*]. Tartu: Eesti Ajalooarhiiv.

Tering, Arvo (2018): *Lexikon der Studenten aus Estland, Livland und Kurland an europäischen Universitäten 1561–1800.* With the collaboration of Jürgen Beyer. Cologne, Weimar, and Vienna: Böhlau.

Troje, Hans Erich (1977): "Die Literatur des gemeinen Rechts unter dem Einfluß des Humanismus: V. Unterrichtsscriften." In: Coing, Helmut (Ed.): *Handbuch der Quellen und Literatur der neueren europäischen Privatrechtsgeschichte: Veröffentlichung des Max-Planck-Instituts für europäische Rechtsgeschichte. Zweiter Band, Neuere Zeit (1500–1800): das Zeitalter des gemeinen Rechts.* Erster Teilband, Wissenschaft, Münster: Beck, 718–730.

Tygielski, Wojciech (1990): *Politics of Patronage in Renaissance Poland. Chancellor Jan Zamoyski, His Supporters and the Political Map of Poland 1572–1605.* Warsaw: Wydawnictwo Uniwersytetu Warszawskiego.

Tygielski, Wojciech (2007): *Listy, Ludzie, Władza: Patronat Jana Zamoyskiego w świetle korespondencij* [*Letters, People, Power: Jan Zamoyski's Patronage in the Light of Correspondence*]. Warsaw: Oficyna Wydawnicza VIATOR.

Viiding, Kristi (2021): "David Hilchen und seine Dichtung." In: Viiding, Kristi and Klöker, Martin (Eds.): *David Hilchen. Sub velis poeticis. Lateinische Gedichte.* Münster: LIT, 11–36.

Viiding, Kristi (2022): "David Hilchen und seine Expertenkorrespondenz." In: Viiding, Kristi, Siimets-Gross, Hesi, Hoffmann, Thomas, and Klöker, Martin (Eds.): *Briefe, Recht und Gericht im polnischen Livland am Beispiel von David Hilchen. Letters, Law and Court in Polish Livonia. The Case of David Hilchen.* Münster: LIT, 17–69.

Viiding, Kristi, Siimets-Gross, Hesi, Hoffmann, Thomas, and Klöker, Martin (Eds.) (2022): *Briefe, Recht und Gericht im polnischen Livland am Beispiel von David Hilchen. Letters, Law and Court in Polish Livonia. The Case of David Hilchen.* Münster: LIT.

Wotschke, Theodor (1929): "Caselius' Beziehungen zu Polen." In: Friedensburg, Walther and Kohlmeyer, Ernst (Eds.): *Archiv für Reformationsgeschichte. Texte und Untersuchungen* (Leipzig) 26, 133–152.

Second Part: **Students' Curiosity and Choices**

Matthias Roick

Aristotle Up-Front: A Student's Notes on the Title Page of Jacques Lefèvre d'Étaple's *Introduction to Aristotle's Ethics*

In memoriam Eckhard Keßler (1938–2018), *responsio mea sera valde*

Abstract: Among the practices of note-taking common in early modern Europe was the annotation of books. Margins and flyleaves provided space for notes, and text pages allowed for interlinear notes. This chapter focuses on a specific case study: the title page of Jacques Levèfre d'Étaples' *In Aristotelis Ethicen Introductio*, printed in Vienna in 1501 by Johann Winterburger. As will be argued, the notes on this title page, dictated in class, circumscribe the text and help students with their intellectual orientation. They show that texts such as the *Nicomachean Ethics* were not isolated entities, but part of the intertextual structure of early modern literary culture. This approach shaped students' reading experiences and their encounters with texts in the Renaissance and the early modern period.

1 Introduction

Among the practices of note-taking common in Renaissance and early modern Europe was the practice of annotating books, and textbooks were no exception. In what follows, I will concentrate on one example of a textbook with students' notes, an annotated copy of Jacques Levèfre d'Étaples' *In Aristotelis Ethicen Introductio*, printed in 1501 in Vienna by Johann Winterburger (Lefèvre 1501). The copy is preserved as part of a *sammelband* in the Herzog August Bibliothek in Wolfenbüttel under the shelfmark A: 41.3 Quod, henceforth the Wolfenbüttel copy (abbreviated as WF). The composition of the *sammelband*, containing a total of 23 works printed between 1494 and 1507, is in itself fascinating but not the topic of the present chapter. It suggests, however, that the notes in the *Introduction* are most probably from the beginning of the 16th century.

Matthias Roick: ORCID: 0000-0001-6214-8666. Institute of Philosophy and Sociology, Polish Academy of Sciences, Warsaw, Poland. The article has been written in the framework of the project "Virtue and Sociability. Teaching Friendship in Early Modern Schools and Universities, 1518–1648", PASIFIC Call 1, No. 46718. This project has received funding from the European Union's Horizon 2020 research and innovation programme under the Marie Skłodowska-Curie grant agreement No 847639 and from the Ministry of Education and Science.

∂ Open Access. © 2023 the author(s), published by De Gruyter. This work is licensed under the Creative Commons Attribution 4.0 International License. https://doi.org/10.1515/9783111072722-007

Unlike other chapters in the present book, I have very little information about the author of the notes in WF. For reasons I will explain below, I am convinced that they were a student listening to the explanations of their teacher. But although more information about the identity of the student would be welcome, especially in establishing the exact teaching context in which they took notes, I take the Wolfenbüttel copy of the *Introduction* as a case study of how students worked with texts, and especially with Aristotle and the *Ethics*, in the Renaissance and early modern period. In general, textbooks offer us a key to understanding "the standard structure of school learning" and "the cultural assumptions and cognitive practices of the period" (Oosterhoof 2019, 20–21). The student's notes in WF confirm this impression, but they also offer a beautiful example how the student, acting as a writer, listener, and reader, enters into dialogue with the text. This is especially true for WF's title page.

2 Lefèvre, Art, and the *Introduction*

Jacques Lefèvre (in Latinized form, Faber Stapulensis) was born between 1450 and 1460 in Étaples, a small port town in Picardy. Little is known about his childhood and youth. He began his studies at the university of Paris around 1474; at the beginning of the 1490s, he appears as a teacher at the Collège du Cardinal Lemoine, a residential college of the university (Rice 1988, 110). During the last decade of the 15th century, he worked mainly on translations, commentaries, and introductions regarding Aristotle's works, becoming the figurehead of what Charles Schmitt, Eugene F. Rice, and others have labelled "humanist Aristotelianism" (Rice 1988, 112; for a discussion of this expression see Lines 2002: 20). Continuing a tradition ushered in by humanists such as Leonardo Bruni and Ermolao Barbaro, Lefèvre took the characteristic traits of this Aristotelianism—among them disenchantment with medieval translations, the rejection of scholastic commentaries, and a greater concern with moral philosophy—and transferred them into the context of the universities. Despite his success, however, Lefèvre did not pursue an academic career until the end of his life. In 1507, he left the university and dedicated himself mainly to biblical studies and the translation of the Bible, giving important impulses to the reformation movements in Europe (Schönau 2017). He died in 1536.

During his Paris years, Lefèvre was surrounded by a circle of students including the Flemish theologian, priest, and humanist Josse van Clichtove and the Alsatian humanist Beatus Rhenanus. Lefèvre's students found themselves in a special situation. The late 1490s and early 1500s were a period of transition between manuscript and print, and both Clichtove and Rhenanus belonged to a new generation who could base their complete *cursus artium* on printed textbooks (Oosterhof 2019,

124). They attended Lefèvre's classes and took notes in them. One of Beatus' textbooks ends, in fact, with the remark that the book "was read and ... set down in letters by me, Beatus Rhenanus" (Oosterhof 2019, 124).[1] Beatus made the book his own, both by the lectures he attended and the annotations he wrote down in the book, leaving visible traces of his intellectual ownership of the volume. At first, notes such as Beatus' were intended for personal use, but they could also develop a dynamic of their own in later years. Clichtove's annotations in the *Introduction to Aristotle's Ethics*, for example, would later be published, among others by Beatus Rhenanus, and find their way into WF.

The *Introduction* was among the most successful works of Lefèvre. It was first printed in 1494 by Antoine Caillaut in Paris as *Ars moralis* and seen through the press by Guillaume Gontier (Rice 1972, 25). The first page of this edition provides the reader less with a title than with a kind of "blurb" laying out the program of moral education intended by Lefèvre's work. It is worth quoting it in full:

> This Art of Ethics teaches the good life both to individuals and to the community which brings individuals together, it shows what to pursue and what to avoid, for virtue must be pursued, but vice avoided, and it makes the moral writings of the philosopher Aristotle plain and clear. And anyone who brought together the throng of moral virtues as one, in the full consonance and unity of wisdom, would see that Aristotle had ascended to the cleansing virtues and the virtues of the purified mind to the fullest and in a most divine manner. In them, and only in them, the happiness of mortals must be placed (while we still live and breathe) (Lefèvre 1494, a1r).[2]

The information given here includes the audience (individuals and society at large) and the main topic (virtues and vices). It also advertises the "plain and clear" treatment of the topic, setting the book apart from other, more obscure approaches. This was an implicit attack on older scholastic translations and commentaries, a critical outlook Lefèvre shared with humanist scholars in the Italian peninsula such as Ermolao Barbaro. Years later, the Italian humanist Mario Equicola would praise Lefèvre for his clarity: "like a risen sun he disperses the clouds of obscurity from every Aristotelian text" (Rice 1970, 132).[3]

---

1 "Lecta est et a me litteris mandata Beato Rhino[wer]."
2 "Hec Ars Moralis cum singulos tum civitatem que ex singulis colligitur ad beatam vitam instruit, seguenda fugiendaque monstrat, virtus enim sequenda, vicium autem fugiendum, et Aristotelis philosophi moralia illustria claraque reddit. Et qui moralium virtutum multitudinem in unam sapentie consonantiam unitatemque colligeret, videret Aristotelem purgatorias animique iam purgati virtutes plenissime divinissimeque attigisse. In quibus vel solis mortalium (dum adhuc mortalem vitam spiramus) felicitas collocanda est."
3 "Tamquam exortus aereus sol tenebras ab omni lectione discutit, fugat, removet" (Rice 1972, 126).

The following reference to "cleansing virtues" and "virtues of the purified mind" was, on the one hand, a respectful nod towards the Platonic tradition and the philosophy of Marsilio Ficino. Lefèvre had met Ficino on his travels to Italy and encountered Florentine Neoplatonism. He certainly knew about Ficino's division of the virtues into political virtues, cleansing virtues, virtues of the purified mind, and exemplary virtues. This division was, in any case, not the Florentine's invention but derived from the philosophy of Plotinus and Porphyry; through Macrobius' *Commentary on Cicero's Dream of Scipio* (*Commentarii in Somnium Scipionis*), it was also known throughout the Middle Ages. In fact, Lefèvre could fall back on a longstanding discussion on the exact relationship between these two classifications, already present towards the middle of the 13th century (Buffon 2008, 18–19).

On the other hand, the reference to cleansing virtues and virtues of the purified mind countered arguments about the lack of a transcendent dimension in Aristotle's moral teachings. One such argument concerned the worldliness of Aristotelian ethics and the low rank of moral virtue as "political" or "consuetudinal," that is, based on habituation. Instead of helping humans to develop the better part of their nature, their spiritual side, Aristotle's moral teachings could bar the path to God. The title information argues against this implicit criticism by setting great store in the unity of virtue. According to the text, the unity of virtues does not culminate in worldly wisdom (*prudentia*), as would be typical for the Peripatetics, but in contemplative wisdom (*sapientia*). It therefore bridges the gap between moral–practical and intellectual–contemplative virtue in Aristotle. The transcendent character of this unity is underlined by the remark that those reaching the state of unification will recognize that Aristotle himself had not stopped at the political virtues but had ascended to higher forms of virtue. Moreover, the title passage is careful to limit the scope of Aristotle's moral writings. The virtues discussed in the *Ethics* concern human happiness in this life and not in the next. As is clearly stated, they regard our *human* nature, although they potentially offer us a path to transcend our limits towards the superhuman.

The first edition of the *Introduction* contains a prefatory letter to Germain de Ganay, one of the most important patrons of Lefèvre and other French humanists (Rice 1972, 20). The letter praises Aristotle for the comprehensive character of his works, covering both theory and practice, calling him a philosopher, a lawyer, and even "a priest and theologian" in his metaphysical writings (Lefèvre 1494, a2r; Rice 1972, 23).[4] Lefèvre, then, discusses the new format of the short introduction (*ars brevissima*). He argues that through its brevity "we might acquire in short time

---

4 "Sacerdos et theologus."

that which without art we could not even have begun to perceive" (Keßler 1989, 16).[5] His teaching technique includes three components: questions, elements, and precepts.

> For in questioning we ask what is worth knowing about every virtue. The elements digest and resolve. The precepts of duty, however, which we may call short sentences, display the duties and resemble certain laws for a life of happiness (Keßler 1989, 16).[6]

After the prefatory letter, the reader finds a table of contents with the arguments that will follow (*sequentium tabula*) (Lefèvre 1494, a2r–v) before the text begins, introduced by the title *Jacobi fabri stapulensis ars moralis in magna moralia aristotelis introductoria* (Lefèvre 1494, a3r). The next editions of the *Introduction* corrected the faulty title, substituting "Great Ethics" (*magna moralia*) with "Nicomachean Ethics" (*Ethicen*). The work finishes with hortatory closing words (*peroratio exhortatoria*) (Lefèvre 1494, b8r).

The second edition of the *Introduction* appears as part of another printing enterprise regarding Aristotle's ethics, *Decem librorum Moralium Aristotelis tres conversiones*, published by Johann Higman and Wolfgang Hopyl in Paris in 1496–1497 (Aristotle 1496–1497). Not only does the volume contain three translations of the *Ethics* by John Argyropoulos, Leonardo Bruni, and the "old translator" Robert Grosseteste, but also Lefèvre's commentary on the *Ethics* as well as Giorgio Valla's translation of the *Great Ethics*. Moreover, it contains Bruni's *Isagoge*, an introductory dialogue to moral philosophy, and Lefèvre's *Introduction*, now entitled *Artificialis Introductio per modum Epitomatis In decem libros Ethicorum Aristotelis* in the list of contents (Aristotle 1496–1497, E6v).

The edition adds new paratexts. Two poems appear for the first time, Lefèvre's *Virtutis Syncriticum carmen* (Aristotle 1496–1497, E6v), addressed to the court historian Paolo Emili, and Battista Mantovano's *Querela Virtutis* (Aristotle 1496–1497, a1r), an excerpt from his *De calamitatibus temporum*, written in 1479 (Mantovano 1916).

The reader also finds a second prefatory letter to Germain de Ganay, in which Lefèvre better explains his concept of the "introductory arts" (*artes introductoriae*) (Aristotle 1496–1497, a2r). He compares them to "paths" (*semitae*) that lead very

---

5 "Parvo tempore ea consequamur quae sine arte vix etiam multo percipere valeamus" (Lefèvre 1494, a2r; Rice 1972, 23).
6 "Quaestionibus enim quae circa unamquamque virtutum cognoscere dignum est sciscitamur. Elementa digerunt atque dissolvunt. Apophthegmata vero officiorum (quas breves sententias dicere possumus) officia praebent suntque tamquam beatae vitae certae leges" (Lefèvre 1494, a2r; Rice 1972, 23).

gradually and without any haste (*ocy[osi]ssime*) to one's destination without making errors on the way (*sine viarum erroribus*). The disciplines, instead, are similar to beautiful fields, but as inviting as they are, one has to know one's way around them. For without any knowledge of the paths leading through them, it is difficult to make progress—or to find our way out (*non facile progressum egressumve reperiamus*) (Aristotle 1496–1497, a2r). The *Introduction* is a guidebook in the literal sense, meant to give readers the conceptual lay of the land.

3 The Wolfenbüttel Copy: Description of the Title Page

The first impression of the Wolfenbüttel copy of the *Introduction* is striking (fig. 1).[7] It is striking because it offers a title page on which the printed parts are almost crowded out by the handwritten notes around the text column. I use the term "title page" for the *recto* page of the first folio in a loose way since, in the strict sense, there is no separation (*Separierung*) between the work's title and its beginning, one of the criteria used to define title pages in early printed books (Rautenberg 2008, 17). Nonetheless, the fact that the page is still firmly embedded in the media ecology of medieval manuscripts only strengthens the argument made about the role the annotations play in its make-up. Their strong presence singles the page out among others, an impression that will be confirmed by the analysis of the annotations' contents.

Before turning to the annotations, a short description of the printed elements on the page is in order. There are three such elements. The first is the book title, set in Rotunda blackletter script: *Compendiaria in Aristotelis ethicen introductio rei litterarie studiosis apprime utilis*. Below is a second title, set in Antiqua script: *Iacobi Stapulensis Introductio in Ethicen Aristotelis, ad studiosum uirum Germanum de Ganay, decanum Bellovacensem et Consiliarium Regium*. This second title belongs to the prefatory letter to Germain de Ganay. In fact, the letter constitutes the third printed element on the page, beginning with the words: [D]*ignissime vir, cum humana vita duobus ...* (Lefèvre 1501, a1r; see Rice 1972, 23–24). The title page contains no metadata on the printer, the place of print, or the year of print. All of this information is found in the colophon: "The present methodical in-

---

7 HF is available as digital copy online. See http://diglib.hab.de/drucke/41-3-quod-4f-8s/start.htm (last accessed July 15, 2022).

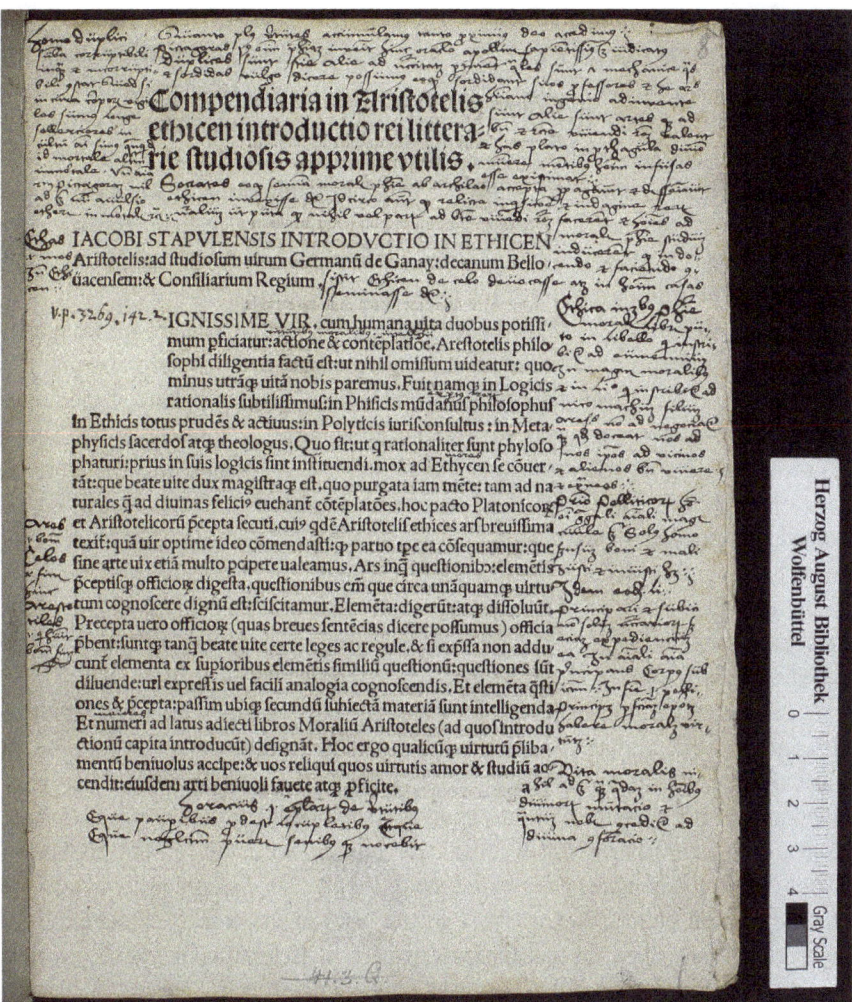

Fig. 1: Jacques Levèfre d'Étaples, *In Aristotelis Ethicen Introductio* (Vienna: Winterburger, 1501), Title Page (Wolfenbüttel, Herzog August Bibliothek, A: 41.3 Quod.)

troduction to the ten books of Aristotle's *Ethics* has been successfully brought to an end in the nourishing University of Vienna, 1501" (Lefèvre 1501: b6v).[8]

---

[8] "Presens Artificialis introductio in decem libros morales Aristotelis feliciter suum fine[m] assecuta est in alma Viennesiium [sic] academia 1501." The colophon is an exact copy of the 1496 version of the *Introductio* in Lefèvre's commented edition of the *Ethics* in three translations (Aristotle 1496–1497, a10v). Winterburger simply substituted "Parhisiorum" with "Viennesiium" as the loca-

Returning to the annotations, they start in the upper left corner of the page, resume on the top margin above the work's title and surround it before they continue on the outside margin and the bottom margin. Some smaller annotations are inscribed on the inside margin. The margins of the page accommodate eleven annotations in total, all in the same handwriting and separated by small labels or flourishes. There is one more annotation in the handwriting of Duke August set in the blank space reserved for the lacking initial letter, referencing the "companion" volume 142.2 Quod., containing Lefèvre's introductory works to Aristotle's natural philosophy, on page 3269 of his book wheel catalogue.[9]

What is certain, however, is that the annotations on the page result from a lesson, most probably a dictation of essential parts of the teacher's presentation. The oral character of the transmission is inferable from the misspelling of the names "Protagoras" as "Prothagula" in note 4 and "Eudemum" as "Eumemium" in note 6. As I will show below, note 4 is taken from another Lefèvre text, the dedicatory letter to Jean de Rely in his 1496–1497 edition of the *Ethics*. Had the student simply copied from the letter, he would not have misspelled the name, a problem common in early modern classrooms. Heinrich Julius Scheurl, for one, teacher of moral philosophy at the University of Helmstedt, reports that his students asked him to dictate his lectures to avoid mistakes regarding proper names (*ne scilicet ... in excipiendis nominibus propriis error forte committeretur*) (Scheurl 1648, (:)2v).

Other signs of their being from a lecture are the very few interlinear annotations and the two annotations on the inside margin. Unlike the other notes on the page, they refer to the printed text. When Lefèvre writes, for example, that a fulfilled human life depends both on action and contemplation (*actione et contemplatione*), the student paraphrases these two concepts with "moral and intellectual virtues" (*virtutibus moralibus et intellectualibus*). When Lefèvre describes Aristotle, the natural philosopher, as "wise in the ways of the world" (*mundanus*), the interlinear note gives the paraphrase "expert in [scientific] matters" (*expertus rerum*). The term "*Ethycen* [sic]" is given a Latin rendering as "*mores*," in concordance with note 12, on the left of the title, which explains that "Ethos stands for custom" (*Ethos, id est mos*) and gives the Greek declension of the term "in the *Ethics*" (*In Ethicen*). The last interlinear annotation regards the advice that "the numbers added in the margins indicate the books of the *Ethics*" (*numeri ad latus adiecti li-*

---

tion. Another hint that Winterburger used the 1496 version of the *Introduction* is hidden in the salutation of Germain de Ganay; while the *editio princeps* addresses him as "royal counsellor and deacon of Beauvais" (Aristotle 1496–1497, a2r), the later imprint reverses these titles and uses the formula "deacon of Beauvais and royal counsellor" (Lefèvre 1496, a1v).

9 This suggests that the *sammelband* containing the *Introduction* came into the duke's possession after 1641 (Katte 1972, 180).

bros Moralium Aristoteles ... designant). The student adds *"maiores"* to *"numeri"* (greater numbers) to clarify that Lefèvre speaks of the Roman numerals in the margins, written with a larger script, and not of the smaller Arabic numerals in the text. The last note with a plain explanatory character is note 11, which is situated in the middle of the inner margin. It gives the (invented) etymology of the name Aristotle, arguing that *"Ares* means *bonum; Telos* means end, therefore [the name] Arestotiles [sic] means he who had a good end."[10]

In what follows, I will read annotations 1–9 on the margins clockwise from the top left corner to the bottom of the page. There is no way to confirm that this is the actual order in which the annotations were written down; as will become obvious, however, they can be read in different directions.

4 A Portion of the Aether

The first note reads:

> Human beings are composed of two substances, that is to say [one that is] corruptible and [one that is] incorruptible. Now if we are attentive to the care of our bodies, let us be much more accomplished in the cultivation of our souls, for one is mortal, the other immortal. Whence, according to Pythagoras, the soul is nothing else but a detached portion of the aether, immortal in kind (WF, a1r).[11]

The twofold nature of human beings is one of the most important concepts of premodern thought about the human being. Nevertheless, there are different ways to conceptualize this duality. Aristotle, for one, is mainly interested in the duality of—and at the same time, the complex interplay between—body and soul. Essentially, the soul is supposed to rule over the body and the rational part of the soul over its irrational parts.

The note does not reflect Aristotle's position, however. Although Aristotle would agree with the note's emphasis on the necessity of cultivating one's soul, the points made about mortality and immortality seem outside the scope of the *Ethics*. Arguments about the immortality of the soul were not exactly a strong suit of Peripatetic thought. In fact, the note evokes a different authority to give support to the close relationship between care for the soul and its immortality, Pythagoras.

---

10 "Ares, idest bonum; Telos, idest finis; hinc Arestotiles, idest qui habuit bonum finem."
11 "Homo duplici substantia, corruptibili inquam et incorruptibili, constat. Quod si in cura corporum vigiles sumus, longe sollertiores in cultum animi simus quiaquidem id mortale, alterum inmortale. Unde anima secundum Pittagoram nil aliud est nisi avulsio etheris inmortalis rationis."

Already in medieval encyclopedias, Pythagoras of Samos (c. 570–c. 500 BCE) appeared as the inventor of philosophy—a point to which we will return—and was thought to have been "one of the first to conceive of the soul as immortal—even though his doctrine on the transmigration of the souls is not Christian" (Robert 2022, 234). Aquinas notes Pythagoras' "interest in the immortality of the soul," albeit critically (Borgo and Costa 2022, 351). Closer to the 16th century, Pythagoras was praised by Marsilio Ficino and others as a believer in the immortality of souls and, through his disciples, as the teacher of Plato, another champion of the immortal soul (Celenza 1999). Nonetheless, to my knowledge, Ficino never speaks of the soul as a detached portion of the aether, but only alludes to a famous Pythagorean maxim in the *Golden Verses*: "If you leave the body and come to the free aether, / You will be deathless, an undying god, no longer mortal" (Laks and Most 2016, R35, 393, and Ficino 2001, 18.8, 120–121).

The passage that the note cites is found in the 3rd-century biographer Diogenes Laertius' *Lives and Opinions of the Eminent Philosophers* (*Vitae et sententiae philosophorum*):

> Everything that partakes of heat is alive, which is why plants are living things. But not all living things have soul. The soul is a detached portion of the aether [ἀπόσπασμα αἰθέρος], partly the hot and partly the cold; and because it participates also in the cold aether the soul is distinct from life. It is immortal, since that from which it has been detached is immortal (Diogenes Laertius 2018, 8.28, 406).[12]

There is little doubt that the note cites Laertius' biographical work directly or indirectly. The central concept, "a detached portion of the aether" (*avulsio aetheris*) is a signature term that clearly indicates its origin. And at the beginning of the 16th century, the Latin translation by Ambrogio Traversari (1386–1439), finished in 1433, had circulated both in manuscript and book form; the *editio princeps* was published c. 1472.

One reason Ficino would not use the theory of "*avulsio*" as an argument for the immortality of the soul might be found in its presence in Stoic philosophy and the problems it brought to light. Similar to the theory of the migration of souls, the idea that the soul was part of the cold, immortal aether had advantages

---

[12] The *editio princeps* of Ambrogio Traversari's Latin translation renders the passage as follows: "Vivere item omnia queque colori [sic] participent atque ideo et arbores esse animantes, animam tamen non habere; omnes animam vero avulsionem etderis [sic]. Differre autem a vita animam esseque illam immortalem quandoquidem et id a quo avulsa est immortale sit" (Diogenes Laertius 1472, 103v). The next editions would correct the misspelling of "*aetheris*". Laertius quotes this and other passages in Book VIII from Alexander Polyhistor's *Successions of the Philosophers*. Alexander, again, reports from the Pythagorean *Hypomnemata* (Laks 2013).

and serious drawbacks, and they became visible in the writings of Seneca and Cicero.

For the Stoics, the rational self was a portion or part of the living cosmos: "[the cosmos] is endowed with a soul, as is clear from the fact that each of our souls is a fragment [ἀπόσπασμα] of it" (Diogenes Laertius 2018, 7.143, 363; see Algra 2003, 176). Seneca falls back on this idea when he discusses the inquisitive disposition (*curiosum ingenium*) of human beings in *On Leisure* (*De otio*). Describing their innate curiosity for hidden truths, he concludes his thoughts with the biggest secret of all: "whether that theory is true which strives especially to prove that man is part of the divine spirit, that some part, sparks, as it were, of the stars fell down to earth and lingered here in a place that is not their own" (Seneca 1932, 5.5, 192–193).[13] At the end of the 16th century, the philologist, scholar, and librarian Jan Gruter (Janus Gruterus; 1560–1627) will comment on this passage in his *Animadversiones*, first published in 1594, with a reference to Pythagoras: "I think that Pythagoras was the first to argue that the soul is a portion or a part of the aether" (Seneca 1605, 256–257).

Gruter was interested in a philological problem, the emendation of *sacrorum* to *astrorum* in Seneca's text, but others were more critical. In his *Scholia* to the *Letters* of Jerome, the Italian humanist and theologian Mariano Vittori (1485–1572) connected the mention of Pythagoras in Letter 133 to Ctesiphon to his theory of *avulsio*. Jerome asks,

> Can there be greater presumption than to claim not likeness to God but equality with Him, and so to compress into a few words the poisonous doctrines of all the heretics which in their turn flow from the statements of the philosophers, particularly of Pythagoras and Zeno, the founder of the Stoic school? (Jerome 1893, 272).[14]

While Jerome strikes out against the Stoic notion of *apatheia*, a state of mind in which one is not disturbed by the passions, Vittori complains that

> Pythagoras ... equated human beings with God, and argued that they were of his substance. Diogenes [Laertius] maintains that Pythagoras argued that the soul was a portion of the aether, and therefore immortal, as it had been taken from something immortal. I think he called

---

13 "An illud verum sit, quo maxime probatur homines divini esse spiritus, partem ac veluti scintillas quasdam astrorumin terram desiluisse atque alieno loco haesisse."
14 "Quae enim potest alia major esse temeritas, quam Dei sibi non dicam similitudinem, sed aequalitatem vindicare, et brevi sententia omnium Haereticorum venena complecti, quae de Philosophorum et maxime Pythagorae et Zenonis principis Stoicorum fonte manarunt?" (Jerome 1845, 1148).

all the stars, and even more so the aether, from which the stars are made, God (Jerome 1565, 395).[15]

Vittori was not wrong. Seneca, for one, fully recognized the divine element in every human being. "Divine seeds are scattered throughout our mortal body," he writes in Letter 73 to Lucilius (Seneca 1920, 73.16, 112–113).[16] Of course, Seneca took the aethereal link to divinity Pythagoras had created not for granted, but attempted to integrate the idea of *avulsio* in spiritual exercises. Still, there was the problem of equating ourselves with God and of forgetting that it was not only the better angels of our nature to guide us.

Ficino seems to have been aware of the dangers connected with not claiming likeness but equality. In the passage on the *Golden Verses* in the *Platonic Theology* mentioned above, he writes: "The soul once born in the aether yearns for the aether, as Pythagoras says, especially if it has conceived in its mind a habit of living and of thinking that resembles that of aethereal minds" (Ficino 2001, 18.8, 120–121).[17] "Resembles," at the heart of the sentence, is a thought of *similitudo* and not of *aequalitas*.

Cicero, too, was aware of Pythagoras' theory of *avulsio*. In the "Stoic" fifth book of the *Tusculan Disputations*, he describes the soul of man as "plucked [*decerptus*] from the divine mind" and argues that it is comparable with "nothing else save God alone"—albeit with caution, "if it is right to say so" (Cicero 1927, 5.39, 464–465).[18] The aim is to show that virtue alone is sufficient for a happy life. In *On the Nature of the Gods*, instead, he turns the problem with the idea of *avulsio* around, not so much worried about the deification of human nature than the humanization of God:

> As for Pythagoras, who believed that the entire substance of the universe is penetrated and pervaded by a soul from which our souls are plucked [*carperentur*], he failed to notice that this severance of the souls of men from the world-soul means the dismemberment and rend-

---

15 "Pythagoras ... hominem Deo aequabat et de eius dicebat esse substantia. Diogenes, aetheris avulsionem esse animam, asserit dixisse Pythagoram, proptereaque immortalem, quod immortale esset id, a quo avulsa esset. Deos, ut sydera omnia, sic magis aethera, a quo sydera sunt, Deum appellasse illum existimo."
16 "Semina in corporibus humanis divina dispersa sunt."
17 "Ad aetherem aspirat anima nata quondam in aethere, ut inquit Pythagoras, praecipue si vivendi et cogitandi habitum aethereis mentibus similem mente conceperit."
18 "Humanus autem animus decerptus ex mente divina cum alio nullo nisi cum ipso deo, si hoc fas est dictu, comparari potest."

ing asunder of god; and that when their souls are unhappy, as happens to most men, then a portion of god is unhappy, which is impossible (Cicero 1933, 1. 27, 30–31).[19]

When the teacher dictated the short note on the immortality of the soul and Pythagoras' theory of *avulsio* in the classroom, neither they nor their students could have been aware of all the valences and theological implications of the citation. (It is probable, though, that the teacher was aware of the passage in the *Tusculan Disputations*, from which he also took the information found in notes 3 and 5). But that was not the point. I tend to see the note as a move, the beginning of a complex dance. And I think that the reason for the note is not sophisticated at all. Aristotle does not talk about the immortality of the soul; Pythagoras does, so let us bring in Pythagoras.

By writing down the note, the student adds something to the book. They begin to make it their own, and they begin to shape an idea about ethics. Ethics is soul-craft, but if the soul is immortal, it is not only about the mortal world. In this sense, the note goes against the careful limitation of ethics as belonging to this world the title page of the 1494 edition of the *Introduction* puts forward. It inscribes a transcendent dimension onto the page, into the text. This thought, however, needs a certain amount of calibration. In fact, the next notes attempt to further calibrate the relation between its various aspects.

5 Short Intermezzo: Moral Psychology

Before turning to note 2 on the title page, one caveat has to be made. So far, the discussion has concentrated on, for lack of a better word, the centrifugal powers of annotations—that is, annotations that do not lead straight into the text but try to give it another direction. As has been said, note 1 does not necessarily reflect Aristotle's position, and it actually does not have to. We are in the midst of inventive thinking, a thinking that lets authorities, thoughts, concepts galvanize each other. But that does not mean that Aristotle's position disappears. It is, as it were, re-established on the next *recto* page. Here, we find the following note in the upper righthand corner:

---

[19] "Nam Pythagoras, qui censuit animum esse per naturam rerum omnem intentum et commeantem, ex quo nostri animi carperentur, non vidit distractione humanorum animorum discerpi et lacerari deum, et cum miseri animi essent, quod plerisque contingeret, tum dei partem esse miseram, quod fieri non potest."

> The student of moral and political knowledge has to discuss the soul in every possible way. For someone who intends to treat the eye must know the body as a whole in some way. Therefore, the moral faculty must consider the soul, which it sets out to attend to, all the more so, as the soul is more estimable and nobler than the body [and] the moral faculty more distinguished than medicine (WF, a2r).[20]

This note, very probably part of a second lesson, echoes Aristotle's statement in the *Ethics* that the "student of political matters [πολιτικός, *civis*] ought to have some acquaintance with psychology, just as a doctor who intends to treat the eye must have a knowledge of the body as a whole" (Aristotle 1976, 88, 1.13.1102a18–21).[21] However, the note does not cite Aristotle, but Lefèvre's commentary on the text; the telltale sign is the substitution of the Latin translation's "*civis*" with the more elaborate "*moralis civilisque discipline studiosus*" in Lefèvre, rendered as "*moralis civilisque scientie studiosus*" in WF's note.[22]

The annotation states very clearly the importance of moral psychology and gets the discourse back on the Aristotelian track. Together with a series of other notes on the parts of the soul, all falling back on the same chapter of the *Ethics*, it offers an inroad into the Aristotelian text. It does so on the same page in which Lefèvre explains his ideas on *ars* as a path into the fields of knowledge. This may be incidental, but there is no doubt that the note interacts with other elements on the page.

The first of these elements is a poem by Master Paul Hug printed below Lefèvre's second dedicatory letter. Hug figures among the teachers of the Viennese arts faculty from 1500 onwards (Maisel and Matschinegg 2007).[23] In his *Hexastichon*

---

[20] "Moralis civilisque scientie studiosus de anima quoquo modo tractare habet. Nam qui curaturus est oculum totumque corpus aliquo pacto debet cognoscere. Igitur tanto magis moralis facultas animum debet considerare quam curare suscipit quanto ipsa honorabilior praestantiorque corpore tanto praestabilior medicinam."

[21] In the translation of John Argyropoulos. "Quae cum ita sint, patet ipsum civilem aliqua ex parte de anima scire oportere, quemadmodum et eum qui curaturus est oculos totumque corpus, de ipsis scire oportet. Et eo magis, quo facultas civilis honorabilor est atque praestabilior medicina. Elegantes etiam medici multa plane circa cognitionem corporis tractant, et civilis igitur ipse de anima contempletur oportet" (Aristotle 1496–1497, b5v).

[22] Lefèvre writes: "Correlarium. Unde fit ut moralis civilisque discipline studiosus quoquo pacto de anima habeat considerare. nam qui curaturus est oculum totumque corpus, ea quoquo pacto debet cognoscere. igitur tanto magis moralis facultas animum ipsum (quem curandum suscipit) habet considerare, quanto ea honorabilior praestantiorque quam ipsa medicina est" (Aristotle 1496–1497, b6r).

[23] The entries regarding Hug are: "11/11/1500 receives key to the library" (no. 22540); "14/2/1502 examiner of the Saxonian nation" (no. 22868); "10/6/1503 Paul Hugonus" is given the "*lectio metaphisices cum exercitio*" as "*stipendiatus collegii Lilii, quod vulgo bursa Lilii appelatur*" (no. 23354); "26/

Magistri Pauli Hug quo philosophia moralis lectorem alloquitur, Hug lets moral philosophy readily admit that she shares some common ground with medicine, but only to underline its superior nature. While medicine cures pale bodies and helps them to recover from their illnesses, moral philosophy seeks to make good the disturbed soul (WF, a2r). The second element is a handwritten note to the left of the poem. "Paulus: the flesh desires what is contrary to the spirit [Gal. 5:17] and sensuality [turns] against reason. If reason wins, virtue breaks forth through continence, and vice versa" (WF, a2r).[24] Like the above note on the crucial role of psychology in moral philosophy and the poem by Hug, this note establishes a clear hierarchy between body and soul, undergirding it with a biblical citation.

6 Closer to You, My God

The second note is shorter than the first. It consists of only one sentence:

The more virtues we accumulate, the closer we will get to God (WF, a1r).[25]

This is a sententious rendering of a passage in the *Dicta Albini de imagine Dei*, a short treatise going back to the late 5th or early 6th century (Bullough 1991). The treatise discusses the passage of Genesis which describes the final creative act of the sixth day of creation: "Then God said, 'Let us make human beings in our image and likeness'" (Gen. 1:26).[26] In fact, parts of the work resurfaced in *Charles' Books* (*Libri Carolini*), a work in four books aimed at refuting the conclusions of the Byzantine Second Council of Nicaea (787) regarding the place of images in Christian worship. It was probably around this time that the little treatise came to the attention of Alcuin of York (735–804), a leading scholar and teacher at the Carolingian court of the mid-790s. Alcuin was nicknamed Albinus and therefore thought to be its author, a hypothesis that has ultimately been discredited in the scholarship (Lebech, McEvoy, and Flood 2009, 4–6).

Regarding their transmission history, the *Dicta Albini* make up part of a group of passages which had their origin at the Palace School of Charlemagne. John Mar-

---

2/1504 examiner of the Hungarian nation (no. 23524); 14/2/1505 deputee of the faculty" (no. 23898); "1/9/1505 Paulus Hugonius "*necessitudinem legendi grisaorio praedicabilia*" (?)" (no. 24147).
24 "Caro concupiscit adversus spiritum et sensualitas contra rationem. Si ratio vincit, continentia virtus emergit, et contrarium e contrario."
25 "Quanto plus virtutes accumulamus tanto proximius deo accedimus."
26 "Et ait Deus: 'Faciamus hominem ad imaginem et similitudinem nostram.'"

enbon named this set of materials "the Munich passages" after the place where the manuscript is most fully preserved (Marenbon 1981, 31–32). Included in the Munich passages is another short treatise on the same topic, the *Dicta Candidi*. Both works began to circulate under the title *On the dignity of the human condition* (*De dignitate conditionis humanae*), "sandwiching the *Dicta Candidi* in between the *Dicta Albini*'s discussion of the image of God (*imago Dei*) and his likeness (*similitudo Dei*)" (Lebech, McEvoy, and Flood 2009, 12).

At the time of the Winterburger edition of Lefèvre's *Introduction*, the *Dicta Albini* was present both in manuscript and print. Following certain strands of the manuscript tradition, however, they did not circulate under the name of Albinus or Candidus in print, but were attributed to Ambrose and Augustine (Marenbon 1981, 148). In the works of St. Ambrose, published in 1492 by Amerbach, the two combined treatises appeared under the title *Qua ratione homini tanta dignitas sit collata* (Ambrose 1492, g2v). They were also printed as *De creatione primi hominis* in the tenth volume of the monumental 1505–1506 edition of St. Augustine's *Opera* (Augustine 1506, X2r).[27] When Erasmus re-edited the *Opera*, in 1529, he still included the *De creatione*, adding the critical remark that "this seems to be a fragment; its author is unknown to me" (Augustine 1529, 810).[28]

Despite this wealth of information, it is difficult to pinpoint the exact origin of note 2, as it is not a direct quotation but takes on the concise form of a maxim. This suggests it could have also been taken from a commonplace book. Still, it should be mentioned that the printed editions follow a version of the text that differs from parts of the manuscript tradition. The text in the Munich passages reads: "The more someone has these virtues in himself, the more he is special [*proprius*] to God, and the greater is the likeness he bears to the Creator" (Lebech, McEvoy, and Flood 2009, 5).[29] The editions of Ambrose and Augustine, instead, both read "the more someone has these virtues in himself, the closer [*propius, propinquior*] he is to God."[30] The saying circulated at least until the second half of the 16th century. The Italian jurist Pietro Folliero (1518–1588) still used it in his *Canonica crim-*

---

27 "Divi aurelii augustini hipponensis episcopi tractatus de creatione primi hominis incipit." The *Opera* are among the most complex editions of the early sixteenth century. Luckily, we have a recent bibliographical description that is both extensive and detailed (Sebastiani 2018, 146–157).
28 "Fragmentum esse videtur nescio cuius."
29 "Quas uirtutes, quanto plus quisque in seipso habet, tanto proprius est Deo, et maiorem sui conditoris gerit similitudinem" (Marenbon 1981, 160).
30 "Quas virtutes quanto plus quisque in seipso habet : tanto propius est deo : et maiorem sui conditoris gerit similitudine" (Ambrose 1492, g3v); "Quas virtutes, quanto plus habet in seipso, tanto propinquior est deo, et maiorem sui conditoris similitudinem gerit" (Augustine 1506, X2r; Augustine 1529, 510).

inalis praxis, where he ascribed it to Plato: "The more everyone is adorned with the other virtues, the closer they get to God, as Plato maintains in the best and wisest way possible" (Follerio 1570, a2v).[31] Around the same time, the maxim still appears in editions of Ambrose's *Works* (Ambrose 1586, D4v).[32]

Returning to the classroom, the teacher and the student reading the *Introduction* obviously did not have all of this background knowledge. My guess is that the teacher had excerpted the saying from Ambrose, or had taken it from a collection of excerpts, as Ambrose appears in still another note in WF.[33] But while teacher and student would have had only a vague idea of the textual tradition from which the note derived, they certainly had a much clearer notion of its doctrinal dimension. The note evokes, after all, a long tradition that connects our likeness to God with our exercise of the virtues (Willeke 2003, 140). As the *Dicta Albini* puts it, this likeness "can be detected in right conduct" (Lebech, McEvoy, and Flood 2009, 25).[34] The sentence taken from the *Dicta* is, in fact, the culmination of an argument regarding the virtuousness that connects God with us humans:

> Just as God, the Creator who created the human being to his likeness, is charity, is good and just, is patient and mild, pure and merciful, and the other distinctive marks of holy virtues which can be read of, so the human being was created in such a way as to have charity, to be good and just, to be patient and mild, pure and merciful (Lebech, McEvoy, and Flood 2009, 25).[35]

Reconnecting this thought to note 1, we have to take care of our immortal soul not so much because it *is* divine but rather because it enables us to come closer to God and, in a sense, *become like* God—Plato's ὁμοίωσις θεῷ, which will make its appearance in note 8. For now, it is important to underline that note 2 is a concise

---

[31] "Quanto enim quisque caeteris est virtutibus ornatior, tanto propius accessit ad Deum, quod optime et sapientissime affirmat Plato."
[32] The "Index rerum et verborum" mentions the saying as "homo quanto virtutibus ornatior est, tanto est Deo vicinior."
[33] "[In] Ambrose [we read:] The Romans wear the figure of the moon, that is *fortuna*, on their shoes" (Ambrosius romani portant figuram Lune, idest fortunam, in calceis) (WF, a3r). I have not been able to identify the origin of this saying in Ambrose. However, the custom is confirmed by other sources. "Plutarch tells us that Romans of his day—in the 1st century CE—wore a lunar-shaped trinket on their shoes as a reminder that the fortunes of humankind are as mutable as the Moon" (Ní Mheallaigh 2020, 64).
[34] "In moribus cernenda est" (Marenbon 1981, 160).
[35] "Vt sicut Deus creator, qui hominem ad similitudinem suam creauit, est caritas, est bonus et iustus, paciens atque mitis, mundus et misericors, et cetera uirtutum sanctarum insignia quae de Deo leguntur, ita homo creatus est ut caritatem haberet, ut bonus esset et iustus, ut paciens atque mitis, mundus et misericors foret" (Marenbon 1981, 160).

expression of the idea that ethics, right conduct, *mores*, are not as mundane as they seem but have a distinct religious dimension, transcending the limits of human existence in this world.

7 The Invention of Morality

The following three notes contain what I would describe as a genealogy of ethics:

> 3. Pythagoras was the first to discover philosophy, hence the Apollinic oracle held him to be the wisest [of all men] (WF, a1r).[36]
>
> 4. There are two kinds of disciplines; some are founded on utility, such are, in fact, the mechanical [arts], commonly said to be sordid because they stain their practitioners, and these arts are an invention of human ingenuity; others are the arts that are good for living well and in the right way, and in the [*Protagoras*] Plato considers them to be granted to the minds of humans by divine gift (WF, a1r).[37]
>
> 5. Because he propagated and scattered the very seeds of moral philosophy he had received from Archelaus, Socrates is said to have introduced ethics [as a discipline]. ... It is said that he called down ethics from the heavens and planted it in human homes.[38]

The genealogy begins with Pythagoras, described as the "inventor" of philosophy according to an anecdote that was best available to readers in Cicero's *Tusculan Disputations* (Cicero 1927, 5.8–10, 433–435) and Augustine's *City of God* (Augustine 1952, 8.2, 22). The source is probably Cicero given that note 5, which mentions Socrates and his teacher Archelaus, also draws heavily on the *Tusculan Disputations*. The remark on the Delphic oracle and its judgement of Pythagoras as the wisest

---

[36] "Pittagoras primus enim philosophiam invenit, hinc oraculo apollinis sapientissimus iudicatus est."

[37] "Duplices sunt scientie, alie ad utilitatem pertinent, quales sunt enim mechanice, quas et sordidas vulgo dicere possumus eo quod sordidant suos professores et he artes humano ingenio adinvente sunt; alie sunt artes que ad bene et recte vivendi rationem valent et has plato in prothagula divino munere mentibus hominum infusas esse existimat."

[38] "Socrates, eo quod semina moralis philosophie ab archilao accepta propagavit et disseminavit, ethicen invexisse dicitur. ... Idcirco autem quod Ethicen de celo deuocasse atque in hominum casas seminasse dicitur." I have only a vague understanding of the middle part of this note, probably because I misread the handwriting: "Idcirco aiunt (?) quod relicta inquisitione et indagine rerum naturalium ut puta quod nihil vel parum ad beate vivendi rationem facerent et homines ad moralis philosophie studium inducerent quod in docendo et faciendo consistit." Based on the expression "*docendo et faciendo*," one probable source for the passage is the *Silvae morales*: "moralemque philosophiam, quam Aethicam vocant, docendo et faciendo instituisset" (Bade van Assche 1492, 4r).

man seems like a misattribution, as the story normally referred to Socrates (Bowden 2005, 82).

Note 4 may be inspired by Pythagoras' remark, reported by Cicero, that he had "no acquaintance with any art, but was a philosopher" (Cicero 1927, 5.8, 432–433).[39] Distinguishing between mechanic and liberal arts, Pythagoras' description of philosophy resembles the idea of liberal arts presented in the note. The description of the mechanical arts as "sordid" is a commonplace of the literature. Clichtove describes them as "servile" (*serviles*) and "impure" (*adulterinae*) in his commentary (Lefèvre 1506, 43). The direct reference to Plato and the *Protagoras*, misspelled as "Protaghula," derives from Lefèvre's dedicatory epistle to Jean de Relay in his edition of the *Ethics* (Aristotle 1496–1497, a1v) and reproposes, albeit in an indirect manner, the bipolarity of an ethics orientated towards what is human and divine in us.[40]

In note 5, Socrates takes the last step towards moral philosophy. As Pythagoras is the inventor of philosophy, he is the inventor of ethics, shifting the focus of philosophical research from an inquiry into the secrets of nature to the good life. The new focus of philosophy is happiness (*beate vivere*).

8 Aristotle's Practical Philosophy

The preceding notes give the prehistory of moral philosophy and set the scene for the protagonist of Lefèvre's *Introductio,* Aristotle. Pythagoras and Socrates create new spaces for thought, one by setting philosophy free from the necessities of daily life and the lower arts, the other by focusing the philosopher's gaze on the human world. It is up to Aristotle, however, to meet the challenge and write an all-encompassing, definitive treatment of ethics:

> 6. Ethics: In the three books on moral philosophy—that is, in the little book entitled [*Eudemian*] *Ethics,* in the *Great Ethics,* and in the book that is entitled *Nicomachean Ethics,* Aristotle's whole business is to teach how to live well with regard to ourselves, our neighbors, and strangers and foreigners (WF, a1r).[41]

---

[39] "At illum artem quidem se scire nullam, sed esse philosophum."
[40] "Platonis in Protagora sententia videtur esse eas artes que ad victum pertinent humanum providentia humanam reperisse, que autem ad bene beateque vivendum summi dei munere mentibus mortalium infusas esse."
[41] "Ethica in tribus philosophie moralis libris, puto in Libello qui inscribitur ad eumemium, in magnis moralibus et in libro qui inscribitur ad nicomachum filium aristoteles non aliud negociatur quam quod doceat nos ad nos ipsos, ad vicinos et alienos [et extraneos] bene vivere." (In the note, "*et extraneus*" is added below "*et alienos*.")

Ethics is not only an individual enterprise but rather a practical activity that concerns the whole of society and even those outside one's familiar surroundings. As a consequence, ethics and politics are closely intertwined, and the *Politics* becomes an essential part of Aristotle's practical philosophy:

> 7. In the first book of the *Politics*, [Aristotle writes that] humans are more political than any gregarious animal. In the same book, [he also writes] that some rule and others be ruled is a thing not only necessary but expedient. In living beings, the soul is the ruling part, and the body is under its authority. At the end of the first book of the *Politics*, [he writes] that the ruler must have perfect moral virtue (WF, a1r).⁴²

The note combines three passages with citations from the *Politics* in the translation of William of Moerbeke.⁴³ The first one regards Aristotle's famous description of the human being as a political animal (ζῷον πολιτικόν). For Aristotle, human beings are "political" to a greater measure than any other animal because they have the gift of speech. While other animals can express pain and pleasure, they cannot form concepts about what is advantageous and harmful to them. Therefore, they do not have a notion of wrong and right. Accordingly, it is the "special property" of human beings that "[they] alone [have] perception of good and bad and right and wrong and the other moral qualities" (*Politics* 1.2.1253a16–18 = Aristotle 1932, 11).⁴⁴

The second passage argues that "authority and subordination are conditions not only inevitable but also expedient" (Aristotle 1932, 1.5 1254a21–24, 19).⁴⁵ Aristotle's statement that all human beings are *not* born equal but "marked out from the moment of birth to rule or to be ruled" (Aristotle 1932, 1.5 1254a21–24, 19) is certain-

---

42 "Primo Polliticorum homo omni gregali animali magis ciuile est. Solus homo sensum boni et mali Justi et iniusti habet. Idem eodem Libro principari et subici non solum necessarium sed etiam expedientium ea. In animali anima principans Corpus subiectum. In fine .1. polli. Principem perfectam oportet habere moralem virtutem."
43 Leonardo Bruni's translation employs a different vocabulary. In rendering *Pol.* 1.5 1254a21–24, for example, he uses *"imperare"* and *"parere"* instead of *"principari"* and *"subiici"* as well as *"utilium"* instead of *"expedientium"* (Aristotle 1568, 5).
44 "Quod autem civile animal homo, omni ape et omni gregali animali magis, palam. Nihil enim, ut aiunt, frustra natura facit: sermonem autem solus habet homo super animalia. Vox quidem igitur delectabilis et tristabilis est signum, propter quod et aliis existit animalibus: usque enim ad hoc enim natura eorum pervenit, ut habeant sensum tristabilis et delectabilis; et hoc significant invicem. Sermo autem est in ostendendo conferens et nocivum. Quare et iustum et iniustum. *Hoc enim ad alia animalia habent, hominibus proprium solum, boni et mali, iusti et iniusti et aliorum sensum habere.* Horum autem communicatio facit domum et civitatem" (Aquinas 1966, 5, my emphasis).
45 "Principari enim et subiici, non solum necessariorum sed etiam expedientium est" (Aquinas 1966, 17).

ly among the most difficult statements to accept in Aristotle's moral and political thought for modern readers, although "the elitism that is present in his ethical theories is usually ignored" (Leunissen 2017, xv). In the case of the present note, the model of authority and subordination is immediately translated to the relationship between body and soul in the individual, following Aristotle's argument that "an animal consists primarily of soul and body, of which the former is by nature the ruling and the latter the subject factor" (Aristotle 1932, 1.2 1254a34–36, 21).[46]

The third passage states that "the ruler must possess [moral] virtue in completeness" (Aristotle 1932, 1.13 1260a15, 63).[47] In the *Politics*, it stands at the end of the discussion of the relationship between natural ruler and subject regarding the question whether "virtue [is] the same for ruler and ruled, or different" (Aristotle 1932, 1.13 1259b33–34, 61). Aristotle's answer is that slaves do not possess the deliberative element (βουλευτικόν, *consiliativum*) at all, while it has no real power in women and still has to be developed in children (Aristotle 1932, 1.13 1260a13–14, 63). Hence, the "completeness" of the free, male, adult ruler's virtue stands in contrast with a variety of "defective" states of virtue in slaves, women, and children.

In the context of the Renaissance reception of Aristotle, these points played no role, and the superiority of some parts of society over others was not questioned. The very notion of virtue implied inequality, as it was used as a marker of social distinction. Teacher and student follow "orthodoxy," in our modern view, uncritically. Nevertheless, their framing of ethics as a social and political, and not merely as an individual enterprise, is remarkable—not to them, but to us. I am not saying this in a nostalgic manner, playing out our individualism against their sense of community and pleading for a return to the old ways. I am saying this to render visible how the simple, seemingly innocent act of writing down a quite ordinary annotation is, at the same time, a tool of extraordinary power. Stroke for stroke, scribble for scribble, the student creates their own miniature and makes the volume in their hands their own. Every annotation, as common as it may be, shapes their view of the world inside and outside the classroom.

---

[46] "Animal autem primum constat ex anima et corpore; quorum haec quidem principans est natura, hoc autem subiectum" (Aquinas 1966, 18).

[47] "Principem quidem perfectam habere oportet moralem virtutem" (Aquinas 1966, 47). The Loeb edition does not follow the manuscript tradition and the early modern printings of the *Politics* and substitutes "moral virtue" with "intellectual virtue" (Aristotle 1932: 62).

9 What Is Good for You?

With note 8, we have arrived at the lower righthand corner of the page. Diametrically opposite note 1, which celebrates the human soul as a detached piece of the immortal aether, it takes up one last time the leitmotif of the annotations, the relationship between human action and divine imprint:

> 8. The moral life is nothing other than an imitation of divine things in humans and, so far as it is allowed to us, a modelling of what is divine (WF, a1r).[48]

The note has, without a doubt, a strong Platonic character. The idea of "modelling what is divine," in Latin *"divina conformatio,"* echoes if not translates Plato's famous idea of ὁμοίωσις θεῷ, a process of assimilation that allows us to "become like God." In the *Theaetetus*, central to all later writings in the Neoplatonic tradition, Socrates argues that

> we ought to try to escape from earth to the dwelling of the gods as quickly as we can; and to escape is to become like God, so far as this is possible; and to become like God is to become righteous and holy and wise (Plato 1926, 176a–b, 128–129).

Ficino translates the central part of the sentence, "to escape is to become like God," as *"fuga autem est, ut Deo similes pro viribus efficiamur"* (Plato 1782, 121). Again, the topic of image and likeness, of *imago* and *similitudo*, implicit in note 2, turns up. To become like God, we need to conduct ourselves in the right way.[49] This means, however, that we are not ethical creatures solely out of necessity. Instead, ethics is at the core of our anthropological make-up. Even though it may sound fanciful, note 8 is, in its own way, an answer to the challenge of the divine spark posed in note 1 and a companion to note 2.

Notwithstanding these observations, there is still a little twist to the note: It is a literal quotation from Lefèvre's commentary on the *Ethics* (Aristotle 1496–97, a3r) when he discusses the question of how exactly to translate the first sentence of the *Ethics:* "Every art and every investigation, and similarly every action and pursuit, is considered to aim at some good. Hence the Good (τἀγαθόν) has been rightly defined as 'that at which all things aim'" (Aristotle 1976, 1.1.1094a1–3, 63). The problem is the translation of "τἀγαθόν"—that is, "ἀγαθόν" with the definite article "τὸ."

---

[48] "Vita moralis nihil aliud est quam quedam in hominibus divinorum imitatio et quantum nobis conceditur ad divina conformatio."
[49] *"Conformatio* is used from early on to speak of the Christian's alignment of will and being with Christ" (Herdt 2019, 29).

Latin lacks definite articles, which led to differing solutions when translating the passage. Leonardo Bruni translates it as "supreme good," "*summum bonum*," for "because of the Greek definite article ... he clearly sensed a higher meaning" (Aristotle 1496–97, a3r). Argyropoulos, instead, rendered τάγαθόν as "good itself," "*bonum ipsum*." Without going into further philological details, Lefèvre sees the occasion to reflect on the idea of imitation and likeness and the divine sense that is, according to him, enclosed in both translations. And although Lefèvre identifies conforming to God as central to the human aspiration for the good life, he is quite aware about its limits. He likens our desire to become like God to someone who observes the world bathed in the light of the sun and sees all things striving for it in a "beautiful competition" (*pulchro certamine*). But despite all efforts, nothing on earth can ascend to the heavens and actually become the sun (Aristotle 1496–97, a3r).

Note 9, set below the printed text at the bottom of the page, seems to heed the call to respect one's role and to remain in the "inferior" world. At the same time, it serves as a kind of epitaph:

> 9. Horace in *Epistles* I on the virtues: It benefits alike the poor, alike the rich / but when neglected will harm alike young and old (WF, a1r).[50]

This is the only note on the page with a precise citation. The citation is typical insofar as it is exhortatory in character and aims at motivating the student to approach his studies for his own good, benefitting from the doctrines of ethics.

10 Conclusion: No Text Is an Island

WF is a brilliant example of the inventiveness of Renaissance note-taking. It clearly shows that a text is not an island unto itself. Texts are always surrounded by paratexts, notes, and other texts. The student annotating WF deals not only with the *Introduction* in their hands. From their notes, we can see a whole text universe. There is the *Introduction*, then the *Ethics*, Lefèvre's commentary on the *Ethics*, and Clichtove's commentary on the *Introduction*. There are the titles, dedicatory epistles, and tables of contents. And as soon as we take into the consideration the notes, still other texts are added, directly or indirectly: Diogenes Laertius, the *Dicta Albini*, the *Politics*, and Horace's *Epistles*. We may find this confusing because the notion of a deep, immersive reading experience, practiced until the ad-

---

50 "Horatius .i. epistolarum de virtutibus: Eque pauperibus prodest, locupletibus eque / Eque neglectum pueris senibusque nocebit" (Horace 2011, 1.1.25–26, 65).

vent of the digital revolution, still influences our ideas about texts and how to pay attention to them, and it leads us to mistrust techniques of reading we perceive of as discontinuous and extractive.

Nothing could be further from the reading experiences of students in the Renaissance and the early modern period. Their encounters with texts did not take place in a study, or some other private space apart from the world, but in the public space of the classroom, under the guidance of a teacher or tutor. In their notes, students would scribble down the lectures of their teachers, following their words and explanations, struggling with the strange Greek names the professors cited, catching up with ideas, scrambling for correct citations from other works, jotting down sententious life advice, and registering remarks about grammar and rhetoric. Learning how to read the Greek and Latin classics was not a cakewalk. Instead of letting students retire from the world, they would plunge students into a torrent of learnedness, competition, and struggle.

In this situation, orientation was essential to students, and the notes on the title page of WF give such orientation. It would be worth seeing if notes on title pages have a special semantics which reflects their special role as vestibules and thresholds (Genette 1997, 2). In the case of WF, there is a difference between the notes on the title page and the rest of the book. The notes on the title page show paths into the texts, but they also open spaces for possible thoughts. They do not define the text but circumscribe it, approach it from different angles, react to each other, and galvanize it.

Bibliography

Primary Sources

Ambrose, Saint (1492): *Opera*. Basel: Johann Amerbach.
Ambrose, Saint (1586): *Opera, sacrae scripturae contextum, ad faciliorem lectorum intelligentiam, ex ipsa sancti Doctoris lectione*. Paris: Jamet Mettayer. USTC 137859.
Aquinas, Thomas, Saint (1966): *In octo libros politicorum Aristotelis*. Rome: Marietti.
Aristotle (1496–1497): *Decem librorum Moralium Aristotelis tres conversiones* [...] Paris: Johann Higman and Wolfgang Hopyl.
Aristotle (1568): *Politicorum sive De republica libri octo Leonardo Aretino interprete cum Thomae Aquinatis explanatione*. Venice: Giunta. USTC 810975.
Aristotle (1932): *Politics*. Harris Rackham (Trans.). Cambridge: Harvard University Press.
Aristotle (1976): *Ethics*. James Alexander Kerr Thomson and Hugh Tredennick (Trans.). London: Penguin Books.
Augustine, Saint (1506): *Decima pars librorum divi Aurelii Augustini quorum non meminit in libris Retractationum*. Basel: Froben. USTC 686497.

Augustine, Saint (1529): *Omnium operum decimum tomus summa vigilantia repurgatorum a mendis innumeris.* Basel: Froben. USTC 625902.
Augustine, Saint (1952): *The City of God. Books VIII–XVI.* Gerald G. Walsh and Grace Monahan (Trans.). Washington, DC: The Catholic University of America Press.
Cicero, Marcus Tullius (1927): *Tusculan Disputations.* John E. King (Trans.). Cambridge: Harvard University Press.
Cicero, Marcus Tullius (1933): *On the Nature of the Gods. Academics.* Harris Rackham (Trans.). Cambridge: Harvard University Press.
Diogenes Laertius (1472): *Vitae et sententiae philosophorum.* Ambrogio Traversari (Trans.). Rome: Georg Lauer, 1472.
Diogenes Laertius (2018): *Lives of the Eminent Philosophers.* Pamela Mensch (Trans.). Oxford: Oxford University Press.
Ficino, Marsilio (2006): *Platonic Theology.* Vol. VI: *Books XVII–XVIII.* Michael B. Allen (Trans.). Cambridge and London: Harvard University Press.
Follerio, Pietro (1570): *Canonica criminalis praxis.* Venice: Francesco Portonari. USTC 830181.
Horace (2011): *Satires and Epistles.* New York: Oxford University Press.
Jerome, Saint (1565): *Epistolae d. Hieronymi Stridoniensis, et libri contra haereticos ex antiquissimis exemplaribus.* Mariano Vittori (Commentary). Rome: Paolo Manuzio. USTC 835738.
Jerome, Saint (1845): *Sancti Hieronymi stridonensis presbyteri opera omnia.* Paris: Vrayet.
Jerome, Saint (1893): *Letters and Select Works.* Oxford and New York: James Parker and Christian Literature Co.
Laks, André and Most, Glenn W. (Eds.) (2016): *Early Greek Philosophy. Western Greek Thinkers. Part I.* Cambridge and London: Harvard University Press.
Lefèvre, Jacques (1494): *Ars Moralis in Magna Moralia [= Ethica Nicomachea] Aristotelis introductoria.* Paris: Antoine Caillaut.
Lefèvre, Jacques (1501): *Compendiaria in Aristotelis ethicen introductio rei litterarie studiosis apprime utilis.* Vienna: Johann Winterburger. USTC 623823.
Mantovano, Battista (1916): *B. Baptistae Mantuani libri tres de calamitatibus temporum.* Rome: Typographia Pontifica.
Plato (1926): *Theaetetus. Sophist.* Harold N. Fowler (Trans.). Cambridge: Harvard University Press.
Scheurl, Heinrich Julius (1648): *Bibliographia Moralis.* Helmstedt: Müller. USTC 2038032.
Seneca, Lucius Annaeus (1605): *Senecae philosophi opera quae extant omnia.* Jan Gruter (Commentary). Antwerp: Plantin. USTC 1005006.
Seneca, Lucius Annaeus (1920): *Epistles.* Vol. II: *Epistles 66–92.* Richard M. Gummere (Trans.). Cambridge: Harvard University Press.

Secondary Sources

Algra, Keimpe (2003): "Stoic Theology." In: Inwood, Brad (Ed.): *The Cambridge Companion to the Stoics.* Cambridge: Cambridge University Press, 153–178. DOI: 10.1017/CCOL052177005X.007
Borgo, Marta and Costa, Iacopo (2022): "Pythagoras Latinus: Aquinas' Interpretation of Pythagoreanism in His Aristotelian Commentaries." In: Caiazzo, Irene, Macris, Constantinos, and Robert, Aurélien (Eds.): *Brill's Companion to the Reception of Pythagoras and Pythagoreanism in the Middle Ages and the Renaissance.* Leiden and Boston: Brill, 350–372.

Bowden, Hugh (2005): *Classical Athens and the Delphic Oracle. Divination and Democracy.* Cambridge: Cambridge University Press.

Buffon, Valeria A. (2008): "The Structure of the Soul, Intellectual Virtues, and the Ethical Ideal of Masters of Arts in Early Commentaries on the *Nicomachean Ethics*." In: Bejczy, István Pieter (Ed.): *Virtue Ethics in the Middle Ages: Commentaries on Aristotle's Nicomachean Ethics.* Leiden and Boston: Brill, 13–30. DOI: 10.1163/ej.9789004163164.i-376.6.

Bullough, Donald A. (1991): "Alcuin and the Kingdom of Heaven." In: Bullough, Donald A.: *Carolingian Renewal: Sources and Heritage.* Manchester and New York: Manchester University Press, 161–240.

Celenza, Christopher (1999): "Pythagoras in the Renaissance: The Case of Marsilio Ficino." In: *Renaissance Quarterly* 52. No. 3, 667–711. DOI: 10.2307/2901915.

Herdt, Jennifer (2019): *Forming Humanity. Redeeming the German Bildung Tradition.* Chicago: University of Chicago Press.

Katte, Marie von (1972): "Herzog August und die Kataloge seiner Bibliothek." In: *Wolfenbütteler Beiträge* 1, 168–199.

Keßler, Eckhard (1999): "Introducing Aristotle to the sixteenth century: The Lefèvre enterprise." In: Blackwell, Constance and Kusukawa, Sachiko (Eds.): *Philosophy in the Sixteenth and Seventeenth Centuries. Conversations with Aristotle.* London and New York: Routledge, 1–21.

Laks, André (2013). "The Pythagorean Hypomnemata reported by Alexander Polyhistor in Diogenes Laertius (8.25–33): A proposal for reading." In: Cornelli, Gabriele, McKirahan, Richard, and Macris, Constantinos (Eds.): *On Pythagoreanism.* Boston and Berlin: De Gruyter, 371–384. DOI: 10.1515/9783110318500.371.

Lebech, Mette, McEvoy, James, and Flood, John (2009): "De dignitate conditionis humanae: translation, commentary, and reception history of the Dicta Albini (Ps.-Alcuin) and the Dicta Candidi." In: *Viator* 40. No. 2, 1–34. DOI: 10.1484/J.VIATOR.1.100420.

Leunissen, Mariska (2017): *From Natural Character to Moral Virtue in Aristotle.* New York: Oxford University Press.

Lines, David (2002): *Aristotle's* Ethics *in the Italian Renaissance (ca. 1300–1650). The Universities and the Problem of Moral Education.* Leiden: Brill. DOI: 10.1163/9789004453333.

Marenbon, John (1981): *From the Circle of Alcuin to the School of Auxerre: Logic, Theology and Philosophy in the Early Middle Ages.* Cambridge: Cambridge University Press. DOI: 10.1017/CBO9780511562327.

Ní Mheallaigh, Karen (2020): *The Moon in the Greek and Roman Imagination: Myth, Literature, Science and Philosophy.* Cambridge: Cambridge University Press. DOI: 10.1017/9781108685726.

Oosterhof, Richard J. (2019): "Apprenticeship in the Renaissance University: Student authorship and craft knowledge." In: *Science in Context* 32, 119–136. DOI: 10.1017/S0269889719000140.

Rautenberg (2008): "Die Entstehung und Entwicklung des Buchtitelblatts in der Inkunabelzeit in Deutschland, den Niederlanden und Venedig—Quantitative und qualitative Studien." In: *Archiv für die Geschichte des Buchwesens* 68, 1–106.

Rice, Eugene F., Jr. (1970): "Humanist Aristotelianism in France: Jacques Lefèvre d'Étaples and his circle." In: Levi, Anthony H. T. (Ed.): *Humanism in France at the End of the Middle Ages and in the Early Renaissance.* Manchester and New York: Manchester University Press and Barnes and Nobles, 132–149.

Rice, Eugene F., Jr. (1972): *The Prefatory Epistles of Jacques Lefèvre d'Étaples and Related Texts.* New York and London: Columbia University Press.

Rice, Eugene F., Jr. (1988): "Humanism in France." In: Rabil, Albert, Jr. (Ed.): *Renaissance Humanism: Foundations, Forms, and Legacy.* Vol. II: *Humanism Beyond Italy.* Philadelphia: University of Pennsylvania Press, 109–122. DOI: 10.9783/9781512805765-005.

Robert, Aurélien (2022): "Pythagoras' Ethics and the Pythagorean Way of Life in the Middle Ages." In: Caiazzo, Irene, Macris, Constantinos, and Robert, Aurélien (Eds.): *Brill's Companion to the Reception of Pythagoras and Pythagoreanism in the Middle Ages and the Renaissance.* Leiden and Boston: Brill, 229–274. DOI: 10.1163/9789004499461_009.

Schönau, Christoph (2017): *Jacques Lefèvre d'Étaples und die Reformation.* Heidelberg: Verein für Reformationsgeschichte.

Sebastiani, Valentina (2018): *Johann Froben: Printer of Basel. A Biographical Profile and Catalogue of His Editions.* Leiden and Boston: Brill.

Willeke, Heike (2003): "Ordo und Ethos im Hortus Deliciarum. Das Bild–Text-Programm des Hohenburger Codex zwischen kontemplativ-spekulativer Weltschau und konkret-pragmatischer Handlungsorientierung." PhD dissertation. Hamburg: University of Hamburg.

Alicja Bielak

The Notebook that Stood Trial for Heresy: Antitrinitarianism among Polish Students in Tübingen in 1550s

Abstract: The aim of the chapter is to show how the theological discussions of the late 1550s influenced students, as evidenced by their personal notes. The corpus of analysis are the manuscripts left after Michał Zaleski, a Polish student who was killed in Tübingen in 1559. During the murder investigation the *Declarationes Iesu Christi Filii Dei*, attributed to the Antitrinitarian Miguel Servet, was found among his belongings. This discovery started a new investigation, this time on heresy. The text bears numerous marginal notes written by various hands. Moreover, Zaleski prepared a commonplace book called by the trial committee *Locus communis de Trinitate*. In addition to being one of the earliest traces of the antitrinitarian discussions among Poles, the materials also demonstrate how confessionalization influenced students' methods of text interpretation and ways of conducting heterodox discussions outside the university walls.

1 Introduction: Education in the Age of Confessionalization

At the turn of 1520 and 1530, both Catholics and Protestants had understood the role of education in the process of confessionalization. Protestants placed their emphasis on exercise in language characteristic of humanistic studies and at the same time saw education as a civil duty. The ideal alumnus was one who serves God and the State and, at the same, time advocates a precise religious confession (dependent on the Bible and a particular creed-specific interpretation). This educational model was grounded on essentially neutral humanist tools like historical inquiry and the philological toolbox that served biblical analysis in the name of the *sola Scriptura* rule. Humanists, in turn, like Erasmus, saw this amalgamate of theology

---

Alicja Bielak: ORCID: 0000-0003-0701-0634. Institute of Philosophy and Sociology, Polish Academy of Sciences, Warsaw, Poland. This research has been made possible thanks to ERC Consolidator Grant n. 864542, "From East to West, and Back Again: Student Travel and Transcultural Knowledge Production in Renaissance Europe (c. 1470–c. 1620)."
Acknowledgements: I would like to sincerely thank Matthias Roick and Martin Rothkegel for their generous comments that significantly improved this article.

Open Access. © 2023 the author(s), published by De Gruyter. (CC BY) This work is licensed under the Creative Commons Attribution 4.0 International License. https://doi.org/10.1515/9783111072722-008

and humanistic curriculum as ideological exploitation and the perversion of the latter (Rummel 2000, 30–49, and McGrath 1993, 49–59). For humanists, philology as a weapon in the hands of Reformation theologians no longer pursued erudition (*paideia*), conceived of as a drive for knowledge, which was understood as a natural inclination of man (Aristotle) and—what Cicero had emphasized—unmercenary instinct (Włodarski 2001, 48–56). One of the reasons for such criticism was that Protestants, while using the methods of the humanists, at the same time rejected their rhetoric of doubt (Rummel 2000, 4). These divisions were reflected in the confessionalization of universities, which attracted specific adherents. The purpose of this chapter is to show how profoundly confessional discussions affected students' methods of reading texts, using the example of two manuscripts that belonged to Polish nobles studying in Tübingen. Emphasis will be placed on their reactions to the texts they read.

At the University of Tübingen in the late 1550s, an increase in the number of students of Polish origin can be observed. The first in this wave was Michał Zaleski, who arrived in the city on November 26, 1556. On November 24, 1559, seven more students enrolled at the university, together with their preceptor Albert Sylvius (Kot 1953, 81).[1] In March of the same year, Zaleski was stabbed to death in Tübingen. The murder case was reported to Prince Christopher of Württemberg (1515–1568) on March 6 by Pier Paolo Vergerio (1498–1565), ex-bishop and Reformation propagator, who was in good relations with the Poles in Tübingen (Kausler and Schott 1875, 196). It was soon to turn out that it was not the murder that was the problem for the Poles. Much to Vergerio's surprise, among belongings of Zaleski, a manuscript of the *Declarationes Iesu Christi Filii Dei* by the Spanish Antitrinitarian theologian Miguel Servet (1511–1553) was found (Kot 1953, 82–84).

The case files—including the Servetian manuscript—were found in the Stuttgart Municipal Archive (A 63 Bü 25/11) by Stanisław Kot (1953), who maintained the attribution of the work to Servet. His article started a discussion concerning both the authorship of the text and the spread of antitrinitarianism at the end of the 1550s. Kot proved that long passages of the work are consistent with some of Servet's *De Trinitatis erroribus* published in 1531 (a photocopy of the manuscript is preserved in the Jagiellonian Library with the annotations of the researcher who meticulously marked these parallel passages).[2] He supposed that it was an intermediary work between *De Trinitatis erroribus* (1531) and *Christianismi restitutio* (1553) in which Servet rejected both the doctrine of the Trinity and the idea of pre-

---

[1] These students were Kiljan Drohojowski, Jan Jaskmanicki, Mikołaj Kotkowski, Stanisław Kula, Jan Pieniążek, Stanisław Pieniążek, and Marcin Strzelecki.
[2] Biblioteka Jagiellońska MS Przyb 87/83, 1–119 (*Fotokopie z rękopisów z bibliotek i archiwów niemieckich: Berlin, Marburg, Królewiec, Stuttgart, Wiesbaden, Wolfenbüttel*).

destination. Ángel Alcalá (2004, lxxii) and Robert H. Bainton (1973, 228–229) in turn suggested that the manuscript from the Stuttgart Archive was an early draft of *De Trinitatis erroribus*. Even though the inscription on the title page suggests Servet's authorship, Peter Hughes and Peter Zerner (2010), who edited and translated the manuscript, were not in agreement about this. The matter was additionally complicated by the fact that the apologetic preface was signed by "Alphonsus Lyncurius Tarraconensis," which was a pseudonym used by Matteo Gribaldi Moffa (1505–1564), an Italian jurist, Servet's apologist, and a propagator of antitrinitarianism. Other propositions included such figures as Martin Cellarius (1499–1564), Celio Secondo Curione (1503–1569), and Laelius Socinus (1525–1562) (Williams 1992, 957). In the discussion over the authorship of the main part of the work, Uwe Plath (1969) proposed that the whole thing was written by Gribaldi, and this trail was followed by Hughes and Zerner (2010, xxviii–xxxiii).

To date, the attention of researchers has focused precisely on establishing authorship and placing the content within the views of a particular theologian (Kot, Williams, Bainton, Alcalá, and Hughes and Zerner). Polish researchers have also been interested in the trial as an example of the significance of Servetianism for Polish students (Kot 1953, Tazbir 1966). So far, no attention has been paid to the notes left in the margins and the *Locus de Trinitate* notebook, which became evidence in the case. The purpose of this article, therefore, will be to analyze the aforementioned sources with special attention paid to the work of the Polish students who kept, passed on, read, and annotated these manuscripts.

2 On the Frontier of Protestant Orthodoxy: Between Padua and Tübingen

Not much is known about the murdered Polish noble. Zaleski was likely studying law in Basel from May 1553 (Wackernagel 1956, 78), but he was also interested in theological matters. In May 1555, he translated into Latin and presented in Basel a declaration of faith by Polish Protestants based on the Augsburg Confession (see Appendix I, Fig. 1).[3] The declaration had been pronounced in Polish during the Sejm in Piotrków on May 3, 1555, probably by Rafał Leszczyński (1526–1592), the starost of Radziejów and one of the leaders of the Polish Reformation. It is likely

---

3 Universitätsbibliothek Basel, MS Fr. Gr. I 2 11: *Compendiaria et succincta confessionis Christianae descriptio, quam amplissimi oratores Poloni in Comitiis Petroronicensibus* [sic] *Regi et universo senatui Polonico exhibuerunt mense Mayo, Latina lingua donata a Michaele Zalewio, Polono, anno Domini 1555* (see Appendix I).

that Zaleski's Latin translation served as the basis for the German edition of the declaration published in Strasbourg, which may suggest that the Polish student had a connection to the printer Thiebolt Berger (d. c. 1570)[4].

This was an important event for the Polish Reformation as the Protestants successfully lobbied for the adoption of a resolution stating that supporters of Lutheranism had the right to observe the Augsburg Confession, and that the nobility was entitled to maintain Protestant clergy on their estates (Finkel 1896, 257–285; Borawska and Małłek 1985, 21; and Wijaczka 2014, 20). It is likely that the nobility's position was based on a confession of faith by Zaleski's relative, Stanisław Lutomirski (1518–1575), who sent it to the King and the Polish episcopate in 1554, and put it in print two years later (Lutomirski, 1556). Marcin Kromer (1512–1589), who was present at the 1555 Sejm as the King's secretary, prepared a refutation of the confession containing the Catholic side's response. In his correspondence with Kromer, Stanislaus Hosius (1504–1579) criticized the 1555 confession, especially the passages contesting Christ's divinity and calling him a "mere creature" (*pura creatura*) (Finkel 1896, 269). The diminishment of Christ's role is best seen in Articles 11 and 12, which state that one should only pray to God the Father.

The Zaleski's translation of the confession confirms that he maintained close relationships with the Polish Protestants and a well-organized network abroad. Evidently, he was able to present the latest news from Poland in Basel and forward them to Strasbourg to be printed. Significantly, at the end of Zaleski's version of the text quotations from writings attributed to St. Augustine (absent in other versions of the Polish confession, but present in the Augsburg Confession) can be found.

Zaleski was part of the inner circle of Italian humanist Celio Secondo Curione (1503–1569) in whose house he lived together with another student from Poland, Mikołaj Uhrowiecki (1537–1557) (Wackernagel 1956, 78–79). Although the Italian professor of rhetoric pretended to be an orthodox Protestant in public, he published his antitrinitarian book *De amplitudine beati regni Dei* (1554) and came in close contact with Matteo Gribaldi (Kutter 1955 and Williams 1992, 953–956). Curione also became a source of radical religious thought for Polish students in Basel, among which were Abraham Zbąski (1531–1577) and Mikołaj Uhrowiecki (Kot 1921, 109–112, and Włodarski 2001, 83–95).

---

[4] *Neüwe Zeyttung und Warhaffte Bekandtnuss der Chrïstlichen Glaubens auff dem Landtag zü Piotrkow durch die gesandten dess Künigreichs Polen. Geschehen auff den dritten tag Maii* (Strasbourg: Thieboldt Berger, 1555). Two more surviving versions of the text are known: a German edition probably printed by Cyriacus Schnauss (1512–1571) in Coburg (a unique copy is preserved in the Princes Czartoryski Library in Krakow) and a manuscript written in Polish preserved in Biblioteka Pawlikowskich in Lviv (see Appendix I and Finkel 1896).

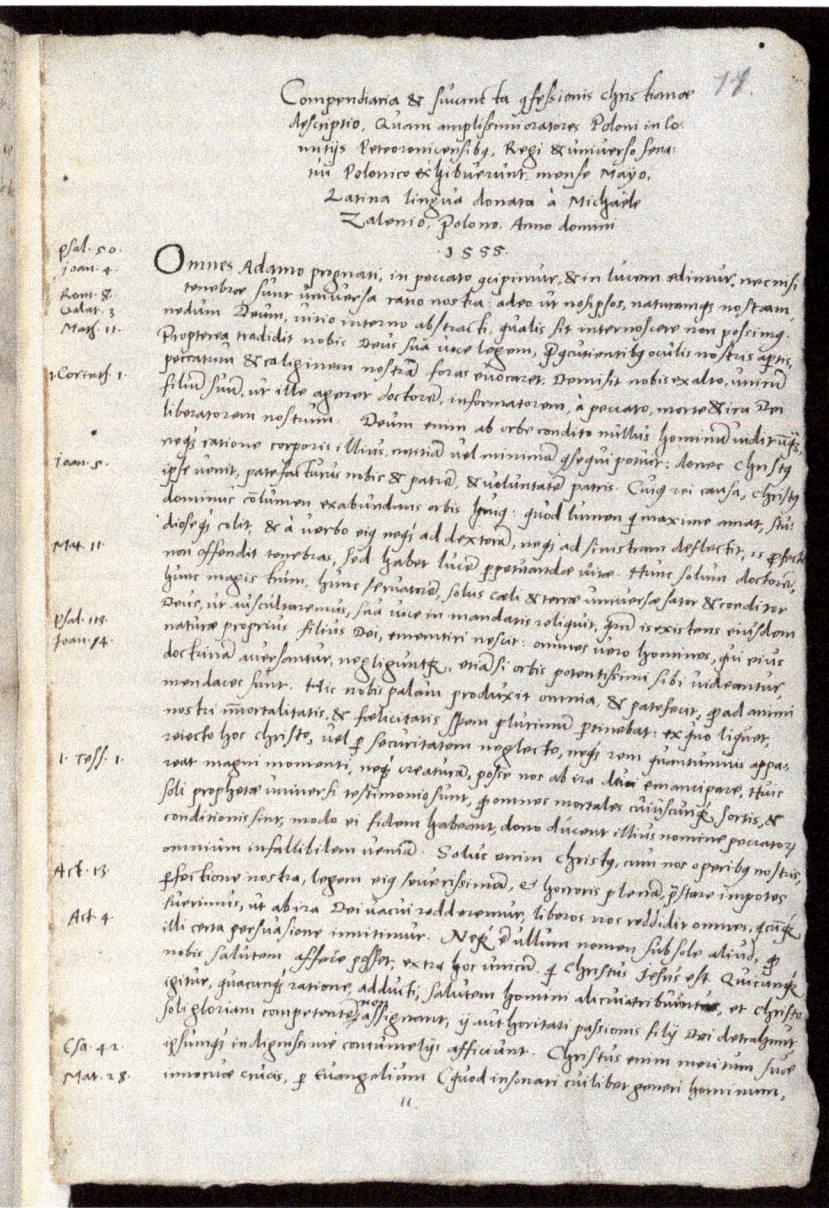

Fig. 1: *Compendiaria et succincta confessionis Christianae descriptio...* translation prepared by Michał Zaleski (Universitätsbibliothek Basel, Ms. Fr Gr I 2, no. 11, 11r)

That is probably where Zaleski became friends with Gribaldi, who at the time was based in Geneva, just at the moment of Servet's trial (Kot 1921, 113). Gribaldi discussed Servet's views openly and broadly trying to convince Johannes Calvin (1509–1564), Johann Heinrich Bullinger (1504–1575), and Vergerio that Servet should not be executed. It was probably then that Gribaldi started to write the *Apologia pro Michaele Serveto* (composed in 1554) while in dialogue with Agostino Curione (1538–1567, son of Celio Secondo), Gonesius, Socinus, and Zaleski in Padua (Plath 1969, 586–590). That was also when Sébastien Castellion (1515–1563) took a clear stand on religious tolerance and published his famous *De haereticis, an sint persequendi* (Basel 1554) under the pseudonym "Martin Bellius," speaking about the freedom of conscience and attacking Calvin's actions against Servet. Together with Gribaldi, they argued that only God can judge one's heart (Gribaldi 2010b, 183, and Castellion 1554). After this hectic period, Zaleski moved together with Gribaldi to Tübingen where he immatriculated on November 25, 1556 (Kot 1921, 113, and Tazbir 1966, 68).

Even though Gribaldi held Protestant views probably from 1542, he knew that he had to hide them in order to maintain his position as lecturer of Roman law at French universities. His approach changed when he started teaching at the University of Padua, well known for its religious toleration. In 1548, he published a piece where he defended a jurist, Francesco Spiera (1502–1548), who had been forced by the Inquisition to recant his beliefs publicly. After this, he came into contact with Peter Paul Vergerio, whom he recommended in a private letter to Johannes Calvin. Vergerio started to gain a leading role in Italian Protestant communities in exile. In the meantime, the Inquisition kept pressing Gribaldi to recant his Protestant beliefs. This time it was Vergerio who helped him. Thanks to his recommendation to the Duke of Württemberg, Gribaldi obtained the position of professor at the University of Tübingen in 1555. In the meantime, Gribaldi read Servet's *De Trinitatis erroribus* and radicalized his theological views. Calvin suspected this change and ostentatiously refused to shake hands with Gribaldi while he visited Geneva. In July 1557, by order of the duke, the senate of the University of Tübingen set a hearing against him. The duke hoped he would acknowledge the orthodox doctrine. Not only did Gribaldi not do so, but less than three weeks later he fled the city on foot (Hughes and Zerner 2010, xxxvii–xlii, and Williams 1992, 622–627).

The modification of *Declarationes Iesu Christi Filii Dei*'s attribution still does not change the fact that Polish students were accused of promoting antitrinitarian content in line with Servet's views, who was burned at the stake along with copies of his *De Trinitatis erroribus* at the Plateau de Champel in Geneva with Johannes Calvin's approval just six years earlier on October 27, 1553. It was probably Gribaldi who introduced Servet's writings to Petrus Gonesius (Piotr of Goniądz; c. 1525–1573), the pioneering propagator of anabaptism and antitrinitarianism in Poland

and Lithuania (Jasnowski 1936, 4, and Szczucki 1981, 398).[5] Petrus Gonesius was Gribaldi's student in Padua, who fled soon after he did. He returned to Poland in 1555, exactly when the first traces of antitrinitarianism in Poland were reported to Francesco Lismanini (1504–1566) in letters by Alexander Vitrelinus (d. 1587) and Felix Cruciger (d. c. 1587), who asked him to come back and help the Calvinistic congregation. When Theodore de Bèze (1519–1605) heard about it, he wrote to Bullinger: "You see, also on the basis of what is reported to us from Poland, Satan is already concentrating his forces for the resumption of this heresy, whose axioms, as Lismanini reported to us, are so similar to Gribaldi's confessions that one could confidently attribute their authorship to him."[6] In Poland, Petrus Gonesius became a Protestant minister under Mikołaj Radziwiłł Czarny ("the Black"; 1515–1565), but when the prince heard of his heretical views on the Trinity, he sent him to the synod in Secemin. On January 22, 1556, the written confession of Gonesius "the new Arian and Servetian" (*novus Ariani et Servetiani*) was read, in which he stated his views on the Trinity. He acknowledged that the very word "Trinity" is an invention, as is the Symbol of Athanasius. He recognized God the Father as "*solum Deum*," which he supported with a quotation from John 17:3.[7] In turn, he considered Jesus to be subordinate to God, as Jesus himself testified to many times in the Bible (e.g., "*Quia tu me misisti*" in Jn 17:23). Moreover, he criticized the doctrine of the two natures of Christ and negated participation in the divinity of the Father. He also followed Servetus in postulating a literal reading of the incarnation: the preexistent Logos was brought into flesh in Mary's womb (Sipayłło 1966, 47, and Ogonowski 2021, 1–5).

Although Gonesius published his work *Doctrina pura et clara de praecipuis Christianae religionis articulis* in 1570 in Węgrów, at least part of it was written —and probably circulated—before 1560, as it mentions Philipp Melanchthon (1497–1560) as still living (Szczucki 1964, 245; Gonesius 1560). Even though contemporaries identified sources of Gonesius' thought in Servet's and Arius' doctrines,[8] it was Gribaldi who was his teacher in Padua. Because of the lack of sources, Gonesius' works (written at a time when he was also among the Polish students of Gribaldi) will serve below as context for the trial manuscripts. Gribaldi based his treatise on Servet's *De Trinitatis erroribus* and following the Spanish thinker he

---

5 On his biography, see Górski (1949), Szczucki (1981), and Jasnowski (1936).
6 Letter from Lousanne, January 1, 1556, quotation after Jasnowski (1936, 10).
7 The *Vulgata Clementina* has "*solum verum Deum*" there.
8 At the Secemin synod, he was called a "new Arian and Servetian," while Vergerio, in a letter to Melanchthon from July 20, 1556, complained about the "installation of Arianism" in Poland by Gonesius' publication *De filio Dei homine Christo Jesu*. Pier Paolo Vergerio a Filippo Melantone (*Königsberg, 20 luglio 1556*), edited by Caccamo (1999, 178).

rejected theological terms such as *persona*, hypostasis, and substance. Unlike Servet, he was not interested in the Holy Spirit and the Word—according to his interpretation, the Word was mentioned in the Bible only to underline the divine origin of Jesus (Hughes and Zerner 2010, xxxiv).

The University of Tübingen was the only Lutheran university in southern Germany and attracted to itself such theologians as Johannes Brenz (1499–1570), Joachim Camerarius (1500–1574, sent there by Melanchthon), Gulielmus Bucanus (d. 603), and Jakob Andreä (1528–1590). Gribaldi gained a position at the University of Tübingen thanks to Vergerio. When Duke Christoph of Württemberg had been informed of his unorthodox views, he commissioned the university to conduct an investigation. When Vergerio heard about the growing Servetianism among Poles in Tübingen, he must have been alarmed and probably started worrying about himself, because any connection to Servet's ideas was now also his problem. Vergerio was known for his good relations with the Poles and his plans to Lutheranize the Polish-Lithuanian Commonwealth. Sometime before the events described, he wanted to gain the young King Sigismund II for the Augsburg confession, and to this end he wanted to gain Mikołaj Radziwiłł Czarny's support for his plan. His project failed, however, and the Helvetic Reformation was developing in the Polish-Lithuanian Commonwealth (Williams 1992, 1013–1014). Additionally, during the hearing, one student testified that Vergerio's servant, Cleophas, also left Zaleski many books in Polish and Italian (Tazbir 1966, 70).

The University of Tübingen Archives preserve the *Protokolle des Akademischen Senats*.[9] The Stuttgart State Archives, in turn, holds a detailed report with the Polish students' testimonies given during the trial.[10] The Rector of the University, Jacob Schegk, and two theologians, Jacob Peurlin (1522–1561) and Diettrich Schnepf (1525–1586), as well as a professor of law, Chilian Vogler, were appointed to this task. The theologians assisted by magister Georgio Heitzler prepared an inventory of Zaleski's books (Wotschke 1908, 200). The two manuscripts, the *Declarationes Iesu Christi Filii Dei*, and a copy of *Locus communis de Trinitate* from Zaleski's notebook were attached to the investigation record as evidence in the case.[11] At

---

9 Universitätsbibliothek Tübingen MS UAT 2/1b: *Protokolle des Akademischen Senats*, 273v–283v (*Sommerhalbjahr 1559. Rektorat Gebhard Brastberger*). http://idb.ub.uni-tuebingen.de/opendigi/UAT_002_1b, last accessed May 14, 2023. See here the dates: 06.05, 11.05, 15.05, 13.06, 16.05; October 10th (fol. 286r) and November 5th (fol. 288r).

10 Hauptstaatsarchiv Stuttgart MS A 63 Bü 25/ 11. The hearing in German edited by Janusz Tazbir (1966, 65–74), and below (Appendix III) I summarize and quote this edition (the translation is my own).

11 Hauptstaatsarchiv Stuttgart MS A 63 Bü 25/ 11.

the hearing, the Polish students were asked the following questions (see Appendix III):
1. Where did dominus Zaleski get this book?
2. What did dominus Zaleski think of it? Did he praise it and encourage you to read it or not?
3. Who made the underlines in said book and notes in the margins?
4. Who gave the book to Vergerio and told him about it?
5. Did this person bring it to Vergerio of his own free will, without prompting, or was it delivered to Vergerio at his request?
6. Did dominus Zaleski have more books of this kind or not?
7. What is this book in Polish written by him (Zaleski)?

One of the Poles, Jan Tomasz Drohojowski (Droievius; d. 1606), who had studied before in Strasburg and Wittenberg, testified that a few days before his death Zaleski said to him and to other Polish students that Servet's book "reveals the true sense and truth of the Gospel" (Tazbir 1966, 66). Moreover, he added that the underlines and notes in the margins were written by Zaleski's hand. According to Drohojowski, Zaleski asked his colleagues to check whether the content of *Declarationes* was correct and corresponded to the truth because he planned to publish it. This information was not confirmed at any print house in Tübingen (the commission asked several printers, Tazbir 1966, 73), but if Zaleski wanted to, he could have had some options to do so in other places thanks to his previously gained contacts in Basel and Strasbourg. Polish students collaborated with Curione in terms of publishing activities. Another Pole from Curione's circle, Zbąski, probably mediated the publication of such works as *De lege coelibatus* (1551) by Stanisław Orzechowski (1513–1566) and *De Republica emendanda* (1554) by Andrzej Frycz Modrzewski (1503–1572) at the famous printing house of Johannes Oporinus (1507–1568). His ability in this regard may be evidenced by the fact that in 1560, Curione advised, for example, Silvestro Teglio (d. 1574) to contact him in regard to publishing his Latin translation of Machiavelli's *The Prince* (Włodarski 2001, 86–87). Accordingly, Zaleski, who was invited by Zbąski to Basel, had the contacts to pursue publication. Drohojowski guessed that he would engage his cousin, Jan Lutomirski (d. 1567), the *secretarius regius* and leader of the Reformation among nobles in Poland (Tazbir 1966, 66).

However, the testimonies of the witnesses were not consistent. According to the statements of Marcin Strzelecki and the preceptor of Polish students, Albertus Sylvius, it was Stanisław Kula who brought the book from Strasbourg to Tübingen to be stored with Zaleski. Just before the murder, Tomasz Drohojowski took this book from Zaleski along with other books by Kula (because of that, it was not present among Zaleski's belongings). Kula was a noble from Mały Książ (in Kraków

Voivodeship), son of Jakub Kula (Boniecki 1909, 13:159). Among his family members, we find Wawrzyniec Kula, a supporter of the Reformation who took part in the mentioned synod in Secemin during which it was decided that Gonesius was falling into the heresy of Servet and needed to consult Melanchthon, to whom he was eventually sent (Sipayłło 1966, 46). It is known that Stanisław Kula had earlier studied in Padua, where in August 1554 he was appointed an advisor (*consigliere*) of the Polish nation. He also came into contact with Gonesius in Padua (Pietrzyk 1997, 61–62).

After a short episode in Padua, Kula continued his studies in Strasbourg under the supervision of the great teacher of Bible exegesis, Valentinus Eritreus (1521–1576). At the same time, Johannes Wolf (1521–1572), Swiss reformed theologian, also recommended Kula (in the name of a sick Bullinger) to Johannes Sturm (1507–1589), the famous German educational reformer (Pietrzyk 1997, 61). In the context of education in these times of confessional divergence, it should be mentioned that Sturm's method was based on philological analysis, which—in his opinion—enabled a deeper understanding of the truths of faith. His method, summarized in the famous pedagogical goal of "wise and eloquent piety" (*eloquens et docta pietas*), was based on studying classical literature and language as divinely inspired. It was not to be weaponized in religious indoctrination (Tinsley 1989, 26–31).

Nevertheless, from the very beginning, Kula was the source of much trouble for his patrons. Among other things, he had been accused of beating and harassing another Polish student, Szymon Żegocki (Pietrzyk 1997, 61). According to the preceptor of the Polish nation, Kula had already returned to Poland at the time of the trial. According to him, the highlights belonged to Kula (obviously it is easier to put the responsibility on someone who is not present at the trial), while Drohojowski claimed that they were written by Zaleski's hand. Sylvius assured, moreover, that he never heard Zaleski discuss the Trinity; he had been rather examining the books of Brenz, a German Protestant theologian (Tazbir 1966, 70).

A comparative analysis of the handwriting is not possible because no other manuscripts by Zaleski's or Kula's hands are known; we can only inform our hypothesis concerning the authorship of the marks and annotations in the text on the basis of Tomasz Drohojowski's testimony, who himself compared the handwriting present in the Servetian manuscript with annotations in Kula's books.

Regardless of the precise person to whom the materials belonged, the entire case revolved around the notebooks that proved to be the reason for the heresy case. It is also known that they were used and read by Polish students, as testified by Drohojowski, who admitted that he, Kula, and "other Poles in Strasbourg at Erithreo" had read it to check whether Gonesius is a Servetianist (Tazbir 1966, 71). Below, I will outline what was highlighted in the aforementioned manuscript and then suggest directions for analysis of the second notebook—that is, *Locus communis de Trinitate*, written by Zaleski.

3 Annotating Heretical Texts: The Case of *Declarationes Iesu Christi filii Dei*

Dissemination of radical religious material outside the print circuit was popular at that time among antitrinitarians. After the banning of Servet's *De Trinitate erroribus*, his works spread in manuscripts (also one is preserved in the University Library in Tübingen that may be further evidence for the development of Servetianism in the city).[12] One can find also editorial comments on works never published, for example the ones by Celio Secondo Curione that were identified in Gribaldi's manuscript *De vera cognitione Dei*,[13] which he left behind while escaping from Tübingen in 1557 (Williams 1992, 952–953). *Declarationes Iesu Christi filii Dei* was also probably preserved in more copies. Certainly, one was in possession of Stanisław Lubieniecki (1623–1675), who quoted it in his *Historia Reformationis Polonicae (History of Polish Reformation)* (Lubieniecki 1685, 98; Hughes and Zerner 2010, lv).

What can we learn from the codicological analysis of the manuscript about its reception and impact? The main text was undoubtedly written by at least two people, because between pages 16 and 17, the color of the ink and handwriting changes significantly; that is exactly where the difference between *Scriptor* A (Hauptstaatsarchiv Stuttgart MS A 63 Bü 25/11, 1–16; 25–54, see Fig. 2) and B (17–24, Fig. 3) is visible. Moreover, between pages 65–80, we can differentiate *Scriptor* C (Fig. 4), and finally, from the beginning of the fifth chapter, between 81 and 93, we can identify *Scriptor* D (Fig. 5), after whom proceeds once again *Scriptor* A (Hauptstaatsarchiv Stuttgart MS A 63 Bü 25/11, 94–119). None of the handwritings match the manuscripts left after Gribaldi[14] or Agostino Curione, to whom he probably dictated *Apologia*[15] (Guggisberg 2003, 99). The *Declarationes Iesu Christi Filii Dei* manuscript could have been rewritten by Polish students after an unknown original. The

---

[12] Universitätsbibliothek Tübingen MS Mc 161: *De Trinitatis erroribus libri septem* (ante 1531); see also: University Library of Oklahoma MS M 3319042–1001: *Michael Servetus. De Trinitatis erroribus libri septem*.
[13] The manuscript has been lost; we know about it from correspondence between Vergerio and Bullinger (Hughes and Zerner 2010, l–li).
[14] See Gribaldi's letters, e.g., in Universitätsbibliothek Basel (MS G I 9: Bl. 29–30, 58–61, 64–65) and *Religionis christianae progymnasmata* (Universitätsbibliothek Basel MS M. A IX, 74, 2a).
[15] *Alphonsi Lyncurii Tarraconensis Apologia pro Michaele Serveto*, Universitätsbibliothek Basel MS Ki. Ar. 26a (with corrections in Agostino Curione's hand).

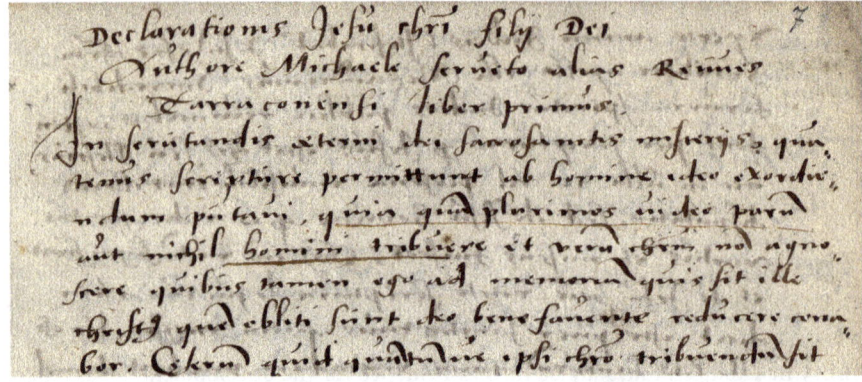

Fig. 2: Scriptor "A" handwriting sample (Hauptstaatsarchiv Stuttgart MS A 63 Bü 25/11, 7)

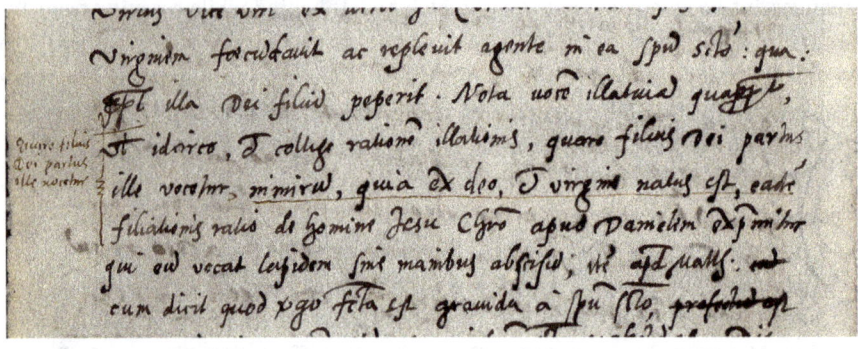

Fig. 3: Scriptor "B" handwriting sample with marginal note by Scriptor "E" (Hauptstaatsarchiv Stuttgart MS A 63 Bü 25/11, 18)

four styles of handwriting can serve as confirmation of Tomasz Drohojowski's testimony about a group of Poles reading the manuscript already in Strasbourg.

Moreover, the notes in the margins were also written by at least two different hands and had two purposes (Fig. 6). The first one was to edit the text (someone changed the order of the words, made minor corrections, etc.), and that was mainly *Scriptor* A. These improvements suggest that the manuscript was indeed being prepared for publication as testified by Tomasz Drohojowski. The second type of annotations, in turn, are traces of reading the text, like highlights and additions of headings that indicate the trajectory of the anonymous annotators' reading, as well as suggesting the themes that particularly caught their attention. Among such marginal notes one can distinguish: added headings (e.g., *"Christus," "Filius*

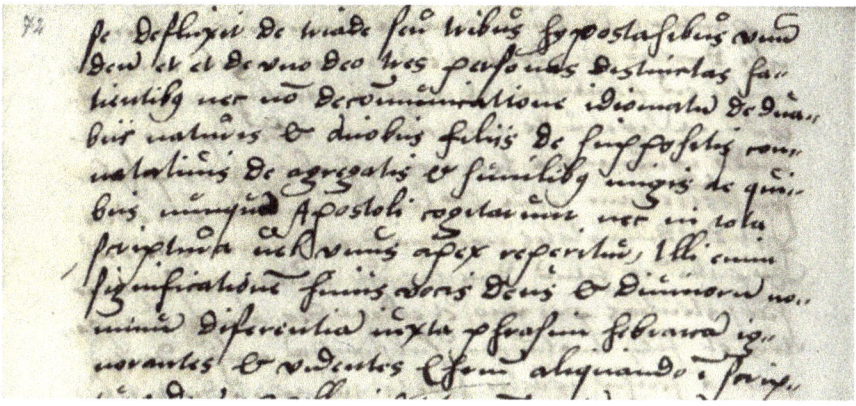

Fig. 4: Scriptor "C" handwriting sample (Hauptstaatsarchiv Stuttgart MS A 63 Bü 25/11, 72)

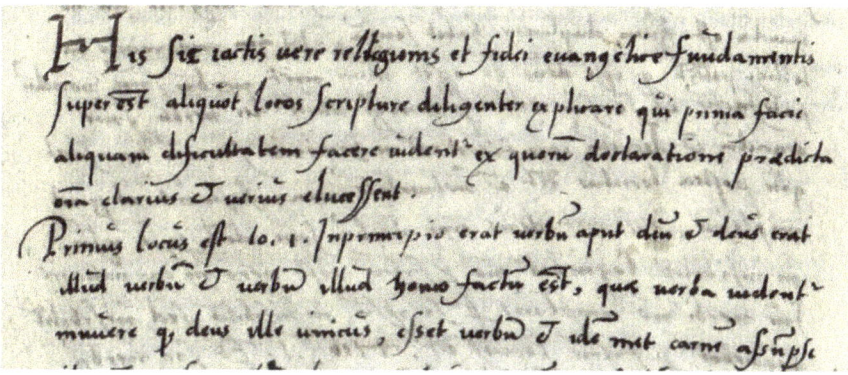

Fig. 5: Scriptor "D" handwriting sample (Hauptstaatsarchiv Stuttgart MS A 63 Bü 25/11, 81)

hominis"), *manicula*,[16] "nota,"[17] as well as two styles of highlights of the whole passages in the margins: linear and dotted, composed of semicircles (Fig. 6, 7).[18] On pages 18 and 19, one note in the margins matches *Scriptor* A's handwriting, who added some details to the text, while the second one must be a different person —*Scriptor* E (Fig. 7). The preface and first chapter of the manuscript contain the most underlined and annotated material, but one of the scribes using bright brown ink (probably E) left his highlights throughout the entire work.

---

16 Hauptstaatsarchiv Stuttgart MS A 63 Bü 25/11: 16 (x2), 20.
17 Hauptstaatsarchiv Stuttgart MS A 63 Bü 25/11: 35, 42, 36.
18 Hauptstaatsarchiv Stuttgart MS A 63 Bü 25/11: 9, 16, 18, 19–25, 29 (linear brackets) and 9–10, 15, 19–20 ("semicircle" brackets).

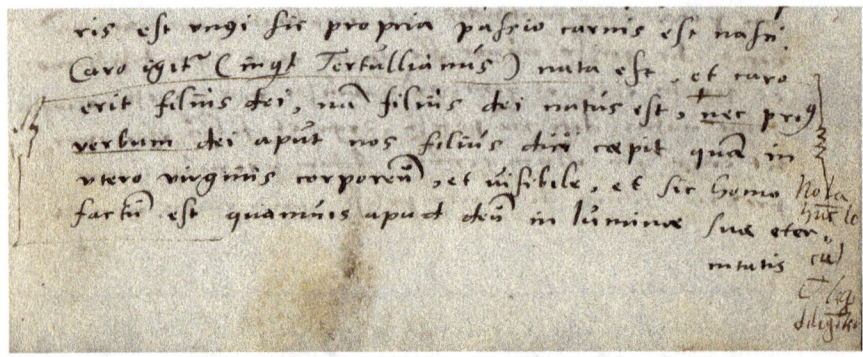

Fig. 6: Sample of handwriting by *Scriptor* E (margins with brighter brown ink, " ☞ Nota hunc locum et lege diligenter"); main text is *Scriptor* A

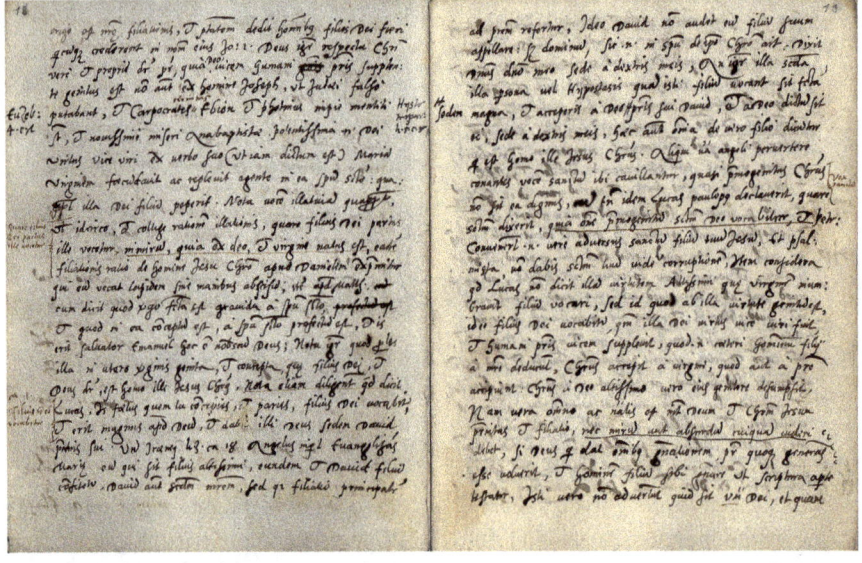

Fig. 7: *Declarationes Iesu Christi Filii Dei* with marginal notes written by different hands: main text and notes above—*Scriptor* A; highlight and notes in the margins in brighter brown ink—*Scriptor* E (Hauptstaatsarchiv Stuttgart MS A 63 Bü 25/11, 18–19)

It should be noted that the corrections and additions are not always and only of an editorial and linguistic nature. For example, when Gribaldi enumerates the ones that falsely claimed that Christ was not begotten by the Joseph in the manuscript, we find enumeration: Carpocrates, Cerinthus, Ebion, and Photinus. It was rewritten from Servet (1531, 6a) with one addition by Gribaldi (Ebion). Nevertheless, in the manuscript, "Cerinthus" is added by a different hand, so one of the students had to have been acquainted with this theological issue and was able to supplement the passage (Fig. 7)[19].

The second kind of annotation is strictly focused on the meaning of the text and highlights the passages in which *Scriptor* E was interested. It should be noted that even the annotators that were mostly focused on editing the text, like *Scriptor* B, a pioneering one in this regard added also the *"nota"* annotations. For example, he left one such marginal note next to a text portion dealing with Math 16:16–17, where Gribaldi suggested that "as God the Father cannot be comprehended except through Jesus the Son, neither can the Son be understood except through the divine revelation of the Father."[20]

Moving to the theological consequences, one may ask what was so disturbing in these notes to have prompted the trial commission to ask the third question: "who made the underlines in the said book and notes in the margins?" The passages highlighted are in particular the ones where Jesus is discussed as a man of human nature, as in the case of the very first one already present in the preface by "Alphonsus Lyncurius Tarraconensis" (the underlines below follow the ones in the manuscript):

Marginal notes and brackets	Main text (with highlights indicated by underscores)
Son of man	There is not a single syllable [in the Old Testament] (as he was wont to say) which does not prefigure that most divine man, Jesus Christ the redeemer.[21]

---

19 Gribaldi 2010a, 24–25 (Hauptstaatsarchiv Stuttgart MS A 63 Bü 25/11, 18). The cross-references (here and below) to page numbers in Servet's *De Trinitatis Erroribus* given after Hughes and Zerner (2010).
20 Gribaldi 2010a, 48–49: "sicut deus pater non nisi per Jesum filium cognosci potest, ita nec filius ipse cognoscitur nisi per divinam patris revelationem" (Hauptstaatsarchiv Stuttgart MS A 63 Bü 25/11, 35).
21 Gribaldi 2010a, 2–3: "[In Veteri Testamento] nullam esse (sic enim loqui solebat) syllabam quae hominem illum divinissimum Iesum christum redemptorem non praefiguraret"; marginal note: "*Filius hominis*" (Hauptstaatsarchiv Stuttgart MS A 63 Bü 25/11, 3).

The marginal note *"Filius hominis"* corresponds with Servet's observation from *De Trinitate erroribus* (1531, 3a): "for the Hebrew expression *Son of Man*, like *son of Adam*, means nothing other than a human being." And the student further marked the passage on the separation of the natures of God the Father and Jesus the Son:

> [Servet] showed beyond a doubt that there is by <u>nature only one</u> God the Father, the creator of all things, and one Son of God, <u>Jesus, the man</u> who was crucified.[22]

> { Since the eternal, unchanging, and inconceivable God wished to reveal the awesome wealth and treasure of his infinite power, wisdom, and goodness, he chose to beget a <u>human</u> son of his own, <u>in whom he would be perceptible, and who would carry out all his will. Through him and by him,</u> God the Father made and created all other things [Heb 2:10].[23]

These statements were also in line with Servet's views described in the *De Trinitatis erroribus* (6a). Another group of headings concern the conception of Jesus and his transformation from the Eternal Word:

> John reveals the way in which Christ was conceived from the incorruptible seed of God: how the *Words of God*, which *was with God* before all creation and *through whom all things were made* [John 1:1–3], acting as God's seed, flowed into the womb of the Virgin.[24]

According to Gribaldi, Jesus did not exist before his transformation from the Eternal Word in the Virgin's womb—these should be understood as two separate beings (Fig. 6):

---

22 Gribaldi 2010a, 4–5: "<u>Unum tantum</u> natura deum patrem scilicet omnium conditorem, et unum dei filium Iesum <u>hominem</u> crucifixum ostendens" (Hauptstaatsarchiv Stuttgart MS A 63 Bü 25/11, 5).
23 Gribaldi 2010a, 20–21: "Deus igitur aeternus, immutabilis, et incomprehensibilis admirabiles suae infinitae potenatiae sapientiae et bonitatis ac thesauros manifestare volens, <u>filium hominem sibi</u> generare decrevit, <u>per quem et perceptibilis fieret et omnem suam voluntatem adimpleret per quem, et propter</u> quem omnia alia deus ipse pater fecit atque creavit" (Hauptstaatsarchiv Stuttgart MS A 63 Bü 25/11, 15).
24 Gribaldi 2010a, 22–23: "Quo modo autem christus ex dei semine incorruptibili conceptus sit, declarat Joannes quia verbum dei quod fuit apud ipsum deum, ante omnem creationem" (Hauptstaatsarchiv Stuttgart MS A 63 Bü 25/11, 16).

Marginal notes and brackets	Main text (with highlights indicated by underscores)
☞ *Note carefully*	"Therefore," Tertullian says, "it was flesh that was born, and that flesh will be the Son of God." For the Son of God was born. We did not begin to call the Word of God the Son until, in the womb of the Virgin, it was made corporeal and visible and thus was made a man. Nonetheless, in God's terms, in light of his eternity, the Son has always existed.[25]

In fact, in his *Adversus Praxean*, Tertullian of Carthage quoted this statement as one in which his opponents (followers of Praxeas) believed (Hughes and Zerner 2010, 276). Nevertheless, Tertulian was the earliest major Christian author writing in Latin, and pioneer of Trinitarian theology. One of the students marked this passage as highly important ("note ... carefully").

What is more, the student was interested in the method of biblical analysis, for which Servet was known—that is, philological and literal interpretation based on the Valla-Erasmus tradition of biblical criticism. Religious beliefs should be then based only on the authority of the Bible, not scholastic dogmatics. As Servet had put it in *De Trinitate erroribus* (1531, 13b): "for you must bear in mind that all things written about Christ took place in Judea and in Hebrew tongue" (Friedman 1978, 28). The student highlighted thus the whole passage concerning Luke 1:35, where the angel addresses Mary: "Therefore the child to be born will be holy and will be called the Son of God." Gribaldi interpreted the Greek inferential word "διό" (therefore) as "*quapropter*" and "*ideo*" in Latin, which means "therefore," "for that reason," etc. (Hughes and Zerner 2010, 275). The translation of this word was already a point of controversy after Servet's *De Trinitate erroribus* (6a–b), where he argued that only Jesus the man—not the Word—can be called the Son of God. This provoked Calvin to respond in his *Defensio orthodoxae fidei de sacra Trinitate* (1554). He explained that heretics like Servet overinterpret the word and, on that basis, believe that Christ became the son of God because he was anointed as a man (Hughes and Zerner 2010, 275). The anonymous student

---

25 Gribaldi 2010a, 37: "Caro igitur (inquit Tertullianus) nata est, et caro erit filius dei, nam filius dei natus est, nec prius verbum dei apud nos filius dici coepit quam in utero virginis corporeum, et visibile, et sic homo factum est quamvis apud deum in lumine suae aeternitatis filius semper fuerit"; marginal note: "? Nota hunc locum et lege diligenter" (Hauptstaatsarchiv Stuttgart MS A 63 Bü 25/11, 27–28).

marked the whole fragment regarding the issue in the manuscript with highlights and marginal notes:

Marginal notes and brackets	Main text (with highlights indicated by underscores)
Why this child is called Son of God	Note the inferential word *quapropter* [because of this] or *idcirco* [therefore], and you will grasp the meaning of the inference whereby the child is called Son of God [Matt. 1:18–23]. <u>Undoubtedly, this was because he was born from God and a virgin.</u> The same understanding of the sonship of the man Jesus Christ is set forth in the book of Daniel, which calls him *a stone cut by no human hand* [Dan. 2:34,45]. ... Note, therefore, that the power that was begotten
It is called Son of God	and conceived in the Virgin's womb, which was the Son of God and is called God, was the man Jesus Christ. Also note carefully what [the angel] says in Luke: "The son whom *you will conceive and bear will be called the Son of* God and *he will be great* in the sight of God" [Luke 1:31–32] (...).[26]

Relying entirely on the Bible also involves a rejection of theological terminology "made up by theologians," as Servet said about the "Trinity." The author of the highlights was interested in the passage where the dogma of hypostatic union and *communicatio idiomatum* (exchange of the properties) is rejected for the same reasons. The latter was applied to Christology by Cyril of Alexandria (d. 444) and meant that even though the divine and human nature of Christ are separate, the attributes can be ascribed to each other through their union in the one person of Christ. It played a significant role in Luther's theology (Christology and views on the Lord's supper) (Lindberg 2002, 385; Michel 1922, 595–602). Theologians who share this view are referred to in the manuscript as "falsely speaking sophists":

---

26 Gribaldi 2010a, 24–25: "Nota vocem illativam quapropter, aut idcirco, et collige rationem illationis, quare filius dei partus ille vocetur, nimirum, quia ex deo, et virgine natus est, eadem filiationis ratio de homine Jesu Christo apud Danielem exponitur qui eum vocat lapidem sine manibus abscisum item; Nota igitur quod potestas illa in utero virginis genita, et concepta, quae filius dei, et deus dicitur, est homo ille Jesus Christus. Nota etiam diligente quod dicit Lucas. Is filius quem tu concipies, et paries, filius dei vocabitur ..."; marginal notes: "Quare filius Dei partus ille vocetur"; "Filius Dei vocabitur" (Hauptstaatsarchiv Stuttgart MS A 63 Bü 25/11, 18).

Marginal notes	Main text (with highlights indicated by underscores)
	Christ was formed from the Word itself, by a process of transformation. In the Virgin's womb, the incorporeal and invisible Word of God, by which all things exist, became corporeal, visible, and capable of suffering. And John, employing words in their usual way, correctly says the Word became flesh [John 1:14]—that is, a human being—not by means of a union, or[27] by communicatio
And the word became flesh	idiomatum, as our theological sophists falsely assert, but in reality and by a process of transformation. Therefore, Christ is nothing other than the Word of God itself, made
Christ—what	corporeal and human.[28]

Gribaldi's approach was based on a literal reading of the Bible and referred to Gospel witnesses and their expertise: "Could it be that these rough-hewn, uneducated men knew anything about hypostases and connotatives, or talked about *communicatio idiomatum*?" (Gribaldi 2010a, 51). At the very same moment, Melanchthon was also criticizing the *communicatio idiomatum* because, according to him, it could not be applied on an ontological level. He kept repeating this statement right through the middle of the 1550s, when a series of regional conflicts on Christology and the Lord's Supper were spreading among Lutherans. In them, Melanchthon took an active position against the radical Lutherans, supporting the Reformed wing. Zaleski and Kula, studying in Germany, must have heard about the so called Second Eucharistic Controversy (*Zweiter Abendmahlsstreit*) and perhaps they were looking for comments on this very topic.[29] Moreover, it is known that Petrus Gonesius travelled with a thick manuscript volume entitled *De communicatione idiomatum nec dialectica, nec physica ideoque prorsus nulla* (Jasnowski 1936, 13). Nikolaus Selnecker (1530–1582), having reviewed it at Melanchthon's behest, concluded that the author was convinced of the antitrinitarian heresy, denied and ridiculed the *communicatio idiomatum*, and regarded Christ as God born of

---

27 In the manuscript, "*sed*" corrected by Hughes and Zerner (2010, 26) without marking to "*sicut*" (Hauptstaatsarchiv Stuttgart MS A 63 Bü 25/11, 20).
28 Gribaldi 2010a, 26–27: "Christus autem ex ipso verbo convertibiliter factus est. Nam ipsum verbum dei per quod omnia constant incorporeum et invisibile, in utero virginis factum est corporeum visibile, et passibile, et Joannes vere, et proprie dixit, et verbum caro, id est homo factum est, non per unionem sed idiomatum communicationem, ut nostri Theosophistae male opinantur, sed proprie et convertibiliter, Christus igitur nihil aliud est, quam verbum dei ipsum corporeum, et homo factum"; marginal note: "Et verbum caro factum est," "*Christus quid*" (Hauptstaatsarchiv Stuttgart MS A 63 Bü 25/11, 20).
29 I thank Marta Quatrale for pointing out this issue. See Quatrale 2022, 143–177; Hall 2014, 185–197.

man (Kot 1963, 76). This may be another trace of the student's examination of whether Gonesius believed in Servetus' heresy (as suggested by Drohojowski during the trial).

Considering Gribaldi's and Servet's commitment to the Bible, it may be said that their close reading of the Holy Scripture does not mean a complete denial of tradition but rather a reaching out to authorities who lived as close as possible to the time of biblical events to grasp their true historical circumstances. One of the Polish students was interested in these early sources because he highlighted references to Irenaeus (c. 140–c. 190), Apollo of Alexandria, and mentioned Tertullian.

The longest underlined section is the entire passage with quotes from Irenaeus (covering three pages of the manuscript) with a heading in the margin "words of Saint Irenaeus."[30] Gribaldi copied longer passages from the third book of Irenaeus' *Adversus Haeres* almost word for word, just as Servet did in *De Trinitate erroribus*.[31] The passage highlighted by the Polish student is a critique of the view of the two natures of Jesus, which begins with a questioning of the dogmas held in theology: "Our theologians, immersed as they are in such palpable darkness and ignorant of Jesus Christ, divide him up and split him into two distinct and separate natures, producing two Christs or two sons."[32] Gribaldi compares the belief that one Christ is visible and suffering and another invisible and incapable of suffering to the heresy of Valentinus (d. 165), the gnostic countered by Irenaeus. Moreover, in the Irenaeus citations, it is strongly emphasized that Jesus became the Christ and that the Word incarnated in him with his conception. This is a second point with respect to which Gonesius could have gone into intellectual debt to his master, since in his *De Deo et Filio eius* and *De uno vero Deo* written in the 1560s, he also invokes the authority of Irenaeus to show the two natures of Christ as well as his limited knowledge: "Irenaeus confesses without distinction that the Father is greater than the Son and that the Son did not know about the day of judgment, yet he was considered orthodox and still is."[33]

---

30 [V]erba S[ancti] Iraenai (Hauptstaatsarchiv Stuttgart MS A 63 Bü 25/11, 21).
31 It should be mentioned that Calvin comments widely on the same *loci* to criticize Servet's heresy, while in Melanchthon's doctrine, Irenaeus played an important role in the theses on the gift of immortality (see Gribaldi 2010a, 94–98, and Meijering 1983, 67).
32 Gribaldi 2010a, 29: "Nostri vero Theologi tenebris palpabilibus immersi et Jesum Christum ignorantes illum dividunt ac solvunt in duas naturas distinctas, et separatas, duos christos aut filios introducentes..." (Hauptstaatsarchiv Stuttgart MS A 63 Bü 25/11, 20).
33 Gonesius 1560a, 65–66: "Irenaeus sine ulla distinctione confitetur Patrem Filio esse maiorem et Filium de die iudicij nescire et tamen pro orthodoxo habitus est et hucusque habetur" (Trans. mine). See also Gonesius 1560b, 78–79, where he quotes *Adversus haereses* II: 2:6, 28:6–8; III: 4:1, 6:4, 9:1, 11:7, 12:11.

Already on the first page of the manuscript, the student marked in the margin sources of thoughts, among which was Apollos of Alexandria, who according to Acts 18 promoted a form of Christianity under Jewish law and therefore was inconsistent with the Paul's mission to the Gentiles:

Marginal notes	Main text (with highlights indicated by underscores)
Math. 1	To begin with, no one has ever denied that the man
Lucae 1	born of the Virgin Mary and crucified by the Jews
	was named Jesus. (…) Just as your name, for instance,
	is Peter, and his, John, so too Jesus (as Tertullian says)
	is a man's proper name. Christ, on the other hand, is
Jesus Christus	a title. The Jews all admitted that he was Jesus, the son
	of Mary, but denied that he was the Christ. And they
	put out of the synagogue all who confessed Jesus to be
Acts 3	Christ [John 9:22]. For this reason Paul the convert,
	publicly and with great zeal, testified to the Jews that
	Jesus was the Christ [Acts 18:28]. Likewise Apollos of
Apollos	Alexandria, with tremendous fervor, confuted the Jews
of Alexandria	in public, showing by the scriptures that Jesus was the
	Christ or the Messiah.[34]

The underlining of the text and the annotations indicate the work of several people familiar with Servetus' thought since they were even able to suggest additions to the text. The themes that caught the attention of the annotators were the human nature of Jesus, his conception, the separation of the divine persons (Father and Son), and ancient accounts (Apollo of Alexandria, Tertullian, Irenaeus). Tomasz Drohojowski's claim that the Polish students wanted to check whether Gonesius was a Servetian actually fits, since, for example, passages from Irenaeus were also cited by Gonesius in his printed works. Regardless, the notebook attests to an interest in Servetian thought mediated by Gribaldi among Polish students.

---

[34] Gribaldi 2010a, 8–9: "In primis hominem illum ex Maria virgine natum et a Judaeis crucifixum dici Iesum nemo unquam negavit id enim nomen proprium, illius est, quod ei adhuc puero iussu angeli ipso die circumcissionis impositum fuit, sicut tibi petrus, et illi Johannes, est enim Jesus (ut ait Tertulianus) nomen proprium viri, et cognomen christus. Judaei illum Mariae filium esse Jesum omnes concedebant, sed christum esse negabant, et alienos a synagoga eos faciebant qui Jesum esse Christum faterentur, unde Paulus conversus magno et apero animo Judaeis testificabatur Jesum esse Christum"; marginal notes: "Math. 1," "Lucae 1," "Jesus Christus," "Apollo Alexandrinus" (Hauptstaatsarchiv Stuttgart MS A 63 Bü 25/11, 7–8).

4 Biblical Commonplaces: The *Locus communis de Trinitate*

When it comes to the second source, it has a very different form. It is a copy of a manuscript commonplace book with listed biblical *loci communes* that belonged to Michał Zaleski. The university's commission assessing whether the notebook dealt with Servet's heresy rewrote only the chapters on the Trinity: *Locus communis de Trinitate excerptus ex locis communibus Michaelis Salevii Poloni* (see Appendix II).[35] Unfortunately, I have not been able to find the Pole's entire notebook,[36] so it is impossible to judge what part of the whole notebook it originally formed and what the scope of the work as a whole was (what the other headings were, themes, whether only theological or also political, etc.). Melanchthon, Calvin, and Bullinger all paid attention to the ordering of the topics they analyzed. The selection of topics and their proper ordering count as a transition from the initial catechism-based phase of Protestantism to the stage of *loci communes* characteristic of the mid-16th century reformers (Earnshaw 2020, 92–96, and Muller 2000, 105–106). Below, I will analyze the extant booklet that is just an extract from a lost notebook or commonplaces-collection.

Among Zaleski's belongings, some additional manuscripts and books were also found: *Defensio orthodoxae fidei de sacra trinitate* by Calvin,[37] *Loci communes* by

---

[35] Hauptstaatsarchiv Stuttgart MS A 63 Bü 25/11: *Locus communis de Trinitate excerptus ex locis communibus Michaelis Salevii Poloni*.

[36] It is known that the materials left by Zaleski were given by the University to a merchant who acted as an intermediary between Tübingen and Poland, but their ultimate destination is unknown to us now. According to the letter sent to Christoph of Württemberg by the University commission, Niklas Varnbüler, professor of law, was authorized by Protten of Augsburg (who lent Zaleski money) to pay everything on his behalf and to pack up all his books, clothes, and his entire legacy and have it sent to Augsburg (Tazbir 1966, 74). About the potential journey of these books, see the entry for May 16, 1559: "Ratione occisi Poloni nuper decretum, ut scribatur in Poloniam ad cognatos Domini Michaelis Saletski. Hoc igitur conceptum in senatu praelectum, mandamus [?] scriptum ad Herbartum [?] Mercatorem in Augsburg ut litteras Poloni mittat in Poloniam. Haec duo scripta per omnia approbata tantum ut ⟨ mutare – F.K.⟩ omittatur vocabulum in latino concepto" (Universitätsbibliothek Tübingen MS UAT 2/1b: *Protokolle des Akademischen Senats*, 274v); as well as the entry for July 15, 1559: "rescripsit princeps super inquisitionis ratione suspectae opinionis habitae, suam Celsitudinem contentam et promittere ut avehentur libri ipsius cum supellectili ad Herbartum Augustanum" (Universitätsbibliothek Tübingen MS UAT 2/1b: *Protokolle des Akademischen Senats*, 275r —I would like to thank Farkas Kiss for transcribing the entries). The mentioned merchant originated probably from the patrician merchant family active in Augsburg (Reinhard 1996, XIV–XV).

[37] Perhaps he got it from his professor, Valentinus Erytreus.

Melanchthon, some books of Brenz,[38] and his own translation (into Polish) of Quintus Curtius' *De rebus gestis Alexandri Magni*. It is known that Kula also passed Zaleski *De elocutione* by Sturm (Tazbir 1966, 68–69, 71). Unfortunately, there is no comparative material by Zaleski's hand, so it is difficult to say whether his copy of Melanchthon's *Loci communes*, which was said to be covered with numerous notes, survived in the Tübingen University Archives.[39] According to Kiljan Drohojowski, who lived with him, Zaleski usually read the Bible, and on holidays, since they did not quite understand the sermons in German, he would explain Brentz' *Homilies*. It is known that "he attended *lectiones iuris* with enthusiasm, but also found in a book after him numerous *epistolas and declamatiunculas*, written *exercitii gratia* to the Polish nobility ... and especially diligently read *historias*" (Tazbir 1966, 72–73).

Certainly, it may be said that Zaleski did study the Bible on his own, using Castellion's translation first printed in 1551 (subsequent editions: 1554 and 1556),[40] as evidenced by some specific vocabulary present in the *loci* typical for Castellion— that is, *sermo* instead of *verbum*, *genius* instead of *angelus*, *lavare* instead of *baptizare* or *Iova* instead of *Deus* (in order to reflect the Hebrew tetragram—YHWH). These shifts resulted in part from Castellion's intention to replace Greek loan words by genuinely Latin expressions, which led Théodore de Bèze and Calvin to ridicule him for such linguistic extravagances (Bainton 1951, 40). We see the echoes of this translation in 1555, when Gribaldi was accused of exalting the first person of the Trinity, because for him "God the highest is like *Jove*, the first among them" (Williams 1992, 953). The choice of this Bible translation could be dictated by the influence of Celio Secondo Curione, who was a friend of Castellion. Significantly, it is known that the Anabaptists in Transylvania (e.g., Ferenc Dávid, c. 1520–1579) also used this translation (Balázs 1998, 67). Zaleski must have used the very first edition from 1551, since in the next ones Castellion changed some of his solutions (e.g., he replaced *lavare* with *baptizare*) after considering the criticism he

---

38 "Libros aliquot Domini Brentii" (Tazbir 1966, 66).
39 Of the 13 surviving copies, only one matches: *Loci communes seu Hypotyposes theologicae Philip. Melan.: recogniti ab auctore*, Argentorati [Strasbourg]: Iohannes Hervagius, 1523. I sincerely thank Nicole Domka for the assistance in browsing the *Loci communes* preserved in the Universitätsbibliothek Tübingen.
40 *Biblia Sacra ex Sebastiani Castallionis interpretatione* (Basel: Joannes Oporinus, 1551). He then published the French translation (Basel 1555). After many controversies, he also wrote the apologetic *Defensio translationum Bibliorum* (Basel: Joannes Oporinus, 1562).

received.⁴¹ Usually, Zaleski rewrote the quotations without changing anything except the conjugation or the word order.⁴²

The order of the notebook was probably of Zaleski's invention. Neither the list of biblical quotes in Calvin's *Institutiones* nor of Melanchthon's *Loci communes* match the Polish student's *loci*. The most telling are the words present in the headings as well as the organization of the notebook's chapters. The headings specified by the student are as follows (including the number of quotations assigned to each heading):

1. *Divinitatis ternio* (Divine triad)—12;
2. *Genitor persona prima divinitatis* (Begetter, the first divine person)—5;
3. *Unigena Patris Deus persona altera* (The only begotten of the father, God the second person)—20;
4. *Spiritus almus Deus persona tertia promanans ab utroque, nec non eius functiones et officia* (God the benevolent Spirit, a third person springing from each of them, and his functions and duties)—74;
5. *Eiusdem potestatis atque aeternitatis divinae sanctus spiritus, minus fuit cognitus usque dum Christus, ass(ur)e(c)tione⁴³ a morte, ira dei suorum gloriosus Victor apparuisset* (The holy spirit, who had the same power and divine eternity, was less recognized until Christ had appeared as the glorious Vanquisher of his people, after rising from the dead)—1;
6. *Rudibus divinarum rerum nulla scientia* (The unlearned have no knowledge of divine things)—1;
7. *Genitus Deo ante omnia secula filius* (The Son was born to God before the ages) —1.⁴⁴

At first glance, one can agree with the commission that Zaleski's notebook does not arouse suspicion from the point of view of the Trinitarian orthodoxy, since three divine persons were mentioned. However, attention should be drawn to the specific vocabulary. Zaleski's philological choices are certainly not accidental. After all, he was a student of Erythreus, Gribaldi, and probably of Sturm (whom he at least read), who strongly emphasized the importance of the words into which thoughts are put. Likewise, Melanchthon—whom he read so eagerly—understood

---

41 About the changes, see Sébastien Castellion, *Defensio suarum translationum Bibliorum* (Basel: Joannes Oporinus, 1562).
42 E.g., in John 14:8–10, "*qui me videt, Patrem videt*" instead of "*qui me vidit, Patrem vidit*" or, in John 16:8, "*arguet mundum*" instead of "*mundum arguet.*"
43 *ass(ur)e(c)tione*—correxi, ac. Assetione.
44 See Appendix II. In the English translations above, I tried to maintain the uniqueness of the terms used in Latin. I sincerely thank Andy Peteermans for his help in the matter.

and asserted that the art of speaking, the way language is used, is fundamental to the comprehension, organization, and transmission of knowledge (Bihlmaier, 46–49, and Moss 1996, 124).

The emphasis is on the bond between God and Jesus, who are not named as in the creeds ("Father" [*Pater*] and the "Son" [*Filius*]) but referred to as "Begetter" (*Genitor*) and the only begotten of the father (*Unigena Patris Deus persona*). In the latter case, it would be more common to simply apply a masculine form, as it was used with regard to Christ (*unigenitus filius*) rather than "*unigena persona.*" Judging by the headings, Zaleski considerably distanced himself from traditional Catholic trinitarian terminology.

Already in the first heading concerning the Holy Trinity, Zaleski does not use traditional terminology, instead calling it "*Divinitatis ternio.*"[45] This choice could already raise suspicion among the trial committee. After all, Servet did not negate the Trinity entirely but dismissed the scholastic terminology linked to it. Naming three of the "divine triad" in the following headings as "persons" also does not mean Zaleski agreed with the "papists." In fact, such a term was used by so called Tritheists (regarded by the Church as heretics)—that is, Christians that did not believe in the unity of the Trinity. They emphasized the individuality of each divine person by calling it "three divinity" (from Greek, τριθεΐα). Tritheism will start developing in the Polish-Lithuanian Commonwealth after August 1559,[46] so Zaleski's notebook may be a trace of even earlier reception. Needless to say, Gribaldi vacillated between Tritheism and Ditheism as he conceived the Father and the Son as two separate beings.[47] Perhaps independently of each other, but at the same time, Gonesius was working on his treatise on the Trinity, published ten years later, in which he used the Polish cardinal numeral in the masculine gender "Trzej" (i.e.,

---

[45] The noun *ternio, -onis* derives from "*terni*" (three each) and signified the "number three on a die" (Isidore 2006, 371 [18,55]) and "a set of three," "ternary," "triplet" (Charlton 1879). According to Aulus Gellius, it signified "triad," which was equivalent to the Greek τριάς (*Attic Nights*, 1.20).

[46] In the Polish-Lithuanian Commonwealth, the source of Tritheism was Francesco Stancaro (1501–1574), who paradoxically presented his ideas on congregation in the spring of 1559; he condemned antitrinitarians and wrote in a letter to Calvin that "the Arians here teach that the Father, the Son, and Holy Spirit are not the one God but three Gods in such a way that they are separate from each other" (December 4, 1560; see Wotschke, *Briefwechsel*, No. 208; the quotation follows Williams 1992, 1028). Thanks to him, some of the Calvinists realized that the concept of Trinity is an error, and there is one God, one Son, and one Holy Spirit (Williams 1992, 1028–1030; Caccamo 1970, 21; and Ogonowski 2021, 57–58).

[47] See Gribaldi 2010c, 225: "See therefore, how the scriptures are always accustomed to distinguish between God and the Son of God. If you look carefully you will see that scripture, except for three or four passages, always simply and absolutely calls the Father "God," and calls Jesus his Christ and Son. However, the divinity of the Son differs from that of other gods."

"Three," as in three men), thus distancing himself from the traditional trinitarian terminology in a similar manner to Zaleski (Gonesius 1570b).

In the *Locus communis de Trinitate*, he was mostly interested in the third person of the Trinity, as evidenced by the length of the fourth chapter on the Holy Spirit, which "springs" (*promanans*) from the "functions and duties" (*functiones et officia*) of God and Jesus (as proven by the 74 listed quotations, which comprise 64% of the whole notebook). The idea of the Holy Spirit following from both the Father and the Son was the subject of the so called *Filioque* ("and from the Son") controversy. The discussion started already in the 4th century, and it became one of the minor disagreements between the Eastern and Western Churches. The conflict was based on the question of whether "Son" should also be included in the Symbol of faith or not. After it had been added to the Creed at the Third Council of Toledo in 589 by the Latin Church in the form: "I believe ... in the Holy Ghost, the Lord and Giver of life, who proceeds from the Father and the Son," the orthodox theologians regarded "and Son" as interpolation (Gill, 913–914; Palmieri, 2310–2343). In this regard, the vocabulary used by Zaleski is also significant. The expression *"persona tertia promanans ab utroque"* (a third person springing from the previous two) seems to be a crypto-quotation from St. Basil's *Homilia de Spiritu Sancto.* Indeed, he was one of the Church Fathers, next to St. Augustine, whose scriptures were the basis for adding "and the Son" (*Filioque*) to the Western Church's creed. Moreover, he was one of the theologians that pointed out the heretical views of Arians and his view on Trinity laid the foundations for the orthodox view on the matter (Kariatlis 2010, 59–62). Usually, in discussing the "procession of the Holy Spirit from God" theologians used the Latin word *procedere* instead of *promanare*, the latter of which was used in the translation of St. Basil's text, which I found exceptional.[48] Even though Melanchthon quoted St. Basil several times in *Loci* against antitrinitarians (Hall, 129–142),[49] he also used the verb *procedere* both in his *Definitiones* (which was added to his *Loci* since the Leipzig edition of 1553) and in *Examen Ordinandorum* (1556).[50]

---

48 Basilius 1547, 144v: "Verum spiritus ex deo promanans eiusdem cum illo est subsistentiae: quae vero ex spiritu proftuunt ipsius sunt operationes. Hunc spiritum sanctum deus opulente in nos per Iesum Christum effudit. Effudit, inquam, non creavit, dedit, non condidit." The guiding metaphor is very clearly the springing (*promano/profluo/πηγάζω*) of water from a source (*fons/πηγή*). I cordially thank Andy Peetermans for explaining the ambiguities in the translation of this passage from Greek to Latin in the 1547 edition.
49 In the 1559 Leipzig edition, 8 times; see Melanchthon (1559, Vol. I, 40, 72, 74, 76, 78 [twice], 134, and 342).
50 See Melanchthon 1558, 705: "Spiritus sanctus est persona tertia divinitatis, procedens ab aeterno Patre et Filio, et ὁμοούσιος eis, et est amor, et laetitia substantialis"; Melanchton 1559, Vol. I, 78–79:

What is more, theologians from the University of Tübingen argued with the Orthodox Church about the precise formulation of the *Filioque* dogma in second half of the 16th century. The starting point for the discussion was the publication of the Greek version of the Augsburg Confession in 1559 (just a few months after Zaleski's murder). Melanchthon probably took part in preparing the creed; he forwarded it to the Joasaph II of Constantinople (d. c. 1565), patriarch of Constantinople. Tübingen theologians taught that the *Filioque* dogma was a crucial part of the doctrine of the Trinity.[51] Lutherans proved the three pillars of the *Filioque* dogma by joining them with biblical quotations. Their defense of this belief was based on reading the biblical text to prove the "surds and absurdities" into which one falls when one undermines them (Marschall 2002, 158). The biblical *loci* quoted by them were Rom. 8:9, Gal. 4:6, Phil. 1:19, and 1 Pet. 1:11, which refer to the Holy Spirit as the Spirit "of Christ" (Marshall 2002, 158). Almost all of those mentioned appear in the fourth chapter of the *Locus communis de Trinitate* by Zaleski. Other quotations listed by the student proffer the same meaning—the Spirit's proceeding also from the Christ. A few years later, this was also a controversial point for the Italian radical reformer Giorgio Biandrata's (1515–1588) manuscript presented in 1566 during the synod in Turda,[52] which was the first discussion on the Trinity dogma in Transylvania, which started the Unitarian controversy (Wilbur 1945, 32–35).

Regardless of these suppositions the use of the term *promanare*, which—in a broader context—may evoke associations with Platonic metaphors, may as well be a sign of Zalewski's humanist training and the need for variation—perhaps he simply wanted to use a more elegant word.

The last heading, with only one quotation, i.e., "The Son was born to God before the ages," is linked to the controversy regarding the two natures of Jesus. Gribaldi and Servet believed that the Son of God had been begotten before the world was created.[53] Gonesius also subscribed to this conviction and believed in the preexistence of Jesus until the end of his life. He expressed this in his work against the

---

"Constantopolitana [doctrina] defendit hunc articulum Spiritum sanctum esse personam procedentem a Patre et Filio."

51 A delegation of theologians from Tübingen, led by Jakob Andreä and Martin Crusius, arrived in Constantinople in 1573 (Benz 1949; Oberdorfer 2006, 55; Reinhard 2015).
52 The manuscript has been lost, but the transcript is preserved in Friedrich Adolph Lampa, *Historia ecclesiae reformatae in Hungaria et Transylvania*, Utrecht: Jacobus van Poolsus, 1729, 149–152.
53 Gribaldi 2010a, 97: "For this you must come to understand the mysteries of the Word, and become acquainted with that most holy man Jesus, the Son of God. *Before* all *the ages* [1 Cor 2:7] and from eternity, he was already God with God the Father, to whom all things are eternally present" See Servet 1531, 53a.

heresy of the Ebionites, entitled *O Synu Bożym iże był przed stworzeniem świata, a iż jest przezeń wszytko uczyniono przeciw fałesznym wykrętom ebiońskim* (*On the Son of God, and that he was before the creation of the world, and that all things were made through him, against the false prevarications of the Ebionites*; Węgrów 1570). Many Polish antitrinitarians shared his views, but they went on to deny this dogma under the influence of Grzegorz Paweł and Faustus Socinus, who rejected the doctrine of Christ's pre-existence (Ogonowski 2021, 39). According to Servet, it was the Word—not Jesus—that existed before creation (Servet 1532, 67b–68b). However, in this form, Zaleski's heading stands also in line with Melanchthon's definition (placed at the end of his *Loci communes* as a sort of dictionary) that is consistent with the traditional view of the Trinity: "The Son, the second divine person, was not created from nothing but was begotten by the Father, his eternal substance" (Melanchthon 1558, 705).[54]

Moving to the biblical commonplaces themselves in terms of confessional differentiations, the Castellion translation used by Zaleski includes the *Comma Johanneum* (1 John 5:7), over which there has been fierce controversy as to whether or not it is an authentic account. It was omitted by Erasmus of Rotterdam (accused afterwards of being Unitarian) in his edition of *Novum Instrumentum* (1516) and restituted in his subsequent editions of the New Testament (McDonald 2016, 13–70). This is the only passage in the Bible where the Trinity is explicitly mentioned.[55] The discussion was based on the fact that in the Greek source the three words are spirit, water, and blood. Soon after, Erasmus excluded it from his edition; it became one of the main points of discord in the age of flourishing biblical scholarship. In 1527, during one of the lectures on the First Letter on John, Luther claimed that Catholic apologists had added it clumsily only to counter the Arians (McDonald 2016, 63). As we have already seen, antitrinitarians like Gribaldi did not deny the existence of the three persons of the Trinity but undermined the identity of their substance, so the presence of the Johannine Comma does not prejudge the confessional views of the excerptor. Its presence in the notebook was already determined by the choice of the Bible edition from which Zaleski excerpted. Nevertheless, what is most important is that Zaleski was interested in the passages concerning the Holy Trinity.

What were the aims of Zaleski's excerpting from the Bible? Was it a response to Melanchthon's *Loci praecipuae theologici*, which he read so attentively, as evi-

---

54 "Filius aeterna est secunda persona divinitatis, non creata ex nihilo, sed a Patre ab aeterno genita de ipsius substantia" (Trans. mine). Even the same formula of *"persona divinitatis"* is present. The creation *"ex nihilo"* was linked with Christ (*logos*) by Arius.
55 "Tres sunt, qui testantur in coelo: Pater, Sermo et Spiritus Sanctus: et hi tres unum sunt" (*Biblia Sacra ex Sebastiani Castallionis interpretatione*, Basel: Joannes Oporinus, 1551, 264).

denced by the many underlined fragments and notes in the margins (what we know from the testimony of his colleagues)? It was not only a scholarly proposition on how to read the Bible, but also evidence of a new use of commonplaces in disputations in the midst of the religious crisis of Reformation Europe (Moss 1996, 136). For Melanchthon, searching and structuralizing *loci* was equal to the preparation of arguments for theological disputes and civil deliberations. It can be assumed that Zaleski was preparing himself for civil service, since orations on civil topics were found among his belongings. The first edition of the *Loci communes* by Melanchthon was focused on the Letter to the Romans, which he called the *"methodus totius scripturae"*—the method for reading all scripture. Melanchthon's *Loci* were to serve students' own readings, although growing concern for certainty in teaching can be seen in Melanchton's works from 1528, especially in ethical matters and the development of *loci* as a method of teaching (Kolb 2012, 31–33). Kusukawa (2003) sees in it a method similar to the catechisms. Catechetical exercise was meant to achieve unity of thought against heresy. Melanchthon's dialectics enabled teaching orthodox statements.

While antitrinitarian positions were spreading also among radical Lutherans, Melanchthon proposed his view on the Trinity and Christ in the second edition in a chapter entitled *De Tribus Personis Divinitatis* and then once again by adding a section entitled *De Filio* to the third edition (1543–1544). What is significant is that the German theologian recommended to his readers in this chapter that "the Christian reader should carefully note for himself other similar passages, I am presenting here only a few, so that one can daily strengthen himself when he is plagued with evil thoughts on this article" (Melanchthon 1555, 21). In the chapter devoted to the "Eternal Son," he enumerated biblical *loci* (mainly from John)[56] and demonstrated the literal differentiation between the Father and the Son by using the grammatical plural forms or listing passages with such words as "son" and "father." At the end, he instructed that "each person should himself carefully note similar passages, for listing them all here would take too long" (Melanchthon 1965, 19). Similar—almost grammatical—issues interested Zaleski. For example, he placed biblical quotes where *filius* appears under the second heading (e.g., Heb. 1:3–4; Ps. 2:7; Mt. 3:17; and Isa. 9:5).

Taking into account the kind of company Zaleski was in (Gribaldi, Curione, and Kula) and the kind of books he had in his apartment (Servet), one can conclude after Melanchthon that he was indeed "plagued with evil thoughts on this article" and should have sought certainty by selecting biblical quotes. Indeed, this aid-character of *Loci* was already praised by Luther, who stated that one should read it "dil-

---

56 Melanchthon 1555, 19–23: John 1:1, 1:14, 1:18, 5:19, 5:21, 8:58, 17:5, 6:17, 10:28, 6:44.

igently as well, until he has its contents fixed in his head. If he has these two [the Bible and Melanchthon's *Loci*] he is a theologian, and neither the devil nor heretic can shake him" (Mayes 2011, xv–xvi). The aim of such commonplace books, according to Melanchthon, besides storing information, was training in methods of systematic investigation, the collection of arguments and quotations for use in disputes, and learning critical reading (Moss 1996, 125). Zaleski's *Locus de Trinitate* is not an example of passive reception. He did not copy the headings nor the quotations from any authority. The structurization of biblical *loci* under specific headings shows Zaleski's individual approach to the Bible, tradition as well as academic and theological discussion. Although it is impossible to judge the exact confessional denomination of the *loci*'s author based solely on its contents, the headings reveal Zaleski's solid understanding of theological disputes and the controversies they were linked to. As Moss (1996, 136) put it, "for many a Protestant schoolboy in the second half of the 16th century, sectarian bias was built into his commonplace-book by appropriately placed quotations from the Bible." In this way, Melanchthon-Luther's conviction on strengthening the orthodoxy through *loci* fails. Zaleski's idiosyncrasy is visible already in the linguistic choices present in the headings that confirm his struggle to find and express the truth through proper language and structure.

5 Conclusion: Manuscript Circulation as a Platform for Heterodox Discussions

Considering that both Vergerio and the university representatives wanted to close the case as quickly as possible, one can doubt their swift verdict that there was no center of Servetianism in Tübingen. The inconsistency of the testimonies is additionally inconclusive. It is also evident that the commission was not interested in the different handwritings in the *Declarationes* that imply that not one but at least five people had written, read, and even edited the manuscript. It is not without significance that, after the investigation, the Poles studying in Tübingen moved to Basel. Moreover, Gribaldi's affair of 1557—when he had to flee Tübingen—and the trial of Polish students in 1599 had an impact on the university, as evidenced by the holding of a disputation at the university a few years later, on July 15, 1566, where Tritheistic views (summarized in accordance with Gonesius' logic) were rejected by the well-known Lutheran theologian Jakob Andreä. A record of the discussion—held in 1566 on the occasion of Mikołaj Krzysztof Radziwiłł's (1549–1616, the son of Mikołaj Radziwiłł Czarny) sojourn at the university—is preserved in the manuscript *Colloquium de Sacro Sancta Trinitate*, which lists in three columns the *loci communes* from the "extreme heretics" proposing that there are two or three gods of the Trinity ("Ditheists," "Tritheists"), through the "moderates," and finally the "minor ones" ("Sabelians").[57]

The analyzed manuscripts represent other types of confessional engagement. The marginal notes and highlights in *Declarationes* betray readers interested in proving the human nature of Christ. The annotations in *Declarationes* can also be seen as a reaction to discussions held in the 1550s in Germany and Poland, like the Secemin synod and Gonesius' excommunication by the Reformed Synod. The statements most likely to be true were those by Drohojowski, who heard that Poles discussed the work and planned to publish it.

Zaleski's *loci communes*, on the other hand, indicate that he was very interested especially in the concept of the Trinity and looked for evidence for the separation of three divine persons in the Bible. Zaleski was acquainted with freethinkers (Curione, Gribaldi); among his relatives, there were antitrinitarians, like Jan and Stanisław Lutomirski (d. 1575, Kot 1921, 113). In preserved part of his notebook, echoes of disputes characteristic of the Tritheistic faction in antitrinitarianism are evident, even before they became entrenched in Poland. Nevertheless, Zaleski's interest in the Holy Spirit points to other sources than the thought of Gribaldi, who was hardly interested in the third person of the Trinity. The fact that they were of interest to a student who was primarily preparing for civil service testifies to the depth of the theological complexities at work, reaching all the way to students who themselves began to penetrate the intricacies of, for example, the Trinity. A search for *similia* in the headings of Zaleski's *loci communes* led first to the conclusion that Zaleski was transcribing Castellion's Bible. A textual analysis of the headings' wording then pointed to Zaleski's philological interests and indirectly revealed his familiarity with discussions held in Reformed congregations in Poland (just in the moment of the separation of the antitrinitarians) as well as between radical Lutherans, Lutherans, and foreign antitrinitarians in Germany from the 1555–1560s period. An extract from the Zaleski's *loci communes* testifies to his search for biblical quotations that could be used as arguments in the discussions of the time (comparison of the notebook with the doubts expressed by Melanchthon in the 1550s and in his *loci* also brought positive results). Notably, the best testimony of Zaleski's personal commitment to the Protestantism movement is his efforts to spread the confession of Polish Reformers from 1555.

---

57 *Colloquium de Sacro Sancta Trinitate praesente Illustrissimo Principe ac Domino, Domino Nicolao Christophero Radziwiell ... breviter et bona fide descriptum*, Thubingae: 15 Julii anno 1566 (Staatsarchiv Zürich MS E II 367: 141–148). See Daugirdas (2012, 66–67). I sincerely thank Wojciech Kordyzon for pointing out the manuscript to me.

All these examples prove that students were important agents for transferring unorthodox ideas and that by examining their notes we can learn what stirred not only their minds but also consciences. It is important to remember that it was through a student (Gonesius) that antitrinitarianism entered the Polish-Lithuanian Commonwealth. Moreover, the analyzed manuscripts represent the earliest written echoes of Tritheistic and Servetian inspiration among Poles, as it is only from 1570 onward that Gonesius started to publish his works. The notes analyzed were produced six years earlier than the official separation of the antitrinitarian Minor Reformed Church (known as the Polish Brethren).

Finally, these notes and the *loci communes* show how the "heretical" discourses were evolving outside the circulation in print. Even here, in the manuscript circuit, authors did not reveal themselves and wrote under pseudonyms or borrowed names (as in the case of the *Declaratio*, written by Gribaldi in the name of Servet). Leaving works in manuscripts, passing along knowledge during private lessons, and at the same time pretending publicly to be orthodox were all part of "Nicodemitic" dissimulation as practised by Gribaldi, Curione, and their students.

Appendix I

Universitätsbibliothek Basel, Ms. Fr Gr I 2, no. 11: 11r–12r[58]
Compendiaria et succincta confessionis Christianae descriptio, quam amplissimi oratores Poloni in Comitiis Petroronicensibus [sic] Regi et universo senatui Polonico exhibuerunt mense Mayo, Latina lingua donata a Michaele Zalewio, Polono, anno Domini 1555

Omnes Adamo prognati in peccato concipimur et in lucem aedimur nec nisi tenebrae sunt universa ratio nostra, adeo ut nos ipsos naturamque nostram, nedum Deum, vitio interno abstracti, qualis sit, internoscere non possimus (Psal. 50). Prop-

---

[58] I sincerely thank Tomasz Płóciennik for verification of the transcription as well as suggestions of necessary corrections. References to the Bible occurring in the manuscript in the margins are placed in round brackets (without any changes). A paragraph division has been introduced to facilitate comparisons with the numbering of the articles contained in the manuscript *Confessio nunciorum cum responso episcoporum. Responsum die 23. Mai 1555 ferebatur* (held in Lviv in Dzieduszycki library, cf. the edition by Finkel 1896, 257–285) and in German translation, i.e., *Ein kurtze Abschrifft der Bekantnus des H. Christlichenn Glaubens so auff den Landtagk zu Peterkoif durch die Legaten des Könnigreichs Poln geschehen ist den Drietten May 1555* ([Coburg: Cyriacus Schnauss 1555]), which is preserved only in a copy now held in Biblioteka Książąt Czartoryskich in Krakow (1552 I Cim).

terea tradidit nobis Deus sua voce legem, quae conniventibus[59] oculis nostris apertis peccatum et caliginem nostram foras evocaret (Ioan. 4; Rom. 8; Galat. 3; Math. 11).

Demisit nobis ex alto unicum filium suum, ut ille ageret doctorem, informatorem, a peccato, morte et ira Dei liberatorem nostrum (1 Corinth. 1).

Deum enim ab orbe condito nullus hominum vidit umquam neque ratione corporis illius notitiam vel minimam consequi potuit, donec Christus ipse venit, patefacturus nobis et patrem et voluntatem patris (Ioan. 5)

Cuius rei causa Christus Dominus conlumen exabundans orbis huius: quod lumen qui maxime amat studioseque colit et a verbo eius neque ad dexteram, neque ad sinistram deflectit, is profecto non offendit tenebras, sed habet lucem perpetuandae vitae (Mat. 11).

Hunc solum doctorem, hunc magistrum, hunc servatorem solus caeli et terrae universae sator et conditor Deus, ut auscultaremus, sua voce in mandatis reliquit, quoniam is existens eiusdem naturae proprius filius Dei ementiri nescit; omnes vero homines, qui eius doctrinam aversantur negliguntque, etiamsi orbis potentissimi sibi videantur, mendaces sunt (Psal. 113; Ioan. 14).

Hic nobis palam produxit omnia et patefecit, quod ad animi nostri immortalitatis et foelicitatis spem plurimum pertinebat. Ex quo liquet reiecto hoc Christo vel per securitatem neglecto neque rem, quantumvis appareat magni momenti, neque creaturam posse nos ab ira Dei[60] emancipare. Huic soli prophetae universi testimonio sunt, quod omnes mortales, cuiuscunque sortis et conditionis sint, modo ei fidem habeant, dono ducent illius nomine peccatorum omnium infallibilem veniam (1 Tess. 1).

Solus enim Christus, cum nos operibus nostris, perfectione nostra legem eius severissimam et horroris plenam praestare impotes fuerimus, ut ab ira Dei vacui redderemur, liberos nos reddidit omnes, quicumque illi certa persuasione innitimur. Neque est ullum nomen sub sole aliud, quod nobis salutem afferre[61] posset, extra hoc unicum, qui Christus Iesus est (Act. 13; Act. 14).

Quicunque igitur, quacunque ratione adducti, salutem homini alicui atribuunt et Christo soli gloriam competentem assignant[62], ii authoritati passionis filii Dei detrahunt ipsumque indignissime contumeliis afficiunt (Esa. 42).

Christus enim meritum suae innocuae crucis per Evangelium (quod insonari cuilibet generi hominum indigenitali, nativa, adeoque propria lingua debet), per sacramenta sua hominibus fidentibus verbo suo proprium facit: ut lotione et

---

59 conniventibus *scripsi* (con)cutientib(us) *ms.*
60 *In ms. correctum e* duci.
61 *In ms. correctum ex* affere.
62 assignant *scripsi* non assignant *ms., sed* non *perperam suprascriptum.*

verbi Dei praedicatione, ut frequenti usu sacrosancti corporis illius, cruci pro nobis crudeliter suffixi, sanguinis denique nostri causa in perpetuam omnium vitiorum condonationem profusi (Mat. 28).

His sacramentis foedus divinum nobiscum est obsignatum, quod resignare vel minima in re infirmare si quis audacia ei [sic] redigitur, execratio est.

Caetera sacramenta nulla alia profitemur neque sacramenti nomine dignamur, nisi ea, quae authoritati verbi divini et oraculis esse innixa comperimus (Exod. 30; Deut. 12).

Etenim reiecto imperio et verbo Dei sub leges humanas, traditiones, somnia et figmenta, hecque loco divino revereri idololatria est.

Praeterea compertum habemus voce nostri caelum incola(n)tis magistri nullis aliis, nisi soli Deo parenti supplicationes precesque habendas esse, cum unicus ille scientia sua incomparabili abdita et penetralia cordium nostrorum pertingat, scrutetur et evolvat, eius vero occulta imperscrutabiliaque mortalium nemo. Praebet nobis evidens huius rei documentum antiquum foedus in ipso statim eloquiorum divinorum primordio, ut qui aliter Deo (praeter Iehovam Israelitarum Deum) supplicationes faceret, eum esse suorum popularium medio scindendum (Math. 26; 3 Reg. 8; Hier. 13; Exod. 22 ; Ioan. 14; 1 Timo. 2).

Apud hunc armipotentem [sic] Deum quo faciliore via aditum habeamus, neque sequestrem, neque mediatorem alium cognoscimus, Christo excepto Domino (Ioan. 2).

Non in postremis ponendum est mentes nostras scientia quoque harum rerum confirmare, Deum sese verbo suo, neque statuae, neque imagini, ad formam hominis mortalis fabraefactae, alligare voluisse (Exod. 20).

Sacramenta sive externa signa lotionis et caenae dominicae nobis fide Christo inauguratis veniam peccatorum in Christo afferunt.

Sine [sic] his nulla alia, et dignitate et energia quae conferri possunt, habent Christiani. Alia popularia munera et functiones, ut matrimonium, ut sacerdotum officia, ut confirmatio, nos non cumulatiores reddunt peccati venia; propterea illa uni caenae exequare renuimus: non quod illa[63] in reprehensionem vocemus, sed ut ea in sua dignitate relinquamus (August. ad Ian. epistula 118; Ambros. de sacramentis; Bernardus de coena Domini)[64].

Mortuis Christianis (qui suum diem obierunt) offensionis alicuius contra Deum consciis neque exequiis, neque pecunia paratis[65] liberationibus et hostiis iusta solvere audeamus: si enim credidere Christo et amplexati illum fuerint,

---

63 *In ms. correctum ex* illam.
64 Cf. Augustinus, *Ad inquisitiones Ianuarii*, epistola 118; Ambrosius Mediolanensis, *De Sacramentis*; Bernardus Claraevallensis, *Sermo in cena domini*.
65 paratis *scripsi* paratur *ms.*

verbo suo foventur (etiam nullis nostris precibus adiuti) in[66] illis divinitus promissa et designata vita; sin minus, in ima tartara tanquam saxa sedebunt. Misse et vigiliae caeteraque humana somnia et instituta non eos liberant[67] (Ioan. 3; Marc. 6).

Ergo qui adiunxit fidem filio, in condemnationem non veniet; qui non adiungit, aeternae morti obnoxius est (1 Ioan. 5). Qui filium Dei possidet, vitam reportat permanentem; qui vero ab eo refugit (etiamsi omnia collegia sacerdotum, omnes conventus rasorum gamratorum in unum accervum preces suas et missas accumulent auxiliares, illis ulla ratione haud poterunt praebere manus), morte plectetur. Qui crediderit et ablutus fuerit, in vita consequenda optatum feret; qui non crediderit, compingetur in tenebras (Marc. 16).

His de rebus cum abunde apostoli, tum etiam sanctorum patrum literis proditum est. Dicit enim Apostolus: "Nolo vos ignorare fratres de his, quae [sic] obdormierunt, ne cruciemini, ut caeteri, qui spem non habent. Si enim credimus Iesum esse mortuum et resurrexisse, ita Deus etiam eos, qui per Christum obdormitant, ducet cum eo" (1 Tess. 4).

Cum in praesenti seculo sumus, sive orationibus, sive consiliis invicem posse nos adiuvari. Cum autem ad[68] tribunal Christi venerimus, nec Iob, nec David, nec nos rogare posse pro quoquam, sed unumquemque portare onus suum (Hiere. 13; Ps. cap. 4).

Hic vita aut amititur ⟨aut tenetur⟩, saluti aeternae cultu Dei et fructu hic providetur. Quando hinc excessuri sumus, nullus locus iam poenitentiae est, nullus satisfactionis effectus.

Morum corrigendorum nullus alius quam hac in vita locus, nam post hanc vitam quisque id habebit, quod in hac vita sibimet conquisivit. Vias duas, unam patentem et laxam, in arctum, coactam angustioremque alteram: hanc ad vitam, illam in exitium vergentem (Aug. epistula 54).

Vox salvatoris et imitatoris discipulique eius Augustini aperuit, ubi servator relicta vulgari per arctam contendendum[69] esse censuit. Augustinus caelum receptaculum piorum docet, Gehennam autem perversorum, cum dicit: "Primum fides catholicorum divina authoritate regnum credit caelorum, unde—sicut dixi[70]— ⟨non⟩ baptizatus excipitur. Secundo Gehennam, ubi omnis apostata vel a Christo

---

66 in *scripsi* an *ms.*
67 *In ms. correctum esse videtur.*
68 *In ms. correctum ex* ante.
69 contendendum *scripsi* (con)tentendam *ms.*
70 *In ms. correctum e* dixit.

fide alienus paenas sustinebit. Tertium penitus ignoramus, imo nec esse e sacris literis comperimus" (Aug. lib. 6 de tempore)[71].

Fidei nostrae symbolum, sive collectam, verbum sacrosanctum iussaque divina amplexamur et doctrinam divinitus traditam, puram et sinceram profitemur.

Nam de figmentis hominum sic servator noster dicit Christus: "Temere me colitis, docentes doctrinas et figmenta hominum"[72]. Item: "Omnis plantatio, quam non plantavit pater meus, radicitus evelletur"[73].

Haec nobis referre de religione, serenissime Rex, quandoquidem tuo iussu et voluntate horum comitiorum initium de ea iactum sit, nominis proceres, optimates, palatini, castellani, pontifices, qui hunc frequentem consessum completis et gravitate vestra augusta et potentia honestatis, visum est; vestrum erit nostrae voluntati et petitioni respondere et, priusquam negotium Reipublicae foelici omine inchoemus, hanc semel susceptam ad suum exitum deducere.

Τέλος.

Appendix II

Hauptstaatsarchiv Stuttgart MS A 63 Bü 25/11
Locus communis de trinitate excerptus ex locis communibus Michaelis Salevii Poloni

1 Divinitatis ternio

Gen 1[:2]	Deum autem terram est atque rudix tenebris officium, profieri dum, et divinis sese super aquas libraret, iussit Deus ut existeret lux et extitit lux.
Gen 1[:26]	Faciamus hominem ad imaginem nostrum, nostril similem, qui dominetur piscibus aquatilibus, volucribus aereis.
Gen 11[:7]	Age iam descendamus et ibi eorum sermonem ita confundamus, ut alii aliorum sermonem non intelligat.
1 Ioann 5[:7]	Tres sunt qui testantur in coelo: Pater, sermo, et Spiritus Sanctus, et hi tres unum sunt.
Matth 18[:28]	Mihi data est omnis potestas in coelo et in terra. Vadite igitur doctum omnes gentes, eosque lavate in nomine patris, Filii et Spiritus Sancti, docentes eos exequi, quaecunque vobis praecepi.

---

71 Cf. Pseudo Augustinus, *Hypomnesticon contra Pelagianos et Caelestianos*.
72 Mt 15:14.
73 Mt 14:13.

Ioann 10[:30]	Ego et Pater unum sumus.
Ioann 14[:8–10]	Cui Philippus: Domine inquit ostende nobis patrem et satis erit nobis. Cui Iesus: Tantum iam tempus vobiscum sum, et tu me non novisti? Philippe, qui me videt, Patrem videt: Qui fit ut dicas, ostende nobis patrem? Non credis et me in patre, et patrem in me esse?
Ioann 14[:11]	Credite mihi et me in Patrem et Patrem in me esse.
Ioann 8[:15–18]	Vos more hominum iudicatis: Ego neminem iudico, et si iudicarem ego iuditium meum verum esset. Ut pote qui non sum satis, sed una mecum etiam adsit, qui misit me Pater. In vestra quoque lege scriptum est, duorum hominum testimonium esse verum. De me et ego ipse testimonium dico et dicit etiam is qui misit me Pater.
Is 11[:1–2]	Existet autem surculus ex caudice Isaei, et ab eius radicibus pullulabit Stolo, in quo residebit Spiritus Iova. Spiritus sapientiae et itteligentiae. Spiritus consilii et fortitudinis etc.
Gen 3[:22]	Cum sit homo, quasi unus de nobis, boni malique sciens periculum est, ne manum admoveat arbori etiam vitali, ut eius decerpto et qustato fructu, vivat in sempiternum.
Gen ⟨5⟩[74][:1–2]	Itaque hominem Deus ad suum, id est, divinam imaginem creavit, scilicet marem et foemmam, quibus foecunditatem dedit.
Eccle 1[:8–9]	Unus est Sapiens creator omnium supremus omnipotens et Rex Potens valde terribilis, sedens in solio suo Dominus et Dominator Deus. Is etiam sancto Spiritu creavit, vidit, enumeravit et mensus est.

2 Genitor persona prima divinitatis

Gen 1[:1]	In principio creavit Deus coelum et terram.
Eph 1[:3–4a]	Concelebrandus est Deus, Pater, Domini nostri Iesu Christi, qui nos fortunavit omni ubertate divina, in rebus Christi coelestibus: Quemadmodum vos in eo elegerat ante orbem conditum
Eph 4[:6]	Unus Deus et Pater omnium, qui est super omnia et per omnia et in omnibus.
Matth 6[:9–10]	Pater qui es in coelis, sancte colatur nomen tuum veniat regnum tuum fiat voluntas tua, ut in coelo sic et in terra.
Matth 11[:27]	Omnia mihi tradita sunt a Patre meo neque quisqam filium suum agnoscit nisi Pater, neque patrem quisquam agnoscit nisi filius et cui voluerit filius patefacere.

---

74 *Gen ⟨5⟩*—correxi, a.c. *Gene 1*.

3 Unigena Patris Deus persona altera

Hebr 1[:3–4]	Filius est divinae gloriae splendor et forma expressa substantiae, serens cuncta potenti sermone, facta per semet ipsum expiatione peccatorum nostrorum, consendit ad dexteram maiestatis sublimi tanto geniis factus praestantior, quanto excellentius quam illi nomen obstruit.
Ps 2[:7]	Narrabo Iovae decretum, qui mihi dixit: Filius meus es, ego hodie genui te.
Ps [2:12]	Osculamimi natum, ne si indignetur, vestras res perdatis, illius ira protiuns incensa: cui foelices quicunque confidunt.
Col 1[:12–16a]	Agimus Patri gratias, qui nos Idoneos reddidit ad participandam sanctorum sortem in luce, qui nos ex tenebrarum potestate vindicatos, transtulit in regnum sui charissimi fili, in quo filio liberationem habemus per eius sanguinem peccatorum veniam, qui imago est inaspectabilis Dei totius rerum naturae primogenitus. Utpote per quem condita sunt omnia, tum quae in coelis, tum quae in terra sunt.
Ioann 1[:1]	In principio erat Sermo, et Sermo erat apud Deum et Deus erat in Sermo. Is erat in principio apud Deum.
Rom 9[:5]	Quorum sunt patres, et ex quibus est Christus, quod ad humanitatem attinet, qui est super omnia Deus collaudandus in sempiternum.
Col 2[:8]	Videte ne quis sit, qui vos philosophia fallaciaque, vana praedetur, ex hominum institutione, mundique rudimentis, non ex Christo, in quo tota divinitatis plenitudo Corporaliter inhabitat.
Matth 3[:17]	Et ecce vox ex coelis dicens: Hic est meis charissimus filius, qui mihi acceptus est.
Matth 17[:5]	Adhuc eo loquente, ecce lucida nubes illos obumbravit, et ex nube vox exstitit, ita dicens: Hic est meus charissimus Filius, qui mihi acceptus est. Hunc audite.
Ioann 6[:57]	Quemadmodum vivit Pater qui me misit, ita et ego per Patrem vivo et qui me nescetur, is quoque per me vivet.
Ps 118[:22]	Lapis ab aedificatoribus improbatus, adhibitus est ad caput anguli, a Iova profectum est hoc, quod nobis mirum videtur.
Is 9[:5]	Puer nobis nascitur, filius nobis datur, qui humeris suis principatum gerit, qui nomine vocabitur admirabilis consiliarius, Deus potens, Pater aeternitatis, Princeps pacis.
Os 3[:5]	Postea rursum quaerent Israelitae Iovam Deum suum, Davidemque suum regem, formidabuntque Iovam, et eius bonitatem postremis temporibus.
Ier 30[:7–9]	Heu quanta, quantaque incomparabilis est illa dies et adversum tempus Iacobeo? Ex quo tamen evadet, eritque dies inquit armipotens Iova, cum ego eius iugum ex tua cervice abrumpam, tuaque vincula dissolvam, nec illi servient amplius alieni, sed Iovae Deo suo servient, Davidique regi suo, quem eis suscitabo.

Ioann 7[:16]	Mea doctrina non est mea, sed eius qui misit me.
Ioann 7[:28-29]	Iesus in sano clamans, docebat huiusmodi verbis: Et vos me nostis, et unde sim nostis: Et ego mea sponte non veni, sed ab eo missus qui verax est, quem vos non nostis. At ego cum novi, quippe quum ab eo sim, cumque is me miserit.
Ioann 1[:3]	Omnia per eum facta sunt, et absque eo factum est nihil quod factum est.
Ioann 3[:31-32]	Qui superne venit super omnes est: Qui a terra est, is et terrestris est, et terrestria loquitur. Qui a coelo venit, supra omnes est: quodque et vidit et audivit, id testatur, et tamen eius testimonium admittit nemo.
Ioann 8[:23]	Vos inferne estis inquit eis, ego superne sum: Vos ex hoc mundo estis, ego non sum ex hoc mundo.
1 Petr 1[:18]	Hanc nos vocem de caelo audivimus delatam, cum una cum eo essemus in sacro monte: Hic est meus charissimus filius, in quo me oblecto.

4 Spiritus almus Deus persona tertia promanans ab utroque, nec non eius functiones et officia

Rom 8[:9]	At vos non estis in carne, sed in Spiritu, siquidem Dei Spiritus habitat in vobis. Quod si quis Christi spiritum non habet. Is Christi non est
Rom 8[:11]	Quod si Spiritus eius, qui Iesum ex mortuis excitavit habitat in vobis, is qui Christum ex mortuis excitavit, etiam vestra mortalia corpora revocabit in vitam, per inhabitantem in Vobis spiritum suum.
Rom 8[:15]	Non enim servitutis Spiritum accepistis, rursus ad metum, sed spem accepistis adoptionis, per quem clamamus Abba Pater. Is Spiritus animis nostris testatur nos esse Dei liberos.
Ephes 1[:13-14]	In quo eodem vos quoque spem collocastis, audita veritatis oratione, hoc est vestrae salutis Evangelio, cui fidem habendo consignati estis sancto Spiritu promisssionis, qui pignus est haereditatis nostrae, ad asserendam partam possessionem, quae res ei gloriosam laudem pariat.
Eph 4[:1-3]	Exhortor ergo vos ego propter Dominum vinctus, ut ita vos geratis, ut dignum est ista conditione, ad quam vocati estis cum omni modestia ac mansuetudine, cum patientia, ferentes alius alium cum charitate Spiritus unitatem pacis vinculo tueri studentes.
Eph 4[:4]	Unum corpus, unusque Spiritus, quemadmodum in unam conditionis vestrae spem estis vocati.
1 Cor 12[:3]	Itaque declaro vobis, neminem esse, qui divino afflatu loquens, Iesum verbis execretur: itemque neminem esse, qui Dominum possit Iesum dicere, nisi per Sanctum Spiritum.

1 Ioann 4[:2]	Hic cognoscite Dei Spiritum: quisquis spiritus Iesum Christum corporatum venisse confitetur is a Deo est.
1 Cor 12[:4–6]	Sed discrimina sunt donorum, cum sit idem Spiritus: et discrimina sunt ministeriorum, cum sit idem Dominus: et discrimina sunt effectionum, cum sit idem Deus, qui omnia efficit in omnibus.
1 Cor 12[:11]	Atque haec omnia efficit unus idemque Spiritus, dispertiens privatim cuiqe ut vult.
1 Cor 12[:13]	Etenim uno Spiritu nos omnes unum in corpus loti sumus et Iudaei, et Graeci, et servi, et liberi, omneque unum Spiritum hausimus.
Matth 3[:16]	Et Iesus simul ablutus est, ascendit ab aqua: et ecce apertis ei caelis, vidit Ioannes Dei Spiritum descendentem, quasi columbam, et in eum venientem.
Act 2[:4]	Repleti sunt omnes Spiritu Sancto et diversis loqui linguis coeperunt, prout eis spiritus fari dabat.
Act 1[:3]	Accipietis vim Spiritus Sancti, qui vos invadet, mihique testes eritis, et Hierosolimae et in tota Iudaea, ac Samaria, denique ad ultimas terras.
Act 4[:31]	Illis comprecatis, contremuit locus, in quo congregati: repletique sunt omnes Spiritu sancto, divinumque sermonem libere eloquebantur.
Act 13[:1–4]	Erant Antiochiae, in ea quae erat ecclesia, vates, et doctores, Barnabas et Simon cognomine Niger, et Saulus. Eis autem Domino operantibus ac ieiunanti, iussit Sanctus Spiritus ut sibi Barnabam ac Saulum segregarent ad id opus, cui destinasset eos. Tum illi, cum ieiunassent ac supplicassent, manus eis imposuerunt, eosque dimiserunt. Atque ii a Sancto Spiritu emissi ad Seleuciam descenderunt et inde in Cyprum navigarunt.
Act 19[:1–6]	Interea dum Apollos Corinthi est, Paulus peragratis superioribus tractibus, venit Ephesum, et quosdam nactus discipulos sic alloquutus est: An Sanctum Spiritum adepti estis, cuum credidistis? Cui illi: Nos vero ne quidem an Spiritus Sanctus sit audivimus. Qua igitur ratione loti estis? Ioannis lotione inquiunt. Et Paulus: Ioannes quidem corrigendae vitae lotionae lavit, vulgo monens, ut venienti post se fidem haberent, hoc est Christo Iesu. Hoc audito illi in Domini Iesu loti sunt. Cumque manus eis Paulus imposuisset, invasit eos Spiritus Sanctus, linguisque loquebantur, ac vaticinabantur.
Ioann 20[:22–23]	Accipite Spiritum Sanctum, si quorum peccata remiseritis, remiseritis, remissa erunt: si quorum tenueritis, tenta erunt.
Matth 10[:20]	Non enim vos eritis qui loquemini, sed Patris vestri Spiritus in vobis loquens.
Ioann 14[:15–16]	Si me amatis, mea percepta servate, ego vero meum patrem exorabo. Ut alium vobis confirmationem det, qui vobiscum perpetuo maneat. Scilicet: veritatis spiritum, quem mundus consequi non potest
Ioann 14[:26]	Sed confirmator Spiritus Sanctus, quem mittet pater nomine meo, is vos omnia docebit et vobis in memoriam revocabit, quemcumque ego vobis dixi.

Ioann 16[:7–8]	E re vestra est, ut ego discedam nisi enim discessero, confirmator ad vos non veniet. Sin abiero eum ad vos mittam: atque ille ubi venerit arguet mundum de peccato, et de iustitia et de iuditio
Ioann 16[:13–14]	Verum cum venerit ille, videlicet veritatis Spiritus, praeibit vobis ad omnem veritatem: Non enim sua sponte loquetur, sed quaecunq auduerit eloquetur et futura vobis praenunciabit. Ille me illustrabit, siquidem de meo sumat, quae vobis exponat.
Ioann 16[:15–16]	Omnia quaecunque Pater habet mea sunt: propterea dixi illum de meo sumpturum esse, quae vobis exponat.
Ioann 15[:26–27]	Cum autem venerit confirmator, quem ego vobis a patre mittam, scilicet Spiritum veritatis, qui a Patrem proficiscetur. Is de me testabitur, quin et vos testes estis, qui mecum fueritis ab initio.
Luc 1[:34–35]	At Maria: Quo pacto fiet istud? Inquit Genio: Cum ego virum nesciam? Et ille respondens: Te Spiritus Sanctus invadet, et supremi vis inumbrabit. Itaque sanctus iste partus dicecur Dei filius.
Gal 5[:17a, 18]	Caro contra quam Spiritus, et Spiritus contra quam caro concupiscit. Quod si Spiriu agemini, non estis sub lege.
Gal 5[:24–25]	Si Spiritu vivimus, etiam Spiritum gradiamur, ne simus gloriosi, invicem provocantes, invincem invidentes.
Ioann 7[:37–39]	Postremo autem die, qui erat festi celeberrimus, consitit Iesus et hisce verbis clamavit: Si quis sitit veniat ad me et bibat. Qui mihi fidem habet, ut perhibent literae, eius ex ventre fluent perennis aquae flumina. Id autem dicebat de Spiritu Sancto, quem accepturi erant.
Ioann 3[:5–6]	Hoc tibi magnopere confirmo, qui ex aqua et Spiritus natus non fuerit, non posse in divinum regnum intrare. Quod ex carne natum, caro est, quod ex Spiritu natum est, Spiritus est.
Ioann 4[:13b–14]	Quisquis ex hac aqua bibit, tum rursum sitit: Sed qui ex aqua, quam ego ei dedero, biberit, is numquam sitiet, quin aqua quam ei dedero, fiet in eo fons scaturiens ad vitam aeternam.
Matth 3[:11b]	Venit post me, qui quidem adeo me praestantior est, ut ego non sim dignus, qui eius calciamenta portem. Is vos sancto Spiritu et igne abluet.
Ioann 1[:32–33]	Vidi Spiritum descendentem veluti columbam de coelo et super eo manentem. Ac equidem non noveram eum, sed qui me ad aqua lavandum misit, is mihi sic dixit: Super quem descendere et manere spiritum videris, is est qui Spiritu Sancto lavat.
2 Cor 3[:17]	Dominus aut Spiritus est: Ubi vero Domini Spiritus est, ibi est libertas.
2 Cor 3[:2–3]	Epistola nostra vos estis, inscripta animis nostris, cognoscenda legendaque cunctis hominibus: Est enim perspicuum, vos esse Christi epistolam, a vobis administratam, non atramento, sed viventis dei Spiritu descriptam.

1 Cor 2[:10–11]	Nobis autem Deus suo Spiritu patefecit. Spiritus enim omnia rimatur, etiam dei abditissima. Nam quis hominum scit hominis negotia, nisi hominis Spiritus, qui in eo est. Sic Dei negotia nullus scit, nisi Dei spiritus.
Eph 3[:14–17]	Huius gratia flecto genua mea ad patrem Domini nostri Iesu Christi, ex quo omnis et in caelo et in terra denominatur cognitio, ut pro sua gloriosa opulentia det vobis fortiter corroborari, per suum Spiritum, in interiorem hominem, quo habitet Christus, per fidem in vestris animis.
Tit 3[:4–6]	Sed postquam benignitas et humanitas extitit Servatoris nostri Dei, non ob iustitiae opera, quae fecimus nos, sed pro sua misericordia servavit nos, lavacro renascentiae renovationisque Spiritus Sancti, quo nos large persudit per Iesum Christum servatorem nostrum.
Gen 1[:2–3]	Quum autem terra esset iners atque rudis, tenebrisque offusum profundum et Divinus Spiritus sese super aquas libraret, iussit Deus, ut existeret lux, et extitit lux.
Ioel 2[:28]	Postea autem perfundam omne genus hominum meo Spiritu: vaticinabunturque vestri filii et filiae, vestri et senes somnia somniabunt, et iuvenes visiones videbunt.
Is 44[:1–4]	Ne metue mi Iacobeae tu probe, quem elegi, nam perfundam aqua sitientes, aridumque solum rivis: perfundam spiritu meo tuam stirpem, meaque beneficentia tuam progeniem, ita ut graminum more pullulent, tanquam ad quam profluentem falices.
Is 12[:3–4]	Cum sit mihi salutaris Deus, confidam intrepidus, postquam mea potentia et cantio. Ia Iova est, qui mihi saluti fuit. Et aquam laeti ex fontibus salutis haurietis, atque ita tum dicetis: Agite Iovae gratias.
Ex 8[:18–19a]	Hanc pediculorum effectionem magi cum suis carminibus imitari frustra tentavissent, pediculis cum homines tum bestias infestantibus, apud Pharaonem confessi sunt digitum esse Dei.
Matth 4[:1]	Tum Iesus a Spiritu subductus est in solitudinem, ut tentaretur a Diabolo.
Ioann 6[:63]	Spiritus est qui vivificat, caro nihil prodest. Verba quae ego vobis loquor, spiritus et vita sunt.
Zach 14[8–9]	Atque illa die manabit vitalis aqua Hierosolima parte sui dimidia ad orientale mare, altera dimidia ad mare postremum, idque et aestate fiet et terram hyeme, et erit Iova rex in universam terram.
1 Petr 1[:10–11]	Quam salutem exquisiuerunt ac persequtati sunt vates qui de conferendo in vos beneficio vaticinati sunt scrutantes quod nam aut quale tempus indicaret Christi Spiritus, quo erant praediti, praesignificans et Christi supplicia, et deinde secuturam gloriam.
2 Petr 1[:21]	Non enim hominis voluntate editum est unquam oraculum, sed Sancti Spiritus inflict locuti sunt homines divini.

Ier 23[:29]	Nonne sic sunt dicta mea, ut ignis, inquit Iova, utque petram diffindens malleus.
Gal 4[,6]	Et quoniam filii estis, misit Deus filii sui Spiritum in vestros animos, qui clamet: Abba pater.
Luc 2[:25-26]	Erat tum Hierosolimae homo nomine Simeon, qui homo iustus erat et religiosus expectans consolationem Israelitarum et Sancto Spiritu praeditus. Huic fuerat sancti spiritus oraculo dictum non prius esse mortem sensurum, quam Domini Christum vidisset.
Rom 5[:3-5]	Neque id solum, sed etiam gloriamur in calamitatibus illud scientes, quod calamitas patientiam parit, patientia probationem, probatio spem: Spes autem non pudefacit, quod Dei amore perfusi sunt animi nostri per spiritum sanctum nobis datur.
Rom 14[:17]	Non est regnum Dei cibus et potio, sed iustitia et pax et gaudium in Spiritu Sancto.
1 Cor 6[:19]	An ignoratis, vestrum corpus templum esse Spiritus Sancti, qui in vobis est, quem a Deo habetis?
1 Thess 1[:5]	Evangelium nostrum non fuit apud vos in verbis dumtaxat positum, sed cum potentia, Sanctoque Spiritu, et certissimis argumentis coniunctum.
2 Tim 1[:15]	Praeclarum istud depositum servato, per Spiritum Sanctum in nobis habitantem.
Tit 3[:5b-6]	Pro sua misericordia servavit nos, lavacro renascentiae. Regenerationisque Spiritus Sancti, qui nos large perfudit, per iesum Christum servatorem nostrum.
Act 10[:44-45]	Adhuc haec verba loquente Petro, invasit sanctus Spiritus omnes eam orationem audientes: Suntque attoniti ii, qui erant a circumcisione fidentes, quicumque cum Petro venerant, quod etiam extranei Sancti Spiritus munere perfusi essent.
Act 15[:28]	Visum est eum Sancto Spiritui, et nobis, nihil amplius vobis oneris imponere, quam haec necessario abstinendum a deastrorum victimis et sanguine, et suffocate, et stupro a quibus si vos continebitis, recte facietis.
Act 16[:6]	Peragrata autem Phrygia et Galatica regione, prohibiti ⟨a⟩[75] Sancto Spiritu verba facere in Asia, in Mitisiam profecti, conabantur per Bithiniam iter facere.
Num 11[:17]	Ego ad colloquendum tecum eo descendam, detrahamque de spiritu quo tu praeditus es, quod eis immittam.
Iudic 6[:33-34]	Cum autem Madianitae et Amalechitae Orientalesque universi, collatis copiis traiecto flumine, castra in valle Israelis fecissent, Gedeon Iovae spiritu cir-

---

75 ⟨a⟩ —correxi, a.c. e.

	cumsusus, tuba clangit, et evocatis Abiezerianis, nunctios dimittit ad omnes Manassenses.
Iudic 11[:28–29]	Huiusmodi verbis Iephthae ad Ammonitarum regem missis cum regi non persuaderetur. Iephta a Iova affatus Galaaditas Manassensesque petit, et ad maspham Galaaditarum progreditur.
Iudic 13[:25]	Puer cum Iova favente adolevisset, Iovae afflatu primum instinctus est in castris daniis, inter Saraam et Estaol.
Iudic 14[:19]	Deinde Iovae afflatu percitus descendit Ascalonem, caesisque inde triginta hominibus, eorum et arma abstulit, et elegantes vestes aenigmatis interpretibus dedit, atque ira accensus, domum patris repetiit.
Iudic 15[:13b–15]	Ita duobus recentibus vinctum loris, ex rupe educunt, qui simulac ad Maxillam venit vociferantibus in occursum eius Palaestinis Iovae afflatus instinctu, loris, quibus constricta brachia habebat, ab ruptis, perinde ac si ustulatum igne linum foret, manibusque solutis ac vinculis tabidam nactus asini maxillam corripit, et ea mille viros occidit.
1 Reg 10[:10]	Atque ubi illo videlicet Gabaam venerunt, occurrit ei caecus vatum, quos inter ipse divinitus afflatus vaticinari caepit.
1 Reg 16[:13]	Tum Samuel sumpto olei cornu, illum inter fratres suos unxit, atque ex illo die deinceps Iovae Spiritu fuit instinctus David.
1 Reg 16[:14]	Saul autem Iovae Spiritu destitutus.
3 Reg 18[:11–12]	Tu mihi nunc Iubes, ut domino nunctiatum eam Eliam adesse? Qui postquam a te digressus fuero, auferet te Iovae spiritus nescio quo.
1 Par 12[:18]	Hic Amasaeus princeps triginta, divino afflatu preditus: Tu vero salve David Isaei fili una, inquit, cum tuo comitatu.
1 Par 15[:1–2]	Tum Azarias odedi filius, divini Spiritus instinctu, Azae obviam egressus, eum sic est alloquutus: Audite me, Aza et omnes Iudaei et Beniamitae, Iova tum vobiscum est, cum vos estis cum eo. Et si eum quaeretis, invenietur vobis: sui eum deseritis, deseret vos.
Iob 4[:14–15]	Accidit mihi terror tremorque tantus, ut quantum est artuum meorum attonitos reddiderit. Et praeter meum conspectum transiens Spiritus mei corporis pilos horrificavit.
Ps 33[:6]	Ad Iovae dictum facti sunt coeli, et ad eiusdem Spiritum omnes eorum copiae

5 Eiusdem potestatis atque aeternitatis divinae sanctus spiritus, minus fuit cognitus usque dum Christus ass⟨ur⟩e⟨c⟩tione[76] a morte, ira dei suorum gloriosus Victor apparuisset

Ioann 7[:39]	Hoc autem dicebat de Spiritu, quem accepturi erant, qui ei fidem haberent. Nondum enim erat Spiritus Sanctus, utpote cum Iesus nondum gloriosus esset factus.

6 Rudibus divinarum rerum nulla scientia

Act 19[:1-2]	Interea dum Appollos Corinthi est, Paulus peragratis superioribus tractibus, venit Ephesum, et quosdam nactus discipulos, sic allocutus est: An spiritum sanctum adepti estis, cum credidistis? Cui ille: Nos vero ne quidem an Spiritus Sanctus audivimus.

7 Genitus Deo ante omnia secula filius

Eccli 1[:4]	Prima omnium creata est sapientia et prudens intelligentia ab aeternitate.
⟨Psalm 2:7⟩[77]	Narrabo Iovae Decretum, qui mihi dixit: Filius meus es, ego te hodie genui.

Appendix III

Hauptstaatsarchiv Stuttgart MS A 63 Bü 25

Summary of the hearing based on a German transcription edited by Janusz Tazbir (1966): "Aus der Geschichte der Propaganda des Servetismus im XVI Jahrhundert: das Verhör polnischer Studenten in Tübingen im Jahre 1559." In: *Archiwum Historii Filozofii i Myśli Społecznej* 12: 65–74.

---

76 *ass⟨ur⟩e⟨c⟩tione—correxi*, a.c. *assetione.*
77 ⟨ *Psalm 2 :7* ⟩ —*supplevi.*

Witness / Question	1. Stanisław Pieniążek	2. Marcin Strzelecki	3. Albertus Sylvius	4. Jan Tomasz Drohojowski	5. Mikołaj Kotkowicki (Kotkowski)	6. Kilian Drohojowski
1. Where did dominus Zaleski get this book?	This book did not belong to Zaleski but was given to him by another Pole to acquaint him with his [Servet's] doctrine (*"ut cognosceret illam doctrinam"*).	It was brought to Zaleski to be read by a Pole from Strasbourg whose name is either "*Steineslaus Kolo*" [Stanisław Kula] or "*Ioannes Jessmannus*" [Jan Jaskmanicki] (both studied under Erythreus).	The book was brought to Zaleski by Stanisław Kula, who was in Strasbourg and has now returned to Poland. He was in Tübingen and when he wanted to return to Poland, he left Zaleski many books, including this one. Before the murder, Tomasz Drohojowski (the fourth witness who had been assigned to keep Stanisław Kula's books) took this suspicious book from Zaleski back (he had the rest of Kula's books with him as well). Additionally, Vergerius' servant, Cleophas, who was quite close to Zaleski, left him numerous books in Polish and Italian (Zaleski, however, did not understand a bit of Italian).	Tomasz brought this book from Strasbourg; it belonged to Stanisław Kula, who had moved from Strasbourg to Tübingen. Kula wanted to leave Tübingen, so he gave many books to Zaleski. A month before Zaleski's murder, Tomasz had taken them from him, so they were not among his belongings.	He had never heard anything about the book. When he came to Zaleski, he did not talk to him about religion but about history.	The book was delivered to Zaleski by a Pole, Jan [Jan Pieniążek?], who was in Strasbourg and returning to Poland via Tübingen. He received it with other books (e.g., Sturm's *De elocutione*). Although he lived with Zaleski, he never saw him reading this book.

Continued

Witness Question	1. Stanisław Pieniążek	2. Marcin Strzelecki	3. Albertus Sylvius	4. Jan Tomasz Drohojowski	5. Mikołaj Kotkowicki (Kotkowski)	6. Kilian Drohojowski
2. What did dominus Zaleski think of it? Did he praise it and encourage you to read it or not?	–	Zaleski never spoke about it, nor about de Trinitate.	Zaleski had never read this book and did not order anyone to read it. Nor did any of Sylvius' disciples know anything about this book. Perhaps only "*Chilianis*" [Kilian Drohojowski].	He had not heard that Zaleski had a good opinion of this book by Servetus, let alone that he had ever praised it or told anyone to read it.	–	
3. Who made underlines in said book and notes in the margins?	–	–	–	Stanislaw Kula. This is the handwriting of Kula and no one else, as Thomas was able to prove "*per collationem litterarum*" from other notes in Stanislaw's books. When he was with Stanislaw and other Poles in Strasbourg at Erithreo's, they read the book themselves to see whether "*Koniesuki*" [Petrus Gonesius] was a Servetian or not.	–	

Continued

Witness / Question	1. Stanisław Pieniążek	2. Marcin Strzelecki	3. Albertus Sylvius	4. Jan Tomasz Drohojowski	5. Mikołaj Kotkowicki (Kotkowski)	6. Kilian Drohojowski
4. Who gave the book to Vergerio and told him about it?	Someone of Vergerius' household saw it at the preceptor's [Albert Sylvius] and carried it to Vergerius'.	Vergerio's cousin [Lodovico Vergerio].	A relative of Vergerius got this book from Thomas and delivered it to Vergerius (without Thomas' knowledge), as the latter did not want to give it to Vergerius but to his relative. About this, said Thomas [Jan Tomasz Drohojowski] will be better able to inform you. Thomas admitted before the university senate that Zaleski disagreed with Servetus' views.	Tomasz himself.	–	–
5. Did this person bring it to Vergerio of his own free will, without prompting, or was it delivered to Vergerio at his request?	–	He took the book without asking from the room of one of the Poles and brought it to Vergerius; they wanted to send the book back to Strasbourg.	–	Thomas sent it at the request of Vergerius through a relative of the latter.	–	–

Continued

Witness / Question	1. Stanisław Pieniążek	2. Marcin Strzelecki	3. Albertus Sylvius	4. Jan Tomasz Drohojowski	5. Mikołaj Kotkowicki (Kotkowski)	6. Kilian Drohojowski
6. Did dominus Zaleski have more books of this kind or not?	–	–	–	–	–	–
7. What is this book in Polish written by him?	–	Curtius translated into Polish by Zaleski.	–	This book in Polish, written by Zaleski's hand, is *Historia De Rebus Gestis Alexandrii Magni Curtii*, which Zaleski translated into Polish.	*Historia Curtii* translated into Polish by Zaleski.	–

Bibliography

Primary Sources

Manuscripts

Biblioteka Jagiellońska, Krakow
MS Przyb 87/83

Hauptstaatsarchiv Stuttgart, Stuttgart
MS A 63 Bü 25/11. http://www.landesarchiv-bw.de/plink/?f=1-1466032, last accessed May 14, 2023.

Staatsarchiv Zürich, Zürich
MS E II 367.

Universitätsbibliothek Basel, Basel
MS Fr. Gr. I 2 11
MS G I 9: 29–30; 40; 43; 46–57; 58–61; 64–65.
MS M. A IX,74, 2a.
MS. Ki. Ar. 26a.

Universitätsbibliothek Tübingen, Tübingen
MS Mc 161. http://idb.ub.uni-tuebingen.de/opendigi/Mc161, last accessed May 14, 2023.
MS UAT 2/1b. DOI: 10.20345/digitue.10762

University Library of Oklahoma, Oklahoma.
MS M 3319042–1001. https://repository.ou.edu/uuid/fcf02087-d672-518f-be63-0f58dc86cc6a#page/3/mode/2up, last accessed May 14, 2023.

Printed Sources

Basilius, Magnus (1547): *Operum D. Basilii Magni ... prior [-secundus] tomus*. Paris: Carola Guillard.
Calvin, Johannes (1554): *Defensio Orthodoxae fidei de sacra Trinitate, contra prodigiosos errores Michaelis Serveti*. [Geneva:] Robert Estienne.
[Castellion, Sebastien] (1551): *Biblia Sacra ex Sebastiani Castallionis interpretatione*. Basel: Joannes Oporinus.
[Castellion, Sebastien] (1554): *De Haereticis, an sint persequendi et omnino quomodo sit cum eis agendum, doctorum virorum tum veterum, tum recentiorum sententiae*. Magdeburg [=i. e., Basel]: Rausch, G. [i. e., Joannes Oporinus].
Castellion, Sébastien (1562): *Defensio suarum translationum Bibliorum*. Basel: Ioannes Oporinus.
Ein kurtze Abschrifft der Bekantnus des H. Christlichenn Glaubens so auff den Landtagk zu Peterkoif durch die Legaten des Könnigreichs Poln geschehen ist den Drietten May 1555. (1555). [Coburg: Cyriacus Schnauss, 1555].

Gonesies Petrus (1560a): *De Deo et Filio eius (um 1560)*. In: Dingel, Irene and Daugirdas, Kęstutis (Eds.) (2013): *Antitrinitarische Streitigkeiten: die tritheistische Phase (1560-1568)*. Göttingen: Vandenhoeck & Ruprecht, 19-68. DOI: 10.13109/9783666560156.19.

Gonesius Petrus (1560b): *De uno vero Deo (um 1560)*. In: Dingel, Irene and Daugirdas, Kęstutis (Ed.) (2013): *Antitrinitarische Streitigkeiten: die tritheistische Phase (1560-1568)*. Göttingen: Vandenhoeck & Ruprecht, 69-97. DOI: 10.13109/9783666560156.69.

Gonesius, Petrus (1570a): *O Synu Bożym iże był przed stworzeniem świata, a iż jest przezeń wszytko uczyniono przeciw fałesznym wykrętom ebiońskim* [*On the Son of God, and that he was before the creation of the world, and that all things were made through him, against the false prevarications of the Ebionites*]. Węgrów: Jan Kiszka.

Gonesius, Petrus (1570b): *O trzech, to jest o Bogu, o Synu jego i o Duchu ś. przeciwko Trójcy sabelliańskiej* [*On the Three, that is, God, his Son, and the Holy Spirit, against the Trinity of the Sabellians*]. Węgrów: Jan Kiszka.

[Gribaldi, Matteo] (2010a): *Declarationes Iesu Christi Filii Dei* [*A Revelation of Jesus Christ, the Son of God*]. In: Gribaldi, Matteo: *Declaratio. Michael Servetus's Revelation of Jesus Christ the Son of God and Other Antitrinitarian Works by Matteo Gribaldi*. Hughes, Peter and Zerner, Peter (Eds.). Zerner, Peter, Hughes, Peter, and Hughes, Lynn Gordon (Trans.). Providence: Blackstone Editions, 1-167

[Gribaldi, Matteo] (2010b): *Apologia pro Michaele Serveto* [*A Defense of Michael Servetus*]. In: Matteo Gribaldi: *Declaratio. Michael Servetus's Revelation of Jesus Christ the Son of God and Other Antitrinitarian Works by Matteo Gribaldi*. Hughes, Peter and Zerner, Peter (Eds.). Zerner, Peter, Hughes, Peter, and Hughes, Lynn Gordon (Trans.). Providence: Blackstone Editions, 169-199.

[Gribaldi, Matteo] (2010c): *De vera Dei et Filii eius cognitione sermo* [*A Discourse on the True Knowledge of God and his Son*]. In: Gribaldi, Matteo: *Declaratio. Michael Servetus's Revelation of Jesus Christ the Son of God and Other Antitrinitarian Works by Matteo Gribaldi*. Hughes, Peter and Zerner, Peter (Eds.). Peter Zerner, Peter Hughes, and Lynn Gordon Hughes (Trans.). Providence: Blackstone Editions, 214-227.

Irenaeus (1857): *Adversus haereses*. In: Migne, Jacques (Ed.): *Patrologiae Cursus Completus, Series Graeca*. Vol. VII. Paris: J.-P. Migne, 433-1224.

Lampa, Friedrich Adolph (1729): *Historia ecclesiae reformatae in Hungaria et Transylvania*. Utrecht (Traiectum): Jacobus van Poolsus.

Lubieniecki, Stanislaus (1685): *Historia Reformationis Polonicae in qua tum reformatorum tum antitrinitariorum origo et progressus in Polonia et finitimis provinciis narrantur*. Freistadt: Johannes Aconius.

Lutomirski, Stanisław (1556): *Confessio, to jest Wyznanie wiary chrześcijańskiej* [*Confessio, that is, the Creed of the Christian faith*]. Königsberg: Hans Daubmann.

Melanchthon, Philipp (1555, 1965): *Loci communes*. In: Manschreck, Clyde L. (Ed. and Trans.): *Melanchthon on Christian Doctrine. Loci communes 1555*. New York: Oxford University Press.

Melanchthon, Philipp (1558): *Loci communes theologici*. Basel: Ioannes Oporinus.

Melanchthon, Philipp (1559): *Loci praecipui theologici*. In: Litwan, Peter and Grosse, Sven (Eds.): *Philipp Melanchthon. Loci praecipui theologici nunc denuo cura et diligentia Summa recogniti multisque in locis copiose illustrati 1559: Lateinisch-deutsch*. Volumes I and II. Leipzig: Evangelische Verlagsanstalt.

Melanchthon, Philipp (1965): *Melanchthon on Christian Doctrine: Loci Communes 1555*. Manschreck, Clyde L. (Ed. and Trans.). New York: Oxford University Press.

Neüwe Zeyttung und Warhaffte Bekandtnuss des Christlichen Glaubens auff dem Landtag zü Piotrkow durch die gesandten dess Künigreichs Polen. Geschehen auff den dritten tag Maii (1555). Strasbourg: Thieboldt Berger.

[Servet, Miguel] (1531, 1932): *De Trinitatis erroribus*. [Hagenau: Johann Setzer]. In: Ropes, James H. and Kirsopp, Lake (Eds.) (1932): *The Two Treatises of Servetus on the Trinity*. Cambridge: Harvard Theological Studies, 1–188.

Vulgata Clementina (1598): Vatican: Typographus Vaticanus. http://vulsearch.sourceforge.net/html/index.html, last accessed May 14, 2023.

Secondary Sources

Alcalá, Ángel (2004): "Introducción." In: Alcalá, Ángel (Ed.): *Miquel Servet. Obras Completas*. Vol. II: *Primeros escritos teológicos*. Ángel Alcalá and Betes Luis (Trans.). Saragossa: Prensas de la Universidad de Zaragoza.

Bainton, Roland H. (1951): "Sebastian Castellio, Champion of Religious Liberty." In: Bainton, Roland H., Becker, Bruno, and Valkhoff, Marius-François (Eds.): *Castellioniana. Quatre etudes sur Sébastien Castellion et L'idée de la Tolérance*. Leiden: Brill, 25–79.

Bainton, Roland H. (1973): *Servet, el hereje perseguido*. Ángel Alcalá (Trans.). Madrid: Taurus.

Balázs, Mihály (1996): *Early Transylvanian Antitrinitarism (1566–1571). From Servet to Palaeologus*. Baden-Baden and Bouxwiller: Éditions Valentin Koerner.

Becker, Bruno (Ed.) (1953): *Autour de Michel Servet et de Sébastien Castellion*. Haarlem: Tjeenk Willink.

Benz, Ernst (1949): *Wittenberg und Byzanz. Zur Begegnung und Auseinandersetzung der Reformation und der östlich-orthodoxen Kirche*. Marburg: Elwert.

Boniecki, Adam (1909): *Herbarz polski: wiadomości historyczno-genealogiczne o rodach szlacheckich* [*The Polish Coat of Arms: Historical and Genealogical News about Noble Families*]. Vol. XIII-I. Warsaw: Warszawskie Towarzystwo Akcyjne S. Orgelbranda.

Borawska, Teresa and Małłek, Janusz (1985): "Reformacja w Polsce w świetle relacji pruskiej i meklemburskiej z sejmu piotrkowskiego 1555 r." In: *Acta Universitatis Nicolai Copernici. Historia* 20, 17–30.

Caccamo, Domenico (1999): *Eretici italiani in Moravia, Polonia, Transilvania (1558–1611): studi e documenti*. Florence: Le lettere.

Daugirdas, Kęstutis (2012): "Petras Goniondzietis. Tradicinių dogmų kritikos pradžia XVI a. LDK ir jos atgarsiai Europoje [Peter Gonesius. The Beginings of the Criticism of Traditional Dogmas in the 16th Century Grand Duchy of Lithuania and its Repercussions in Europe]." In: *Senoji Lietuvos literatūra* 33, 53–74.

Dingel, Irene and Daugirdas, Kęstutis (Ed.) (2013): *Antitrinitarische Streitigkeiten: die tritheistische Phase (1560–1568)*. Göttingen: Vandenhoeck & Ruprecht.

Earnshaw, Rebekah (2020): *Creator and Creation according to Calvin on Genesis*. Göttingen: Vandenhoek & Ruprecht. DOI: 10.13109/9783666540837

Fiedman, Jerome (1978): *Michael Servetus: A Case Study in Total Heresy*. Geneva: Droz.

Finkel, Ludwik (1896): "Konfesja podana przez posłów na sejmie piotrkowskim w r. 1555." In: *Kwartalnik Historyczny* 10. No. 2, 257–285.

Florovsky, Georges (1959): "The Greek Version of the Augsburg Confession." In: *Lutheran World* 6. No. 2, 153–155.

Gill, Joseph (1967): "Filioque." In: *New Catholic Encyclopaedia*. Vol. V. Washington, D.C: The Catholic University of America.

Górski, Konrad (1949): "Piotr z Goniądza." In: *Studia nad dziejami polskiej literatury anty-trynitarskiej XVI w* (*Studies on the History of Polish Anti-trinitarian Literature of the Sixteenth Century*). Krakow: Polska Akademia Umiejętności, 54–57.

Guggisberg, Hans R. (2003): *Sebastian Castellio, 1515–1563: Humanist and Defender of Religious Toleration in a Confessional Age*. London and New York: Routledge.

Hall, Aschley (2014): *Philip Melanchthon and the Cappadocians: A Reception of Greek Patristic Sources in the Sixteenth Century*. Göttingen: Vandenhoeck & Ruprecht.

Hughes, Peter and Zerner, Peter (Eds.) (2010): *Declaratio. Michael Servetus's Revelation of Jesus Christ the Son of God and Other Antitrinitarian Works by Matteo Gribaldi*. Peter Zerner, Peter Hughes, and Lynn Gordon Hughes (Trans.). Providence: Blackstone Editions.

Isidore of Seville (2006): *The Etymologies of Isidore of Seville*. Stephen A. Barney, Wendy J. Lewis, Jennifer A. Beach, and Oliver Berghof (Eds. and Trans.). Cambridge: Cambridge University Press. DOI: 10.1017/CBO9780511482113.

Jasnowski, Józef (1936): "Piotr z Goniądza. Życie, działalność i pisma. Studjum z dziejów ruchu religijnego w Polsce w drugiej połowie. XVI stulecia [Peter of Goniadz. Life, Activities and Writings. A Study in the History of the Religious Movement in Poland in the Second Half of the Sixteenth Century]." In: *Przegląd Historyczny* 33. No. 1, 5–58.

Kariatlis, Philip. (2010): "St. Basil's Contribution to the Trinitarian Doctrine: A Synthesis of Greek Paideia and the Scriptural Worldview." In: *Phronema* 25, 57–83.

Kausler, Eduard and Schott, Theodor (Eds.) (1875): *Briefwechsel zwischen Christoph, Herzog von Württemberg und Petrus Paulus Vergerius*. Stuttgart: Stuttgart Litterarischer Verein.

Kolb, Robert (2012): "The Pastoral Dimension of Melanchthon's Pedagogical Activities for the Education of Pastors." In: Dingel, Irene (Ed.): *Philip Melanchthon: Theologian in Classroom, Confession, and Controversy*. Göttingen: Vandenhoeck & Ruprecht, 29–42. DOI: 10.13109/9783666550478.29.

Kot, Stanisław (1921): "Polacy w Bazylei za czasów Zygmunta Augusta. U źródeł polskiej myśli krytycznej XVI wieku" [Poles in Basel in the Reign of Sigismund Augustus. At the Origins of Polish Critical Thought in the Sixteenth Century]". In: *Reformacja w Polsce. Organ Towarzystwa do Badania Dziejów Reformacji w Polsce* 1. No. 2, 105–138. [German translation: Kot, Stanisław (1942): "Polen in Basel zur Zeit des Königs Sigismund August (1548–1572) und die Anfänge kritischen Denkens in Polen." In: *Basler Zeitschrift für Geschichte und Altertumskunde* 41, 105–153.]

Kot, Stanisław (1953): "L'influence de Michel Servet sur le mouvement antitrinitarien en Pologne et en Transylvanie." In: Becker, Bruno (Ed.): *Autour de Michel Servet et de Sébastien Castellion*. Haarlem: H.D. Tjeenk Willink, 72–115.

Kusukawa, Sachiko (2003): "Uses of Philosophy in Reformation Thought." In: Friedman, Russell L. and Nielson, Lauge O. (Eds.): *The Medieval Heritage in Early Modern Metaphysics and Modal Theory, 1400–1700*. Dordrecht: Kluwer, 143–164. DOI: 10.1007/978-94-017-0179-2_8.

Lindberg, Carter (Ed.) (2002): *The Reformation Theologians. An Introduction to Theology in the Early Modern Period*. Oxford: Blackwell.

Marschall, Bruce D. (2002): "The Defense of the Filioque in Classical Lutheran Theology. An Ecumenical Appreciation." In: *Neue Zeitschrift für Systematische Theologie Und Religionsphilosophie* 44. No. 2, 154–173. DOI: 10.1515/nzst.2002.009.

Mayes, Benjamin T. G. (2011): "Introduction to the Second Edition." In: Melanchthon, Philipp: *Loci praecipui theologici 1559. The Chief Theologian Topics*. Jacob A. O. Preuss (Trans.). Saint Louis: Concordia Publishing House.

McDonald, Grantley (2016): *Biblical Criticism in Early Modern Europe: Erasmus, the Johannine Comma and Trinitarian Debate*. New York: Cambridge University Press. DOI: 10.1017/CBO9781316408964.004.

McGrath, Alister E. (1993): *The Intellectual Origins of the European Reformation*. Oxford: Blackwell.

Meijering, Eginhard P. (1983): *Melanchthon and Patristic Thought: The Doctrines of Christ and Grace, and the Trinity and the Creation*. Leiden: Brill.

Michel, Alain (1922): *Idiomes (Communicatio des). Dictionnaire de théologie catholique*. Vol. VII-I. Paris: Librairie Letouzey et Ané, 595–602.

Moss, Ann (1996): *Printed Commonplace-Books and the Structuring of Renaissance Thought*. Oxford: Clarendon Press. DOI: 10.1093/acprof:oso/9780198159087.003.0006.

Muller, Richard A. (2000): *The Unaccommodated Calvin: Studies in the Foundation of a Theological Tradition*. Oxford: Oxford University Press.

Oberdorfer, Bernd (2006): "*Who Proceedeth from the Father and the Son:* The Problem of the Filioque." In: Helmer, Christine and Higbe, Charlene T. (Eds.): *The Multivalence of Biblical Texts and Theological Meanings*. Atlanta: Society of Biblical Literature, 145–159.

Ogonowski, Zbigniew (2021): *Socinianism: History, Views, Legacy*. Marcin Turski (Trans.). Rome: Edizioni di Storia e Letteratura.

Palmieri, Aurelio. (1913): "Filioque." In: *Dictionnaire de théologie catholique*. Vol. V. Paris: Librairie Letouzey et Ané, 2309–2343.

Pietrzyk, Zdzisław (1997): *W kręgu Strasburga: z peregrynacji młodzieży z Rzeczypospolitej polsko-litewskiej w latach 1538–1621* [*In the Circle of Strasbourg: From the Peregrinations of the Youth of the Polish-Lithuanian Commonwealth in the Years 1538–1621*]. Krakow: Biblioteka Jagiellońska.

Plath, Uwe (1969): "Nocheinmal *Lyncurius*. Einige Gedanken Zu Gribaldi, Curione, Calvin Und Servet." In: *Bibliothèque d'Humanisme Et Renaissance* 31. No. 3, 583–610.

Quatrale Marta (2022): "Educating the Lutheran Laity in "Right" Doctrine. Polemical and Philological Paths in the Reactions against the Dresden Consensus (1571)." In: Burton, Simon J. G. and Baines, Matthew C. (Eds.): *Reformation and Education Confessional Dynamics and Intellectual Transformations*. Leiden: Vandenhoeck & Ruprecht, 143–176. DOI: 10.13109/9783666560552.143.

Reinhard, Flogaus (2015): "Eine orthodoxe Interpretation der lutherischen Lehre?: Neue Erkenntnisse zur Entstehung der Confessio Augustana Graeca und ihrer Sendung an Patriarch Joasaph II." In: Flogaus, Reinhard and Wasmuth, Jennifer (Eds.): *Orthodoxie im Dialog: Historische und aktuelle Perspektiven*. Berlin, Munich, and Boston: De Gruyter, 3–42. DOI: 10.1515/9783110421415-003.

Reinhard, Wolfgang (Ed.) (1996): *Augsburger Eliten des 16. Jahrhunderts Prosopographie wirtschaftlicher und politischer Führungsgruppen 1500–1620*. Berlin: Akademie.

Rummel, Erika (2000): *The Confessionalization of Humanism in Reformation Germany*. Oxford: Oxford University Press.

Sipayłło, Maria (Ed.) (1966): *Akta synodów różnowierczych w Polsce* [*Records of the Dissenting Synods in Poland*]. Vol. I: *1550–1559*. Warsaw: Wydawnictwa Uniwersytetu Warszawskiego.

Szczucki, Lech (1964): *Marcin Czechowic. Studium z dziejów antytrynitaryzmu polskiego XVI w.* [*Marcin Czechowic. A Study in the History of Polish Anti-trinitarianism in the Sixteenth Century*]. Warsaw: Państwowe Wydawnictwo Naukowe.

Szczucki, Lech (1981): "Piotr z Goniądza [Piotr of Goniądz]." In: Rostworowski, Emanuel (Ed.): *Polski Słownik Biograficzny [Polish Biographical Dictionary]*. Vol. XXVI. Krakow and Wrocław: Zakład Narodowy im. Ossolińskich and Wydawnictwo Polskiej Akademii Nauk, 398-400.

Tazbir, Janusz (1966): "Aus der Geschichte der Propaganda des Servetismus im XVI Jahrhundert: das Verhör polnischer Studenten in Tübingen im Jahre 1559." In: *Archiwum Historii Filozofii i Myśli Społecznej* 12, 65-74.

Tinsley, Barbara Sher (1989): "Johann's Sturm's Method for Humanistic Pedagogy." In: *The Sixteenth Century Journal* 20. No. 1, 23-40. DOI: 10.2307/2540521.

Von Dunin Borkowski, Zbigniew Stanislaus (1931): "Untersuchungen zum Schrifttum der Unitarier vor Faustus Socini." In: *75 Jahre Stella Matutina. Festschrift*. Vol. II. Feldkirch: Selbstverlag Stella Matutina, 103-137.

Wackernagel, Hans Georg von (Ed.) (1956): *Die Matrikel der Universität Basel, 1460-1818*. Vol. II: 1532/1533-1600/1601. Basel: Verlag Universität.

Wijaczka, Jacek (2014): "Reformacja w Koronie w XVI w.—sukces czy niepowodzenie?" In: *Gdański Rocznik Ewangelicki* 8, 13-34.

Wilbur, Earl Morse (1945): *A History of Unitarianism: In Transylvania, England, and America*. Boston: Beacon Press.

Williams, George Hutson (1992): *The Radical Reformation*. Kirksville, MO: Truman University Press.

Włodarski, Maciej (2001): *Dwa wieki kulturalnych i literackich powiązań polsko-bazylejskich 1433-1632 [Two Centuries of Cultural and Literary Connections Between Poland and Basel 1433-1632]*. Krakow: Universitas.

Wotschke, Theodor (1908): *Der briefwechsel der Schweizer mit den Polen*. Leipzig: M. Heinsius Nachf.

Farkas Gábor Kiss

Transmission and Transformation of Knowledge: Valentine Nádasdi's Miscellany from the University of Paris or the Chances of Christian Kabbalah and Neoplatonism on the Ottoman Frontier

Abstract: This chapter analyses a miscellaneous manuscript of a 16th century Franciscan, Valentine Nádasdi, and interprets its contents in the light of the possibilities and limits of knowledge transmission between central and peripheral knowledge communities. Nádasdi moved between Paris, and the border zone of Hungary and the Ottoman Empire. In France, he collected books during his studies, and made compilations from his readings, which he tried to make use of in Hungary as a preacher. While acting in an overwhelmingly Protestant country, he tried to engage his readers with his new cultural ideas (e.g. Christian Kabbalah) by re-contextualizing these texts as model letters and preaching. I argue that his main strategy of knowledge transmission was a "covert recontextualization" of his cultural ideals, in which he tried to avoid confessional conflicts and reframed their original arguments in a covert form to save their contents.

1 Introduction: A Franciscan Miscellany from the Mid-16th Century

This chapter analyses a miscellaneous manuscript of a 16th century Observant Franciscan, Valentine (Bálint) Nádasdi, now kept in the Hungarian National Library (Oct. Lat. 1220), and interprets its contents in the light of the possibilities and limits of knowledge transmission between central and peripheral knowledge communities (*lieux de savoir*). Nádasdi, the manuscript's owner, moved between Paris, one of the centers of 16th century scholarship and the border zone of Eastern Hungary, Transylvania, and the Ottoman Empire. In Paris, he collected books, which he imported to his home country, and made different kinds of compilations

---

Farkas Gábor Kiss: ORCID: 0000-0002-8632-5855. Institute of Philosophy and Sociology, Polish Academy of Sciences, Warsaw, Poland. This research has been made possible thanks to ERC Consolidator Grant n. 864542, "From East to West, and Back Again: Student Travel and Transcultural Knowledge Production in Renaissance Europe (c. 1470–c. 1620)."

∂ Open Access. © 2023 the author(s), published by De Gruyter. [CC BY] This work is licensed under the Creative Commons Attribution 4.0 International License. https://doi.org/10.1515/9783111072722-009

from his readings, which he tried to make use of in the Nyírség region of Hungary, where he was a court preacher of Andreas Báthory, the military chief of the region. In Paris, he was imbibed with a strong enthusiasm for contemporary pedagogical literature (Erasmus, Fortius Ringelberg), rhetoric (Ravisius Textor, Jean Pellisson), the church fathers (Tertullian, John Damascene, Ignatius of Antiochia, Anselm of Canterbury), and most importantly, Christian Neoplatonism (Giovanni Pico della Mirandola and Francesco Zorzi). My aim here is to examine the strategies Nádasdi tried to employ in order to apply his learning and high cultural standards in his native environment and how he transformed these ideals. How did a 16th century Hungarian Franciscan try to cope with the difference of intellectual climates and the limitations of political and cultural infrastructure? What happened to these readings after they were transferred to a culturally new environment?

2 The Intellectual Landscape in Hungary after 1526

After the Battle of Mohács (1526) and the fall of Buda (1541), the physical and intellectual infrastructure of the Catholic church was greatly damaged in the country. From the twelve bishoprics of the country, seven had fallen under Ottoman rule, and the strife between the two competing kings, Ferdinand I (who held his court in Vienna) and King John Szapolyai (who mostly resided in Transylvania, in Alba Iulia), created further conflicts by appointing parallel candidates to the surviving bishoprics. In this often-anarchic situation, the Protestant Reformation offered a reasonable alternative for the spiritual care of believers, as it was less centralized and the local communities could take charge of choosing their own pastor. In the frontier areas, monasteries and friaries were dissolved, libraries were dispersed, and their educational centers ceased to exist (Pálffy 2021, 92). From among the religious orders, the Franciscans were the strongest order before the Battle of Mohács and the coming of Protestantism: they had 70 friaries around 1500, and the number of friars was high even in an international comparison (Romhányi 2013, 4950). They were the only order which survived the political and religious turmoil of the 1520s and 1530s in significant numbers and saved some of their convents in this new period, even under Ottoman rule (de Cevins 2008, 406–470). After 1535–1537, four convents remained with some 50 friars in them (Romhányi 2013, 50).

The life of friars who continued to work under these circumstances was often in danger and the remaining members of the order registered their martyrs on a list entitled "Friars killed in the province of Hungary" (Bunyitay, Rapaics, and Karácsonyi 1904, 531–534; *Fratres interfecti in provincia Hungariae*). While most deaths seem to have been caused by Ottoman Turks (*per Turcos*) (de Cevins 2008a, 413–417), often it was "Lutherans" (*Lutherani*), "bandits" (*latrones*), "Hungarians" (*Hungari*), "Ruthenians" (*Rutheni*), "Romanians" (*Volachi*), or servants of a local fief who killed the remaining Franciscans. Apparently, being a Catholic and a Franciscan preacher in mid-16th century Hungary carried the dangers of incurring the wrath of other confessions, be it Lutheran or Eastern Orthodox, and the most important safeguard of their security was not the king or the—by then largely nonexistent—Catholic hierarchy, but a locally important landlord. By the middle of the 1560s, even some of these remaining convents and custodies, like that of Várad (Oradea) and Szalárd (Sălard), were annihilated and disappeared from the charters of the order (Karácsonyi 1922).

Bálint Nádasdi began his career as an Observant Franciscan (who were called "Salvatorians" in Hungary) and preached in Tasnád in 1542 and in Nyírbátor in 1544 (Alszeghy 1935; Vizkelety 1990). In 1546, he became the court chaplain of Andreas Báthory, the comes (*ispán*) of Szabolcs county and military captain of the country. He refers to himself in one of his books in this function: "friar Valentine, preacher of the illustrious Lord Andreas Báthory" (Soltész 1965–66, 116; *frater Valentinus concionator magnifici domini Andreae de Bathor*). Thus, despite being an Observant Franciscan, he was closely connected to a secular court, and his career can be compared to Catholic court priests around the same period. From 1561, he also held the office of a guardian as an Observant friar. He also stood out among his brethren because between 1550 and 1552 he was able to study theology in Paris with the support of Báthory. In one of his letters, which he addressed to his fellow friar, Valentine Dirnbach, he wrote about his appreciation of the "Academy of Paris" in the following words: "Guided by the love of profound virtue, I was attracted to the academy of Paris, the voracious river of wisdom, and the pride of the entire Christianity, which nurtures the profound speculations of your philosophy" (Molnár 2022, 650; my translation). We do not know, however, what exactly Nádasdi meant by the academy of Paris. Through his connections with the Franciscan order, he surely could have studied at the Franciscan *studium generale*, but he probably would not have referred to that as the "Academy of Paris." It is more probable that he meant the theological faculty of the university or the newly founded Collège Royal (1530). The latter possibility might be strengthened by the fact that the cultural and intellectual scope of his writings in his miscellany shows clear parallels to the educational ideals of the Collège Royal. As we will see, he often cited Greek authors in Greek, and he occasionally copied Hebrew words into his miscellany and his books. His relatively good knowledge of Greek, his ability to read and write Hebrew, and his familiarity with the works of Petrus Ramus (Pierre de la Ramée) make it likely that he studied at the Collège Royal. His miscellany reveals that he was in Paris in 1551 (1551 Parisiis, OSZK Oct. Lat. 1220, 27v), and the further remarks ("*frater Valen[tinus] Na[dasdi] in achademia Parisina* ... 1552" OSZK Oct. Lat. 1220, 256v and "*frater Va. Na. ... in vigilia apostolorum Philippi et Jacobi in achademia parisina attingit* 1552" OSZK Oct. Lat. 1220, 269v) make it clear that he remained there at least until May 3, 1552, when he composed theological disputations.

3 Nádasdi in Paris and Ramus

In the years preceding Valentine Nádasdi's visit to Paris, a number of famous Hebrews and Hellenists (Jacques Toussain, Paul Paradis, Agacio Guidacerio, François Vatable) taught biblical languages at the Collège Royal (Irigoin 2006). Most importantly, Petrus Ramus was appointed as a royal professor of eloquence and rhetoric at the College in 1551, exactly at the time when Nádasdi was taking courses at the university. Significantly, in one of his works, entitled the "Duty of the Princes" (*De munere principum*; Vízkelety 1990, 123–128), which he compiled from the texts he collected and copied in Paris during his visit, Nádasdi claimed that the princes have to take heed of two major doctrines. First, they have to practice clemency and remain moderate and forgiving towards the faults of their subjects. He cited a famous quote from Virgil's *Aeneid*, according to which the Roman Empire's political program is to "spare the conquered and battle down the proud" (Virgil, *Aeneid* 6, 853; parcere subiectis et debellare superbos). Later, he added another Greek quotation from the end of Plato's *Sophist* (311b–c), where he claims that statesmanship has to harmonize all the virtues and must "complete the most magnificent and best of all fabrics." Surprisingly, both quotations appear together in a speech by Petrus Ramus, which he delivered in front of King Henry II in 1551 and addressed to Charles de Guise, Cardinal of Lorraine (Ramus 1580, 8). Nádasdi added some orthographical mistakes to Ramus' Greek text, but he included them in a structurally similar position, to where the oration divides the subject matter into two areas, and he introduced this dichotomy with the same words ("there are two major arts and doctrines" in Nádasdi vs. "there are two major arts" in Ramus), which clearly shows its dependence on the French philosopher. Ramus' oration was already edited in 1551 in a small separate print (Ramus 1551 and Bruyère 1984, 316), and Nádasdi must have acquired this version of the text. But it is very probable that he attended the inaugural oration of Ramus, as he supplemented his text with further quotations from Cicero's speech on Marcus Marcellus, and Ramus' oration was an introductory speech to a course on Cicero (Ramus 1551, 35). Thus, it is more than probable that Nádasdi employed the word "academia" in the same sense as Ramus did in his inaugural speech, referring to the entirety of the university. In fact, as Marie-Dominique Couzinet and

Jean-Marc Mandosio claim, the Collège Royal was not a physically existing institution in the 16th century; the term rather referred to the chairs financed by the king, and Ramus' lectures actually took place in the Collège de Presles after his nomination as a professor in 1551 (Couzinet and Mandosio 2004, 11).

4 His Miscellany and His Library

There exist two main sources for Nádasdi's studies in Paris: his miscellany and his library. His miscellany is a thick, 345-folio manuscript volume, which includes several kinds of texts. The paper of the miscellany is identical throughout the entire volume, but it was rebound in 1785, when a sketchy table of contents was added to the beginning. Most reading manuscript is written by Nádasdi's hand, although there are some minor texts added later, probably at the beginning of the 17th century, which are partly in Hungarian (Alszeghy 1935, 36–37). The original owner of the codex is identified by a note on the first page: "I carry the small packages entrusted to me by the friar Valentine Nádasdi by his own hands in Paris, so that he support his unstable memory" (Sarcinulas fero per f[rat]rem Valentinum Nadasdinum propriis manibus michi Parisiis pro sua labiliist memoria stipanda impositas Anno gratiae quingentesimo quinquagesimo primo). Thus, the miscellany's original aim was to collect the texts in Paris that he deemed important and store them for his later career. None of the texts are course materials, college textbooks, or study notes. The miscellany consists of three major parts: the first one contains holy sermons and festive speeches on various subjects (12r–93v), including "On the Offices of Princes" (*De munere principum*, 12r–24v), "The Dignity of Priesthood" (*De sacerdotum dignitate*, 25r–27v), the Praise of St. Francis (*De divo patre Francisco*, 71r–74v), and on the Election of the Minister of the Observant Franciscans (*De electione ministri*, 82r–89v). Some of these were surely composed in Paris, as they bear the date 1551 (e.g., "The Dignity of Priesthood" or the anti-Lutheran sermons against the idea that faith alone is enough for salvation, 45v–71r). On fols. 230v–269v, we find two theological questions, dated to 1552, the first one with the title "Are there beings who are called Gods, either in the heavens or on the earth" (230v–239r; Suntne qui dicantur dii, sive in coelo, sive in terries?) and the second "Where did Paul study and what did he teach?" (240r–269v; Unde Paulus didicit et quid docuit?). These two questions suggest that in the second year of his studies, he was involved in theological studies in Paris. Whereas the first of these questions seems not much more than an exercise in collecting some occurrences of the word God or Father in the Bible and does not make a clear statement, the second one has a reasonable argument: it provides a theological commentary, mostly based on the late antique and medieval Christian tradition (Ambrose, *Glosa ordinaria*),

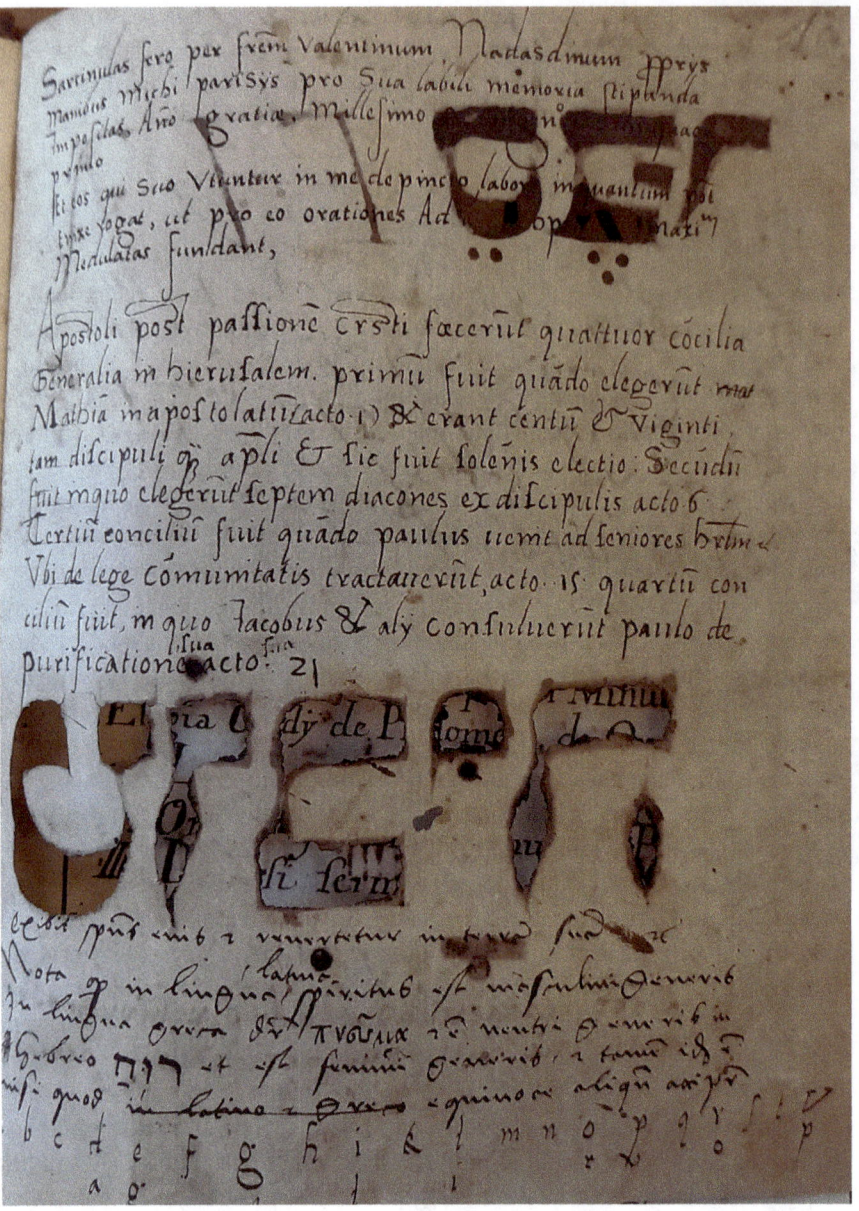

Fig. 1: First leaf of the manuscript of Valentine Nádasdi (Hungarian National Library, MS Oct. Lat. 1220, 1r)

on some claims made by Paul, some of which had strong repercussions in the times of the Reformation (e.g., predestination or the question of virginity). The third major part includes a collection of model letters which Valentine Nádasdi composed for his order's use (287v–334v). The model letters are followed by documents which attest to Nádasdi's political contacts in Hungary and his friendly relations with Enguerrand Escombard, the provincial of the *France parisienne* province of the Franciscans (Molnár 2022, 652). Escombard's personality offers an insight into Nádasdi's immediate religious environment in Paris: the French provincial was counted among the Franciscans who still kept the strictness of religious observance and who could be called "true Observants" according to a member of the order (Moracchini 2005, 183).

The miscellany is primarily written in Latin, but it embraces the two other holy languages, Greek and Hebrew, as well. In addition to the many short Hebrew quotations, the abbreviation of the owner's name, "F[rater] V[alentinus] N[ádasdi]," occurs throughout the volume in Hebrew several times (OSZK Oct. Lat. 1220, fol. 1r; Fig. 1). His grasp of the Greek language must have been more confident, although he did not master using it in the cursive script: the longer Greek quotations written in the volume imitate the ligatures of the printed Greek letters to the point that they look like printed text (OSZK Oct. Lat. 1220, fol. 239r). Still, he quotes the New Testament in Greek regularly in the theological questions (*Quaestiones theologicae*), which he wrote in 1552. This linguistic ideal, which comprises Latin, Greek, and Hebrew letters, fully reflects the educational ideals of the Collège Royal.

The other most important source is his significant library, part of which survives to this day and was identified in the Franciscan library of Gyöngyös (Hungary) and in smaller numbers in the libraries of Martin (Slovakia), Satu Mare, and Csíksomlyó (Romania). Currently, 35 volumes are known to have belonged to him. This large personal collection started to be built up early in his career: the first dated purchase is known from 1539, Dionysius Carthusianus' commentary on the four Gospels (Gyöngyös, Ant. 527). In 1546, he received a donation from his main patron, Andreas Báthory (on him, see Pálffy 66), from which he bought a number of books, including Anselm of Canterbury's explanations on the Epistles of Paul and the sermons of Johann Fabri and Friedrich Nausea, earlier bishops of Vienna. The greatest enrichment of his library came in 1551 and 1552, during his studies in Paris, where he acquired at least ten of his surviving books (Soltész 1965–1966, 118–119). Judging from these purchases, his interest seems to have been focused on early Christian authors and medieval theologians (Ambrose, Rupert of Deutz, Albert the Great), but he also bought contemporary commentaries on the book of Ecclesiastes by Johann Wild and Franciscus Titelmans. Nevertheless, it needs to be emphasized that only a fragment of his library survives and that he purchased other texts as well.

The wide scope of his readings is witnessed by the model letters at the end of the volume (287v–344v). Without mentioning the name of the original authors, Nádasdi created model letters to be used in his order from a number of authors he read and approved of. These included both actual epistles (e.g., some of Cicero's letters) and collections of model letters which were popular in Nádasdi's time: Erasmus' sample letters from his *De conscribendis epistolis*, Gasparino Barzizza's early 15th century letter collection, the popular textbook on model letters by Johannes Ravisius Textor, and even the medieval letter collection of Pierre de Blois, which remained popular in the late 15th and early 16th century, appear among the texts imitated and copied by Nádasdi (Kiss 2017, 356–371). Still, he not only employed letters that were composed in order to be imitated but also added texts that he found worthy of attention from a stylistic viewpoint or because of their content. Some of these selections seem to be unusual, as the dedication letter of St. John Damascene to his commentary on the *Trisagion* hymn (Damascenus 1546) or a letter of the 3rd century bishop St. Martialis, which was published in 1546 (Martialis 1546). Nádasdi appropriated some texts from the early Christian author Novatian and presented them as letters; he inserted some segments of a dialogue on grammar by the French schoolmaster Jean Pellisson and interpreted them as letters. A portion of Joachim Fortius Ringelberg's popular pedagogical dissertation, *De ratione studii* (1529), also served as a model letter, and this choice suggests that he was involved in pedagogy and may have performed educational duties as a Franciscan.

Nádasdi's process of cultural transposition and reshaping can be demonstrated with the example of how he transformed a text by Andrea Guarna into a praise of his home country, Hungary. Guarna's *Bellum grammaticale* was a unique pedagogical effort at renewing the teaching of Latin grammar by turning it into a battle (hence the title) between the Nouns and the Verbs. The warfare is followed by peace negotiations which are decided by a jury, consisting of three ancient and three modern grammarians (Bolte 1908 and Butler 2010). The work was especially popular in France, where at least 26 editions are noted between 1512 and 1557 (Pettegree and Walsby 2012, 911). It was written in a story-like form, full of comical dialogues, and its main subject, grammar, was introduced by a praise at the beginning, as if it were a country:

> Not a single person who is even half-educated doubts that the province of Grammar is the most beautiful and fortunate of all the provinces in the world. It is so because, on the one hand, it remains second to none in the pleasantness of its location, by the health of its climate, by the abundance of all the fruits, and other things, of which human life should not be de-

prived, and on the other, it has always been the nourisher and parent of illustrious men (Bolte 1908, 4; all translations are mine).

Nádasdi must have felt tempted by this richly adorned account of the land of Grammar, and it immediately reminded him of his homeland, Hungary, or Pannonia. Hence, he created a model praise for his native country by turning Guarna's allegorical praise of Grammar into a rhetorical exercise on the fertility of Pannonia:

> Not a single person who is even half-educated doubts that the province of Pannonia is the most beautiful and fortunate of all the provinces in the world. It is so because, on the one hand, it remains second to none by the pleasantness of its location, by the health of its climate, by the abundance of all fruits, and other things, of which human life should not be deprived of, and on the other, it has always been the nourisher and parent of illustrious men (OSZK Oct. Lat. 1220, 323v).

Nádasdi leaves off the praise only at the point where it turns towards the description of the neighboring countries of Grammar (Dialectics, Theology) and the two kings of Grammar, the noun *Poeta* and the verb *Amo*. There is no indication of the origin of these phrases in Nádasdi's version: it was clearly the linguistic richness and elegance of the text that was to be studied and passed on to his students, and not the authority of the grammarian who created it.

While the use of Erasmus' or Ravisius Textor's epistolaries might seem natural when composing a collection of model letters, Nádasdi also selected several authors because of his personal preference for their writings. His choice of letters by Marsilio Ficino and Giovanni Pico della Mirandola is particularly interesting. From among Pico della Mirandola's letters, he selected fifteen for his Franciscan letter collection. He first copied the letter to Pico's nephew, Gianfrancesco, almost in its entirety, where Pico encourages him not to be afraid of the devil and to keep his trust in God, Christ, and the Gospel (Pico 1498, fol. Tvi^v–Vii^r). Pico's pious admonitions can be reinterpreted in the framework of the fight against heresy, a topic that often returns throughout the volume. Pico's letter to Ermolao Barbaro depicts an ideal philosophical community which transcends the idle fables of poetry and deals with the causes of human and divine matters instead (Pico 1498, Viii^v) while also praising his friend for following these ideals. Later on in this letter, Pico emphasizes the complete opposition between philosophy and rhetoric, and dismisses the latter: rhetoric is not worthy of a true philosopher—as Pico repeats the Platonic ideal. Transposed into the Hungarian frontier zone, this letter gains a new and simpler meaning: only Ermolao's praise remains, and the condemnation of rhetoric is omitted. What is originally a combative defense of philosophy against rhetoric in Pico's letter here becomes a simple example of stylistic elegance that is worthy of being imitated and applied by any knowledgeable member of the Hungarian Franciscan order. We have seen above that the influence of Ramus was important for him in 1551: it might perhaps not be an exaggeration to see this omission of the triumph of philosophy against rhetoric as a consequence of the teachings of Ramus, who equaled dialectics with rhetoric in the oration that Nádasdi excerpted and that was delivered in the same year. The imitation of good style is of primary importance to Nádasdi, and he does not consider it to obstruct philosophical investigations.

In Nádasdi's sermons, there emerges a unique mixture of Neoplatonic teachings and medieval Christian theology, which hark back to the Franciscan ideals of the later Middle Ages. The language of the sermons is classicizing and often Ciceronian. God is often referred to as the *"deus optimus maximus"* in accordance with the humanist custom. Nevertheless, he does not cite pagan authors: his main authorities are church fathers and medieval theologians (Eusebius, Jerome, Isidore of Seville on fol. 27r–30r; Dionysius Areopagite, Bernard of Clairvaux on 39r). The peculiar duality of his Christian and ancient cultural ideals is best characterized by his sermon on Francis of Assisi. There, the founder of his order is compared to pagan historical personalities and philosophers alike:

> When their princes won a war, or served their country well, the Romans exalted them with praises… Whom should we consider similar to our Francis? Hercules, who visited several regions of the world? Alexander the Great? Achilles or Hector? Julius Caesar or Augustus? Should we compare him to Pompeius Magnus or to Marcellus? … But let us turn to the words of worldly wisdom: To Aristotle? To Plato, Pythagoras, Socrates, Zeno, or finally to Solomon? About whom the holy texts mention that he was furnished with so many gifts of the soul that by his wisdom and glory, there was, there is and there will be no one among the mortals who would be equal to him (OSZK Oct. Lat. 1220, 72r; my translation).

In Nádasdi's sermons, classical antiquity serves as an inferior though noble antecedent to Christian history, but linguistically, it is his main model. It is the stylistic aspect, the elegant mode of expression, which encompasses his text and often defines and directs its subject matter. Despite the ecclesiastic themes discussed in the stricter Observant branch of the Franciscan order, he feels confident in using comical expressions from the Roman comedian Plautus: in his speech "On the election of the minister" (*De electione ministri*), the bad, biased father is called a "sixpence man," a *"triobolaris homuncio"* (OSZK Oct. Lat. 1220, 82r–89v). The primary driving force of his textual composition is the imitation of Classical rhetoric prose style, especially that of Cicero. His Ciceronian ideal reflects the contemporary landscape of Neo-Latin prose style in France, where Cicero was the favorite author. It is especially true for Étienne Dolet, whose commentary on Terence (323r–v) Nádasdi quotes, and for Ramus, whom he probably heard lecturing. In his *Ciceronianus*

(1557), Ramus exposed an eclectic application process of Cicero's style that can be easily compared to Nádasdi's imitative practices: although Ramus disagreed with Cicero's theoretical views on rhetoric, he endorsed his philosophical approach, and considered his style the primary model of Latin writing. Ramus' Ciceronianism—just like Nádasdi's—is not exclusive: it can be enriched with an eclectic choice of words and expressions from other archaic (early Roman) or late antique authors that have a classical touch. The main criterion is not the model's authority but rather one's own judgment (Meerhoff 1986, 31–32, and Fumaroli 2002, 454–462, especially 456).

5 Christian Kabbalah

One more important influence reached Nádasdi during his studies in Paris. His miscellany reveals that he had a strong interest in works of Christian Kabbalah, especially those written by Franciscan authors. On the one hand, this tendency is consistent with his interest in Hebrew studies, but on the other hand, it adds a new twist to the eclectic intellectual journey of an Observant Franciscan who was influenced by both Ramus and Pico della Mirandola at the same time. Nádasdi's miscellany includes a preface at the beginning with the title "Ad lectorem" (10r), which seems to suggest that Nádasdi, as the compiler of the manuscript, envisaged it as a volume that has a meaning and a message on its own, and will function as an independent intellectual resource. In fact, this preface is derived from the *Secrets of the Catholic Truth* (De arcanis catholicae veritatis, 1518), a bulky work by the Observant Franciscan Pietro Galatino (1460–1540). Galatino's aim was to offer an introduction to the secrets of Hebrew Kabbalah for the Christian reader and to support the efforts of Johann Reuchlin in finding the Christian revelation in the Kabbalistic writings of the Jews (Campanini 2010). Galatino claimed that the writings of the ancient rabbis contained prophecies of the Virgin Mary, Jesus, the Catholic doctrine of the Eucharist, the finding of the True Cross, and many other teachings of the Catholic church (Grafton and Weinberg 2011, 37–39). To Nádasdi, it must have been an interesting text not only because of its Kabbalism—for which he seemed to have had a penchant—but also because its arguments could be turned against the heretics—that is, Lutheran heretics, whose theological opinion on the role of faith in salvation he refuted in several sermons of the miscellany. Nevertheless, Nádasdi's treatment of this text is very similar to how he treated Ramus' inaugural lecture on Pico's epistles. He quoted only the first few paragraphs of Galatino's preface, which scolded all heresies, and removed all references to the name of his fellow Franciscan or to the Kabbalistic approach of his book. Thus, he created a new preface for his own miscellany from Galatino's work, which nevertheless seems to have been among his favorites because of its Christian Hebraism. Although Nádasdi's copy has not survived, he most probably owned the 1550 Basel edition that had recently come out of the press at the time when he was in Paris.

6 Nádasdi and the Protestant Reformation

The fight against the representatives of the Protestant Reformation does not occupy a central place in the miscellany, but it still appears as an important subject several times. The volume contains a list of Luther's various opinions on purgatory collected from several works of his (7r–7v). In fact, this is an excerpt from "The purgatory fire of the souls" (*De animarum purgatorio igne*) by Johann Cochlaeus, a German Catholic humanist and canon of Wrocław (1479–1552), in which he called attention to the contradictions of Luther's opinions about the subject (Cochlaeus 1544, fol. C1r–C1v). Furthermore, two longer sermons focus on the question of salvation and faith, which were central issues of the religious controversies of the mid-16th century. The first one bears the title "That faith alone, which is pure credulousness, cannot be enough for salvation" (45v–54r: Quod sola fides, quae est pura credulitas minime sufficit ad salutem). This text follows a bipartite structure: it starts with a rhetorical introduction which encourages the audience to pay attention to the religious message. Then the biblical pericope of the sermon is given: "And they that have done good things, shall come forth unto the resurrection of life; but they that have done evil, unto the resurrection of judgment" (John 5:29, Douay-Rheims translation). Nádasdi's biblical theme from the Gospel of John is about the judgment of good and evil after the resurrection, and therefore it fits the theme of salvation by faith alone, as the Gospel makes it clear that it is necessary to "have done good things" for the salvation of the soul. Afterwards, his "controversist" stance against the Lutheran position consists of nothing but stressing the importance of Christian law. As according to Nádasdi, the Gospel clearly states that good works (*opera bona*) are necessary for salvation, believers only need to accept that the words of Jesus are true. Hence, he argues:

> These words are the very words of our Savior, Jesus Christ, by which he eagerly strives for the salvation of our souls: Not only is Christ's law truthful, but also those things that he taught proved to be completely true. First, because his doctrine emanated from the fountain of truth, which is the Father, as he explained when he said: He that sent me is true [Jn 8:26]. For I have not spoken of myself; but the Father who sent me, he gave me commandment, what I should say, and what I should speak [Jn 12:49]. Thus, this doctrine, which arose from the paternal fountain, descended by the first canal of truth to create the deepest sea of highest wisdom, which is the Son—so that we speak like the Jews do. Therefore he himself

says it again: My doctrine is not mine, but his that sent me [Jn 7:16]. It is mine because I inherited it, it is mine because I learned it, but not mine because it originates from elsewhere. ...

Thus, the Truth itself says about the Devil: He was a murderer from the beginning, and he stood not in the truth [Jn 8:44], because whoever has taught against the teachings of Christ and his apostles, he has not only moved away from truth, but also from the teaching of Christ and all the apostles (OSZK, Quart. Lat. 1220, 45v).

Nádasdi aims to emphasize that the teaching of Christ is the true law, so we must accept the Gospel's claim that salvation requires good deeds in addition to faith. Again, however, he did not write the passage himself but copied it almost entirely from the "Harmony of the world" (*De harmonia mundi*), a Neoplatonic work, first published in 1525 by the Christian Kabbalist Francesco Zorzi (Fig. 2):

How is the teaching of Christ completely true?

In Christ, not only is the law truthful, but also those things that he taught proved to be completely true. First, because his doctrine emanated from the fountain of truth, which is the Father, as he explained when he said: He that sent me is true [Jn 8:26]. For I have not spoken of myself; but the Father who sent me, he gave me commandment, what I should say, and what I should speak [Jn 12:49]. Thus, this doctrine, which arose from the paternal fountain, descended by the first canal of truth to create the deepest sea of highest wisdom, which is the Son—so that we speak like the Jews do. Therefore he himself says it again: My doctrine is not mine, but his that sent me. [Jn 7:16]. It is mine because I inherited it, it is mine, because I learned it, but not mine because it originates from elsewhere. ...

Thus, the Truth itself says about the Devil: He was a murderer or killer from the beginning, and he became death itself, as he stood not in the truth [Jn 8:44], because receded from Christ, moreover, he intended to revolt against him, when it was revealed to him in heaven in advance that he will be born from a woman clothed with the Sun and crowned by twelve stars (Zorzi 1545, 258v–261r; Zorzi 2010, 1420–1422, my translation).

As one can see, the words are almost identical. But Nádasdi's choice is surprising: in Zorzi's original text, the context is entirely different. Rather than salvation by good deeds, Zorzi tried to prove that the manifestations of Christ are equal to those of the Father, thus emphasizing the unity of the Hebrew Bible, which serves as the foundation of Kabbalah, and the Christian Gospels. Only by accepting the divine power and dignity of Christ's word one is able to consider the New Testament as part of the Kabbalistic tradition, the mystical interpretive method of the Bible. Nevertheless, Nádasdi borrows Zorzi's words only to reinforce the truth of the Biblical pericope of his sermon in praise of the "good works", and he limits his argument to sustaining the undeniable truth of it.

To this thought Nádasdi added the second part of his speech, in which he claims that anyone who disputes the importance of good deeds for salvation violates God's law:

> But that is the teaching of Christ and all the apostles, that it should be supposed that no one achieves salvation without good deeds. Thus, whoever precludes good deeds from believers, he stands against truth. Second, faith alone without good works does not reach justification. I ask those who claim that faith alone is able to justify, whether the people who violate and pollute the sacred laws of God are just in front of God and worthy of eternal life if they have faith and defend themselves by the protection of faith against the infidels. But no one is so silly and mad, and mentally diminished, that he would say that such people are just (OSZK, Quart. Lat. 1220, 46r–46v).

Nádasdi's anti-Protestant agenda is clear and his reference to those who "defend themselves by the protection of faith against the infidels" might refer more to the delicate confessional situation in Hungary than to the religious realities of the Franciscans in Paris. Hungarian Protestants may be the ones who break the divine laws (*sacras dei leges*) but still claim to have faith, and fight the infidels under the protection of faith. If that is so, Nádasdi adds a clever argument here: even if they fight against the infidel through their faith, how could they be justified if they commit evil deeds too? After formulating this idea, he supports his statement with two Old Testament and three Gospel quotations and then draws the following conclusion:

> This is what was taught to us by our teacher, Christ, that we should not only believe but also act according to what we believe and what we profess. So not only faith justifies us (OSZK, Quart. Lat. 1220, 46v).

Again, Nádasdi's use of his sources is peculiar: he quoted a detail from Zorzi which supports a relatively simple idea and does not help him to sharpen his argument. Furthermore, this is a secondary idea in Zorzi's work too, where it serves only to prove that the teachings of Christ match the Hebrew Bible (for him, the Old Testament), and Zorzi's main agenda is to maintain the Christian character of the Hebrew Bible. As we have seen in the cases of quotations from Ramus, Pico, and Galatino, Nádasdi selects the thematically less significant but rhetorically well-formed parts of his sources for imitation.

In Nádasdi's subsequent speeches, which deal with the question of salvation by faith, he comes even closer to the text of Zorzi's *Harmony of the World* and transforms entire chapters of it into sermons. First, the sermon "To the refutation of all their badly established arguments" (*Ad evellenda omnia illorum male collocate fundamenta*, 48v–51v) is entirely based on Zorzi's chapter entitled *Eliminatio illorum fundamentorum*, just like the following one on the "Solution of the great difficulty which are brought along by the words of St. Paul in the Epistle to the Romans" (51v–52v: *Solutio magnae difficultatis quam adferunt dicta Pauli in epistola ad Romanos*), and the sermon on "How to understand those authorities who seem to attribute salvation only to faith" (54v–56v: *Quomodo intelligantur authoritates quae fidei tantum tribuere videantur*). In these cases, Nádasdi follows Zorzi almost word for word, only abbreviating the original text occasionally. In fact, as Zorzi writes in plural throughout his work, it was easy for Nádasdi to transform his text into sermons which speak to a community.

Why was Francesco Zorzi (Franciscus Georgius; 1466–1540) so important to Nádasdi? First of all, he was a fellow Franciscan from Venice, who proposed that the universe was created by God using a universal system of musical proportions and that these proportions are mathematical. Furthermore, he was a fervent student of Christian Kabbalah, and claimed that Kabbalah is able to prove the truth of Christianity. The work consists of 3 parts, or "canticles," which all contain 8 "tones" (an octave), each focusing on a theological or philosophical subject. The first greater part is about God, the second about Christ and the Holy Trinity, while the third is about the human soul, the virtues, and the sacraments. Importantly, it was republished in Paris in 1545, though without any new paratextual elements that would help us identify the most important supporters of Zorzi's teachings in Paris. Zorzi himself had no personal connection to Paris, as he retreated to the convent of Asolo, continuing his studies from 1517 until his death in 1540. We might guess that it was Nádasdi's interest in Christian Hebraism, the *Hebraica veritas* of the Bible, which made his fellow Franciscan's work so dear to him. It is significant, however, that Zorzi's Neoplatonic and Kabbalistic orientation, for which he was widely known, is not conspicuous at all in the passages Nádasdi borrowed from him. It was precisely the lack of Neoplatonic or Kabbalistic ideas in these chapters which allowed Nádasdi to rework Zorzi's text and transform it into sermons for his fellow friars. However, his predilection for Zorzi's work is clear from his surviving copy in the library of Gyöngyös, on the first leaf of which he drew the three monumental letters "F[rater] V[alentinus] N[ádasdi]" in Hebrew.

7 Conclusion: Covert Recontextualization Instead of Transmission

Strictly speaking, Valentine Nádasdi's miscellany is not a collection of notes taken down in a classroom. It is rather a collection of personal annotations, often transformed into new works (sermons and epistles) while he was studying theology and holy languages in Paris in 1551 and 1552. The miscellany comprises an eclectic se-

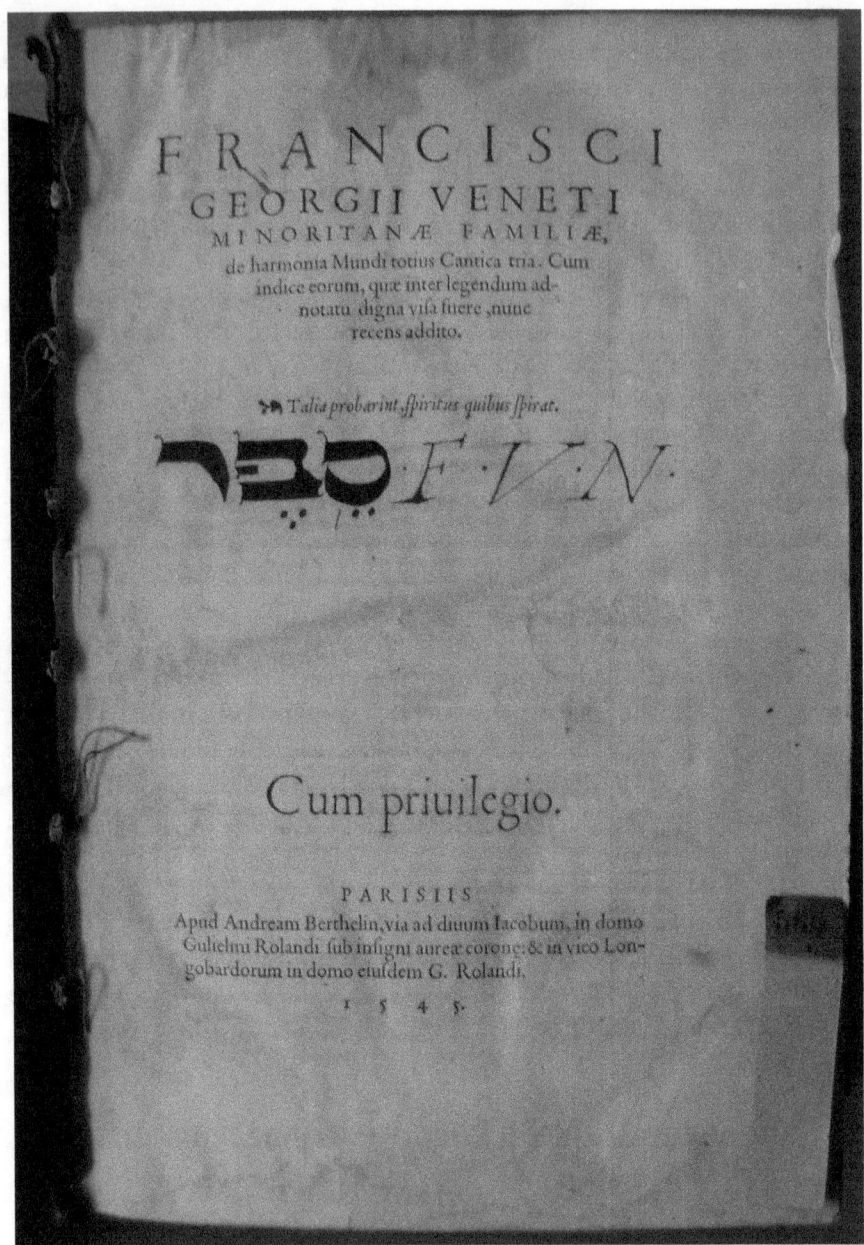

Fig. 2: Title page of Nádasdi's copy of Francesco Zorzi's De harmonia mundi (Gyöngyös, Franciscan Library, Ant. 566)

lection of very different texts, which are all filtered through Nádasdi's intellectual preferences. Significantly, he did not simply copy the texts and did not refer to their authors: there is not a single text presented as they usually appear in a commonplace book—with their authors named and quoted in their full form. Instead, he kept the authors' names under cover and made use of their texts for his own purposes, creating completely new contexts. Guarna's allegory of Grammar would become a praise of Hungary, Ramus' panegyrics to Henry II, King of France, would serve as the basis of an oration of about the duties of princes, and Zorzi's Kabbalism would make ground to anti-Lutheran polemics. Nádasdi's sources were always transformed into the shape he needed, be it a sermon or a model letter, keeping the authors' names covert. The primary aim of his study process was interiorization through transformation, and his transformed texts served exactly this purpose. In describing this process, he called these portions of transformed knowledge "packages" (*sarcinulas*) he carried home from Paris. In fact, one might guess that through the interiorization process, these "packages" were rather internally stored and memorized, and his rewriting practice aided the memorization of the ideas. Surely, he supposed that on the Christian-Ottoman border, very few readers and listeners would be able to appreciate the authority and fame of the original authors, but he still infiltrated their ideas to his local audience in the hope that they would enchant the public by their power and authenticity.

Unlike classroom textbooks and study notebooks, Nádasdi's miscellany is not an organized unit of knowledge transmission. It contains all kinds of materials from all kinds of authors, sometimes borrowed from contexts that seem haphazard, for instance, including editorial introductions and dedications. The impression of diversity is further strengthened by the philosophical and—to a certain extent— even confessional variety of his sources. His eclectic approach to philosophy made it possible for Ramus, the Ciceronian (and later Protestant) rhetorician, and Kabbalist Franciscan authors, like Pietro Galatino or Francesco Zorzi, to find their way into the same notebook. It is possible that Nádasdi, as a foreigner, was not well-versed in the intellectual trends of Paris and did not know about the conflicts between Ramus and the theological faculty of the university. But this lack of acquaintance with the local philosophical climate and lack of prejudices could have made him receptive to both Ramus and Franciscan Kabbalism. His own intention of taking back big "parcels of knowledge" to his home country, which he could later employ for practical uses, was actually consistent with Ramus' focus on practicality and with his efforts of uniting dialectics and eloquence. Nádasdi's aims were primarily practical (creating a new Ciceronian style for the Franciscan model letters in Hungary, or applying the wisdom of his favorite Christian Kabbalists in the fight against heretics) and could easily be aligned with Ramus' practical philosophy. It was most likely the lack of multilayered cultural infrastructure (the lack of Catholic institutions of higher education, and the dispersal of cloister schools) which had a fundamental influence on how he tried to cope with the difficulties of knowledge transmission in an environment which was deeply divided confessionally and politically. While acting in an overwhelmingly Protestant country, he tried to engage his readers with his cultural ideas by recontextualizing their texts as model letters and preaching. The most significant strategy of knowledge transmission was a "covert recontextualization" of his cultural ideals. In this process, he tried to avoid confessional conflicts and reframed the original arguments in a form which proved to be useful for his local community, thus saving his "ideals," although in a covert form. Thus, in his case, instead of knowledge transfer, we might speak of knowledge transformation in the meaning as Michel Espagne exposed the term "cultural transfer": a reinterpretation that prioritizes the perception, recontextualization and re-semantization of a cultural object in a new environment (Jørgensen and Lüsebrink 2021).

Appendix:
Currently known books of Nádasdi's library

1. Albertus Magnus (1536): *In XII prophetas minores enarrationes.* Cologne. Gyöngyös, FL, Ant. 564. (Annotation: 1551)
2. Ambrose of Milan (1540): *Commentarii in Pauli epistolas.* Antwerp. Gyöngyös, FL. (Annotation: 1551).
3. Anselm of Canterbury (1533): *In Pauli epistolas enarrationes.* Cologne. Gyöngyös, FL, Ant. 496. (Annotation: 1546).
4. Antonius a Königstein (1540): *Postillae.* Cologne. Gyöngyös, FL, Ant. 24. (Annotation: 1544).
5. Beda (1541): *Homiliae.* Cologne. Gyöngyös, FL, Ant. 567, 567a.
6. *Biblia* (1547). Paris. Gyöngyös, FL, Ant. 787.
7. Clemens of Alexandria (1536): *Recognitiones.* Basel. Gyöngyös, FL, Ant. 494.
8. Denyse, Nicolaus (1516): *Opus super sententias valde egregium in disciplina Theologie.* Lyon, Simon Bevilacqua. Martin, Slovak National Library (Supralibros: F. Valentinus de Nadasdi).
9. Dionysius Carthusianus (1542): *Enarratio epistolarum.* Cologne. Gyöngyös, FL, Ant. 528.
10. Dionysius Carthusianus (1542): *In evangelium Matthaei enarratio.* Paris. Csíksomlyó (Miercurea Ciuc, RO), Franciscan Library. (Annotation: 1546).
11. Dionysius Carthusianus (1533): *In IV evangelistas enarrationes.* Cologne. Gyöngyös, FL, Ant. 527. (Annotation: 1539).
12. Dionysius Carthusianus (1541): *In VII epistolas canonicas.* Paris. Gyöngyös, Franciscan Library. (Annotation: 1546).
13. Eck, Johann (1537): *Homiliarum* tom. I., s.l. Gyöngyös, FL, Ant. 574. (Annotation: 1545).
14. Eck, Johann (1538): *Homiliae.* Cologne. Gyöngyös, FL, Ant. 584.
15. Euthymius Zigabenus (1547): *Commentaria in sacrosancta quatuor Christi evangelia.* Paris. Library of the Bishopric of Satu Mare, Q 98. (Supralibros: F.V. N.).
16. Fabri, Johann (1541): *Homiliae.* Cologne. Gyöngyös, FL, Ant. 493. (Annotation: 1546).

17. Fischer, Johann (1527): *De veritate corporis Christi.* Gyöngyös, FL, Ant. 568. (Annotation: 1546).
18. Haymo von Halberstadt (1531): *Commentariorum in Apocalypsim.* Cologne, Eucharius Cervicornus. Martin, Slovak National Library ("Emptus... f. Valen[tinus Nádasdi]").
19. Hugo von Ripelin (1485): *Compendium theologicae veritatis.* Venice. Gyöngyös, Franciscan Library (hence: FL), Inc. 85.
20. Junius, Hadrianus (1548): *Lexicon Graecolatinum.* Basel. Gyöngyös, FL, Ant. 409.
21. Nausea, Friedrich (1536): *Sermones.* Cologne. Gyöngyös, FL, Ant. 495. (Annotation: 1546).
22. Nausea, Friedrich (1536): *Sermones.* Cologne. Gyöngyös, FL, Ant. 494.
23. Petrus Lombardus (1507): *Sententiae.* Venice. Gyöngyös, FL, Ant. 646. (Annotation: 1544).
24. *Psalterium* (1538). Lyon. Gyöngyös, FL, Ant. 314. (Annotation: 1546).
25. Quinquarboreus, Jean (1549): *De re grammatica Hebraeorum.* Paris. Gyöngyös, FL, Ant. 791.
26. Rolewinck, Werner (c. 1940): *Fasciculus temporum.* Strassburg. Gyöngyös, FL, Inc. 34. ("Concessus ad usum fratris Valentini de Nadasd 1545").
27. Rupertus Tuitensis (1541): *Commentarii in Apocalypsim.* Cologne. Gyöngyös, FL, Ant. 564. (Annotation: 1551).
28. Rupertus Tuitensis (1526): *In Cantica Canticorum commentarii.* Cologne. Gyöngyös, FL, Ant. 564. (Annotation: 1551).
29. Rupertus Tuitensis (1517): *Morale reductorium super Bibliam.* Basel. Gyöngyös, FL, Ant. 564. (Annotation: 1551)
30. Theophylactus (1542): *In quatuor evangelia enarrationes.* Cologne. Library of the Bishopric of Satu Mare, S184/Coll.1. (Annotation: F. V. N.).
31. Tillman, Godfroy (1550): *De septem sacramentis liber unus.* Paris. Library of the Bishopric of Satu Mare, S98. (Supralibros: F. V. N.).
32. Titelmann, Franciscus (1552): *Commentarii in Ecclesiasten Salomonis.* Paris. Gyöngyös, FL, Ant. 16.
33. Titelmann, Franciscus (1544): *De consideratione dialectica.* Paris. Gyöngyös, FL, Ant. 571. (Annotation: 1551).
34. Wild, Johann (1551): *In Ecclesiasten Salomonis annotationes.* Paris. Gyöngyös, FL, Ant. 16.
35. Zorzi, Francesco (Franciscus Georgius) (1545): *De harmonia mundi.* Paris, Berthelin. Gyöngyös, FL, Ant. 566. (Annotation: 1551).

Bibliography

Primary Sources

Manuscripts

Nádasdi, Bálint: *Omniarium.* National Széchényi Library, Ms. Oct. Lat. 1220.

Printed Sources

Anselmus Cantuariensis (1549): *Omnia Anselmi Cantuariensis... opuscula.* Antonius Democharis Ressonaeus (Ed.). Venice: ad signum Spei.

Barzizza, Gasparino (1723): *Epistolae ad exercitationem accommodatae.* In: Barzizza, Gasparino: *Opera.* Vol. I. Joseph Alexander Furiettus (Ed.). Rome: J. M. Salvioni, 220–336.

Bunyitay, Vince, Rapaics, Rajmund Rapaics, and Karácsonyi, János J. (Eds.) (1904): *Egyháztörténeti emlékek a magyarországi hitújítás korából* [Sources on church history from the time of the religious reform in Hungary]. Vol. II. Budapest: Szent István Társulat.

Cochlaeus, Johann (1544): *De animarum purgatorio igne epitome, contra novas sectas quae Purgatorium negant.* Ingolstadt: Weissenhorn.

Damascenus, Joannes (1546): "De trisagio. Epistola de eo quod ecclesia canit 'Sanctus Deus, sanctus fortis, sanctus immortalis.'" In: Damascenus, Joannes: *Universa quae obtineri hac vice potuerunt opera.* Henricus Gravius (Ed.). Cologne: Petrus Quentel.

Galatinus, Petrus (1550): *Opus de arcanis Catholicae veritatis.* Basel: Hervagius.

Georgius, Franciscus Venetus (Zorzi, Francesco) (1544): *De harmonia mundi totius cantica tria.* Paris: Berthelin.

Martial of Toulouse, Saint (1546): "Epistola beati Martialis ad Tolosanos." In: *Epistolae D. Ignatii, Polycarpi, Martialis, Antonii magni, vetustissimorum scriptorium.* Ed. Symphorien Champier. Venice: Ad signum spei. Fols. 49–57.

Pico della Mirandola, Giovanni (1498): *Omnia opera.* Venice: Bernardinus Venetus.

Ramus, Petrus (1551): *Oratio initio suo professionis habita anno 1551 octavo Calend. Septemb.* Paris: Matthaeus David.

Ramus, Petrus (1580): *Praelectiones in Ciceronis orationes octo consulares, una cum ipsius vita.* Basel: Petrus Perna.

Velcurio, Johannes and Schegk, Jacob (1544): *In universam physicam Aristotelis—Dialogus de animae principatu.* Lyon: Gryphius, 1544.

Zorzi, Francesco (1545): *De harmonia mundi totius cantica tria.* Paris: Berthelin.

Secondary Sources

Alszeghy, Zsolt (1935): "Ismeretlen magyar dráma a 17. század elejéről [Unknown Hungarian drama from the beginning of the 17th century]." In: *Egyetemes Philologiai Közlöny* 59, 34–64.

Bolte, Johannes (1908): *Andrea Guarnas Bellum grammaticale und seine Nachahmungen.* Berlin: Hofman.

Bruyère, Nelly (1984): *Méthode et dialectique dans l'oeuvre de La Ramée.* Paris: Vrin.

Butler, Erik (2010): *The Bellum Grammaticale and the Rise of European Literature.* Farnham and Burlington: Ashgate.

Campanini, Saverio (1999): "Le fonti ebraiche de De harmonia mundi di Francesco Zorzi." In: *Annali di Ca' Foscari* 38. No. 3, 29–74.

Campanini, Saverio (2010): "Quasi post vindemias racemos colligens. Pietro Galatino und seine Verteidigung der christlichen Kabbala." In: Kühlmann, Wilhelm (Ed.) *Reuchlins Freunde und Gegner. Kommunikative Konstellationen eines frühneuzeitlichen Medienereignisses.* Ostfildern: Thorbecke, 69–88.

Couzinet, Marie-Dominique and Mandosio, Jean-Marc (2004): "Nouveaux éclairages sur les cours de Ramus et de ses collègues au collège de Presles d'après des notes inédites prises par Nancel." In: Meerhoff, Kees and Magnien, Michel (Eds.): *Ramus et l'Université.* Paris: Éditions Rue d'Ulm, 11–48.

De Cevins, Marie-Madeleine (2008): *Les franciscains observants hongrois de l'expansion à la debacle.* Rome: Istituto storico dei Cappuccini.

Emődi, András (2013): "Gyöngyösi ferences könyvek 16. századi possessorai a Szatmári Római Katolikus Püspökség Egyházmegyei Műemlékkönyvtárából [16th century owners of Franciscan books from Gyöngyös in the Library of the Catholic Bishopric of Satu Mare]." In: Medgyesy-Schmikli, Norbert, Ötvös, István, and Őze, Sándor (Eds.): *Nyolcszáz esztendős a ferences rend.* Budapest: Magyar Napló, 1184–1204.

Fumaroli, Marc (2002): *L'âge de l'éloquence. Rhétorique et "res literaria" de la Renaissance au seuil de l'époque classique.* Geneva: Droz.

Grafton, Anthony and Weinberg, Joanna (2011): *"I have always loved the Holy Tongue." Isaac Casaubon, the Jews and a Forgotten Chapter in Renaissance Scholarship.* Cambridge: Belknap Press of Harvard University Press.

Irigoin, Jean (2006): "Les lecteurs royaux pour le grec (1530–1560)." In: Tuilier, André (Ed.) *Histoire du Collège de France.* Vol. I. Paris: Fayard, 233–256.

Jørgensen, Steen Bille and Lüsebrink Hans-Jürgen (2021): "Introduction: Reframing the Cultural Transfer Approach." In: Jørgensen, Steen Bille and Lüsebrink Hans-Jürgen (Eds.) *Cultural Transfer Reconsidered. Transnational Perspectives, Translation Processes, Scandinavian and Postcolonial Challenges.* Leiden: Brill, 1–20.

Karácsonyi János (1922): "A váradi káptalan megrontása [The destruction of the Chapter of Várad]." In: *Századok* 56, 440–451.

Karácsonyi János (1924): *Szent Ferenc rendjének története Magyarországon 1711-ig [The history of the Order of St Francis in Hungary until 1711].* Vol. II. Budapest: Magyar Tudományos Akadémia.

Kessler-Mesguich, Sophie (2013): *Les études hébraiques en France, de François Tissard à Richard Simon (1508–1680).* Geneva: Droz.

Keveházi, Katalin and Monok, István (1985): "XVI.–XVII. Századi könyvgyűjtők kötetei a csíksomlyói ferences rendház könyvtárában [Volumes of 16th and 17th century book collectors in the Franciscan convent of Csíksomlyó]." In: *Acta historiae litterarum Hungaricarum* 21, 121–128.

Maillard, Jean-François and Flamand, Jean-Marie (Eds.) (2010): *La France des humanistes. Hellénistes II.* Turnhout: Brepols.

Meerhoff, Kees (1986): "Ramus et Cicéron." In: *Revue des Sciences philosophique et théologiques* 70. No. 1, 25–35.

Meerhoff, Kees (2011): "Petrus Ramus and the Vernacular." In: Reid, Steven J. and Wilson, Emma Annette (Eds.): *Ramus, Pedagogy and the Liberal Arts: Ramism in Britain and the Wider World.* Burlington and Farnham: Ashgate, 133–152.

Molnár, Antal (2014): "Formulari francescani della provincia Ungherese dei frati Minori Osservanti del primo Cinquecento." In: Bartolacci, Francesca and Lambertini, Roberto (Eds.): *Osservanza francescana e cultura tra Quattrocento e primo Cinquecento: Italia e Ungheria a confronto. Atti del Convegno Macerata-Sarnano, 6–7 dicembre 2013.* Rome: Viella, 73–86.

Molnár, Antal (2022): *Die Formelsammlungen der Franziskaner-Observanten in Ungarn (ca. 1451–1554).* Rome: Quaracchi.

Moracchini, Pierre (2005): "Les Observants de la province de France parisienne face aux réformes franciscaines (1574–1612)." In: Meyer, Frédéric and Viallet, Ludovic (Eds.): *Identités franciscaines à l'âge des Réformes.* Clermont-Ferrand: Presses Universitaires Blaise-Pascal, 165–184.

Pálffy, Géza (1997): "A török elleni védelmi rendszer néhány alapkérdése a XVI. Század első felében [Fundamental issues of the defense against the Ottoman Turks in the first half of the 16th century]." In: Petercsák, Tivadar (Ed.): *Hagyomány és korszerűség a XVI–XVII. században.* Eger: Heves Megyei Múzeumok Igazgatósága, 59–74.

Pálffy, Géza (2021): *Hungary between Two Empires, 1526–1711.* David Robert Evans (Trans.). Bloomington: Indiana University Press.

Pettegree, Andrew and Walsby, Malcolm (2012): *French Books III & IV. Books Published in France before 1601 in Latin and Languages Other Than French.* Vol. I. Leiden: Brill.

Romhányi, Beatrix F. (2013): "Le fonctionnement matériel des couvents mendiants dans le royaume de Hongrie aux XIIIe–XVIe siècles: aperçu des sources et de l'historiographie." In: *Études franciscaines* ns. 6, 47–56.

Sanchi, Luigi Alberto (2006): *Les commentaires de la langue grecque de Guillaume Budé.* Geneva: Droz.

Soltész, Zoltánné (1965, 1966): "XVI. századi könyvgyűjtők kötetei a gyöngyösi műemlék-könyvtár antikva-gyűjteményében [Volumes of 16th century book collectors among the 16th century prints of the library of Gyöngyös]." In: *Az Országos Széchényi Könyvtár Évkönyve* 10, 115–148.

Soltész, Zoltánné (1993): "A gyöngyösi ferences könyvtár ősnyomtatványainak possessorai [Ownership marks in the incunable prints of the Franciscan library of Gyöngyös]." In: *Magyar könyvszemle* 109, 129–145.

Vasoli, Cesare (1988): "Marsilio Ficino e Francesco Giorgio Veneto." In: Vasoli, Cesare: *Filosofia e religione nella cultura del Rinascimento.* Naples: Guida Editori, 233–256

Vízkelety, András (1990): "Nádasdi Bálint omniáriuma és beszéde a fejedelmi tisztről [The miscellany of Bálint Nádasdi and his oration on the Office of the Prince]." In: Szerk. Géza Galavics, Herner, János and Keserű, Bálint (Eds.) *Collectanea Tiburtiana. Tanulmányok Klaniczay Tibor tiszteletére.* Szeged: József Attila Tudományegyetem, 121–128.

Wursten, Dick (2011): "François Vatable, so much more than a 'name.'" In: *Bibliothèque d'Humanisme et Renaissance* 73, 557–591.

Zorzi, Francesco (2010): *L'armonia del mondo.* Saverio Campenini (Ed. and Trans.). Milan: Bompiani.

Zvara Edina (2005): "XVI.–XVII. századi könyvgyűjtők kötetei a szakolcai ferences könyvtárban [The volumes of 16th and 17th century book collectors in the Franciscan library of Szakolca]." In: Őze, Sándor and Medgyesy-Schmikli, Norbert (Eds.): *A ferences lelkiség hatása az újkori Közép-Európa történetére és kultúrájára.* Vol. I. Piliscsaba-Budapest: METEM, 539–560.

Index of Names

Accius, Lucius 49
Achilles 238
Ács, Pál 35
Agricola, Rudolph 2, 9–10, 12–14, 18–19, 23–24, 30, 38, 44
Albert the Great 235
Albinus, see Alcuin of York
Alcalá, Ángel 175
Alcuin of York 159–160
Alexander the Great 238
Almási, Gábor 30, 48
Alszeghy, Zsolt 231, 233
Amantius, Bartholomaeus 48
Ambrose, Saint 160–161, 233, 235
Amerbach, Johann 130, 160
Andreä, Jakob 180, 199, 202
Anselm of Canterbury 230, 235
Apollos of Alexandria 193
Aquinas, Thomas 154, 164–165
Archelaus 162
Archidamus, King of Sparta 106
Argyropoulos, John 149, 158, 167
Aristo of Chio 103
Aristotle 4, 17, 36–38, 44, 46–47, 69, 72, 75–76, 82, 95, 102, 104, 128–130, 145–153, 157–158, 163–167, 174, 238
Arnold, Matthieu 40
Ashmann, Margreet J.A.M. 81
Athanaeus Naucratites 20
Augustine, Saint 11, 160, 162, 176, 198
Aurnhammer, Achim 71
Avicenna 71

Bacon, Francis 30
Bade, Josse 162
Bainton, Robert H. 175, 195
Bak, János M. 32
Bánovszky, Martin 37
Bánovszky, Simon 37
Baranyai Decsi, János 41
Barbaro, Ermolao 146–147, 237
Barbirianus, Jacobus 13
Bartholin, Caspar 74

Bartoniek, Emma 33
Barzizza, Gasparino 236
Basil, Saint 198
Báthory, András 5, 230–231, 235
Béla I, King of Hungary 51
Béla IV, King of Hungary 51
Bellius, Martin (pseud.) see Castellion, Sébastien
Bentz, Johann 40–41
Berg, Heinrich 120
Berger, Thiebolt 176
Bergmann, Benjamin 122
Bergmann, Gustav 122
Bernard of Clairvaux 238
Bersman, Gregor 103
Bertalot, Ludwig 2, 10
Biandrata, Giorgio 199
Birkowski, Szymon 95
Blaese, Hermann 120, 122–124
Blair, Ann M. 10, 70, 87, 94, 97, 100, 112
Bocskai, István 31
Bodin, Jean 30, 33, 49–50, 52
Bolte, Johannes 236–237
Bonfini, Antonio 48
Bónis, György 31, 33–34, 36, 41–42
Böthführ, Heinrich Julius 125
Braakhuis, Henricus A. G. 38
Brassicanus, Johannes Alexander 34
Brenz, Johannes 180, 182, 195
Brunfels, Otto 13
Bruni, Leonardo 2, 10, 146, 149, 164, 167
Bruyère, Nelly 232
Bucanus, Gulielmus 180
Buchholtz, Arend 123
Bukowska, Krystyna 95
Bullinger, Johann Heinrich 178–179, 182–183, 194
Bunyitay, Vince 230
Burgersdijk, Franco 74
Burski, Adam 95, 99
Butler, Erik 236
Buttay-Jutier, Florence 29

Caecina, Aulus 43

Caesar, Julius 129, 238
Caillaut, Antoine 147
Calvin, Jean (Johannes) 49, 178, 189, 192, 194–197
Camerarius, Joachim 180
Campanini, Saverio 239
Candidus 160
Cardano, Girolamo 75
Carpocrates 186
Cartwright, Kent 108
Casaubon, Isaac 129
Casmann, Otho 69, 71, 75, 81–82
Castellion, Sébastien 178, 195–196, 200, 203
Catherine of Aragon, Queen 15
Catilina, Lucius Sergius 42, 47
Cerinthus 186–187
Cesarini, Giulio 50
Cevolini, Alberto 30, 52, 87
Chachaj, Marian 95
Christopher of Württemberg 174, 178, 180, 194
Cicero, Marcus Tullius 24, 29–30, 36, 40–49, 53, 99, 102–103, 105, 108, 110–111, 129, 135, 148, 155–157, 162–163, 174, 232, 236, 238–239
Cicero, Quintus Tullius (the orator's brother) 45
Ciekliński, Piotr 100
Clavius, Christophorus 39
Clichtove, Josse van 146–147, 163, 167
Cluentius Habitus, Aulus 45
Cochlaeus, Johann 240
Conley, Thomas M. 99, 101
Coron, Antoine 33
Couzinet, Marie-Dominique 30, 232–233
Crassus, Lucius Licinius 103
Cruciger, Felix 179
Crusius, Martin 199
Ctesiphon 155
Cummings, Brian 30
Curione, Agostino 178, 183
Curione, Celio Secondo 175–176, 178, 181, 183, 195, 201, 203–204
Curtius, Quintus 195, 221
Cuspinianus, Johannes 34

da Fonseca, Pedro 125
Dachtler, Gottlieb 41
Dąmbska, Izydora 95

Daneau, Lambert 33–34
Dávid, Ferenc 195, 207
de Bèze, Theodore 179, 195
de Cevins, Marie-Madelaine 230–231
de Guise, Charles 232
Décultot, Élisabeth 52
Demaratus, King of Sparta 106
Demosthenes 42, 44, 46
Des Freux, André 35–36
Desan, Philippe 33
Destrez, Jean 9
Dibon, Paul 78
Diodorus Siculus 48
Diogenes Laertius 154–155, 167
Diomedes 16
Dionysius Areopagite 238
Dirnbach, Valentin 231
Dolet, Étienne 238
Dreiling, Caspar 120
Drezner, Tomasz 95, 98, 104, 129
Drohojowski, Jan Tomasz 181–182, 184, 192–193, 203, 218–221
Drohojowski, Kiljan 174, 195, 218–221
Du Rieu, Willem Nicolaas 71
Dyjakowska, Marzena 95

Ebion 186
Eckhardt, Sándor 41–42
Eglin, Raphael 85
Emili, Paolo 149
Episcopius, Eusebius 238
Equicola, Mario 147
Erasmus, Desiderius 2, 9, 11–21, 23, 30, 33–35, 41, 44, 160, 173, 200, 230, 236–237
Eritreus, Valentinus 182
Escombard, Enguerrand 235
Espagne, Michel 246
Estreicher, Karol 100
Eusebius 238

Fa(h)rensbach, Theodor 129
Fabri, Johann 235, 246
Facca, Danilo 3, 69, 95, 112
Fantappiè, Irene 12
Faucher, Nicolas 39
Ferdinand I, King of Hungary and Bohemia, Emperor 230

Fernel, Jean   69, 71, 75, 82
Ficino, Marsilio   148, 154, 156, 166, 237
Flügel, Johann   120
Folliero, Pietro   160
Fonseca, Pedro da   125
Forner, Fabio   10
Fortius Ringelberg, Joachim   230, 236
Francis of Assisi   238
Franklin, James   30
Friedenthal, Meelis   69
Friedrichs, Johann   120
Frycz Modrzewski, Andrzej   181
Fumaroli, Marc   35, 239
Fundárková, Anna   32

Galatino, Pietro   239, 242, 245
Galen   71
Gall, Franz   36
Ganay, Germain de   148–150, 152
Gargan, Luciano   10
Garin, Eugenio   10, 20–21
Gastgeber, Christian   48
Gaziński, Radosław   76
Gellius, Aulus   19–20, 23, 197
Gerézdi, Rabán   35
Geri, Lorenzo   12
Gindhart, Marion   69
Gmiterek, Henryk   95, 100, 108, 130
Goclenius, Rudolf sr.   73
Godek, Sławomir   124
Golius, Theophilus   44
Gonesius, Petrus (Piotr of Goniądz)   178–179, 181, 191–193, 197–199, 202–204, 219
Gontier, Guillaume   147
Grafton, Anthony   25, 112, 239
Graseck, Paul   41
Grasser, Joannes   37
Grendler, Paul F.   36, 41
Gribaldi, Matteo Moffa   4, 175–176, 178–180, 183, 186–193, 195–197, 199–204
Gruter, Jan   155
Gryko-Andrejuk, Beata   129
Grześkowiak-Krwawicz, Anna   107
Guarini, Guarino   20
Guarna, Andrea   236–237, 245
Guevara, Antonio   33
Guidacerio, Agacio   232

Hector   238
Heitzler, Georgio   180
Henry II, King of France   232, 245
Hercules   238
Hermogenes of Tarsus   99, 108–109
Higman, Johann   149
Hilchen (Heliconius), David   3–4, 98, 119–136
Hiltebrand, Andreas   71, 82, 85
Hintelmann, Ludwig   120
Hoffmann, Thomas   122–123
Hopyl, Wolfgang   149
Horace   24, 105, 167
Horn, Ewald   69, 122
Horodyski, Bogdan   95
Hosius, Stanislaus   176
Hotson, Howard   78, 81, 86
Hrabecius, Raphael   34
Hug, Paul   158–159

Ignatius of Antiochia   230
Ignatius of Loyola   35
Imre, Mihály   41
Irenaeus   192–193
Irigoin, Jean   232
Isidore of Seville   238
Iunius, Melchior   40–43, 45–47

Jacchaeus, Gilbertus (Jack, Gilbert)   74, 86
Jardine, Lisa   12, 19, 25, 112
Jaskmanicki, Jan   174, 218
Jerome, Saint   155–156, 238
Jessenius, Johannes   71
Jesus Christ   179–180, 187–190, 192–193, 197–200, 239–240
Joasaph II of Constantinople   199
Johannes de Sacrobosco   37, 39
John Damascene   230, 236
John (Evangelist)   179, 188, 191, 193, 196, 200–201, 240
Jørgensen, Steen Bille   246
Jovaiša, Liudas   120
Junius, Melchior   29, 106, 247
Justinian I, Eastern Roman Emperor   95, 98, 101, 106, 109, 129, 131

Kainulainen, Jaska   35
Kallendorf, Craig   10

Karácsonyi, János   230–231
Keckermann, Bartholomäus   69, 71, 73–74, 78, 81–86
Keßler, Eckhard   145, 149
Kieltika, Johannes   124
Kiris, Advig   120
Kiss, Farkas Gábor   5, 48, 194, 229, 236
Klecker, Elisabeth   48
Klöker, Martin   122
Köbler, Gerhard   121, 131, 136
Kochanoreski, Stanislaus   124
Kochanowski, Jan Karol   95
Kocówna, Barbara   110
Koletai, Ioannes   124
Komjáti, Benedek   35
Kooiman, Elly   13
Kot, Stanisław   174–176, 178, 192, 203
Kotkowski, Mikołaj   174, 219–221
Krokier, Jan   129–130
Krokier, Paweł   129–130
Kromer, Marcin   176
Kula, Jakub   182,
Kula, Stanisław   174, 181–182, 191, 195, 201, 218–219
Kula, Wawrzyniec   182
Kumor, Bolestaw   95
Kundert, Ursula   69
Kuryłowicz, Marek   95

Lackner, Christoph   33
Laínez, Diego   35
Lambin, Denis   43
Lang, Joseph   40
Lascaris, Constantine   16
Lavéant, Katell   108
Leesment, Leo   120
Lefèvre d'Étaples, Jacques   38–39
Leliwa, Stanisław   122
Lepri, Valentina   1, 9, 95, 98–99, 107–108, 112
Leszczyński, Rafał   175
Levèfre d'Étaple, Jacques   145
Liebler, George   76–77
Lipsius, Justus   30–31, 33, 73, 86
Lismanini, Francesco   179
Livy   41
Locher, A.   20
Lubieniecki, Andrzey   130
Lubieniecki, Stanisław   183
Lucian   12
Ludwig, Hawenreuter Johann   40
Lüsebrink, Hans-Jürgen   246
Luther, Martin   35, 190, 200–202, 240
Lutomirski, Jan   181
Lutomirski, Stanisław   176, 203
Luts-Sootak, Marju   121–122
Lycosthenes, Conrad   41, 44

Machiavelli, Niccolò   181
Mack, Peter   12, 18–19, 24
Macrobius   19–20, 148
Magirus, Johannes   73–76
Mahling, Madlena   123
Makowski, Tomasz   95, 97
Mandosio, Jean-Marc   233
Maniscalco, Lorenzo   104
Manlius, Christophorus   50
Mantovano, Battista   149
Manuzio, Paolo   35
Marcellus, Marcus   232
Marenbon, John   160–161
Margolin, Jean-Claude   20
Marti, Hanspeter   69
Martial of Toulouse, Saint   236
Mary I, queen of England   15, 21
Mary, mother of Christ   36, 179, 189, 193, 239
Mary Tudor, sister of Henry VIII   11
Matthias, Archduke of Austria, Holy Roman Emperor, King of Hungary as Matthias II   31–32
Mazheika, Hanna   96
Meerhoff, Kees   239
Melanchthon, Philip   12, 19, 25, 74–75, 121, 179–180, 182, 191–192, 194–196, 198–203
Melani, Igor   50
Mercenario, Arcangelo   75
Milo, Titus Annius   45
Moerbeke, William of   164
Molensis, Joannes   35–37
Molnár, Antal   231, 235
Moracchini, Pierre   235
Mosellanus, Petrus   17
Moss, Ann   10, 17–19, 21, 25, 30, 40, 197, 201–202
Mountjoy, Charles   15

Mountjoy, William 15
Muller, Richard A. 194
Mundt, Hermann 69
Murad II 50
Murano, Giovanna 9
Murena, Lucius Licinius 41, 47
Muret, Marc-Antoine 104–106, 108–109
Muszynska, Krystyna 110
Mycio, Andrzej 69, 71
Myk, Sławomir 95

Nádasdi, Valentin (Bálint) 5, 229–247
Najemy, John M. 30
Nanus Mirabellius, Dominicus 40, 48
Naprágyi, Demeter 36
Narbutas, Sigitas 123
Narbutienė, Daiva 123
Nausea, Friedrich 235, 247
Nauta, Lodi 12, 38
Negruzzo, Simona 41
Nelles, Paul 10
Niemcewicz, Julian Ursyn 108

Oestmann, Peter 119
Okolski, Jan Ursyn 100
Olelkowicz Słucki, Alexander 123
Oporinus, Johannes 181, 195–196, 200
Orzechowski, Paweł Jun. 129–130
Orzechowski, Paweł Sen. 130, 181
Orzechowski, Stanisław 129, 181

Pálffy, Géza 32, 230, 235
Papy, Jan 38
Paradis, Paul 232
Passerat, Jean 105–106, 108–109
Patrizi, Francesco 85
Paul, Apostle 35, 158, 233, 235, 243
Pauw, Pieter 71
Pękacka-Falkowska, Katarzyna 85
Pellisson, Jean 230, 236
Pereira, Bento 75
Pesti, Gábor 35
Petrarca, Francesco 12
Pettegree, Andrew 236
Peurlin, Jacob 180
Photinus 186
Piccolomini, Aeneas Silvius 12

Pico della Mirandola, Gianfrancesco 237
Pico della Mirandola, Giovanni 12, 230, 237, 239
Piechnik, Ludwik 125
Piechowicz, Szymon 112
Pieniążek, Jan 174, 218
Pieniążek, Stanisław 174, 218–221
Pierzchalski, Stanislaus 124
Pietrzyk, Zdzisław 123, 182
Pihlajamäki, Heikki 119
Plath, Uwe 175, 178
Plato 17, 46, 48, 154, 161–163, 166, 232, 238
Plautus 16, 100, 238
Pliny the Elder 20
Plotinus 148
Plutarch 24, 41, 44, 46, 161
Pocock, John Greville Agard 30
Poklaterzki, Ioannes 124
Poliziano, Agnolo 18, 20
Pollard, Graham 9
Pölnitz, Götz von 124
Porphyry 17, 37, 148
Protagoras 152, 162–163
Protten of Augsburg 194
Pseudo Plutarch 24

Quera, Miguel Bertrán 15
Quintilian 12, 14, 16–17, 24

Raczinski, Foelix 124
Radecke, Matthias (Radecius, Matthaeus) 85
Radziwiłł, Mikołaj "Czarny" (the Black) 179–180, 202
Radziwiłł, Mikołaj Krzysztof 202
Ramus, Petrus 40, 75–77, 231–233, 238–239, 242, 245
Rapaics, Rajmund 230
Ravisius Textor, Johannes 230, 236–237
Reberterie, Jean de la 101
Rely, Jean de 152
Rennenkampf, Paul 120
Reuchlin, Johann 239
Reusner, Nikolaus 48
Révay, Péter 2–3, 29–37, 39–53, 56
Rhenanus, Beatus 146–147
Riccucci, Marina 12
Rigemann, Dietrich the Elder 124

Rigemann, Theodor (Dietrich) the Younger   124–125, 128
Rimay, János   31
Ritoókné Szalay, Ágnes   35
Romhányi, Beatrix   230
Roques, Magali   39
Roscius Amerinus, Sextus   45–46
Roşu, Felicia   107
Rudolph II, Holy Roman Emperor, King of Hungary   31
Ruestow, Edward   74, 86
Rummel, Erika   12, 174
Rupert of Deutz   235
Ryczek, Wojciech   95

Salliot, Natacha   35
Sambucus, Joannes   47–48
Sand, Christophorus   130
Sapieha, Jan Stanisław   128–129
Sapieha, Lew   130
Scaligero, Giulio Cesare   75
Schegk, Jacob   180
Scheurl, Heinrich Julius   152
Schlegelmilch, Ulrich   71, 79, 81–82
Schmidt, Oswald   119
Schmitt, Charles B.   84, 146
Schnepf, Diettrich   180
Schott, Clausdieter   174
Seidel, Robert   69
Selnecker, Nikolaus   191
Seneca, Lucius Annaeus   46, 155–156
Servet, Miguel   4, 173–175, 178–183, 186–190, 192–194, 197, 199–202, 204, 217–220
Setzer of Haguenau   12
Sigowski, Georg   124
Siimets-Gross, Hesi   122
Skorsieski, Abraham   124
Snell, Rudolf   86
Socinus, Laelius   175, 178
Socrates   162–163, 166, 238
Solomon   238
Soltész, Zoltánné   231, 235
Sophia Jagiellonica (Zofia Jagiellonka)   123
Spiera, Francesco   178
Spitz, Lewis William   40, 108, 113
Sredziński, Andrzey (Andreas)   3, 94, 97–102, 104, 107–112, 113, 182, 195–196, 217
Sredzinski, Faelix   100
Sredzinski, Stanisław   100
Stannifex, Joannes   38–39
Starowolski, Simon   122
Stephen I, King of Hungary   32
Stobaeus, Joannes   44
Strzelecki, Marcin   174, 181, 217–221
Sturm, Johann   29, 31, 40–44, 52, 95, 108
Sturtz, Christoph   120
Susenbrotus, Johannes   17
Sylvester II, Pope   32
Sylvius, Albert   174, 181–182, 218–221
Szelepcsényi Pohronc, Ferenc   37
Szenci Molnár, Albert   41
Szentmártoni Szabó, Géza   50
Szuhay, István   36
Szymanski, Mikołaj   95
Szymonowić, Szymon   100

Tarraconensis, Lyncurius (pseud.) see Gribaldi, Matteo
Tazbir, Janusz   85, 175, 178, 180–182, 194–195, 217
Tecno(n), Johannes   120
Teglio, Silvestro   181
Tering, Arvo   120, 125
Tertullian of Carthage   189
Teszelszky, Kees   32–33
Theodorus Gaza   16
Thompson, Craig   12
Timienski, Petrus   124
Timienski, Wsiemborius   124
Tinsley, Barbara Sher   40, 108, 113, 182
Titelmans, Franciscus   235
Tóth, Gergely   33–34, 36, 41
Toussain, Jacques   232
Traversari, Ambrogio   154
Trisna, Alexander   124
Tucker, George Hugo   30
Tygielski, Wojciech   100, 130

Uhrowiecki, Mikołaj   176

Vadian, Joachim   34
Valerius, Cornelius (Woutersz, Cornelis)   44, 73–74
Valerius Maximus   44

Index of Names

Valla, Lorenzo 38, 189
Valleriola François 71, 75
Valles, Francisco 71, 75, 82
Van der Poel, Marc 38
Vannozzi, Bonifacio 107
Varnbüler, Niklas 194
Vasoli, Cesare 12, 25, 30
Vatable, François 232
Vergerio, Pier Paolo 174, 178–181, 183, 202, 220
Veronese, Guarino 20, 24, 112
Vesalius, Andreas 71, 75
Vestring, Heinrich 120
Viiding, Kristi 3–4, 98, 119, 122–123, 130
Vine, Angus 1, 20, 25
Vitre, Pierre 14, 20
Vitrelinus, Alexander 179
Vittori, Mariano 155–156
Vives, Juan Luis 2, 9, 11–13, 15–16, 21–24
Vizkelety, András 231–232
Vogler, Chilian 180
Von Lohn, Georg 120
Von Ramm-Helmsing, Herta 122
Vorstius, Aelius Everhardus 85
Vulpius, Heinrich 120

Walsby, Malcolm 236
Waszink, Jan 30
Wehrmann, Martin 76
Weijers, Olga 69
Weinberg, Joanna 239
Welling, Gotthard 120
Wild, Eberhard 247
Wild, Johann 235
Winterburger, Johann 145, 151–152, 160
Witkowski, Wojciech 95
Wituski, Johannes 124
Władysław I, King of Hungary (III as King of Poland) 50
Wolf, Johannes 182
Wotschke, Theodor 129, 180, 197

Yeo, Richard 1, 25

Zabarella, Jacopo 69, 71, 75, 82
Zaleski, Michał 4, 173–178, 180–183, 191, 194–203, 218–221
Zamoyski, Jan 94, 96, 100, 122–123, 130
Zamoyski, Tomasz 97, 107, 110
Zbąski, Abraham 176, 181
Zborowski, Petrus 124
Żegocki, Szymon 182
Zeno 155, 238
Żółkiewski, Jan 130
Żółkiewski, Stanisław 130
Zorzi (Georgius), Francesco 230, 241–245, 247
Zum Dahlen, Heinrich 120
Zvara, Edina 36

www.ingramcontent.com/pod-product-compliance
Lightning Source LLC
Chambersburg PA
CBHW050521170426
43201CB00013B/2033